NOAH TRADITIONS IN THE DEAD SEA SCROLLS

Conversations and Controversies of Antiquity

SBL
Society of Biblical Literature

Early Judaism and Its Literature

Judith H. Newman,
Series Editor

Number 26

NOAH TRADITIONS
IN THE DEAD SEA SCROLLS

Conversations and Controversies
of Antiquity

NOAH TRADITIONS IN THE DEAD SEA SCROLLS

CONVERSATIONS AND CONTROVERSIES OF ANTIQUITY

Dorothy M. Peters

Society of Biblical Literature
Atlanta

NOAH TRADITIONS
IN THE DEAD SEA SCROLLS

CONVERSATIONS AND CONTROVERSIES
OF ANTIQUITY

Copyright © 2008 by the Society of Biblical Literature

All rights reserved. No part of this work may be reproduced or transmitted in any form or by any means, electronic or mechanical, including photocopying and recording, or by means of any information storage or retrieval system, except as may be expressly permitted by the 1976 Copyright Act or in writing from the publisher. Requests for permission should be addressed in writing to the Rights and Permissions Office, Society of Biblical Literature, 825 Houston Mill Road, Atlanta, GA 30329 USA.

Library of Congress Cataloging-in-Publication Data

Peters, Dorothy M., 1958-
  Noah traditions in the Dead Sea scrolls : conversations and controversies of antiquity / Dorothy M. Peters.
    p. cm. — (Early Judaism and its literature ; no. 26)
  Includes bibliographical references and index.
  ISBN 978-1-58983-390-6 (paper binding : alk. paper)
  1. Noah (Biblical figure) 2. Dead Sea scrolls. 3. Judaism—History—Post-exilic period, 586 B.C.-210 A.D. I. Title.
BS580.N6P48 2008
296.1'55—dc22

                                                    2008043301

15 14 13 12 11 10 09 08   5 4 3 2 1
Printed in the United States of America on acid-free, recycled paper conforming to ANSI /NISO Z39.48–1992 (R1997) and ISO 9706:1994 standards for paper permanence.

For Greg

With whom I find my rest and consolation

וקרא את־שמו נח לאמר זה ינחמנו
ממעשנו ומעצבון ידינו

Genesis 5:29

Contents

Abbreviations xiii
Preface xxi

CHAPTER ONE
INTRODUCTION

Noah in the Dead Sea Scrolls: Starting the Conversation 1

Noah in the Literature of Early Judaism and Early Christianity 3

Conversations about Noah among the Scholars 8

Noah Traditions in the Dead Sea Scrolls: New Directions 11

CHAPTER TWO
NOAH IN THE BIBLICAL TEXT

Introduction: Noah Enters the Ancient Near Eastern Conversation 13

Texts and Observations 15
    The Genesis Scrolls at Qumran: A Few Words on Noah 15
    The Introduction of Noah in Genesis: The Beginnings of Traditions 17
    Noah in Exile: Ezekiel and Deutero-Isaiah 22

Continuing the Conversation: Within the Gaps of the Noah Narrative 26

CHAPTER THREE
NOAH IN THE ARAMAIC ENOCH TEXTS AND
THE *ARAMAIC LEVI DOCUMENT*

Introduction 29

Texts and Observations 31

CONTENTS

1 Enoch: Who Walks with the Angels?........................... 31
 The Texts... 34
  Astronomical Book...................................... 34
  Book of Watchers....................................... 35
  Book of Giants... 39
  Dream Visions.. 39
  Apocalypse of Weeks.................................... 40
  Birth of Noah.. 43
  Book of Parables....................................... 44
 Enoch: The Preferred Righteous Flood Survivor?............. 46
 The Ebb and Flow of Noah and His Righteousness in *1 Enoch*... 49
Aramaic Levi Document: Noah as Ancestor of Priests............. 52
 The Text... 53
 Levi as a Literary Ancestor of Noah?....................... 55

Continuing the Conversation 59

CHAPTER FOUR
NOAH IN THE HEBREW PRE-SECTARIAN TEXTS (1): WISDOM TEXTS AND *JUBILEES*

Introduction.. 63

Texts and Observations.. 64
 4QInstruction: Righteous... Distinguishing between Good and Evil... 64
 Ben Sira: "For his sake there was a remnant"............... 68
 Jubilees: Toward Becoming an Ancestor like Moses......... 72
  The Text... 72
  Signposts to a New Noah: Reordering and Expansion...... 75
   Noah as "New Adam": Listening to the "Right" Source... 76
   Noah: The Repentant Righteous One Escapes Judgment... 79
   Noah as Priest: Covenant Redefined................. 80
   Noah and Progeny: How to Be Rightly Planted in the Land.... 85
  The Scope and Timing of Revelation to Noah............. 88

Continuing the Conversation 93

CHAPTER FIVE
NOAH IN THE *GENESIS APOCRYPHON* AND OTHER ARAMAIC TEXTS

Introduction.. 97

Texts and Observations...98
   In the Aramaic Levi and Aramaic Daniel Traditions 98
   4QNaissance de Noé ar: Chosen One of God 101
   The *Genesis Apocryphon*: An Enochic and Levitic Noah?.............106
     Text..106
       Introduction of Themes? (0, 1 – I, 29).....................107
       Origin of Noah: Seed and True Planting (II, 1 – V, 27) 108
       Noah, Righteous, Wise, Visionary Priest (V, 29 – XII, 17) 110
       Visions of Imminent and Eschatological Destinies
         (XIII, 8 – XVII, 19)......................................114
   Noah: A Different Kind of Righteous One.........................115
   Noah: Lamech's Son and Abraham's Ancestor....................117
   Noah as "Writer": Was There a "Book of Noah"?..................121

Continuing the Conversation 124

CHAPTER SIX
NOAH IN THE HEBREW PRE-SECTARIAN TEXTS (2)

Introduction 129

Texts and Observations..130
   4QExposition on the Patriarchs (4Q464): A Confusion of Languages...130
   1QBook of Noah (1Q19): Glorified among the Sons of Heaven 132
   4QTanḥumim (4Q176): The Name of Noah and Consoling Words 134
   4QFestival Prayers[b] (4Q508): Covenant, Atonement, and Judgment 135
     "To distinguish between the righteous and the wicked"
       (4Q508 1 1) 136
     "You know our inclination" (4Q508 2 5) 137
     "We have done wickedly" (4Q508 3 1) 137
     "You established your covenant for Noah" (4Q508 3 2) 138
   4QParaphrase of Genesis and Exodus (4Q422):
     Creation and Re-creation 139
     "Whom/what God chose (it) (אשר בחר בה אל)"? (4Q422 II, 6) 142
     "To raise water upon the earth (לעלות מים על הארץ)"
       (4Q422 II, 7) 143
     "It shone on the heavens ... the earth ... as a sign for future
       generations of eternity" (4Q422 II, 9–11).................143
   4QAdmonition Based on the Flood (4Q370):
     Survival of the "Made Righteous"............................144
     "He judged them ... according to their ... inclination" (1 I, 3a)....146
     God "thunders" and the earth "trembles" (1 I, 3b-4)..............146

"Giants (הגבורים), too, did not escape (מלט)" (1 I, 1–9) 146
God "makes righteous (יצדיק)" (1 II, 1–4) 147
"Forevermore (עולם) he will have compassion (רחם)"
 (4Q370 1 II, 6) 147

Continuing the Conversation 148

CHAPTER SEVEN
NOAH IN THE HEBREW SECTARIAN TEXTS

Introduction 151

Texts and Observations... 152
   The *Damascus Document*: The Missing Noah................... 152
   4QAges of Creation (4Q180–181): The *Serek* of the Sons of Noah 154
      "This is the rule/order of the sons of Noah" (4Q180 1 4).......... 155
      "Council of the sons of heaven and earth" (4Q181 1 2)............ 157
      "Guilt in the *Yaḥad* . . . a wicked *Yaḥad*" (4Q181 1 1–2) 157
   4QCommentary on Genesis A – D (4Q252–254a):
      Distinguishing between the Righteous and the Wicked........ 158
      4Q253 and 4Q253a: Noah Understood alongside Malachi?........ 158
      4Q254: More Blessings and Curses............................ 161
      4Q254a: "At their appointed time" 162
      4Q252: Another "First" for Noah 163
   5QRule (5Q13): The Levites Remember Noah........................ 166

Continuing the Conversation 169

CHAPTER EIGHT
CONCLUSIONS

Conversations among Traditions and Tradents of Noah 173
   Noah in the Earlier Hebrew and Aramaic Sources 174
      Genesis, Ezekiel, and Isaiah.................................. 174
      The Books of Aramaic Enoch.................................. 176
      The *Aramaic Levi Document* 177
   Ongoing Aramaic Conversations about Noah 177
      A Trajectory of Noah in "Levi Priestly" Traditions 177
      The *Genesis Apocryphon*..................................... 178
   Ongoing Hebrew Conversations about Noah 180

    Hebrew Pre-sectarian Texts 180
    Hebrew Sectarian Texts 183

Bilingual and Bicultural Noah: Noah Traditions in Hebrew and Aramaic ... 184

The Conversation: To Be Continued 188

Bibliography 191

Indexes
    Biblical and Apocryphal Books 227
    Dead Sea Scrolls and Related Texts 233
    Other Ancient Literature 245
    Modern Authors 247

Abbreviations

Primary Literature

In most instances, abbreviations and matters of style in this study follow *The SBL Handbook of Style*, edited by Patrick H. Alexander, John F. Kutsko, James D. Ernest, Shirley A. Decker-Lucke, and David L. Petersen (Peabody, Mass.: Hendrickson, 1999).

1QapGen^{ar}	*Genesis Apocryphon*
1QH^a	*Hodayot^a* or *Thanksgiving Hymns^a*
1QpHab	*Pesher Habakkuk*
1QM	*War Scroll*
1QS	*Rule of the Community*
1QSa	*Rule of the Congregation* (Appendix a to 1QS)
1QSb	*Rule of the Blessings* (Appendix b to 1QS)
ALD	*Aramaic Levi Document*
Bar	Baruch
2 Bar.	2 Baruch
Ben Sira	Ben Sira (Hebrew)
CD	Cairo Genizah copy of the *Cairo Damascus Document*
DSS	Dead Sea Scrolls
1 En.	*1 Enoch (Ethiopic Apocalypse)*
2 En.	*2 Enoch (Slavonic Apocalypse)*
Gen. Rab.	*Genesis Rabbah*
HB	Hebrew Bible
Josephus	
Ant.	*Jewish Antiquities*
J.W.	*Jewish War*
Jub.	*Jubilees*
Justin Martyr	
2 Apol.	*Apologia 2*
L.A.B.	*Liber antiquitatum biblicarum* (Pseudo-Philo)
L.A.E.	*Life of Adam and Eve*
1–2 Macc	1–2 Maccabees
Pesh.	Peshitta

Philo
    Det.   *Quod deterius potiori insidiari soleat*
    Hypoth.   *Hypothetica*
    Praem.   *De praemiis et poenis*
    Prob.   *Quod omnis probus liber sit*
    QG   *Quaestiones et solutiones in Genesin*
Pliny the Elder
    Nat.   *Naturalis historia*
Ps.-Eup.   Pseudo-Eupolemus
SP   Samaritan Pentateuch
Sib. Or.   *Sibylline Oracles*
Sir   Sirach/Ecclesiasticus (Greek)
Tg. Neof.   *Targum Neofiti*
Tg. Onq.   *Targum Onqelos*
Tg. Ps.-J.   *Targum Pseudo-Jonathan*
T. 12 Patr.   *Testaments of the Twelve Patriarchs*
T. Jos.   *Testament of Joseph*
T. Levi   *Testament of Levi*
Vulg.   Vulgate

Enochic Books

AA   *Animal Apocalypse*
AB   *Astronomical Book* (Aramaic)
AW   *Apocalypse of Weeks*
BG   *Book of Giants*
BW   *Book of Watchers*
DV   *Dream Visions*
EE   *Epistle of Enoch*
Birth   *Birth of Noah (1 Enoch)*
Giants   *Book of Giants*
Luminaries   *Book of Luminaries* (Ethiopic)
Parables   *Book of Parables*

Secondary Literature

General

AB   Anchor Bible
ABD   *The Anchor Bible Dictionary.* Edited by David Noel Freedman. 6 vols. New York: Doubleday, 1992.
ABRL   Anchor Bible Reference Library
AbrN   Abr-Nahrain

ANET	*Ancient Near Eastern Texts Relating to the Old Testament.* Edited by James B. Pritchard. 3rd ed. Princeton: Princeton University Press, 1969.
APOT	*The Apocrypha and Pseudepigrapha of the Old Testament.* Edited by R. H. Charles. 2 vols. Oxford: Clarendon, 1913.
BAR	*Biblical Archaeology Review*
BASORSup	Bulletin of the American Schools of Oriental Research: Supplement Series
BBR	*Bulletin for Biblical Research*
BDB	Brown, F., S. R. Driver, and C. A. Briggs. *A Hebrew and English Lexicon of the Old Testament.* Oxford: Clarendon, 1906.
BETL	Bibliotheca Ephemeridum Theologicarum Lovaniensium
BHS	*Biblia Hebraica Stuttgartensia.* Edited by K. Elliger and W. Rudolph. Stuttgart: Deutsche Bibelstiftung, 1983.
BWA(N)T	Beiträge zur Wissenschaft vom Alten (und Neuen) Testament
CBC	Cambridge Bible Commentary
CBET	Contributions to Biblical Exegesis and Theology
CBQ	*Catholic Biblical Quarterly*
CBQMS	Catholic Biblical Quarterly Monograph Series
CQS	Companion to the Qumran Scrolls
CRINT	Compendium rerum iudaicarum ad Novum Testamentum
CSCO	Corpus scriptorum christianorum orientalium.
DBSup	*Dictionnaire de la Bible: Supplement.* Edited by L. Pirot and A. Robert. Paris. Letouzey et Ané, 1928-
DDD	*Dictionary of Deities and Demons in the Bible.* Edited by K. van der Toorn, B. Becking, and P.W. van der Horst. Leiden: Brill, 1995.
DJD	Discoveries in the Judaean Desert
DSD	*Dead Sea Discoveries*
EncJud	*Encyclopedia Judaica.* 16 vols. Jerusalem, 1972.
ETL	*Ephemerides theologicae louvanienses*
GCS	Die griechische christliche Schriftsteller der ersten [drei] Jahrhunderte
HSS	Harvard Semitic Studies
HTR	*Harvard Theological Review*
HUCA	*Hebrew Union College Annual*
Hen	*Henoch*
ICC	International Critical Commentary
Int	*Interpretation*
IOS	*Israel Oriental Studies*
Jastrow	Jastrow, M. *A Dictionary of the Targumim, the Talmud Babli and Yerushalmi, and the Midrashic Literature.* 2d ed. New York: Pardes, 1903.

JBL	*Journal of Biblical Literature*
JBQ	*Jewish Bible Quarterly*
JDS	Judean Desert Studies
JJS	*Journal of Jewish Studies*
JNES	*Journal of Near Eastern Studies*
Joüon	Joüon, P. *A Grammar of Biblical Hebrew.* Translated and revised by T. Muraoka. 2 vols. Subsidia biblica 14/1–2. Rome: Biblical Institute Press, 1991.
JQR	*Jewish Quarterly Review*
JSem	*Journal of Semitics*
JSJSup	Journal for the Study of Judaism: Supplement Series
JSNTSup	Journal for the Study of the New Testament: Supplement Series
JSOR	*Journal of the Society of Oriental Research*
JSOT	*Journal for the Study of the Old Testament*
JSOTSup	Journal for the Study of the Old Testament: Supplement Series
JSP	*Journal for the Study of the Pseudepigrapha*
JSPSup	Journal for the Study of the Pseudepigrapha: Supplement Series
JSS	*Journal of Semitic Studies*
JSSSup	Journal of Semitic Studies: Supplement Series
JTS	*Journal of Theological Studies*
Jud	Judaica
JWSTP	*Jewish Writings of the Second Temple Period: Apocrypha, Pseudepigrapha, Qumran Sectarian Writings, Philo, Josephus.* Edited by M.E. Stone. CRINT 2.2. Assen/Philadelphia, 1984.
HALOT	Koehler, L., W. Baumgartner, and J. J. Stamm. *The Hebrew and Aramaic Lexicon of the Old Testament.* Translated and edited under the supervision of M. E. J. Richardson. 5 vols. Leiden: Brill, 1994–99.
LCL	Loeb Classical Library
LSTS	Library of Second Temple Studies
Maarav	*Maarav*
Mus	*Muséon: Revue d'études orientales*
NETS	*A New English Translation of the Septuagint.* Edited by Albert Pietersma and Benjamin G. Wright. New York/Oxford: Oxford University Press, 2007.
NIB	*The New Interpreter's Bible*
NICOT	New International Commentary on the Old Testament
NIDB	Douglas, J. D., and M. C. Tenney, eds. *New International Dictionary of the Bible.* Grand Rapids: Zondervan, 1987.
NIDOTTE	VanGemeren, W. A., ed. *New International Dictionary of*

	Old Testament Theology and Exegesis. 5 vols. Grand Rapids: Zondervan, 1997.
NTS	*New Testament Studies*
NovT	*Novum Testamentum*
OTL	Old Testament Library
OTP	Charlesworth, James H., ed. *The Old Testament Pseudepigrapha*. 2 vols. New York: Doubleday, 1983, 1985.
PEQ	*Palestine Exploration Quarterly*
PVTG	Pseudepigrapha Veteris Testamenti Graece
RB	*Revue biblique*
RevQ	*Revue de Qumran*
SBL	Society of Biblical Literature
SBLDS	Society of Biblical Literature Dissertation Series
SBLEJL	Society of Biblical Literature Early Judaism and Its Literature
SBLMS	Society of Biblical Literature Monograph Series
SBLSP	*Society of Biblical Literature Seminar Papers*
SBTS	Sources for Biblical and Theological Study
SEÅ	*Svensk exegetisk Årsbok*
SJLA	Studies in Judaism in Late Antiquity
SOTSMS	Society for Old Testament Studies Monograph Series
SPB	Studia Post Biblica – Supplements to the Journal for the Study of Judaism
STDJ	Studies on the Texts of the Desert of Judah
SUNT	Studien zur Umwelt des Neuen Testaments
SVTP	Studia in Veteris Testamenti pseudepigrapha
Tarbiz	*Tarbiz*
TDNT	Kittel, G., and G. Friedrich, eds. *Theological Dictionary of the New Testament*. Translated by G. W. Bromiley. 10 vols. Grand Rapids: Eerdmans, 1964–76.
TDOT	Botterweck, G. J., and H. Ringgren, eds. *Theological Dictionary of the Old Testament*. Translated by J. T. Willis, G. W. Bromiley, and D. E. Green. 8 vols. Grand Rapids: Eerdmans, 1974–
Text	*Textus*
TSAJ	Texte und Studien zum antiken Judentum
TWOT	Harris, R. L., and G. L. Archer, Jr., eds. *Theological Wordbook of the Old Testament*. 2 vols. Chicago: Moody, 1980.
TynBul	*Tyndale Bulletin*
VT	*Vetus Testamentum*
VTSup	Vetus Testamentum Supplements
WBC	Word Biblical Commentary
Williams	Williams, Ronald J. *Hebrew Syntax: An Outline*. 2nd ed. Toronto: University of Toronto Press, 1976.

Reference Works and Official Editions of the Dead Sea Scrolls

BE	Milik, J. T. *The Books of Enoch: Aramaic Fragments of Qumran Cave*. Oxford: Clarendon, 1976.
Book of Giants	Stuckenbruck, L. T. *The Book of Giants from Qumran: Texts, Translation, and Commentary*. Tübingen: Mohr Siebeck, 1997.
DJD I	Barthélemy, D., and J.T. Milik. *Qumran Cave 1*. Discoveries in the Judaean Desert I. Oxford: Clarendon, 1955.
DJD III	Baillet, M., J. T. Milik, and R. de Vaux. *Les "petites grottes" de Qumrân*. Discoveries in the Judaean Desert III. Oxford: Clarendon, 1962.
DJD V	Allegro, J. M. *Qumran Cave 4.I (4Q158–186)*. Discoveries in the Judaean Desert V. Oxford: Clarendon, 1968.
DJD VII	Baillet, M. *Qumrân Grotte 4.III (4Q282–5Q520)*. Discoveries in the Judaean Desert VII. Oxford, Clarendon, 1982.
DJD IX	Skehan, P. W., E. Ulrich, and J. E. Sanderson. *Qumran Cave 4.IV: Palaeo-Hebrew and Greek Biblical Manuscripts*. Discoveries in the Judaean Desert IX. Oxford: Clarendon, 1992.
DJD XII	Ulrich, E., F. M. Cross, J. R. Davila, J. Jastram, J. E. Sanderson, E. Tov, and J. Strugnell. *Qumran Cave 4.VII: Genesis to Numbers*. Discoveries in the Judaean Desert XII. Oxford: Clarendon, 1994.
DJD XIII	Attridge, H. W., T. Elgvin, J. T. Milik, S. Olyan, J. Strugnell, E. Tov, J. VanderKam, and S. White, in consultation with J. C. VanderKam. *Qumran Cave 4.VIII: Parabiblical Texts, Part I*. Discoveries in the Judaean Desert XIII. Oxford: Clarendon, 1994.
DJD XIV	Ulrich, E., F. M. Cross, S. W. Crawford, J. A. Duncan, P. W. Skehan, E. Tov, and J. Trebolle Barrera. *Qumran Cave 4.IX: Deuteronomy to Kings*. Discoveries in the Judaean Desert XIV. Oxford: Clarendon, 1995.
DJD XVI	Ulrich, E., F. M. Cross, J. A. Fitzmyer, P. W. Flint, S. Metso, C. M. Murphy, C. Niccum, P. W. Skehan, E. Tov, and J. Trebolle Barrera. *Qumran Cave 4.XI: Psalms to Chronicles*. Discoveries in the Judaean Desert XVI. Oxford: Clarendon, 2000.
DJD XVIII	Baumgarten, J. M. *Qumran Cave 4.XIII*. Discoveries in the Judaean Desert XVIII. Oxford: Clarendon, 1996.
DJD XIX	Broshi, M., E. Eshel, J. A. Fitzmyer, E. Larson, C. Newsom, L. Schiffman, M. Smith, M. Stone, J. Strugnell, and A. Yardeni, in consultation with J. C. VanderKam. *Qumran Cave 4.XIV: Parabiblical Texts, Part 2*. Discoveries in the Judaean Desert XIX. Oxford: Clarendon, 1995.
DJD XXII	Brooke, G. J., J. Collins, P. Flint, J. Greenfield, E. Larson, C.

	Newsom, É. Puech, L. H. Schiffman, M. Stone, and J. Trebolle Barrera, in consultation with J. C. VanderKam, partially based on earlier transcriptions by J. T. Milik and J. Strugnell. *Qumran Cave 4.XVII: Parabiblical Texts, Part 3.* Discoveries in the Judaean Desert XXII. Oxford: Clarendon, 1996.
DJD XXIII	García Martínez, F., E. J. C. Tigchelaar, and A. S. van der Woude. *Manuscripts from Qumran Cave 11 (11Q2–18, 11Q20–30).* Discoveries in the Judaean Desert XXIII. Oxford: Clarendon, 1997.
DJD XXV	Puech, É. *Textes Hebreux (4Q521–4Q528, 4Q576–579): Qumran Cave 4.XVIII.* Discoveries in the Judaean Desert XXV. Oxford: Clarendon, 1997.
DJD XXIX	Chazon, E., T. Elgvin, E. Eshel, D. Falk, B. Nitzan, E. Qimron, E. Schuller, D. Seely, E. Tigchelaar, and M. Weinfeld in consultation with J. VanderKam, and M. Brady. *Qumran Cave 4.XX: Poetical and Liturgical Texts, Part 2.* Discoveries in the Judaean Desert XXIX. Oxford: Clarendon, 1999.
DJD XXXI	Puech, É. *Qumrân Grotte 4.XXII: Textes Araméen, Première Partie, 4Q529–549.* Discoveries in the Judaean Desert XXXI. Oxford: Clarendon, 2001.
DJD XXXIV	Strugnell, J., D. J. Harrington, and T. Elgvin in consultation with J. A. Fitzmyer. *Qumran Cave 4.XXIV: Sapiential Texts, Part 2, 4QInstruction: 4Q415ff.* Discoveries in the Judaean Desert XXXIV. Oxford: Clarendon, 1999.
DJD XXXVI	Pfann, S. J., P. Alexander, M. Broshi, E. Chazon, H. Cotton, F. M. Cross, T. Elgvin, D. Ernst, E. Eshel, H. Eshel, J. Fitzmyer, F.García Martínez, J. C. Greenfield, M. Kister, A. Lange, E. Larson, A. Lamaire, T. Lim, J. Naveh, D. Pike, M. Sokoloff, H. Stegemann, A. Steudel, M. Stone, L. Stuckenbruck, S. Talmon, S. Tanzer, E. J. C. Tigchelaar, E. Tov, G. Vermes, and A. Yardeni. *Qumran Cave 4. XXVI: Cryptic Texts and Miscellanea, Part 1.* Discoveries in the Judaean Desert XXXVI. Oxford: Clarendon, 2000.
DJD XXXIX	Tov, E. with contributions by M. G. Abegg, Jr., A. Lange, U. Mittmann-Richert, S. J. Pfann, E. J. C. Tigchelaar, E. Ulrich, and B. Webster. *The Texts from the Judaean Desert: Indices and an Introduction to the Discoveries in the Judaean Desert Series.* Oxford: Clarendon, 2002.
DSSR 3	Parry, Donald W., and Emanuel Tov, eds. *The Dead Sea Scrolls Reader.* Part 3, *Parabiblical Texts.* Leiden: Brill, 2005.
DSSB	Abegg, Martin, Jr., Peter W. Flint, and Eugene Ulrich. *The Dead Sea Scrolls Bible.* New York: HarperSanFrancisco, 1999.
DSSSE	García Martínez, Florentino, and Eibert J. C. Tigchelaar, eds.

	and transs. *The Dead Sea Scrolls Study Edition*. 2 vols. Leiden: Brill, 1997, 2000.
TALD	Greenfield, Jonas C., Michael E. Stone, and Esther Eshel. *The Aramaic Levi Document: Edition, Translation, and Commentary*. Leiden: Brill, 2004.
WAC	Wise, Michael, Martin Abegg, Jr., and Edward Cook. *The Dead Sea Scrolls: A New Translation*. 2 vols. New York: HarperSanFrancisco, 1996, 2005.

Preface

Noah wends his way through the Hebrew and Aramaic Dead Sea Scrolls, across the genres, and in compositions spanning the centuries. For this reason, many scholars and friends over the past six years have joined me for parts of the journey, speaking into and shaping my own contribution to this ongoing and invigorating discussion. Once this particular story is heard, I look forward to even more "conversation and controversy" with these modern-day "women and men of Qumran."

Martin Abegg was the one who first named him in his question, "What about Noah"? Under his direction, I was completing a master's thesis at Trinity Western University and still puzzling over one of the many detours that the study of the Day of Atonement in the Dead Sea Scrolls had drawn us into: How were the sectarians at Qumran who "atoned for the land" connected to Noah, the only character in the Dead Sea Scrolls who also "atoned for land"? Not long after, Professor Abegg arranged a meeting for us with Devorah Dimant at the annual meeting of the Society of Biblical Literature in Toronto, and we spent a memorable Saturday afternoon in discussion of all things Noah. The course was now set.

The initial exploration was a short dissertation at the University of Oxford for a Master of Studies funded by the Oxford Centre for Hebrew and Jewish Studies. In the early stages, I enthusiastically envisioned a "struggle for center stage" between Noah and Moses at Qumran. Each scroll was doing its part in contributing to the development of a composite portrait of Noah, who was becoming formidable in my mind, poised to take over from Moses himself as the authoritative figure for Qumran! Thankfully, Alison Salvesen, under whom this early work began at Oxford, knew when thoughts needed time and space for creative exploration and when they had to undergo disciplined and cautious testing. Her own interests in the larger thought world of the Second Temple period and the literatures of early rabbinic Judaism and early Christianity prompted me to explore the contexts within the time and throughout the time into which Noah traditions in the Dead Sea Scrolls could be placed. Somewhat regretfully at the end, I was forced to conclude that Noah did not, indeed, replace Moses at Qumran. However, the good thing was that, because he was proving to be a much more intriguing and complex character than even originally imagined, Noah could now keep me happily occupied for four more years.

During the next stage, George Brooke provided patient and meticulous oversight for my doctoral work at the University of Manchester. Under his supervisory care, the composite construction of the character of Noah that I had so lovingly created was dismantled as we began to undertake close, literary readings of each text, allowing each to speak with its own, distinctive voice. Only after this detailed work was complete and Noah lay in pieces on the table, was it possible to arrange and rearrange the pieces in order to explore the tentative relationships of one text to another text, of texts to authors, and of authors to movements within their cultural contexts. We worked within an intense and creative tension between my own drive to find an interpretative home for each piece in the overall story and Professor Brooke's respect for the diversity of oddly shaped individual texts that must be listened to and that could not and should not be forced to fit the multiple story lines that I was busily constructing and reconstructing.

Michael Knibb and Philip Alexander examined the dissertation, encouraging its publication while generously providing extensive critical feedback for what was still a somewhat "rough and ready" study. Their interest in questions not yet addressed in the work encouraged me to take that extra year for additional research, writing, and thorough revision.

Further shaping and refinement came from scholars and friends on the conference circuit in the year that followed. I am especially indebted to the participants of the Fourth Enoch Seminar that met in Camaldoli in 2007, the VIth Congress of the International Organization of Qumran Studies in Ljubljana, the 2007 meeting of the Canadian Society of Biblical Studies in Saskatoon, and the Dead Sea Scrolls Symposium 2007 at Trinity Western University. Most particularly, Gabriele Boccaccini, Esther Chazon, Henryk Drawnel, Esther Eshel, Hanan Eshel, Daniel Falk, Crispin Fletcher-Louis, Maxine Grossman, John Kampen, Hindy Najman, George Nickelsburg, and Cecilia Wassen have triggered new ways of thinking about Noah in texts that speak about him and communities that thought about him. Our conversations (and our disputes!) over papers in group sessions and seminars, on walks, around dinner tables, and at outdoor cafes, shaped and informed the story lines of this book in ways that cannot even be traced.

Several important doctoral dissertations now address texts containing Noah traditions at Qumran and I am grateful that Ariel Feldman, Daniel Machiela, and Matthias Weigold have freely shared their own work with me. Furthermore, I am never at a loss for dialogue partners in my academic home at Trinity Western University. Martin Abegg and Peter Flint, co-directors of the Dead Sea Scrolls Institute, together with Craig Allert, Kyung Baek, Craig Broyles, Dirk Büchner, Kent Clarke, Tony Cummins, C. J. "Kippy" Davis, Jonathan Dawn, Tom Hatina, Rob Hiebert, Joel Lohr, Joanne Pepper, James Scott, and Casey Toews are the best of colleagues. Their fingerprints and those of my colleagues in the West Coat Qumran Study Group, especially Daniel Falk and Robert Kugler, are to be found in unexpected places all over this work.

Judith Newman has been a most enthusiastic, careful, and skilled editor, demonstrating a keen interest in every detail. She has overseen the process of transforming a dissertation originally meant to satisfy the examiners into a book meant to be inviting and hospitable to the broader community of scholars. My research assistant, Emily Lim, carefully prepared the indexes at the eleventh hour, and the able assistance of the editorial and production staff at the Society of Biblical Literature meant that this technologically challenged grandmother was not required to produce camera-ready copy!

Finally, I belong to a storytelling and story-loving family. I am thankful for my parents, Leonard and Esther Doerksen, at whose feet I first learned to love the story of Noah, and for my children, Dorolen, Jonathan, David, and Matthew, and my grandchildren, Livia, Matthew, and Nathan, to whom I have been privileged to recount it. My deepest gratitude is for Greg, builder and sailor, who has cheerfully welcomed Noah into our breakfast conversations and who has embarked with me on each leg of our journey from the time we were high school sweethearts. May he yet build the boat of his dreams!

CHAPTER ONE

Introduction

Then I, Noah, went out and I walked upon the land,
over the length of it and the breadth of it
"Eden" in their leaves and in their fruit.
The land, all of it, was filling with new grass, herbs and grain.
Then I blessed the Lord of [Heaven, for] it is he who works praise forever
and the glory belongs to him.
Genesis Apocryphon (1Q20 XI, 11–13)[1]

Noah in the Dead Sea Scrolls: Starting the Conversation

Noah appears as a powerfully magnetic subject of lively and persistent interest in the texts represented in the Dead Sea Scrolls. However, as father of all humanity and not exclusively of Israel, he was a somewhat problematic ancestor for the Jews in the Second Temple period. They knew from the Genesis narrative that Noah was a righteous, covenant-making survivor of the primordial flood, distinguished from the wicked by God in the judgment that blotted out the violence and wickedness on the earth. Except for one isolated incident of drunkenness and self-exposure, Noah could have been enthusiastically claimed as their very own flood survivor hero. Instead, some texts of the Second Temple period and beyond exhibit a decided uneasiness with Noah. Noah embodied the tensions for Jewish groups that were struggling to understand their distinctive self-identities within Judaism and their relationship to the nations that had dominated them and among whom they must live.

One would think that the collection of the Dead Sea Scrolls, preserved in caves by sectarians, would exhibit a more unified and coherent interpretation

---

1. Unless indicated otherwise, all translations of the Dead Sea Scrolls are adapted from English translations in *Accordance Bible Software* modules. Likewise, Hebrew and Aramaic texts from the Dead Sea Scrolls are cited from *Accordance Bible Software* modules in consultation with the appropriate official editions in the Discoveries in the Judaean Desert series. See Martin G. Abegg, Jr., James E. Bowley, and Edward M. Cook with Casey Toews, "QUMBIB-M/C," 2006; Martin G. Abegg, Jr., James E. Bowley, and Edward M. Cook, "QUMENG," 2006; Martin G. Abegg, Jr., "QUMRAN," 2006.

of Noah than is found within Second Temple Judaism as a whole. However, anything but a unity is found. Noah is variously elevated as a "second Adam" on a renewed earth, a wise and righteous "second Enoch" receiving visions of imminent and eschatological judgment, a "first priest" like Levi, or the worthy, covenant-making ancestor of Moses. His priesthood and even the nature of his righteousness are debated, and, at times, Noah is merely acknowledged as the flood survivor or even passed over entirely in favor of more distinctively Israelite ancestral heroes such as Abraham, Isaac, or Jacob.

The ancient conversations and controversies implicit in the portrayals of Noah in the Dead Sea Scrolls are certainly not as easily defined as the polemic betrayed by the harsh contrasts in some later rabbinic and Christian characterizations of Noah in which he is, on the one hand, castrated and disqualified from the priesthood, while, on the other hand, identified as an archetype of Jesus himself. Yet a close reading of the Noah texts in the Dead Sea Scrolls does yield certain implied "questions" and various "answers" about how the Noah traditions were handled.[2]

The following three questions will be in the background of our text-by-text exploration. First, How and to what extent is Noah portrayed as an archetype for a particular interpretation of what it meant to be Jewish? Second, What does God reveal to Noah and how does he do it? Finally, To what extent is Noah claimed as a "distinctly Jewish" ancestor or, alternatively, claimed as a common ancestor shared with the Gentiles? We first allow each text to speak with its own, distinctive voice and, along the way, bring the texts into discussion with one another in the hope that they might illuminate the different types of conversations and controversies that were engaging their authors within the movements of which they were a part.

For Second Temple Jews, Noah was an eminently suitable character through which Jewish identity within the diversity of Judaism and the surrounding nations might be explored and defined. The characterizations, roles, and identities that made up his "archetype" as portrayed in each text prove to be signposts reflecting the diversity of Jewish belief and praxis in the Second Temple period. For example, Noah's character resemblance to either Enoch or Moses might, by extension, suggest the tradent's view of the relative authority of the texts traditionally associated with Enoch or Moses. His various priestly attributes might point to a debate over what was to characterize an ideal priest. Even Noah's absence in a retelling of Israel's history might suggest a particular stance toward those nations outside of Israel.

Implicit within the framing of these questions is that interpreters saw, in the Noah of Genesis, the raw potential for an "archetype" for their own movements

---

2. In this study, the term "Noah tradition" normally describes a speech, action, event, or character trait associated with Noah in more than one text. A "theme" recurs within a given text and may extend beyond Noah to formulations within the text.

and that they responded by variously constructing his personality as a reflection of either the existing character or the idealized character of their movement. This study, however, is less intent on linking specific Noah traditions to separate movements than on exploring *what types* of questions provoked *what kinds* of debate among the conversation partners through the centuries of the composition of the Dead Sea Scrolls.

As will be seen, there is simply not a one-to-one correspondence between the mere utilization of a Noah tradition and the answer to an implied question behind the interpretation, much less a one-to-one correspondence between the tradition and a specific group. Instead, Noah traditions were continually recontextualized and reinterpreted in highly nuanced ways within texts whose authors frequently took new directions with the source traditions.

Noah in the Literature of Early Judaism and Early Christianity

In the literature of the Second Temple Period and in the literature of Christianity and rabbinic Judaism, named and unnamed authors or groups transmitted, composed, and recorded Noah traditions.[3] The following overview identifies some points along trajectories that may have had their origins in the Second Temple period and developed into what appears to be a more clearly defined polemic within subsequent Christian and rabbinic interpretation.

The Hellenistic Jewish writers Philo and Josephus represent what Jack Lewis observes as "different degree[s] of penetration of the Greek spirit into Judaism."[4] Therefore, it is not surprising that the portrayals of Noah betray a knowledge of

---

3. For a comprehensive catalogue of Noah traditions in the texts of Second Temple Judaism, Christianity, and rabbinic Judaism, see Jack P. Lewis, *A Study of the Interpretation of Noah and the Flood in Jewish and Christian Literature* (Leiden: Brill), 1968. See also James L. Kugel, *Traditions of the Bible: A Guide to the Bible as It Was at the Start of the Common Era* (Cambridge, Mass./London: Harvard University Press), 1998. For further helpful discussion on Christian and rabbinic Noah traditions, see Naomi Koltun-Fromm, "Aphrahat and the Rabbis on Noah's Righteousness In Light of the Jewish-Christian Polemic," *The Book of Genesis in Jewish and Oriental Christian Interpretation* (ed. J. Frishman and L. Van Rompay; Leuven: Peeters, 1997), 56–71; Wout J. van Bekkum, "The Lesson of the Flood: מַבּוּל in Rabbinic Tradition," in *Interpretations of the Flood* (ed. F. García Martínez and G. P. Luttikhuizen; Themes in Biblical Narrative 1; Leiden: Brill, 1998), 124–33; and H. S. Benjamins, "Noah, the Ark, and the Flood in Early Christian Theology: The Ship of the Church in the Making," *Interpretations of the Flood*, 134–49.

4. Lewis, *Study*, 42. For an insightful study into the innovative perceptions of the flood story within a Jewish Hellenistic milieu, see Matthias Weigold, "The Deluge and the Flood of Emotions: The Use of Flood Imagery in 4 Maccabees in Its Ancient Jewish Context," in *The Book of the Maccabees: History, Theology, Ideology: Papers of the Second International Conference on the Deuterocanonical Books, Pápa, Hungary, 9–11 June, 2005* (ed. G. G. Xeravits and J. Zsengellér; JSJSup 118; Leiden: Brill, 2007), 197–210.

and an interaction with Greek story and philosophy. Philo identifies Noah with Deucalion, the Greek flood survivor hero (*Praem.* 23), and in his retelling of Noah and the flood, Josephus appeals to the histories written by Berosus the Chaldean, Hieronymus the Egyptian, and Mnaseas, identifying "the man of whom Moses wrote" with the survivor of the deluge in the account recorded by Nicolaus of Damascus (*Ant.* 1.93–94). Early Christian interpretation reveals a tension concerning Noah's identification with Deucalion. Justin identified Noah with the Greek flood survivor hero (*2 Apol.* 7.2), but, on the other hand, Tatian's chronology "would make it impossible for him to identify Deucalion with Noah."[5]

Interpreters of Noah in the New Testament and subsequent Christian writings reinterpreted the righteousness of Noah but in ways different from the Qumran sectarians. The Letter to the Hebrews links Noah's righteousness to faith, the salvation of his household, and condemnation of the world (Heb 11:7). Noah is called a "herald of righteousness" (2 Pet 2:5; cf. 1 Pet 3:19–20) and the "days of Noah" are compared to imminent judgment in the days of the "son of man" (Luke 17:26–27).[6] In the centuries that followed, Noah evolved from the new Adam into an archetype of Christ himself, possessing an even more fully enhanced righteous character.[7]

The flood as a metaphor for symbolic cleansing by baptism (1 Pet 3:18–19) recalls Philo's interpretation of the flood as a metaphorical cleansing of the soul (*Det.* 170) and stands in contrast to the more literal interpretation of a flood that concretely cleanses the earth from the effects of oppression and sin (*1 En.* 10:20). Nowhere in the New Testament is it stated that Noah called his generation to repentance, although the concept might be implied by the designation "herald of righteousness" (2 Pet 2:5) and the fact that Noah was the one through whom the world was condemned (Heb 11:7). Repentance, more subtly associated with Noah in the Dead Sea Scrolls,[8] is more explicitly found in Josephus (*Ant.* 1.74), Targum

---

5. Lewis, *Study*, 107. See Tatian, *Pros Hellenas* 39.2.

6. For a thought-provoking study of the implicit connection between Noah and Melchizedek in the Letter to the Hebrews, see Andrei Orlov, "The Heir of Righteousness and the King of Righteousness: The Priestly Noachic Polemics in 2 Enoch and the Epistle to the Hebrews," *JTS* 58 (2007): 45–65.

7. Lewis (*Study*, 158–60) traces this development, originating with Philo's Noah who is the τέλος of one race and the ἀρξή of another (*QG* 1.96), as "one of the main links of typology." Lewis cites, among others, Tertullian (*Mon.* 5.5), Pseudo-Clementines (*Rec.* 1.29; 4.12; *Hom.* 8.17), Origen (*Cels.* 4.21), Ambrose (*Off.*), Gregory of Nazianzus (*Or. Bas.* 28.18; 43.70); Jerome (*Jov.* 1.17), Justin (*Dial.* 92.2). For Christ as the "true Noah" see Cyril of Jerusalem in *Catech.* 17.10 (*PG* 33:981A); for Noah as the type of Christ, see Ephraem Syrus, *Hymns on the Nativity* 1 (*NPNF* 2, 13:225).

8. See *Jub.* 5:6–19; 4QFestival Prayers^b (4Q508 2 1–3 2), and 5QRule, possibly a variant covenant renewal ceremony that would have incorporated confession.

Pseudo-Jonathan 7.4, *Sibylline Oracles*,[9] and in the literature of rabbinic Judaism and later Christianity.

Rabbinic interpretation frequently restricted the righteousness of Noah, presenting him as righteous *only* in comparison to the wicked of his generation (*Gen. Rab.* 30.9; cf. Gen 6:9). Furthermore, Noah is compared unfavorably with Moses, who was said to be greater than Noah because he could save his whole generation while Noah saved only his family (*Deut. Rab.* 11.3). Noah was pronounced guilty not only for his own "uncovering" (יתגל) (Gen 9:21) but also for causing the exile of the ten tribes and of Judah and Benjamin (*Gen. Rab.* 36. 4). God even regrets making Noah, who becomes the victim of creative, reworked punctuation: "For I regretted making them and Noah" (*Gen. Rab.* 28.8; cf. Gen 6:7b–8a).

Rabbinic and Christian interpreters also puzzled over Noah's apparently limited fertility. In stark contrast to his ancestors who became fathers much earlier—Enoch at 65, Methuselah at 187, and Lamech at 182 (Gen 5:21–28)—Noah was remarkably slow in fulfilling his part of the primeval mandate (Gen 1:28) to be fruitful and multiply! It was not until his five-hundredth year that he fathered Shem, Ham, and Japheth (Gen 5:32) and, although Noah lived another 350 years following the flood, he fathered no more children despite the reiterated primeval command, "Be fruitful and multiply and fill the earth" (Gen 9:1).[10]

Various explanations ensued. *Genesis Rabbah* links Gen 5:32 to Psalm 1, identifying Noah with the "happy man" who has not "walked in the counsel of the wicked" and further identifies him with the tree that "brings forth fruit [Shem] in season" (*Gen. Rab.* 26.1). Elsewhere, Noah neglects the command to be fruitful prior to the flood (*Num. Rab.* 14.12) and, after the flood, is either emasculated by Ham (*b. Sanh.* 70a) or maimed by a lion (*Gen. Rab.* 30.6; 36.4). Either way, he is unfit to offer sacrifices and is disqualified from the priesthood.[11]

According to the fourth-century Aphrahat, Noah chose to remain celibate so that his children would not be corrupted by the evil generation. Naomi Koltun-Fromm points out that this virginity was the "real criterion for Noah's righteousness" and that Noah became a "proto-monk" in the Syriac church.[12] She adds that "[w]hile the rabbis do not abandon certain central characters, like Abraham or Moses, they can easily decentralize less important lights like Noah. . . . In perhaps indirect reaction to Noah's 'christianization,' the rabbis demote him from righteous man to castrate; a judgment, perhaps, not only on Noah, but

---

9. The prophetess Sibyl, a self-proclaimed daughter-in-law of Noah (*Sib. Or.* 3.818–28), speaks of Noah who entreats the wicked to repent (*Sib. Or.* i.147–98).

10. Unless otherwise noted, all biblical quotations are based on the NRSV.

11. Noah is a priest in *Num. Rab.* 4.8, wearing the high priest's garments handed down from Adam.

12. Koltun-Fromm, "Aphrahat and the Rabbis," 59–61. Cf. Ephrem, *Commentary to Genesis* 6:1, in which Noah's celibacy is an example for his children.

on those Christians who idealize him."[13] Generally speaking, it would seem that an increasingly pronounced parting of the ways between Christianity and Judaism was accompanied by sharper debate over the role of their common ancestor. This raises a questions that surfaces from time to time in this study: Is the extent to which a portrayal of Noah either overlaps or remains distinct from another portrayal indicative of the degree of separation among the movements building a particular archetype of Noah?

Noah's genitals were a focus for yet another debate over whether or not he was circumcised. One rabbinic tradition states that he was born circumcised (ʾAbot R. Nat. 2) implying that Noah was obedient to the Torah even before it was given on Mount Sinai.[14] Justin, however, utilized the very fact that Noah was *not* circumcised to argue that the Law was not necessary for righteousness (*Dial.* 19.4). Good evidence for the existence of polemic and debate involving Noah is the dialogue between Justin and Trypho concerning whether righteousness apart from the Law was possible and whether Noah could be saved without keeping the Law (*Dial.* 46).

It is not surprising to find clear-cut Noah archetypes that exemplified ideal or less-than-ideal behavior for groups such as rabbinic Judaism or a fourth-century monastic community that had identifying boundary markers defined by praxis. Neither is the resulting polemic expressed through competing portrayals of Noah unexpected as groups became increasingly more distinct from one another in the centuries following the Second Temple period. However, questions remains: Did the portrayals of Noah function in the same way in the Dead Sea Scrolls, as archetypes for clearly defined groups? To what extent did variant portrayals reflect outright competition and polemic between distinct groups with serious disputes, and to what extent were they evidence of a family-style conversation and debate among the movements within Judaism?

The Dead Sea Scrolls have confirmed the complexity and diversity of movements within Second Temple Judaism; specific components of praxis and belief represented in the Second Temple period cannot anachronistically be parceled out as the exclusive property of one group or another whether they be Pharisees, Sadducees, Essenes, Zealots, the "fourth philosophy," the Sicarii, or the early Jesus movement. While specific practices and ideas tended to travel with certain movements, ideas in conversation with other ideas seem to have passed back and forth easily through the boundaries set by praxis, taking root as new and intriguing plantings.

Even the term "community" can be a misleading one, implying that a single group of people, such as the Essenes, was characterized by ideological unity and

---

13. Koltun-Fromm, "Aphrahat and the Rabbis," 71.

14. Early attestations of Noah's behavior that prefigured Torah obedience are found in *Jubilees*.

stability over time. It must be recognized that within the Judaism of the Second Temple era, ideas and systems of thought were not likely birthed in isolation but rather within and among "groups" and "movements" of people who may well have known each other. Although a movement or group could self-consciously distinguish itself from another group to a greater or lesser extent by means of a different praxis or thought system, this did not necessarily prevent ongoing conversation, whether friendly or adversarial, among them.

The Essenes, known to us from descriptions by the Jewish philosopher Philo, from the Jewish historian Josephus, and from the Roman Pliny the Elder,[15] shared practices and beliefs similar to those attested in the *Community Rule* of the Dead Sea Scrolls. Broadly speaking, at least some Essenes were not of the marrying kind, renounced pleasures, shared their property, and went through an initiation period for two or three years before being allowed entrance into the community. Some Essenes, according to Pliny, had located themselves on the west coast of the Dead Sea with "only palm trees for company" (Pliny, *Nat.* 5.15.73).

What the Dead Sea Scrolls revealed about the beliefs and practices of the community at Qumran did not conform, in every instance, to previously known descriptions of the Essenes.[16] However, although the conversation is ongoing and scholars understand that the Qumran community does not necessarily have to be identified with the Essenes, some kind of integral relationship between them is generally accepted.

In this study, the term "*Yaḥad* sectarians" is used when linking that particular movement to traditionally defined sectarian texts with the understanding that the *Yaḥad* sectarian movement may have originated well before the removal of some of the group to Qumran. The terms "community," "group," or "movement" are used loosely and interchangeably, in recognition of the fact that the boundaries among them were often fluid and differences of belief and even praxis reflected in different texts do not necessarily demand multiple divisions into different "communities" based on these differences. Over time, movements were in conversation with other movements, sharing common borders at some points

---

15. Josephus, *J.W.* 2.119–66; *Ant.* 13.171–73; 18.11–22; Philo, *Prob.* 75–91; *Hypoth.* 11.1–11; Pliny, *Nat.* 5.15.73.

16. For further helpful discussions on the Jewish groups in Second Temple Judaism, the relationship of the Essenes to the Qumran sect, and the case for the "Essene Hypothesis" and beyond, see George W. E. Nickelsburg, *Ancient Judaism and Christian Origins: Diversity, Continuity and Transformation* (Minneapolis: Fortress Press, 2003), 147–84; James C. VanderKam, *The Dead Sea Scrolls Today* (Grand Rapids: Eerdmans, 1994), 71–98; Philip R. Davies, George J. Brooke, and Phillip R. Callaway, *The Complete World of the Dead Sea Scrolls* (London: Thames & Hudson, 2002), 54–63; Florentino García Martínez and Julio Trebolle Barrera, *The People of the Dead Sea Scrolls: Their Writings, Beliefs and Practices* (trans. W. G. E. Watson; Leiden: Brill, 1995) and Gabriele Boccaccini, *Beyond the Essene Hypothesis: The Parting of the Ways between Qumran and Enochic Judaism* (Grand Rapids: Eerdmans, 1998).

and creating distinct boundaries at others. Accompanying the movements in their growth and development were new and nuanced archetypes of Noah.

Conversations about Noah among the Scholars

More recently, the figure of Noah has evoked renewed interest in scholarly conversations and debates. This current overview is necessarily brief, highlighting just the discussions most pertinent to this study.

First and foremost, any work on the history of Noah traditions is deeply indebted to Jack Lewis's 1968 comprehensive compilation of Noah traditions in the Jewish and Christian literature, which includes the biblical versions, Apocrypha and Pseudepigrapha, Philo, Josephus, the New Testament, patristic works, the targums, and rabbinic literature as well as the few Dead Sea Scrolls that had been published at that time.[17]

While the entire known extant corpus of the Dead Sea Scrolls has now been published in the official editions of the DJD series, the interpretation of the figure of Noah in the Dead Sea Scrolls has not yet been the subject of a full-length, thoroughgoing analysis.[18] Most scholarly attention to date has focused on the texts themselves—on the publication of critical editions, translations, and commentaries addressing issues of dating, textual variants, reconstructions, and the ordering of fragments. In dating the composition of a text, scholars have recognized the complex interplay among factors such as the sources of texts and their ongoing redactions and the parallels with and the contrasts to other Second Temple texts.

Determining a text's provenance, authorship, and the implied "community behind the text," continues to be a complex and challenging task. However, the observed compositional history of a text such as *1 Enoch*, for example, reveals that diversity and debates concerning Noah were allowed to coexist even within a single collection and, even more decidedly, within the entire Qumran corpus.

Calendar and chronology, the parallels observed between Noah and Eden traditions, and the so-called *Book of Noah* are among the few traditions associated with Noah that have received the most persistent scholarly attention. Following the discoveries at Qumran, scholars have used the various calendars represented in the texts to link flood chronology to textual traditions,[19] analyzing

---

17. Lewis, *Study*.

18. However, see Ariel Feldman's fresh editions of and commentaries on 1Q19, 4Q370, 4Q422, 4Q464, and 4Q577 in his recently completed dissertation ("Noah and the Flood in the Non-Sectarian Texts from Qumran," [Ph.D. diss., University of Haifa, 2007]). In addition, Matthias Weigold is currently completing a full-length study of the "Book of the Words of Noah" in the *Genesis Apocryphon* as his Ph.D. dissertation at the University of Vienna entitled, "Noah bricht sein Schweigen: Das 'Buch der Worte Noahs' im Genesis-Apokryphon aus Qumran (1QapGen ar v 29–xviii 23)."

19. Concerning the correlation of the flood chronology in *1 Enoch* and *Jubilees* with that

them as parts of larger studies on ancient hermeneutics.[20] Others have looked for the origins of the calendar within Babylonian, Greek, or Jewish movements.[21]

The Dead Sea Scrolls that bring the creation and flood narratives in Genesis into a more clearly defined relationship have also been the focus of scholarly attention. For example, Eibert Tigchelaar has explored the Eden motif, and Torleif Elgvin has outlined the similarities of language in the creation, flood, and plague narratives in 4QParaphrase of Genesis and Exodus (4Q422), demonstrating how the language forms a bridge between the creation and flood stories.[22]

Little, if any, attention has been paid to the creation of idealized biblical figures in the Dead Sea Scrolls until relatively, recently although early modern scholars laid some important foundations. Already in 1902, R. H. Charles made exploratory comments concerning the transfer of function from one ideal figure to another in early Jewish and Christian interpretation: "Just as these Christian writers transferred Enoch's functions to Seth, so Jewish writers after the Christian era, though on different grounds, transferred them variously to Moses, Ezra, and Elijah."[23] Charles's observation alerts us to the possibility of other examples of "transfer of function" among Noah, Enoch, Levi, and Moses in the Dead Sea Scrolls and prompts us to compare Noah's characterizations in the Dead Sea Scrolls with that of his ancestors and descendants.

---

of the Samaritan Pentateuch, see Daniel K. Falk, "Reconstructions in *Genesis Apocryphon*," (paper presented at the annual meeting of the West Coast Qumran Study Group, Newport, Ore., Oct. 23, 2003). For the correspondence in the variations between the P flood chronology in the MT and the LXX of *Jubilees*, see Ronald S. Hendel, "4Q252 and the Flood Chronology of Genesis 7-8: A Text-Critical Solution," *DSD* 2 (1995): 72-79.

20. Timothy Lim has compared the flood chronologies in 4Q252, MT, LXX, and *Jubilees*, exploring the reasons for the differences in the chronologies ("The Chronology of the Flood Story in a Qumran Text [4Q252]," *JJS* 43 [1992]: 288-98, here 297).

21. Roger T. Beckwith, "The Earliest Enoch Literature and Its Calendar: Marks of Their Origin, Date, and Motivation," *RevQ* 10/3 (1981): 365-403; James C. VanderKam, "Calendrical Texts and the Origins of the Dead Sea Scroll Community," in *Methods of Investigation of the Dead Sea Scrolls and the Khirbet Qumran Site: Present Realities and Future Prospects* (ed. M. O. Wise; New York: New York Academy of Sciences, 1994), 371-88, here 384-85. Philip R. Davies argues that the disruption in Judaism over the solar versus luni-solar calendar occurred already during the Babylonian exile and that the luni-solar calendar was subsequently used by some postexilic Jews. In his discussion, Davies responds to Jerome Murphy-O'Connor's proposition that part of the reason for the relationship between *Enoch*, *Jubilees*, CD, and 1QS may be the Babylonian origin of the Essenes. Philip R. Davies, "Calendrical Change and Qumran Origins: An Assessment of VanderKam's Theory," *CBQ* 45 (1983): 80-89; cf. Jerome Murphy-O'Connor, "The Essenes and Their History," *RB* 81 (1974): 221-22.

22. Eibert J. C. Tigchelaar, "Eden and Paradise: The Garden Motif in Some Early Jewish Texts (1 Enoch and Other Texts Found at Qumran)," in *Paradise Interpreted: Representations of Biblical Paradise in Judaism and Christianity* (ed. G. P. Luttikhuizen; Leiden: Brill, 1999), 37-62; Torleif Elgvin, "The Genesis Section of 4Q422," *DSD* 1 (1994): 180-96.

23. R. H. Charles, *The Book of Jubilees or Little Genesis* (London: SPCK, 1902), 35.

Geza Vermes, in 1951, may have been the first to recognize Noah as an "ideal figure" in the Dead Sea Scrolls:

> Comme du déluge d'eau, Noé et sa famille, "huit âmes", sont sortis indemnes parce qu'ils s'étaient trouvés justes au milieu d'un monde complètement perverti, il en sera de même pour cette communauté de pénitents qui se sont séparés des habitants de la "région d'iniquité," pour se mettre à la suite du Docteur de justice . . . alors le Docteur de Justice est représenté comme un nouveau Noé, mandaté par Dieu pour convertir ses contemporains.[24]

In Noah, who was found righteous in the midst of a corrupt world, Vermes visualized a new symbolic image for Qumran. According to Vermes, the Teacher of Righteousness was like a "new Noah" called to convert his contemporaries. Now, Noah as a "preacher of repentance" was not subsequently found in the scrolls but an archetypical Noah may have been, in some interpretations, created as a retrofit that was patterned after a wise and righteous priestly teacher known to the author.

More recently, there have been studies on other idealized archetypical figures such as Adam,[25] Enosh,[26] Enoch,[27] Levi,[28] and Joseph.[29] However, while there has been growing interest in the figure of Noah, published scholarly discussion thus far has been confined to conference papers, journal articles, essays, and seminar papers. Most importantly, James C. VanderKam identified Noah as a righteous priestly figure in *1 Enoch*, *Jubilees*, and the *Genesis Apocryphon*,[30] and Devorah Dimant observed that Noah was an emblematic figure for Qumran whose "biography served as a vehicle for the community's distinctive theology." She argued that Noah's naming, birth, priestly role, and the catastrophic nature of the prototypical flood explained Noah's appeal to the Qumran community.[31] Florentino García Martínez provided a summary overview of the allusions to the

---

24. Geza Vermes, "La communauté de la Nouvelle Alliance d'après ses écrits récemment découverts," *ETL* 27 (1951): 70–80, here 73.

25. Crispin H. T. Fletcher-Louis, *All the Glory of Adam: Liturgical Anthropology in the Dead Sea Scrolls* (STDJ 42; Leiden: Brill, 2002).

26. Steven D. Fraade, *Enosh and His Generation: Pre-Israelite Hero and History in Postbiblical Interpretation* (SBLMS 30; Chico, Calif.: Scholars Press, 1984).

27. James C. VanderKam, *Enoch, A Man for All Generations* (Studies on Personalities of the Old Testament; Columbia: University of South Carolina Press, 1995).

28. Robert A. Kugler, *From Patriarch to Priest: The Levi-Priestly Tradition from Aramaic Levi to Testament of Levi* (SBLEJL 9; Atlanta: Scholars Press, 1996).

29. Robert A. Kugler, "Joseph at Qumran: The Importance of 4Q372 Frg. 1 in Extending a Tradition," in *Studies in the Hebrew Bible, Qumran, and the Septuagint Presented to Eugene Ulrich* (ed. P. W. Flint, E. Tov, and J. C. VanderKam; VTSup 101; Leiden: Brill, 2006), 261–78.

30. James C. VanderKam, "The Righteousness of Noah," in *Ideal Figures in Ancient Judaism: Profiles and Paradigms* (SBLSCS 12; ed. J. J. Collins and G. W. E. Nickelsburg; Chico, Calif.: Scholars Press, 1980), 13–32.

31. Devorah Dimant, "Noah in Early Jewish Literature," in *Biblical Figures Outside the*

flood narrative in the Dead Sea Scrolls, and Moshe J. Bernstein examined Noah traditions within the genres, showing that the way that the scrolls handled the Noah material depended on the goal of the work.[32]

To conclude this section, the extant Dead Sea Scrolls have now been published, and their reconstructions, dating, compositional histories, and provenance have been thoroughly discussed in the official editions and other scholarly publications. Scattered and selected Noah traditions have been treated in shorter essays, but this particular study carries the discussion further by means of close literary readings of each of the Dead Sea texts that handles Noah traditions. Along the way, the rich and diverse kinds of conversations that authors and texts may have participated in are illuminated by the rich and diverse portrayals of Noah within the scrolls.

NOAH TRADITIONS IN THE DEAD SEA SCROLLS: NEW DIRECTIONS

Chapters 2 through 7 focus on texts in which the figure of Noah, whether named or unnamed, is present; however, we also consider scrolls in which the figure of Noah is detached from traditions normally associated with him, such as the primordial judgment by flood, the Watchers story, and "atoning for the land." Finally, chapter 8 summarizes the findings and explores the extent to which there may have been a "Hebrew Noah" as distinct from an "Aramaic Noah" in the Dead Sea Scrolls.

Texts are categorized as either Hebrew[33] or Aramaic,[34] are read for the Noah traditions they contain, and are analyzed for indicators of possible sources and

---

Bible (ed. M. E. Stone and T. A. Bergren; Harrisburg, Pa.: Trinity Press International, 1998), 123–50.

32. Florentino García Martínez, "Interpretations of the Flood in the Dead Sea Scrolls," in *Interpretations of the Flood* (ed. F. García Martínez and G. P. Luttikhuizen; Themes in Biblical Narrative 1; Leiden: Brill, 1998), 86–108; Moshe J. Bernstein, "Noah and the Flood at Qumran," in *The Provo International Conference on the Dead Sea Scrolls: New Texts, Technological Innovations, and Reformulated Issues* (ed. D. W. Parry and E. C. Ulrich; STDJ 30; Leiden: Brill, 1999), 199–231.

33. Noah and flood traditions mentioned in Hebrew texts represented in the Dead Sea Scrolls include Genesis, Ezekiel, Isaiah, Chronicles, Tobit (4Q200) (also found in four copies in Aramaic), Ben Sira (2Q18), *Jubilees* (1Q17–18, 2Q19–20, 3Q5, 4Q176a, 4Q216–224, 11Q12), 4QFestival Prayers[b] (4Q508), 4QTanhumim (4Q176), 4QExposition on the Patriarchs (4Q464), 4QParaphrase on Genesis and Exodus (4Q422), 4QAdmonition on the Flood (4Q370), 4QAges of Creation[a-b] (4Q180–181), *Damascus Document* (4Q266–273), 4QCommentary on Genesis A–D (4Q252, 4Q253, 4Q254, 4Q254a and see 4Q253a), 5QRule (5Q13), and 1QNoah (1Q19).

34. Noah and flood traditions mentioned in Aramaic texts represented in the Dead Sea Scrolls include Tobit (4Q196–199) (also extant in one Hebrew copy), Enochic *Book of Watchers, Dream Visions, Apocalypse of Weeks, Birth of Noah* (4Q201, 4Q202, 4Q204, 4Q205, 4Q206, 4Q207, 4Q212), *Aramaic Levi Document* (1Q21, 4Q213, 4Q213a, 4Q213b, 4Q214, 4Q214a, 4Q214b), 4QVisions of Amram (4Q547), 4QNaissance de Noé(?) (4Q534), *Genesis Apocryphon* (1Q20), and 4QPseudo-Daniel[b] (4Q244).

for the way the received tradition was transmitted and reinterpreted. The specific approach to any given text is determined partially by its state of preservation.

When a text containing Noah traditions was known prior to the Qumran discovery and for which portions are now available in the original language of composition, it is possible to establish a relatively secure literary context for the Noah traditions within the larger work. Such texts include Genesis, Ezekiel, Isaiah, Ben Sira, Tobit, some of the books of *1 Enoch*, the *Aramaic Levi Document*, *Jubilees*, and the *Damascus Document*. Literary structure, unifying themes in recurring words and phrases, reordering of material, omissions, expansions, thematic parallels, idiomatic grammatical constructions, and harmonizations may be studied in the available Hebrew or Aramaic text as supplemented by the work in translation.

When a text such as Genesis or the *Book of Watchers* is itself found within a larger collection of books, the Noah traditions in one part of the collection may be studied in conversation with traditions in another part of the collection. Where there are multiple copies of one text, the variants may be significant, especially if they appear to be interpretative in nature.

Texts containing Noah themes and traditions known only from the Dead Sea Scrolls include the *Genesis Apocryphon*, 4QTestatment of Qahat, 4QVisions of Amram, 4QTanḥumim, 4QFestival Prayers, 4QAdmonition Based on the Flood, 4QAges of Creation, 4QCommentary on Genesis A–D, 4QNaissance de Noé, 4QInstruction, and 4QPseudo-Daniel. Most challenging are the extremely fragmentary texts that offer few hints of the context of the Noah traditions or of the extent of the original content. These include 4QExposition on the Patriarchs, 1QBook of Noah, 4QParaphrase of Genesis and Exodus and 5QRule. Even so, extant individual words and phrases, idiosyncratic grammar, and alternative ordering of the fragments are often instructive about the development of Noah traditions in the text.

Noah first appears in the texts of the Hebrew Bible and in the Aramaic copies of *1 Enoch* within which the process of reinterpreting and recontextualizing existing flood survivor stories had already begun. It is to the Hebrew Bible that we now turn.

CHAPTER TWO

NOAH IN THE BIBLICAL TEXT

And the waters swelled on the earth for one hundred fifty days.
But God remembered Noah
Genesis 7:24–8:1

INTRODUCTION: NOAH ENTERS THE ANCIENT NEAR EASTERN CONVERSATION

When Noah first came onto the scene as a "flood survivor" in the earliest Hebrew narrative, a story something like his had already been recounted in different languages and across cultures for centuries in the ancient Near East. In Genesis, elements of these stories were variously adapted and contextualized within new frameworks and within new stories about Israel's God and about his relationship with the people he had created. Students of Genesis may disagree over the origin of a particular line or feature, but few would argue that Genesis does not bear the imprint of the DNA from its sources.[1]

The Babylonian Gilgamesh Epic and its parent version, the Atrahasis Epic, a "history of the human race from creation to the flood" that likely "survived into Hellenistic times" and was "Grecized by Berossus,"[2] were likely known, in some version, by the Hebrew narrators. The narrators of the Genesis account variously adopted, adapted, or polemicized the theologies expressed in these ancient Near

---

1. For a historical overview of the history of composition of Genesis, see Victor P. Hamilton, *The Book of Genesis Chapters 1–17* (NICOT; Grand Rapids: Eerdmans, 1990), 11–38. Among the many studies of Genesis based on an analysis of its purported sources, see Erich Bosshard-Nepustil, *Vor uns die Sintflut: Studien zu Text, Kontexten und Rezeption der Fluterzählung Genesis 6–9* (BWANT 165; Stuttgart: Kohlhammer, 2005); Hermann Gunkel, *Genesis* (trans. M.E. Biddle; Macon, Ga.: Mercer University Press, 1997); E.A. Speiser, *Genesis: Introduction, Translation, and Notes* (AB 1; New York: Doubleday, 1964); Gerhard von Rad, *Genesis: A Commentary* (OTL; Philadelphia: Westminster, 1972); Claus Westermann, *Genesis 1–11: A Commentary* (trans. J. J. Scullion; Minneapolis: Augsburg, 1984).

2. Nahum M. Sarna, *Genesis* (JPS Torah Commentary; Philadelphia: Jewish Publication Society, 1989), 48.

Eastern stories in the formation of their own flood survivor narrative.³ The very creation of their own flood survivor stories would have brought the ancient biblical narrators into the kinds of conversations and controversies between Israel and its ancient Near Eastern neighbors that resulted in the sharpening of the distinguishing boundaries between them. Even so, Noah, as ancestor of all humanity and not only of Israel, could never be perceived as belonging to Israel alone. Therefore, from the time of its earliest origins and into the Second Temple period, the Noah narrative was heard against a background of competing flood survivor stories.

The recontextualization of ancient Near Eastern Noah traditions into the Hebrew narrative was not the end of engagement with and response to foreign myth and story. At least some Jews in the Second Temple period continued to respond to Mesopotamian and Greek flood survivor stories alongside the narrative in Genesis. Therefore, the figure of Noah was well suited for his role as a magnetic conversational centerpiece around which a lively and ongoing discussion could revolve concerning topics of persistent interest such as what it meant to be a people of God, how God revealed himself to his people, and to what extent should a people of God remain distinct from its surrounding culture.

The final form of Genesis presents a skillful weaving together of the earliest Israelite Noah traditions into a coherent literary unity that allowed the individual sources or voices to be heard in conversational tension.⁴ Later in this chapter, an

---

3. Helge S. Kvanvig makes a good case for Genesis' knowledge of the Atrahasis version of the flood story. He gives two reasons. Both present a "large primaeval history with three basic elements: Creation – destruction – new world order" and, secondly, each presents a creator or creatress who is remorseful. Helge S. Kvanvig, "The Watchers Story, Genesis and *Atrahasis*, a Triangular Reading," *Hen* 24 (2002): 17–21, here 19. In a similar vein, see Gordon J. Wenham, *Genesis 1-15* (WBC 1; Nashville: Thomas Nelson, 1987), xlvi-l; Umberto Cassuto, *A Commentary on the Book of Genesis* (trans. I. Abrahams; 2 vols.; Jerusalem: Magnes, 1978), 1:4–29; David T. Tsumura, "Genesis and Ancient Near Eastern Stories of Creation and Flood: An Introduction," in *"I Studied Inscriptions from before the Flood": Ancient Near Eastern, Literary, and Linguistic Approaches to Genesis 1-11* (ed. R. S. Hess and D. T. Tsumura; Sources for Biblical and Theological Study 4; Winona Lake, Ind.: Eisenbrauns, 1994), 44–57.

4. For scholarship that gives consideration to viewing Genesis as a unified and coherent narrative, see Ronald Hendel, "The Nephilim Were on the Earth: Genesis 6:1–4 and Its Ancient Near Eastern Context," in *The Fall of the Angels* (ed. C. Auffarth and L. T. Stuckenbruck; Themes in Biblical Narrative 6; Leiden: Brill, 2004), 11–34; Gordon J. Wenham, "The Coherence of the Flood Narrative," in *"I Studied Inscriptions from before the Flood": Ancient Near Eastern, Literary, and Linguistic Approaches to Genesis 1-11* (ed. R. S. Hess and D. T. Tsumura; Sources for Biblical and Theological Study 4; Winona Lake, Ind.: Eisenbrauns, 1994), 436–47; Cassuto, *Commentary on Genesis*, 1:1–18; Robert Alter, *The Five Books of Moses: A Translation with Commentary* (New York: W. W. Norton, 2004). These approaches give appropriate credit to the craft of the ancient writers, a significant development from the work of Gunkel, who, perhaps influenced by an evolutionary model, perceived a "primitive construction" to the legends and with respect to the plausibility of the narrative stated that "the auditor of ancient times doubtless did not ask such questions; he was more willing to surrender to the narrator, and was more easily charmed; he was also more credulous than we are" (Hermann Gunkel,

exploration of the beginnings of Noah traditions that were variously developed in the texts represented in the Dead Sea Scrolls reveals that Noah's interpreters were likely familiar with a version of the story as preserved in Genesis. However, even among the textual witnesses of the earliest compositions found in the caves, Noah is an enigmatic figure.

Texts and Observations

The Genesis Scrolls at Qumran: A Few Words on Noah

The nineteen or twenty Genesis manuscripts from Caves 1, 2, 4, 6, and 8 are "generally very close to the traditional Hebrew text" with only a few variants "best classified as mixed, or 'nonaligned.'"[5] In contrast to the various extant editions of Exodus, Leviticus, Numbers, and Deuteronomy, the Qumran Genesis texts display a remarkable degree of conformity to each other and also to the MT.[6] Therefore, a relatively stable text of Genesis was in existence during the Second Temple period and was likely available for interpretation.

Somewhat puzzling is that there is no witness to Noah, no attestation of Genesis 6–10[7] in Caves 1, 2, and 8, or in the ten Cave 4 Genesis manuscripts that contain often substantial portions of Genesis 1–4; 13; and 17–50.[8] Eight full words and several partial words from the Noah narrative (Gen 6:13–21) are preserved in

---

The Legends of Genesis: The Biblical Saga of History [trans. W. H. Carruth; New York: Schocken Books, 1964], 47, 72; trans. of *Die Sagen der Genesis* [1901]).

5. *DSSB*, 3–4. The types of variants listed in the official editions—DJD I, III, IX, and XII—largely support this assessment, as do the recent fragments of 4QGen[f] and 8QGen published by Esther Eshel and Hanan Eshel in "New Fragments from Qumran: 4QGen[f], 4QIsa[b], 4Q226, 8QGen, and XQ papEnoch," *DSD* 12 (2005): 134–57. Of the fifty-one variants in the so-called 4QpaleoGen-Exod[l], twenty-four disagree with the MT (DJD IX, 25). However, in this scroll, Genesis is represented only by two "probable" letters and a question mark accompanies the reference Genesis 50:26 in the official edition (DJD IX, 25).

6. Although each of the other four books of the Pentateuch generally follows the MT, some variants reveal a dependence on other textual traditions. For example, 4QExod[b] is "a collateral witness to the textual family which provided the *Vorlage* of the Old Greek translation" but the variants of 4QExod[c] agree sometimes with MT, sometimes with SP, with LXX, with another Exodus scroll, or preserve a unique reading (DJD XII, 84, 103). 4QExod-Lev[f] contains Aramaicisms and its "filiation . . . is with the Samaritan tradition" (DJD XII, 136). 4QNum[b] contains a significant number of expansions and unique readings and is more closely related to the LXX and the SP than to the MT (DJD XII, 215). 4QDeut[q] more often agrees with the LXX than with the MT (*DSSB*, 146). It should also be noted that 4QGen-Exod[a] closely follows the MT. The Genesis portion has six variants—including orthographic differences—that disagree with the MT in 79 lines of text; the Exodus portion has nine variants that disagree with the MT in 103 lines of text. The text preserves portions of Exodus 1–9 and Genesis 22; 27; 34; 35; 36; 37; 39; 45; 47; 48; and 49.

7. Only "Kenan" (קינן) survives from Gen 5:9 or 10 (4QGen[b] 3 II, 1).

8. טהר and עוד are in unidentified frg. 47 of 4QGen-Exod[a] (see J. R. Davila, DJD XII, 29) but attributed to Gen 8:20–21 in *DSSB*.

6QpaleoGen (6Q1), a text in paleo-Hebrew script dated to 250–150 B.C.E.[9] Cave 6 also housed a copy of the Book of Giants (6QpapEnGiants ar (6Q8), 6QGen? ar (6Q19) that mentions the "sons of Ham."[10]

Copies of the Septuagint found in Cave 7 included texts of Exodus, Leviticus, Numbers, Deuteronomy, and the Epistle of Jeremiah. The presence of the other four books of the Pentateuch suggests that Genesis was also known and available. Most of the LXX variants in the flood story may be accounted for as examples of "translation Greek," harmonization among texts within the narrative, avoidance of anthropomorphisms, and clarification of ambiguities and difficulties in the text such as those presented by ancestral life spans and chronologies.[11] There are several interesting interpretative variants, however, that may reveal questions of interest for the interpreters and translators of the Hebrew narrative.

First, "angels of God" for בני אלהים (Gen 6:2) in Codex Alexandrinus and "giants" for נפלים (Gen 6:4) are readings preserved in the Greek that are found also in Enochic traditions. Second, humankind's responsibility for the inclination of the human heart is more heightened in the LXX than in the MT in Gen 8:21. Whereas the translation of the Hebrew MT reads "the inclination of the human heart is evil from youth," the translation of the LXX reads as follows: "the mind of humankind applies itself attentively to evil things from youth."

Finally, the LXX either harmonizes Gen 9:1 with 1:28 or reflects a variant text of Genesis: "And God blessed Noe and his sons and said to them, 'Increase, and multiply, and fill the earth, and subdue it'" (Gen 9:1). The phrase "and subdue it" is lacking in all Hebrew texts of Gen 9:1 but is found in the Hebrew text of 1:28 in the context of God's blessing of the primeval couple: "Be fruitful and multiply, and fill the earth and subdue it." As Daniel Falk has pointed out, the LXX is not the only tradition that reads Gen 9:1–3 as a "restatement of the prom-

---

9. DJD III, 105–6. The reconstructed למי[ניהם (6Q1/Gen 6:20) with the plural suffix yields a variant that is found also in the SP, but this is only the slimmest of evidence that Noachic interpretation in the Dead Sea Scrolls followed an SP-like text rather than a proto-Masoretic text.

10. A tiny Aramaic fragment containing "of the sons of Ham" (די בני חם) and "the peoples" is titled 6QGen? ar (6Q19) in DJD III; however, the Hebrew equivalent in Gen 10:20 is חם אלה בני. The fact that one of the four extant words would be a strange variant makes this text an unlikely candidate for Aramaic Genesis.

11. For some examples of these, see Jack P. Lewis, *A Study of the Interpretation of Noah and the Flood in Jewish and Christian Literature* (Leiden: Brill, 1968), 82–88. Robert J. V. Hiebert notes that the "overall picture assessment of Greek Genesis is that, lexically and syntactically, it is a strict, quantitative representation of its source text." Hiebert, "Genesis," in *A New English Translation of the Septuagint and Other Greek Translations Traditionally Included under That Title* (ed. A. Pietersma and B. G. Wright; New York/Oxford: Oxford University Press, 2007), 1–42, here 1. All translations of LXX are taken from *NETS*, unless otherwise indicated.

ise to Adam" or as a "restoration of a lost dominion to Noah."[12] This developing tradition of the restoration of dominion to Noah is studied in more detail in chapter 5. In the meantime, we move away this very brief discussion of sources, variants, and translation and into the Genesis Noah narrative as it is preserved its final form in the Hebrew MT.

The Introduction of Noah in Genesis: The Beginnings of Traditions

Second Temple interpreters of Genesis most likely approached the text with a slightly different set of questions in mind than modern interpreters do and one wonders whether they sought out its "structure" in quite the same way! However, the interpreters of antiquity did notice patterns, repetitions, and apparent superfluities within what they still perceived to be a coherent and purposeful narrative. They thought deeply and creatively about how the Noah story was related to what preceded it (the creation and the Cain and Abel stories), to what followed it (the Tower of Babel and the arrival of Abram), and about how each part related to the whole.

The structure proposed here has the Dead Sea Scrolls interpreters of the Genesis narrative in mind and their concerns in view. Its divisions highlight the Noah narrative's connections to what precedes and follows, ways the narrative demonstrates its coherence, and how themes and repetitions play out in ways later interpreters may have noticed and reinterpreted in the texts of Qumran.[13]

STRUCTURE OF THE NOAH NARRATIVE IN GENESIS 5–10

I. Prelude: Doomed First Creation (5:1–6:8)
   A. First Creation Rehearsed (זה ספר תולדת אדם) (5:1–32)
      1. Creation of first "Adam" through to Jared (vv. 1–20)
      2. Enoch, who walked with God (האלהים), and Methuselah (vv. 21–27)
      3. Lamech fathers and names Noah; Noah fathers Shem, Ham, and Japheth (vv. 28–32)
   B. Origin of the Cosmic Enemies (6:1–4)
      1. Sons of gods intermarry with daughters of men (vv. 1–2)
      2. God responds with hints of the coming end (v. 3)
      3. "Fallen ones" (הנפלים) and "mighty ones" (הגברים) on the earth (v. 4)
   C. Destruction of the First Creation Imminent and Promised (6:5–8)
      1. God recognizes the inclination (יצר) of humankind for evil (v. 5)
      2. God regrets (וינחם) making humankind and promises to blot out them out from the earth, along with the animals (vv. 6–7)
      3. Introduction of the exception: "But Noah" (ונח) (v. 8)

---

12. Daniel K. Falk, *The Parabiblical Texts: Strategies for Extending the Scriptures among the Dead Sea Scrolls* (CQS 8; LSTS 63; New York: T&T Clark, 2007), 62.

13. For a more detailed structure and analysis, see Dorothy M. Peters, "Noah in the Dead Sea Scrolls" (Ph.D. diss., University of Manchester, 2006), 46–51, 254–57.

II. Creation Destroyed and Renewed (6:9–9:29) (אלה תולדת נח)
   A. First Creation Destroyed; A Remnant to Be Preserved (6:9–7:24)
      1. God instructs Noah the righteous (צדיק); Noah obeys (6:9–7:12)
         a. Earth filled with violence prompting the "end" (6:9–13)
         b. Noah constructs the ark; Noah gathers the animals (6:14–7:5)
         c. Noah enters ark with family and animals; floodwaters come upon the earth (7:6–12)
      2. Recapitulation, variations, and developments (7:13–18)
         a. Noah enters ark: recapitulation (vv. 13–14)
         b. Noah enters ark: first and second variations on a theme (vv. 15–16)
         c. Floodwaters increase (וירבו) and prevail (ויגברו) (vv. 17–18)
      3. Coda: crescendo and intensification (והמים גברו) (7:19–24)
         a. Waters prevail (גבר) more and more (מאד מאד) (vv. 19–22)
         b. Every living thing is blotted out except for Noah (v. 23)
         c. Waters prevail (גבר) for 150 days (v. 24)
   B. Creation Renewed for the "New Adam" (8:1–9:29) (ויזכר אלהים את־נח)
      1. Days 1–3: earth prepared for habitation—wind, waters, dry ground, and vegetation (8:1–14)
         a. Day 1: God remembers Noah; wind over the waters (v. 1)
         b. Day 2: separation of waters (vv. 2–5)
         c. Day 3: emergence of dry ground and vegetation (vv. 6–14)
      2. Days 4–6: heavens, animals, and humans restored (8:15–9:17)
         a. Transition: Leaving the ark; reentering the land (8:15–19)
         b. Day 4: seasons reestablished (8:20–21)
         c. Days 5–6: humans and animals in covenant with God and primeval blessings renewed (9:1–17)
      3. Noah as "second Adam" on a renewed earth (9:18–28)
III. Finale: Primeval Blessing Unfulfilled and Sons of Noah Scattered (10:1–32)

This structure also reflects natural divisions—unexpected breaks in the narrative sequence—that would have been particularly noticeable in an oral retelling. The narrative proceeds in normal fashion as a series of clauses beginning with *waw-consecutive* verbs but occasionally interrupted at critical junctures by a clause beginning with a noun or pronoun either accompanied or unaccompanied by a preceding *waw*. These interruptions in the narrative flow would have alerted ancient listeners to a shift in subject, emphasis, or setting.

The occasional use of musical terminology in the structural headings evokes the poetic and even musical nature of the myths from which the Hebrew story was adapted and recontextualized.[14] Initial statements of theme as well as the fugal recapitulations and variations are respected as purposeful and integral

---

14. On poetry and "music" in the Noah narrative in Genesis, see Alter, *Five Books of Moses*, 44, who notes the "regular practice of biblical narrative to introduce insets of verse at moments of high importance.... The grand flourish of this line of poetry is perfectly consonant with the resonant repetitions and measured cadences of the surrounding prose." Sarna suggests that the occurrence of unique or rare words and the repetition of others indicate that

components to the piece. The final result is a structure that is informed by the narrative itself but that includes "grace notes," fragments of the story that do not fall easily within our structure, and that function to remind the modern interpreter that outlines should be fitted retrospectively onto an ancient story only with gentleness and caution.

The Noah narrative in Genesis 5:1–10:32 is divided into three main sections, each introduced by a תולדת formula, introducing the generations of Adam (5:1), of Noah (6:9), and of the sons of Noah (10:1). Part I, "Prelude: Doomed First Creation" (5:1–6:8), selectively rehearses the history of humankind, introducing words and details or leitmotifs that anticipate renewal of creation and the removal of the curse and that would be echoed later in the narrative proper. For example, "God created" (ברא) (5:1) is repeated in 6:7; "in the image of" (בדמות) finds the synonym בצלם in 9:6; זכר ונקבה (5:2) is repeated in 7:16, and ברך (5:2) is paralleled in 9:1. The word order of a phrase is reversed for Noah so that Enoch "walked with God" (ויתהלך חנוך את־האלהים) (5:22) but "with God walked Noah" (את־האלהים התהלך־נח) (6:9).

Lamech names his son "Noah," adding that he would bring relief (ינחמנו) from the work and toil (עצבון)[15] that had come about from God's curse (ארר)[16] on the ground (5:29). Noah's name is later echoed is other intriguing ways. For example, God regrets (וינחם) that he made humans (6:6–7); the ark rests (ותנח) on the mountains of Ararat (8:4); the dove finds no place to rest (מנוח) its foot (8:9), and God smells the soothing aroma (הניחח) of Noah's sacrifice (8:21).

While the lines of Gen 6:1–4 concerning the marriage of the "the sons of gods" to the "daughters of men," are, by their very juxtaposition with the Noah narrative, implicitly linked to it, they are still rather oddly and awkwardly placed. The narrator makes no explicit evaluative comment on this mismatched marital alliance but, in a foreshadowing of what would come, God pronounces that he would no longer suspend judgment upon humankind (באדם) (6:3).[17] At this criti-

---

a poetic version of the story may be discernible beneath the present prose narrative (*Genesis*, 49).

15. עצבון "does not mean 'labor' but rather 'pain,' and is the crucial word at the heart of Adam's curse, and Eve's. Given that allusion, the two terms in the Hebrew—which reads literally, 'our work and the pain of our hands'—are surely to be construed as a hendiadys, a pair of terms for a single concept indicating 'painful labor.' " Alter adds that עצבון "appears only three times in the Bible (other nominal forms of the root being relatively common)—first for Eve, then for Adam, and now for Noah." Alter, *Five Books of Moses*, 37.

16. "The curse referred to in 5.29 refers to 'toil' (עצבון) and the provision of a regular seasonal cycle in 8.22 also implies alleviation of agricultural labours." Philip R. Davies, "Sons of Cain," in *A Word in Season: Essays in Honour of William McKane* (ed. J. D. Martin and P. R. Davies; JSOTSup 42; Sheffield: JSOT Press, 1986), 35–56, here 36.

17. Terence E. Fretheim notes the verbal links between Gen 6:2: "sons of gods" see (ראה) the fair (טוב) daughters and take (לקח) them. These same three words, "see, fair, and take" also describe Eve's eating of the fruit (3:6) (*NIB*, 382). This, together with God's statement that his spirit would not abide with mortals forever (6:3), points to the undoing of God's

cal point, there is break in narrative sequence, reflecting a "certain epic heightening" that raises the suspicion that "these words are either a citation of an old heroic poem or a stylistic allusion to the epic genre." The "fallen ones" (הנפלים) are introduced together with "heroes of yore"[18] or "mighty ones" (הגברים). The verbal root גבר is reused repeatedly in the narrative describing the floodwaters that prevailed (גבר) over the earth (Gen 7:18, 19, 20, 24), a wordplay with significant potential that did not escape the attention of the story's interpreters.

The presence of "the fallen ones" or Nephilim on the earth is noted without comment other than that they existed at the same time as the sons of gods "went into" the daughters of humans (6:4). However, the juxtaposition of these lines with God's recognition of the human inclination for evil, his regret that he made humans, and his stated intention he would blot out all human beings and animals that he created (6:5–7) suggests an implicit causal link between the two parts. A second break in the narrative sequence introduces the exceptional hero of the story, the one who, together with his family, would survive the planned destruction: "But Noah (ונח) found favor in the eyes of the LORD" (6:8).

Part II, "Creation Destroyed and Renewed," begins with Part A, "First Creation Destroyed: A Remnant to Be Preserved" (6:9 – 7:24), in which Noah's character is more clearly defined as the righteous, blameless one who walks about with God. God speaks to Noah, revealing specific knowledge about his intention to destroy the earth. He offers him practical instruction on how to build the ark and commands him to collect the animals. Throughout this part of the account, we hear nothing from Noah. He does not speak, and the narrator does not record his thoughts. The narrative simply states that Noah did everything that God commanded him to do (Gen 6:22).

The section continues in ch. 7 with a recapitulation and additional variations and expansions in longer and shorter versions. Types and numbers of animals are specified; God shuts the door; and the waters prevail. A "coda" opens with yet another break in narrative sequence, dramatically intensifying the difference in the balance of power between the death-dealing prevailing waters and Noah; "And the waters prevailed (והמים גברו) more and more upon the earth" (7:19). The waters prevailed (גברו) and rose fifteen cubits higher (7:20); all flesh perished (7:21); everything within whom was the breath of life died (7:22); God blotted out every living thing and, finally, "they were blotted out" (7:23a). The narrative returns to Noah but only very briefly as if to emphasize the solitude and apparent helplessness of those in the ark who were floating on top of the waters: "Only Noah was left" (וישאר) (7:23b). Immediately, the narrative returns to the waters that "prevailed (גברו) upon the earth for one hundred and fifty days" (7:24).

---

impartation of the breath of life to humans in Gen 2:7 and the onset of destruction of creation by the flood. God's decision to wipe out the human race (6:7) employs the same two verbs (ברא and עשה) "that are used in the original Creation (1:26–27) but transposed in order to symbolize the reversal of the process" (Sarna, *Genesis*, 47).

18. Alter, *Five Books of Moses*, 39.

The storyteller has, by means of initial statement, recapitulation, variations, and coda, built tension and suspense in waves, increasing the dissonance between the vulnerability of Noah and the unleashed power of the floodwaters in the face of the silence of God. God's communication with Noah had already ended in Gen 7:4, and the reader is now left to wonder whether God could regain control over the waters now that they had prevailed so mightily.

In the beginning of section B, "Creation Renewed for the 'New Adam'" (8:1–9:29),[19] God reenters the narrative with "But God remembered Noah" (ויזכר אלהים את־נח),[20] a phrase signaling the beginning of the reversal of creation's destruction and the beginning of a new creation. Linguistic parallels and word substitutions of language from the creation account are suggestive of a "creation, destruction of creation, re-creation" motif that unifies the primeval history.[21]

First, days 1–3 of creation in Gen 1 are renewed (8:1–14). God sends a wind over the waters separating them once again. Dry land appears, followed by vegetation on the earth. In an interlude, Noah's family and the animals leave the ark and step out to reenter the land.

Second, days 4–6 see the restoration of the "heavens" and of animals and humans to their proper functions (8:15–9:17). God did not need to re-create humans and animals, for he had already preserved them upon the ark, but he responds favorably to Noah's sacrifice, promising never again to curse the ground[22] or to cut off all flesh from the earth. The days and seasons are reestablished, and both humans and animals enter into a covenant with God that includes certain blood prohibitions.[23] In a restatement of the primeval blessing (Gen 1:28), God

---

19. Wenham concludes that, in the Genesis narrative, the flood ("de-creation") began on a Sunday and concluded on a Friday, affirming that the Genesis flood was deliberately contrasted to the Genesis creation story and was, therefore, a vehicle for theological ideas ("Coherence," 345). Second Temple interpreters would notice the connection.

20. Wenham points to Gen 8:1 as the turning point of the narrative around which two halves of his palistrophe are formed. The numbers of the chronology (7 days, 40 days, 150 days) make their appearances in corresponding positions in each half ("Coherence," 337–43).

21. For a discussion of "creation, un-creation, and re-creation," see P. J. Harland, *The Value of Human Life: A Study of the Story of the Flood (Genesis 6–9)* (VTSup 64; Leiden: Brill, 1996), 89.

22. The verbal discrepancies between this word for curse (קלל) (Gen 8:21) and the curse uttered in Gen 3:17 (ארורה) and 4:11 (ארור) speaks both to an allusion to the curse in Eden and to an interpretation of the curse. Davies identifies the Noah curse story as a "*recapitulation* of Gen 2–3 but one in which contrasts are emphasized" ("Sons of Cain," 38). "The text does not state the curse is revoked, only that there will be no further curse.... The problem of the curse is resolved, but the curse itself is not revoked. What occurs is a *volte face* in which the original, negative curse is 'resolved' by a positive 'counter-curse' ... the blessing of the seasonal cycle" (ibid., 37).

23. The lists of the types of animals throughout the Noah narrative vary in order but mirror the lists in the creation account: Gen 6:20; 7:14; 9:2; 9:10; cf. 1:21, 24–25.

instructs humans to be fruitful and multiply (Gen 9:1) and gives them plants and animals for food (Gen 9:3; cf. Gen 1:29).

Third, humans and animals begin their new life on the renewed earth (9:18–29). Noah cultivates the ground, plants a vineyard, and drinks of the wine. Ham sees Noah as he lies drunk and uncovered in his tent, but it is not God who intervenes in order to curse and punish. In his first recorded speech, it is Noah who blesses and curses.[24] Judgment of sin is no longer solely God's responsibility, and humans are given the role of distinguishing between those who should be blessed and those who should be cursed.

Part III, "Primeval Blessing Unfulfilled and Sons of Noah Scattered," is the finale to the narrative.[25] God had earlier commanded Noah and sons to be fruitful and multiply and to fill (מלא) the earth (9:1); however, as Carol Kaminski has demonstrated, Genesis 10 does *not* fulfill the primeval blessing. Rather than "fill" the earth, Noah's sons פרד and פוץ, words that she translates negatively as "scatter" or "disperse."[26]

We turn now to Noah traditions elsewhere in the Hebrew Bible. While possible points of contact with the flood story are scattered throughout the Hebrew Bible, Noah is specifically named in Ezekiel 14, Isaiah 54, and 1 Chronicles.[27]

Noah in Exile: Ezekiel and Deutero-Isaiah

Noah's inclusion in a list of three righteous people in Ezekiel and in the context of the promised judgments immediately raises two questions: First, why are Noah, Daniel, and Job chosen as examples of righteous ones rather than Israel's more generally acknowledged ancestors, Abraham, Isaac, or Jacob? Second, does the list of judgments allude back to the primordial judgment in some way?

> Mortal, when a land sins against me by acting faithlessly, and I stretch out my hand against it, and break its staff of bread (שברתי לה מטה־לחם) and send

---

24. Cf. 4Q252–254a and its emphasis on blessing and curses, in particular, the curses of Noah. Devora Steinmetz has argued that the vineyard story marks an increase in human involvement and a corresponding decrease in God's involvement. For the first time, a human being curses ("Vineyard, Farm, and Garden: The Drunkenness of Noah in the Context of Primeval History," *JBL* 113 [1994]: 193–207, here 205–6).

25. For the idea that *Jubilees* and the *Genesis Apocryphon* understood Gen 9:1 and 10:32 as forming an "*inclusio* with regard to filling the earth" and the intervening story about Noah's sons as a dispute over land boundaries, see Falk, *Parabiblical Texts*, 65.

26. Carol Kaminski, *From Noah to Israel: Realization of the Primaeval Blessing after the Flood* (London: T&T Clark International, 2004), 30–59. Cf. the expansion of the command to be fruitful: ואתם פרו ורבו שרצו בארץ ורבו־בה (Gen 9:7). On p. 79, Kaminiski adds that the reordering of the brothers with Shem in the final position indicates that he is the one through whom the blessing would eventually be fulfilled.

27. Noah is the tenth person in a genealogy beginning with Adam (1 Chr 1:4). Noah is tenth in Gen 5, but Lamech is sixth in the Gen 4 genealogy.

famine (רעב) upon it, and cut off from it human beings and animals, even if Noah, Daniel, and Job, these three, were in it, they would save only their own lives by their righteousness says the LORD God. If I send wild animals (חיה רעה) . . . even if these three men were in it . . . they alone would be saved, but the land would be desolate. Or if I bring a sword (חרב) upon that . . . and I cut off human beings and animals from it; though these three men were in it. . . . Or if I send a pestilence (דבר) into that land, and pour out my wrath upon it with blood, to cut off humans and animals from it; even if Noah, Daniel, and Job were in it, as I live, says the LORD God, they would save neither son nor daughter; they would save only their own lives by their righteousness. Yet, survivors shall be left in it, sons and daughters who will be brought out; they will come out to you. When you see their ways and their deeds, you will be consoled (נחם) for the evil that I have brought upon Jerusalem, for all that I have brought upon it. They shall console (נחם) you, when you see their ways and their deeds. (Excerpted from Ezek 14:13–23)

The righteousness of Noah, Daniel, and Job is questioned but is simply assumed. All three lived in times of death and disaster, when people were literally or metaphorically "cut off" or living apart outside of the land. In this forecast judgment, not even sons and daughters would be covered by the righteousness of another. Even so, there is the promise that "survivors" would escape (פלט) and Israel would be consoled (נחם) (Ezek 14:22–23), a wordplay that could be read intertextually with the naming of Noah (Gen 5:29). Consolation would follow the judgment, and survivors would be reestablished in the land.

It is curious that Abraham and Moses are not mentioned in this list of notable righteous figures. They had campaigned on behalf of a people whom God intended to destroy, Abraham for Sodom and Gomorrah (Gen 18:16–33) and Moses for Israel (Exod 32:11). In anticipation of our exploration of the Aramaic scrolls in chapters 3 and 5, we might just mention here that Aramaic texts focus on biblical characters who lived at least part of their lives outside of the land, the pre-Mosaic characters of Enoch, Noah, Abraham, Jacob, Joseph, Levi, Qahat, and Amram, as well as Daniel and Job.[28] It would seem that Ezekiel stands at the beginning of a trajectory of tradition idealizing biblical figures—including Noah—as archetypes for a people in "exile," a tradition that intensified in its development in the Aramaic scrolls at Qumran.[29]

---

28. Although Moses was never "in the land," the interpretive texts concerning Moses are written in Hebrew. However, because of Moses' inescapable bond to the Mosaic Torah, this is not unexpected.

29. Job is one of only two biblical books preserved as an Aramaic targum at Qumran, surviving in two copies (11Q10; 4Q157). A targum of Leviticus is also preserved (4Q156). Leviticus 26 is rich in themes that are associated with Noah in Genesis and in later traditions: possession/dispossession of land, blessings and curses, judgment, effect of sin on the land, repentance, and covenant. For example, the words "smell . . . pleasing odors" (ריח . . . וירח הניחח) (Gen 8:21) are found elsewhere only in Lev 26:31–33 (ולא אריח בריח ניחחכם).

Finally, consistent with God's promise in Genesis that he would never again send a flood to destroy all flesh (Gen 9:15), Ezekiel's judgments exclude "floodwaters." Within the exegetical gaps of Gen 9:15, there was still divine permission for flesh to be destroyed and cut off from the land by famine, sword, and pestilence.[30] Ezekiel specifies that both human beings *and animals* would be "cut off" from the land, whereas Genesis uses the more general "all flesh" (Gen 9:11; cf. 7:23). Only cattle (בהמה), animals associated with human habitation of the land, are mentioned in Ezekiel, whereas בהמה are one specific group in a list of animals that were blotted out in the flood (Gen 7:23).[31] Zephaniah forecasts an even more extensive eschatological cosmic judgment that may have intentionally echoed the primordial one: "I will sweep away humans and animals (בהמה); I will sweep away the birds of the air and the fish of the sea. I will make the wicked stumble. I will cut off humanity from the face of the earth, says the LORD" (Zeph 1:3).

Ezekiel elsewhere demonstrates sensitivity to the parallels between his current situation and that of Noah's day. According to Ben Zion Wacholder, Ezek 7:2, 3, 6 describes an end (קץ) "comparable in scope only to the Deluge in the days of Noah."[32] The chapter describes a land full (מלא) of crimes of blood and a city full of violence (חמס) (Ezek 7:23), implying a parallel between the judgment for violent crimes in the days of Noah and a judgment that would be coming. These examples from Ezek 7 and 14 point to the beginnings of concepts of *Urzeit-Endzeit* and "periods of judgment" later developed in the Enochic books, wisdom literature, and right into the *Yaḥad* sectarian scrolls. Later interpreters living in virtual exile surely were drawn to Ezekiel with its appeal to Noah as a righteous figure living in the midst of land-defiling sin.[33]

---

30. Ezekiel's list of four judgments is paralleled in Leviticus: "I will let loose wild animals (חית השדה) against you.... I will bring the sword (חרב) against you, executing vengeance for the covenant; and if you withdraw within your cities, I will send pestilence (דבר) among you.... When I break your staff of bread (בשברי לכם מטה־לחם)..." (Lev 26:22–26). Leviticus 26 is also rich in themes that are associated with Noah in Genesis and in later traditions: possession/dispossession of land, blessings and curses, judgment, effect of sin on the land, repentance, and covenant.

31. Concerning the phrase "cut off humans and animals," see also Ezek 25:13; 29:8; Jer 51:62.

32. Ben Zion Wacholder, "Ezekiel and Ezekielism as Progenitors of Essenianism," in *The Dead Sea Scrolls: Forty Years of Research* (ed. D. Dimant and U. Rappaport; STDJ 10; Leiden: Brill, 1992), 186–96, here 188.

33. Noah's "atoning for the land" sacrifice in *Jub.* 6:2 and in the *Genesis Apocryphon* X, 13 portrays Noah as a priestly archetype of a people who lived at a time when the "land" sinned and when the sins of the people defiled the land (Dorothy M. Peters, "'Atoning for the Land' in the Dead Sea Scrolls: A Trajectory of Distinction between the Insiders and Outsiders," in *Studies in Biblical Law* (ed. G. J. Brooke; JSSSup 25; Oxford: Oxford University Press, 2008), forthcoming. את־הארץ (Gen 6:13) is understood as "with the earth" in LXX, Vulg., Pesh., Tg. Onq., and Tg. Ps.-J. "Gen Rabba 31:7 interprets that the topsoil of the earth is to be removed. This reflects the biblical idea that moral corruption physically contaminates the earth, which must

We end this section with a brief note on the appearance of Noah in Deutero-Isaiah, another prophetic text from the exilic period:[34]

> For a brief moment I abandoned you,
>   but with great compassion (רחמים) I will gather you.
> In a flood of wrath (בשצף קצף) for a moment
>   I hid my face from you,
> but with *my*[35] everlasting love I will have compassion on you,
>   says the LORD, your Redeemer.
> This is like the days of Noah to me:
>   Just as I swore that the waters of Noah (מי־נח)
>   would never again go over the earth,
> so I have sworn that I will not be angry with you *again*[36]
>   and will not rebuke you.
> For the mountains may depart
>   and the hills be removed,
> but my steadfast love (חסדי) shall not depart from you,
>   and my covenant of peace (ברית שלומי) shall not be removed,
>   says the LORD, who has compassion on you (Isa 54:7-10)

The poet here interprets the "waters of Noah" as a metaphor for exile. During the flood, Noah and animals were physically "exiled" from the physical earth. God's momentary abandonment of Israel could be compared to God's temporary loss of memory concerning Noah and the animals during the time that the waters prevailed, and that may have been inferred from "but God *remembered* Noah" (Gen 8:1).

Finally, violence, sacrifice, covenant, and intermarriage in the Hebrew Bible are prevalent and multivalent themes attaching themselves to numerous biblical characters and events, not just to Noah.[37] Yet there are other promising Noah and flood allusions. Biblical apocalyptic and poetic texts, in particular, make effective use of a metaphor of a storm of waters that may derive from the flood story,

---

be purged of its pollution" (so Sarna, *Genesis*, 51). Leviticus 18:27-28; 20:22; Num 35:33-34; Isa 24:5-7; Jer 3:1, 2, 9; and Ps 106:38 are references noted by Sarna (*Genesis*, 356).

34. These verses appear in a collection of "words of comfort" (תנחומים) in 4QTanḥumim (4Q176).

35. "My" is attested in 1QIsaᵃ and 4QIsaᶜ but not in the MT. Cf. Isa 54:10, which collocates "my steadfast love" with covenant, as does 4Q463 1, 3.

36. 1QIsaᵃ attests עוד.

37. For example, Ezra's condemnation of the improper marriages of priests and Levites and his fear that God would destroy the people "without remnant or survivor" are some of the many warnings throughout the Bible concerning intermarriage with the Gentiles (Ezra 9). Cf. Neh 13:23-31 concerning those who had defiled the priesthood, including a son of the high priest.

describing the tribulations of the righteous and acting as a type of the end of the world.[38]

Continuing the Conversation:
Within the Gaps of the Noah Narrative

The Noah narrative in Genesis in its final form represents an internal conversation among its sources, yet it was preserved as a relatively stable text by the time copies of Genesis were collected at Qumran. The paucity of Qumran biblical scrolls containing the Noah narrative is puzzling, although there is no obvious reason to believe that the authors of the Dead Sea Scrolls were not familiar with the Noah story as it appears in Genesis. The very fact of the high interpretative interest in Noah speaks otherwise.

The composition of Genesis itself betrays a certain stance toward Israel's ancient Near Eastern neighbors, an acknowledgment of their shared ancestor who had survived a primordial flood. Genesis had already recontextualized and reinterpreted Mesopotamian and Egyptian flood and flood hero legends from other languages into a Hebrew narrative about Israel's God and promoted a conception of God in relationship to human beings that was different from the conception resident in the ancient Near Eastern source texts. This hermeneutical strategy of adaptation and recontextualization continues as a noble tradition in the interpretative texts of the Dead Sea Scrolls so that Noah traditions appearing in an early text may be traced through a series of recontextualizations and reinterpretations in later Hebrew and Aramaic traditions.

The similarities between the Hebrew and ancient Near Eastern flood narratives could not have escaped the notice of Jews in the Second Temple period. Unlike the explicit polemics against Baal in the Deuteronomistic history, the polemic in Genesis against the gods of the ancient Near East was subtle and only implied from differences and adaptations of the narrative. One might expect, however, that a segment of Judaism that was increasingly nationalistic and intent on defining religious and cultural boundaries may have become uneasy with the

---

38. Lewis notes Ps 29:10 and Job 22:15–20 as possible allusions to flood and Isa 24:1, 4–5, 18; 29:20–21; Nah 1:8; Ps 18:16[15]; 65:6–9[5–8]; 69:2[1]; 93:3; and Dan 9:26 as possible motifs (*Study*, 8–9). For the "deep" and acts of judgment or disaster, see Gen 7:11; 8:2; Exod 15:5, 8; Ezek 26:19; 31:15; Amos 7:4; Jonah 2:5; Hab 3:10; Ps 42:7. Cf. the waters fear and the deep trembles when God sees them (Ps 76:17[77:16]). Cf. Sir 16:18–19/SirA 6v:23–25. See Isa 44:27: "Who says to the deep, 'Be dry—I will dry up your rivers.'" David M. Gunn suggests a "hierarchy of connotations": "the evidence appears to point to the probability of multiple allusion in this verse: creation (but not the *Chaoskampf*) and flood, the stories in which the primaeval play a significant role, *are most strongly indicated* [emphasis mine]; there are hints also of the Reed-Sea event, though this is a less obvious referent." Cf. Isa 50:2 and 51:10, where God dries up the sea or great deep. David M. Gunn, "Deutero-Isaiah and the Flood," *JBL* 94 (1975): 493–508, here 499.

more universalistic Noah, turning its attention more readily to figures that were exclusively Israel's own, such as Moses the lawgiver.

Traditions always have a genesis. Within the Genesis narrative were many gaps and silence that served as "conversation starters" in later interpretation. In the table below, traditions that had an afterlife in the Dead Sea Scrolls and had their origins within the Hebrew Bible are listed and organized under three main questions.[39]

TABLE: THE ORIGINS OF NOAH TRADITIONS IN GENESIS

How and to what extent is Noah portrayed as an archetype for a particular interpretation of what it means to be Jewish?

Noah's generation
Sons of God marry daughters of men (Gen 6:1–4)
Noah within a generation of wickedness (רעה), corruption (שחת), violence (חמס) (Gen 6:5, 11–13)
Sinful inclination (יצר) (Gen 6:5; 8:21)

The differentiation of Noah from those in his generation; distinction among Noah's progeny
Noah's birth and naming (5:29)
Noah, the righteous (Gen 6:9; 7:1; Ezek 14:14)
Noah walks with God/proper paths (Gen 6:9)
Waters prevail (גבר)/waters as the enemy (Gen 7:18–20, 24; cf. Isa 54:9)
"Sons of Noah"; curse on Canaan (Gen 9:25); division of land (Gen 10:1–32)

Noah as participant in carrying out God's plan of judgment
Ark-building; collecting the animals (6:14–7:5)

Noah the survivor
Noah, the one who is left (Gen 7:23)

Noah, the new Adam
Noah reenters the land as "new Adam" (Gen 8:18–19); dominion (LXX Gen 9:1)
Post-judgment "new creation": Reestablishment of times and seasons (Gen 8:22)

Noah, the potential priest
Participates in the chronology of flood events (Gen 7:4–8:14)
Noah offers sacrifices (Gen 8:20)
Division of land (Gen 10)
Blessings and curses (Gen 9:25–27)

---

39. The table will be reorganized in chapter 8 with special attention to how the traditions were variously developed in Hebrew and Aramaic texts.

What does God reveal to Noah and how does he do it?

God speaks directly to Noah,
Announcement of imminent judgment: God tells Noah that he will make an end (קץ) to all flesh (6:13)
God gives Noah practical instruction regarding the construction of the ark (6:14–16)
"Never again curse (קלל) the ground" (Gen 8:21)
Blood prohibitions: eating and shedding (Gen 9:4–7)
God establishes his covenant with Noah (Gen 9:8–17)
God remembered Noah: cessation of water (acts of nature?)? (Gen 8:1)
Sends Rainbow (Gen 8:12–17)

To what extent is Noah claimed as a "distinctly Jewish" ancestor or, alternatively, claimed as a common ancestor of all humanity shared by the Gentiles?

The composition of the narrative itself as a response to ancient Near Eastern flood tradition implies the acknowledgment of a flood survivor who was an ancestor of all of humanity.
Noah and flood within history of the world (genealogies of Gen 5, 10)

The gaps and silences in Genesis would provoke even more debate and creative interpretation than the more explicit characterizations of Noah, Enoch, and Levi did. The interpreters of antiquity found themselves invited into conversations and controversies that had been ongoing for millennia in the ancient Near East. They believed that the story also had relevance for them and, although they were sometimes wary in their handling of the character of Noah, their interest in him was persistent. Noah next appears, in translation, in the Aramaic traditions of Enoch and Levi.

CHAPTER THREE

NOAH IN THE ARAMAIC ENOCH TEXTS AND THE *ARAMAIC LEVI DOCUMENT*

And Enoch took up his discourse . . .
"[U]ntil my time righteousness endured.
After me there will arise a second week, in which deceit
and violence will spring up,
and in it will be the first end, and in it a man will be saved."
4QEnochᵍ 1 III, 24–25/1 Enoch 93:3–4

For thus my father Abraham commanded me
For thus he found in the writing of the book of Noah concerning the blood
Aramaic Levi Document 10:10

INTRODUCTION

Noah's great-grandfather Enoch and his priestly descendant Levi take center stage in the Aramaic Enoch books and in the *Aramaic Levi Document*. Foundational to and in conversation with other Noah traditions in the Dead Sea Scrolls, these documents mention Noah only briefly. However, a study of the characterizations of Enoch and Levi is essential to the understanding of the formation of interpretations of Noah elsewhere and for the way in which a set of attributes could be transferred from one character to another.

In *1 Enoch*,[1] Enoch becomes wise through numerous angelic revelations, transmitting what he has learned about coming judgments to the next generations, both orally and in writing. If a particular characterization of Noah resembles a characterization of Enoch elsewhere, the significance of the shared characteristics might be explored with an attempt to discern the direction of dependence:

---

1. The term, "*1 Enoch*" is used here to designate the contents of the Enochic corpus in its final Ethiopic form, but it may also be more generally extended to include translations and Aramaic *Vorlagen*. The term "Aramaic Enoch" denotes specifically the extant Qumran fragments representative of the hypothetical text available to its interpreters.

Was it more likely that an earlier characterization of Noah was transferred to Enoch in the Aramaic Enoch books or were Enoch's characteristics transferred to Noah in later interpretation?

Likewise, in the *Aramaic Levi Document* (*ALD*), Levi is a wise, visionary figure. However, in the *ALD*, Levi is more unambiguously priestly than Enoch is in *1 Enoch*. He receives and transmits priestly lore that originated from Noah and was reliably handed down from generation to generation. In the Dead Sea Scrolls alluding to Noah's specifically priestly character, Noah resembles Levi. Yet who was the first literary priestly archetype, Levi or Noah? We will explore whether it is more likely that a priestly Levi was fashioned after an existing interpretation of a priestly Noah or whether it may have been the other way around, that a priestly Noah was patterned after a priestly Levi.

These questions, which explore the literary relationship of Noah to both his ancestor Enoch and his descendant Levi, have important implications for the debate concerning the existence of a *Book of Noah*[2] prior to the books of Enoch and the *Aramaic Levi Document*, a debate that still thrives after a century of discussion. Furthermore, how archetypes were characterized differently and for what reason characteristics were transferred from one character to another sheds light on the self-identity of the people who were creating these portraits and may say something about the types of questions and conversations that were driving these literary explorations.

The gaps and silences in the Noah narrative in Genesis had already given plenty of room for interpretative play. To borrow a metaphor from *1 En.* 10:16, a "righteous planting" of interpretation flourished in the spaces between the "rocks" in the garden, the Genesis text. About Enoch, however, even less is said, and what *is* said is so provocative that many stories were constructed around this figure who lived 365 years, whose death was never recorded, and who, like Noah, walked with God (Gen 5:21–24).

In Genesis, Levi did not function as a priest, yet the tradents of the Aramaic Levi traditions found enough exegetical room in between Genesis and Malachi (in which Levi is the only figure apart from Enoch and Noah in the Hebrew Bible who "walked" with God) to legitimate the character of Levi himself for the priesthood and to create for him a priestly ancestor in Noah.

1 Enoch and the *Aramaic Levi Document* were known before the discoveries of the Dead Sea Scrolls; therefore, we will comment not only on the Aramaic fragments surviving at Qumran but also on the text as a whole as it survived in translation. We begin with some observations on texts of individual books or portions of books from the Enochic corpus followed by an exploration of some of the reasons why the Enochic writers may have been uneasy about idealizing

---

2. Generally, the italicized term *Book of Noah* is employed when discussing the hypothetical literary work. The term "Book of Noah," in quotation marks, is used when citing primary texts that refer to the "Book of Noah" such as the *ALD* and the *Genesis Apocryphon*.

Noah as a flood survivor and why Enoch would have been perceived as a better candidate for idealization. The section on *1 Enoch* concludes with discussion of Noah's changing role within the compositional history of the corpus with particular attention to his "righteousness." Following a few brief notes on the text of the *Aramaic Levi Document*, the priestly themes associated with Levi are identified and comparison made to priestly themes associated with Noah in the *Genesis Apocryphon*.

TEXTS AND OBSERVATIONS[3]

1 Enoch: WHO WALKS WITH THE ANGELS?[4]

The beginnings of a dispute concerning Noah vis-à-vis his renowned great-grandfather Enoch may already be discerned in the compositional history and variants of the Enochic books. Mining *1 Enoch* for a coherent biography of Noah is complicated by several issues, including the number of textual variants and the apparent ease with which the writers of antiquity transferred characteristics from one biblical character to another. Originally written in Aramaic and translated into Greek[5] and Ethiopic, *1 Enoch* in its entirety survives only in Ethiopic.

---

3. Patrick Tiller has compiled a useful review of scholarship of nineteenth- and early-twentieth-century texts, translations, and commentaries on *1 Enoch* that includes the groundbreaking work of R.H. Charles, F. Martin, G. Beer, E. Schürer, J. Fleming and L. Radermacher. See Tiller, *A Commentary on the Animal Apocalypse of I Enoch* (SBLEJL 4; Atlanta: Scholars Press, 1993), 4–13. Once Aramaic copies of Enochic books were discovered at Qumran, fresh editions and commentaries began to appear. By the time of the publication of Black's *Apocalypsis Henochi Graece* in 1970, only two of the Aramaic fragments had been published. Black incorporated the collated and checked Greek manuscripts, Greek citations of Enoch in patristic sources, and provided a fresh collation of the Syncellus fragments. Black, *Apocalypsis Henochi Graecae* (PVTG 3; Leiden: Brill, 1970). In 1976, Jozef T. Milik presented a transcription, translation and notes for Aramaic fragments of Enoch from Qumran Cave 4 and was the first to provide a more nuanced commentary that interpreted the data to argue particular theses. Jozef T. Milik, *The Books of Enoch: Aramaic Fragments of Qumran Cave 4* (Oxford: Clarendon, 1976). Following the publication of the Aramaic texts, Michael A. Knibb released a new edition of Ethiopic Enoch in 1978 that accounted also for the Aramaic texts, the new Chester Beatty-Michigan Greek papyrus and other Ethiopic manuscripts that had come to light. Knibb, *The Ethiopic Book of Enoch: A New Edition in Light of the Aramaic Dead Sea Fragments* (Oxford: Clarendon, 1978). Translations of *1 Enoch* include E. Isaac, "(Ethiopic Apocalypse of) Enoch," in *OTP*, 1:5–89; and George W. E. Nickelsburg, *1 Enoch 1: A Commentary on the Book of 1 Enoch: Chapters 1–36; 81–108* (Hermeneia; Minneapolis: Fortress, 2001). The official editions of texts of the Enochic books at Qumran include 1Q23, 1Q24 in DJD I and DJD XXXVI; 4Q201, 4Q202, 4Q203, 4Q204, 4Q205, 4Q206, 4Q206, 4Q207, 4Q208, 4Q209, 4Q210, 4Q211, and 4Q212 in DJD XXXVI.

4. For an earlier version of this part of the study, see Dorothy M. Peters, "The Tension between Enoch and Noah in the Aramaic Enoch Texts at Qumran," *Hen* 29 (2007): 11–29.

5. Greek manuscripts (Akhmim, George Syncellus's *Chronography*, Codex Vaticanus

Michael A. Knibb argues that while the Ethiopic translators almost certainly used a Greek text, they also made use of an Aramaic *Vorlage* at points.[6] His examination of the differences, mostly minor, that exist between the Aramaic and the translations suggests that "the Greek and the Ethiopic texts provide a not too unreliable guide to the Book of Enoch as it was known at Qumrân."[7]

The evidence of any significant Greek witness to *1 Enoch* at Qumran is less than compelling. In his assessment of the evidence for a Greek *Epistle of Enoch* in Qumran Cave 7,[8] George Nickelsburg records his skepticism that the tiny number of extant letters in the fragments of 7Q4, 7Q8, and 7Q12 should be identified with *1 En.* 103:3–8, since its reconstruction is based on the "notoriously corrupt" Chester Beatty-Michigan papyrus with unaddressed "important text-critical problems."[9] The presence of a Cave 7 copy of the Greek *Epistle* as early as 100 B.C.E. is, therefore, by no means proven.

Although the Enochic books drew from older traditions,[10] dates by which they received their final forms may be suggested.[11] That at least some of the books were of value to at least some of the members of the community at Qumran is confirmed by the fact that later copies continued to be collected long after the time of their original composition.[12]

Gr. 1809 and Chester Beatty-Michigan papyrus) attest 1:1–32:6; 6:1–10:14; 15:8–16:1; 97:6–104; 106; 89:42–49. See Black, *Apocalypsis Henochi Graecae;* and Nickelsburg, *1 Enoch 1,* 12–13 for the Greek textual evidence.

6. Knibb, *Ethiopic Book of Enoch*, 37–46.

7. Ibid., 13.

8. See Émile Puech, "Sept fragments de la lettre d'Hénoch (1Hén 100, 103 et 105) dans la grotte 7 de Qumrân," *RevQ* 18/70 (1997): 313–23. Peter W. Flint argues that "at least seven fragments [including 7Q4, 7Q8, 7Q11, 7Q12, 7Q13, 7Q14] belong to a manuscript which is classified as pap7QEn gr," and he reconstructs "7Q4.1, 7Q8, and 7Q12 as preserving portions of 1 Enoch 103:3–8" ("The Greek Fragments of Enoch from Qumran Cave 7," in *Enoch and Qumran Origins: New Light on a Forgotten Connection* [ed. G. Boccaccini; Grand Rapids: Eerdmans, 2005], 224–33, here 231–33).

9. George W. E. Nickelsburg, "Response: Context, Text, and Social Setting of the Apocalypse," in Boccaccini, *Enoch and Qumran Origins*, 237–39. He also notes that the 7Q4 1–2 fragments are "too small to allow a certain identification" with a Greek manuscript of the *Epistle* (Nickelsburg, *1 Enoch 1*, 14 n. 49).

10. For studies on the original and separate mythical "Shemihazah" and "Asael" strands, see Devorah Dimant, "1 Enoch 6–11: A Methodological Perspective," in *SBL Seminar Papers 1978* (SBLSP 13; Atlanta: Scholars Press, 1978): 323–39; Corrie Molenberg, "A Study of the Roles of Shemihaza and Asael in I Enoch 6–11," *JJS* 35 (1984): 136–146; Nickelsburg, *1 Enoch 1*, 165–73; James C. VanderKam, *Enoch, Man For All Generations* (Studies on Personalities of the Old Testament; Columbia: University of South Carolina Press, 1995), 41–42; Patrick Tiller, "The 'Eternal Planting' in the Dead Sea Scrolls," *DSD* 4 (1997), 312–35, here 318.

11. Compositional dates follow George W. E. Nickelsburg and James C. VanderKam, *1 Enoch: A New Translation* (Minneapolis: Fortress, 2004), 1–14.

12. The *Astronomical Book* and the *Book of Giants* are extant in copies dated to the

TABLE: LIST OF ENOCHIC BOOKS AND DATE OF COMPOSITION

Date of Composition	Ethiopic Enoch/Aramaic Enoch
3rd c. B.C.E. or earlier[13]	*Book of Luminaries* (Ethiopic) (chs. 72–82)/ Aramaic *Astronomical Book* (*AB*) 4QEnastr ar^{a-d}: 4Q208–211
mid- or late 3rd c. B.C.E.[14]	*Book of Watchers* (*BW*) (chs. 1–36) 4QEn^a ar: 4Q201 1 I-VI 4QEn^b ar: 4Q202 1 II-VI 4QEn^c ar: 4Q204 1 I-XIII 4QEn^d ar: 4Q205 1 XI-XII 4QEn^e ar: 4Q206 1 XXII-XXVII XQ8
late 3rd c. – 164 B.C.E.[15]	*Book of Giants* (*BG*) 1QEnGiants^{a-b} ar: 1Q23–1Q24 2QEnGiants ar: 2Q26 4QEnGiants^a ar: 4Q203 4QEnGiants^{b-d} ar: 4Q530–532 4QEnGiants^e ar 4Q533 or 4Q556[16] 4QEn^e ar: 4Q206 2–3 [reedition] (Stuckenbruck) 6QpapEnGiants ar: 6Q8 [reedition] (Stuckenbruck)
164–160 B.C.E.	*Dream Visions* (*DV*) (chs. 83–90) 4QEn^c ar: 4Q204 4 4QEn^d ar: 4Q205 2 I-III 4QEn^e ar: 4Q206 4 I-III 4QEn^f ar: 4Q207 1

Herodian period. 2QEnGiants ar (2Q26) is dated between 30 B.C.E.–68 C.E. and 4QEnastr^c ar (4Q209) is dated between 30 B.C.E.–70 C.E.

13. John J. Collins asserts that the *Astronomical Book* "presupposes an astronomical system that is found in the Akkadian text MULAPIN, which certainly predates the Babylonian exile." He suggests that the book "was not composed to address an inner-Jewish dispute about the calendar.... It was rather a correction of its Akkadian prototype" ("Theology and Identity in the Early Enoch Literature," *Hen* 24 [2002]: 57–62, here 58–59).

14. Nickelsburg connects the wars of the Diadochi (323–302 B.C.E.) to the "battles of the giants" with a date around "the end of the fourth century B.C.E." for *1 En.* 6–11 ("Apocalyptic and Myth in 1 Enoch 6–11," *JBL* 96 [1977]: 383–405).

15. For *BG* dependent on *BW*, see Loren T. Stuckenbruck, *The Book of Giants from Qumran: Texts, Translation, and Commentary* (Tübingen: Mohr Siebeck, 1997), 25.

16. For the numeration of this scroll as 4Q566, see Stuckenbruck, *Book of Giants*, 185–86.

Date of Composition	Ethiopic Enoch/Aramaic Enoch
mid 2nd c. B.C.E.	*Epistle of Enoch* (*EE*) (chs. 91–105) including the *Apocalypse of Weeks* (*AW*) (chs. 93:1–10; 91:11–17) 4QEnᵍ ar: 4Q212 1 I-V
prior to mid 1st c.	*Birth of Noah* (*BN*) (chs. 106–7) 4QEnᶜ ar: 4Q204 5
turn of the era	*Book of Parables* (chs. 37–71)
1ˢᵗ c. C.E.	*A Final Book by Enoch* (ch. 108)

The Aramaic Enoch texts from Qumran, including the *Book of Giants*, reveal a tension concerning the status of the figure of Noah throughout the composition, transmission, and translation of the books in the corpus.¹⁷ Hints of this tension are preserved in relevant minor but significant variants represented in the Aramaic. These are surveyed below with particular attention to textual variants, pluses or minuses, and the ordering of the textual material concerning Noah.

THE TEXTS

Astronomical Book

The Ethiopic *Book of Luminaries* is cast as an angelic revelation from the angel Uriel, to Enoch (*1 En.* 72:1), but it contains only a "highly truncated" and epitomized form of the *Astronomical Book*, of which thirty-six fragments survived at Qumran.¹⁸ James C. VanderKam notes that, whereas other books in the Enochic tradition often drew heavily on biblical sources, the *Astronomical Book* is more subdued in its appeal to scripture. Therefore, while the calendar in *Jubilees* is "intimately connected with the roster of festivals," there is silence concerning Passover, Weeks, Tabernacles and even the Sabbath in the *Astronomical Book*, except for an allusion to "feasts" in 82:7, 9. VanderKam adds that the author does make of use of Gen 1:14–18—the creation of the luminaries as signs—and Isa 30:26, reading "the Genesis creation story in the context of other scriptural givens, including Isa 30:26."¹⁹

---

17. The following are the official editions: 1Q23–24 (DJD I); 2Q26, 6Q8 (DJD III); 4Q530–5Q533 (DJD XXXI); Cave 4 manuscripts: Milik, *BE*. Reeditions were issued for the following: 1Q23–24, 2Q26, 4Q201, 4Q203, 4Q206, 6Q8 (L. Stuckenbruck, DJD XXXVI); 4Q203 (DJD, XXXI) 4Q208 and 4Q209 (E. J. C. Tigchelaar and F. García Martínez, DJD XXXVI). See also Stuckenbruck, *Book of Giants*.

18. VanderKam, *Enoch: Man for all Generations*, 22.

19. James C. VanderKam, "Scriptures in the Astronomical Book of Enoch," in *Things Revealed: Studies in Early Jewish and Christian Literature in Honor of Michael E Stone* (ed. Esther G. Chazon, David Satran, and Ruth A. Clements; JSJSup 89; Leiden: Brill, 2004), 89–103. For further discussion on the Aramaic fragments and the Ethiopic text, see also James

Although the *Astronomical Book* is not as overtly "priestly" to the same extent as the *Aramaic Levi Document* is, its concern with calendar does betray some priestly influence together with an interest in astronomical science. In subsequent interpretation, *Jubilees*, originally composed in Hebrew, would link calendar and the first celebration of the Feast of Weeks to Noah within a revelation given to Moses on Mount Sinai.

Book of Watchers

Noah features in what is likely the oldest layer of *Watchers* (*1 En.* 6–11), a layer that entirely omits mention of Enoch. It is now commonly understood that the Shemihazah myth, in which the angels bound themselves with an oath to take wives among women, and the Asael myth, in which Asael's instruction of humanity led to the seduction of angels by women, were interwoven into a composite explanation for the origin of evil.[20]

> Then the Most High said, and the Great Holy One spoke. And he sent Sariel to the son of Lamech, saying, "Go to Noah and say to him in my name, 'Hide yourself.' And reveal to him that the end is coming, that the whole earth will perish; and tell him that a deluge is about to come on the whole earth and destroy everything on the earth. Teach the righteous one (קשטה) what he should do, the son of Lamech how he may preserve (לנצלה) himself alive and escape forever. From him a plant will be planted, and his seed will endure for all the generations of eternity." (4Q201 1 V, 3–4/*1 En.* 10:1–3)[21]

While the "sons of gods" story in Gen 6:1–4 is not clearly linked to the following Noah narrative in Genesis, the *Book of Watchers* brings the Noah story and the reinterpreted angel story into a much more intimate relationship. As Devorah Dimant has demonstrated in her work, both versions of the legend of the angels' sin that make up the composite narrative in chs. 6 and 7 of the *Book of Watchers* were based on the same text of Gen 6:1–4. Most interesting is Dimant's further observation that the combination of the elements of both of these versions is constructed to fit a list of seven "Noachide Laws" and that ch. 8 of *BW* provides "yet another explanation based on Noachide Laws, this time only of the

---

C. VanderKam, *Calendars in the Dead Sea Scrolls: Measuring Time* (London: Routledge, 1998), 17–27, 91, 97.

20. Dimant separates out the instruction traditions as elements that later "contaminated" the earliest Shemihazah myth, the myth that was not originally associated with the flood. With the introduction of Asael, the need for punishment of humans by the flood entered the narrative (Dimant, "1 Enoch 6–11," 327). For more discussion on the composition of *Watchers*, see Siam Bhayro, "Noah's Library: Sources for *1 Enoch* 6–11," *JSP* 15 (2006): 163–77; Nickelsburg, *1 Enoch 1*, 171–72; Molenberg, "Study of the Roles."

21. Unless otherwise noted, translations of *1 Enoch* are adapted from Nickelsburg, *1 Enoch 1*.

three which form the ancient basis of all the lists," the three basic prohibitions—against fornication, murder, and idolatry.[22]

Therefore, the sins of the Watchers appear to be limited to those derived from the Noah narrative in Genesis itself[23] rather than derived from the transgressions of the laws contained in the books of the Mosaic Torah most observably connected to Moses, that is, Exodus through Deuteronomy.[24] "Defilement with women" (*1 En.* 7:1), "evil" (רשעה), and "violence" (חמסה) (4Q201 1 IV, 7-8/ XQ8 3[25]/*1 En.* 9:1) can easily be derived from Gen 6:1-12; "bloodshed" (9:1) and the drinking of blood (7:5)[26] are acts that are potentially derived from the blood prohibitions in Gen 9:4-6.

That Noah is twice identified as the "son of Lamech" had several implications. The more obvious in light of the "remarkable birth" narratives in *1 En.* 106

---

22. Devorah Dimant, "'The Fallen Angels' in the Dead Sea Scrolls and in the Apocryphal and Pseudepigraphic Books Related to Them" (English summary of Ph.D diss., Hebrew University, 1974), 4-7.

23. Nickelsburg has noted that the three concepts of blood, the earth, and the cry that went up to heaven (*1 En.* 7:5-6; 8:4; and 9:1-2) may recall Gen 4:10-11, "to which the author may be alluding as he construes the violence of Gen 6:6 and 13 in terms of murder" (*1 Enoch 1*, 187). Nickelsburg finds similar patterns in Deut 32:43 and its interpretations in *T. Mos.* 9:7 and 2 Macc 8:3-4. If one were to argue that *1 Enoch*'s Noah was adapted not from Genesis but from the same sorts of not-explicitly-righteous Mesopotamian flood heroes that the *biblical* Noah was based on, more compelling evidence for both a late dating for Genesis *and* earlier dating for the *Enoch* traditions would be required than has been marshaled to this point. For one such attempt, see Margaret Barker, *The Older Testament: The Survival of Themes from the Ancient Royal Cult in Sectarian Judaism and Early Christianity* (London: SPCK, 1987).

24. On the use of Genesis in *1 Enoch*, VanderKam comments: "Sin is not reckoned by failure to conform to Moses' Torah which was meant for Israel; the sin involved disobedience to the fundamental divine laws of existence" ("The Interpretation of Genesis in *1 Enoch*," in *The Bible at Qumran: Text, Shape, and Interpretation* [ed. P. W. Flint; Grand Rapids: Eerdmans, 2001], 129-48, here 142). Further, "The story in *1 Enoch* applies to all nations, not just to the Jewish people. The laws violated by the people living before the flood . . . were a version of the Noachic laws, which were meant for all" (ibid.). However, Annette Yoshiko Reed cautions that *1 En.* 6-11 makes no mention of idolatry, adding that Dimant's hypothesis "falls short . . . as an explanation for the topics of instruction in *1 En.* 8:1-2" (Reed, *Fallen Angels and the History of Judaism and Christianity: The Reception of Enochic Literature* [Cambridge: Cambridge University Press, 2005], 38).

25. This tiny papyrus fragment of *Watchers*, XQpapEn, may preserve a different version of *1 En.* 9:1: [. . . the whole earth was filled with e]vil (ר[שעה]) and violence (חמסה) against the ones who were killed (די קטיליא) (XQ8 3/*1 En.* 9:1). Esther Eshel and Hanan Eshel, *DSSR* 3, 470-71. Upon examining the photographs at the annual meeting of SBL, Atlanta, Nov. 21, 2004, Moshe J. Bernstein observed that what was read as the first *yod* in קטיליא may be better read as *waw*, (קטוליא): "[. . . the whole earth was filled with the e]vil and violence of the *murderers*. . . ." Cf. 4Q530 1 I, 3-5.

26. "They drank blood" (*1 En.* 7:5) was the "ultimate abomination and violation of created life (Gen 9:5-6; cf. the exegetical expansion in *Jub.* 7.27-34 and 21:18-20; cf. also *1 En.* 98:11)" (Nickelsburg, *1 Enoch 1*, 186).

and the *Genesis Apocryphon* is that the author knew of and was responding to a tradition in which the human flood survivor had supernatural parentage. Less obvious, but possible, is an allusion to Noah's naming derived from reading Gen 5:29 alongside 2 Sam 7:10-11, in which Israel would be "planted" (נטע) and given "rest" (נוח) from her enemies.[27]

The *Book of Watchers* has links to Genesis in other ways. In Genesis, God revealed the coming destruction to Noah and instructed him how to build the ark (Gen 6:13-21) while in *BW*, Noah receives supernatural instruction from God's messenger, an angel. Revelatory communication between divine beings and humanity in *BW* is presented as absolutely essential for the preservation of humans, and Noah is thus implicitly contrasted with those who received illegitimate instruction from the wrong sorts of angels.[28]

What the Watchers brought to humans was not false knowledge but, rather, forbidden knowledge, as Philip Alexander has pointed out.[29] The sectarian text 4QAges of Creation would later use the Watchers story as a polemic against those who belonged to a "wicked *Yaḥad.*" In this way, while Noah could be perceived as an archetype of the righteous ones who would survive a coming judgment, the Watchers could and did become the archetypical enemies of those who transmitted the wrong kind of knowledge in the wrong sorts of ways.

Noah was the first person to be declared "righteous" (צדיק) in Genesis, but that would change in the *Book of Watchers*. Noah is called "righteous" (קשטא) in *BW* but the title of "plant" (*1 En.* 10:3) or "righteous plant" (נצבת קושטא)[30] (*1 En.* 10:16/4Q204 1 V, 4) is reserved for his progeny.[31] Once the Noah narrative in *BW* (chs. 6–11) was recontextualized into the final form of *BW* (chs. 1–36), it was Enoch who appeared in the text as the first "righteous man" (קשט) (*1 En.* 1:2), an attribution that remained with Enoch throughout the compositional history of the books at the same time that Noah's righteousness was subsumed or even suppressed.

---

27. For an excellent discussion of "planting" themes in the Qumran corpus, see Tiller, "Eternal Planting," 312–35.

28. Reed asserts that "the redactors preserve a range of different approaches to the fallen angels." In particular, the polysemy of *Watchers* allowed for the adoption of angelic descent "by a variety of later Jews and Christians for a surprisingly broad range of different aims" (*Fallen Angels*, 27).

29. Philip S. Alexander, "Enoch and the Beginnings of Jewish Interest in Natural Science," in *The Wisdom Texts from Qumran and the Development of Sapiential Thought* (ed. C. Hempel, A. Lange, and H. Lichtenberger; BETL 159; Leuven: Leuven University Press, 2002), 234. Cf. James M. Scott, *On Earth as in Heaven: The Restoration of Sacred Time and Sacred Space in the Book of Jubilees* (JSJSup 91; Leiden: Brill, 2005), 5–7.

30. The translation based on the Ethiopic text attests "righteousness and truth" but this may well be a double translation of קושטא. Nickelsburg and VanderKam, *1 Enoch*, 30.

31. The plant metaphor survives in Syncellus but not in the Gizeh text; the Ethiopic attests "his seed might remain." "Plant," although not extant in the Aramaic, is consistent with the text of Syncellus. Tiller, "Eternal Planting," 317.

Whether the *Book of Watchers* expressed priestly concerns and, by extension, whether Noah is to be considered within a priestly context, is under debate. David Suter understands *BW* as a polemic against the Jerusalem priesthood from the period before the Maccabean revolt and has argued that, in this text, Enoch possessed both scribal *and* priestly characteristics;[32] however, John Collins has yet to be convinced "that the tradents of the Enoch literature were priests."[33] Whatever the context and ideology of the texts, neither Noah nor Enoch possesses priestly qualities in *1 Enoch* in the same way that Noah and Levi do in the *Aramaic Levi Document*. *BW*'s focus is on transgressions of ordained boundaries between the heavenly and earthly realms that included defiling intermarriage but also forbidden instruction. Enoch contrasts the luminaries who did not transgress (עבר) their appointed order (4Q201 1 II, 1/*1 En.* 2:1) with those who would transgress against God (4Q201 1 II, 13/*1 En.* 5:4), a theme explicated in the *Birth of Noah* in which the Watchers transgressed (עבר) by marrying women (*1 En.* 106:13/4Q204 5 II, 17–19).[34]

Finally, if a *Book of Noah* served as a source for chs. 6–11 of the *Book of Watchers*, it was written in "third person style and not, as one would expect of a *Book of Noah* or an *Apocalypse of Noah*, in an autobiographical style."[35] Noah does speak in first person in the *Book of Parables* (below) and in the *Genesis Apocryphon*, a fact that is at least suggestive of the possibility that Noah's speeches were patterned after Enoch's speeches in the earlier Enochic books.

---

32. David W. Suter, "Fallen Angel, Fallen Priest: The Problem of Family Purity in 1 Enoch 6–16," *HUCA* 50 (1979): 115–35, here 130–31. While the problem of priestly marriages is clearly central in *T. Levi* and CD, for example, the priestly concern, if any, in *1 En.* 6–16 is much less apparent. Suter later nuances his initial position by acknowledging significant disagreement over the specifics of the priestly issues in *BW* such as whether scribes were also priests ("Revisiting 'Fallen Angel, Fallen Priest,'" *Hen* 24 [2002]: 137–42, here 140–41). For a discussion of the notion that priests should marry only women from priestly families, something that *BW* shares with the *ALD* and 4QMMT, see Martha Himmelfarb, "The Book of the Watchers and the Priests of Jerusalem," *Hen* 24 (2002): 131–35, here 133.

33. Collins, "Theology and Identity in the Early Enoch Literature," 60–61.

34. In *Dream Visions*, stars represent the angels who fell to the earth (*1 En.* 86:1–3). On personification of stars in the ancient Near East and the Hellenistic world and *1 En.* 18:15 referring to "transgressing" stars, see Nickelsburg, *1 Enoch 1*, 288–89. Cf. 1Q34[bis] 3 II, 1–4.

35. Devorah Dimant, "Two 'Scientific' Fictions: The So-Called *Book of Noah* and the Alleged Quotation of *Jubilees* in CD 16:3–4," in *Studies in the Hebrew Bible, Qumran and the Septuagint Presented to Eugene Ulrich* (ed. P. W. Flint, E. Tov, and J. C. VanderKam; VTSup 101; Leiden: Brill, 2006), 230–49, here 234. On two cosmic judgments that demonstrate a unity between the Enoch and Noah portions so that the "Noah apocalypses" are not to be treated as a "foreign body" within the Enoch saga, see Matthew Black, *The Book of Enoch, or, 1 Enoch: A New English Edition with Commentary and Textual Notes* (SVTP 7; Leiden: Brill, 1985), 8.

Book of Giants

Jozef T. Milik assigned the Aramaic *BG* found at Qumran to the earliest "Enochic Pentateuch"[36] adding that *Giants* "in all probability" followed the *Book of Watchers* in 4QEnoch^c,[37] a text that included Aramaic fragments of *Dream Visions* and the *Birth of Noah*. *Giants* regales the reader with "inside information" on the giants: their names, their violent deeds that undo the original creation, their conversations with each other and with Enoch, their dreams and their fears of coming judgment. There is no mention of Noah in the extant text; in fact, though sought for everywhere, a righteous man (צדיק) was *not* found (4Q531 22 1).

Loren T. Stuckenbruck argues that the two hundred trees and the large shoots that came out of their roots and were watered by "gardeners"[38] refers to the birth of the giants who had been "watered" by the Watchers. He links the surviving "three shoots" in 6Q8 2 1-3 with another tradition in *Midrash of Shemhazai and 'Aza'el* in which an angel cuts down a garden except for one tree having three branches (אילן אחד של שלשה ענפים),[39] possibly a tradition of a flood survivor with three children.

Closely tied to the world of foreign myth, the *Book of Giants* names Gilgamesh[40] and concerns itself more with the Watchers and Giants than with the fate of humans in the flood. Not enough remains of *BG* to show whether or how it adopted, adapted, or reinterpreted the flood-survivor-as-giant traditions, but it may be that *BG* proved to be just too "foreign" to qualify as part of the Enochic corpus. If, as Milik claims, *BG* was copied onto the same scroll as the *Birth of Noah*, then any ambiguity concerning Noah's parentage in *BG* would have been clarified in its new context within the entire collection.

Dream Visions

In *1 Enoch* as it survives in the Ethiopic, Noah (a white bull) and Moses (a sheep) are selected for transformation into men (representing "angels"); however, Aramaic Enoch is more selective regarding who is worthy to attain angelic status.

---

36. Milik, *BE*, 58. Dimant disputes this, arguing that "the basic Enochic collection, comprising *BW*, *AB*, *BD*, *EE* and the Appendix, was assembled in such a way as to give a synopsis of Enoch's deeds and teachings in the sequence as they occurred" ("The Biography of Enoch and the Books of Enoch," *VT* 33 [1983]: 14-29, here 27-28). Stuckenbruck states, "The importance of the antediluvian patriarch in the story is without doubt the reason why BG may have been included within a copy of other Enochic works." He refutes Milik, saying "it is nowhere clear from the extant fragments that BG is regarded as a story recorded by Enoch" (Stuckenbruck, *Book of Giants*, 25-26).
37. Milik, *BE*, 5-6.
38. 4Q530 2 II+6-12(?), 7-8.
39. Stuckenbruck, *Book of Giants*, 202.
40. 4Q530 2 II+6-12(?) 1; 4Q531 22 12.

Moses transformed (4Q204 4 10/*1 En.* 89:36), but Noah does not attain angelic status even where there is ample opportunity within the extant text.

1 Enoch 89:1 preserves "It [i.e., Noah] was born a bull but became a man," a phrase strikingly missing in Aramaic Enoch (4Q206 4 I, 13-14). Furthermore, later in the text, there is no space for "he became a man" in the Aramaic (4Q206 4 II, 4-5) where the Ethiopic reads "That white bull that became a man" (*1 En.* 89:9).[41] Whether or not there was originally an Aramaic *Vorlage* for a longer Ethiopic recension,[42] it appears that 4Q206's scribe, even if aware of such a *Vorlage*, deliberately avoided transmitting "that white bull became a man." As we shall explore in more detail below, it is perfectly possible that the scribe was aware and wary of Babylonian stories of gigantic flood survivors who had supernatural fathers and so avoided attributing angelic status to Noah.

Apocalypse of Weeks[43]

Human history does not begin with Adam in the *Apocalypse of Weeks*, a text that divides history into ten weeks. It is Enoch's birth that is the notable event in Week 1. In Week 2, Noah appears as an unnamed man. "After me there will arise a second week, in which deceit (שקרא) and violence (חמסא) will spring up (יצמח), and in it will be the first end, and in it a man will be saved, and after, iniquity will increase, and a law will be made for sinners" (4Q212 1 III, 24-25/*1 En.* 93:4).

In the Aramaic text, the text breaks off at "deceit and violence will spring up" and resumes again in Week 7 but with a surprising difference from the previously known Ethiopic version. Long before the discoveries at Qumran, scholars had noted the strange dislocation in the ordering of weeks in the Ethiopic version. The block of material containing Weeks 8-10 that should logically have followed Weeks 1-7 in *1 En.* 93:10 was positioned earlier, in *1 En.* 91:1-10.[44] The discovery of the Aramaic text of 4Q212 revealed the positioning of several lines originally belonging to Week 7 that had been subsequently, in the Ethiopic version, severed, modified, expanded, and then relocated together with Weeks 8-10 to their new context in 91:1-10.[45] This has significant implications for understanding how the Enochic author viewed his own "week" (Week 7) in comparison to the "week" of Noah (Week 2). The lines restored to Week 7 are noted in italics:

---

41. Black, *Book of Enoch*, 262.

42. For a suggestion that the Ethiopic could represent a longer recension of the Aramaic in these cases, see Black, *Book of Enoch*, 262.

43. Only fragments of *Apocalypse of Weeks*, contained in the *Epistle of Enoch*, survived at Qumran. Gabriele Boccaccini argues that the "sectarian community preserved only a much shorter mid-second-century-BCE text" and that an interpolation was made at the original text at 94:5 that continues to 104:6 (*Beyond the Essene Hypothesis: The Parting of the Ways between Qumran and Enochic Judaism* [Grand Rapids: Eerdmans, 1998], 105, 111).

44. Nickelsburg, *1 Enoch 1*, 414-15.

45. Nickelsburg and VanderKam, *1 Enoch*, 142.

And at its conclusion [of the seventh week], the chosen will be chosen, as witnesses of righteousness from the eternal plant of righteousness (נצבת קשט עלמא) to whom will be given sevenfold wisdom (חכמה) and knowledge (מדע) (4Q212 1 IV, 12–13/*1 En.* 93:9–10) *and they will uproot the foundations of violence and the structure of deceit* (אשי חמסא ועבד שקרא) *in it, to execute judgment* (4Q212 1 IV, 14/*1 En.* 91:11).

In the Aramaic text, "violence" and "deceit" occur only in Weeks 2 and 7 of *AW*, suggesting that the author's week is being compared to the week of Noah. The villainous counterfoil to the "eternal plant of righteousness" in Week 7 is thus the implied "weed" of "violence and deceit"[46] that also springs up in Week 2.[47] It does seem odd that Noah is not named as a corresponding archetypical "eternal plant of righteousness" in Week 2 since "righteousness" or "righteous" is liberally used elsewhere in Weeks 1, 3, 4, 8, and 9 of *AW*. This oversight would be remedied by later interpreters who would decide that Noah was, indeed, planted for righteousness.[48] "Deceit," perhaps already inferred from the "illegitimate instruction" motif in *BW*, was here made explicit.

4Q212 also contains material in Enoch's exhortation to his sons not found in the Ethiopic: "and [the] ear[th] will rest (תנוח) . . . all generations of eternit[y] (כל דרי עלמין)" (4Q212 1 II, 13–17). That the earth would finally "rest" after judgment has echoes in the naming of Noah (Gen 5:29), which would intensify once the *Apocalypse of Weeks* joined the interpretation of Noah's naming as "remnant" and "rest" in the *Birth of Noah* (4Q204 5 II, 23–24/*1 En.* 106:18) as part of the Enochic collection.[49]

In sections preceding and following *AW*, Enoch speaks about the "way of righteousness" and ways of "violence" and "iniquity."[50] In Genesis, Noah and Enoch were the only ones in the Hebrew Bible of whom it was said that they "walked about with האלהים," but it was only Noah who was characterized by righteousness in a generation noted for its wickedness and violence (Gen 5:24; 6:5–11). However, in the *Epistle of Enoch*, it is Enoch who instructs his children to choose the way of righteousness (ארחת קשטא) and to avoid the paths of wickedness and violence.

---

46. See the occurrence of "deceit" (שקרה) in conjunction with the deluge in 4Q533 4, 1–3 (DJD XXXI, 110). But see Stuckenbruck (text numerated as 4Q566), who restores יכעל: "everything upon the earth" (*Book of Giants*, 185–91).

47. Based on descriptive statements of worldwide judgment and destruction of evil humans, VanderKam suggests a parallel between weeks 2 and 9 (*Enoch: A Man for All Generations*, 67). It might be argued that the whole time period between the *end* of Week 7 through to Week 10 could find its parallel prototype to the "first end" in Week 2. The parallel I am suggesting is based on the language of "deceit and violence" and refers to a time contemporaneous with the writer that finds its prototypical time in the days of Noah.

48. See 1QapGen VI, 1.

49. Cf. "son of Lamech" in *BW* and *BN* (*1 En.* 10:1; 106:16–18).

50. 4Q212 1 II, 18–21/*1 En.* 91:18–19; 4Q212 4 V, 24–25/*1 En.* 94:1.

Gabriele Boccaccini argues for a "Proto-Epistle of Enoch" with a later interpolation made at the original text at 94:5 that continues to 104:6, a redactional verse that "resumes the thread that the interpolated material interrupted."[51] Eibert Tigchelaar's observation of a column height of sixteen lines for 4Q212 and a "relatively short scroll" without the middle section of the *Epistle*[52] provides some support for this hypothesis.

The portion of the *Epistle* excluded by Boccaccini from the "proto-Epistle" includes a tradition associated with Noah in Genesis and again associated with Noah in later Hebrew traditions at Qumran but that had not appeared in the Enochic books until this point.[53] In Genesis, God makes a covenant with Noah and, later, in his first recorded words, Noah blesses and curses. In the *Epistle*, "woes" are placed into Enoch's mouth throughout the purported expansion, including "Woe to you who alter the true words and pervert the everlasting covenant" (*1 En.* 99:2). Nickelsburg's assessment of the use of "covenant" in this line is that reference to the covenant with Moses is "doubtful" and that the "corpus tends to ignore it."[54]

The extent of humanity's participation in divine judgment upon the wicked may have been a topic of the inner-Enochic conversation. Noah is a passive participant and observer to the primordial cosmic judgment in Genesis, the *Book of Watchers*, *Dream Visions*, and the *Apocalypse of Weeks*. In *1 Enoch*, God normally initiates and personally enacts his judgment. During Week 8, however, the sword is given to the righteous to "execute righteous judgment (דין קשוט) upon all the wicked (רשיעין)" (4Q212 1 IV, 15–17/*1 En.* 91:12–13).[55] The righteous ones are assured that they would be given the sword of judgment for a brief period of time at the end of the era. Subjected to time limits—once the final judgment was complete and the new "house" was constructed, the sword is put away (*1 En.* 90:34)—this notion of placing the sword in human hands does not resurface again even

---

51. Boccaccini, *Beyond the Essene Hypothesis*, 111. Boccaccini notes the shifts between the present time and the eschaton at the beginning and at the end of the interpolation. This is noteworthy, for a similar eschatological insertion may have occurred as *T. Levi* reinterpreted traditions found in the *ALD* and 4QApocryphon of Levi[b].

52. Eibert J. C. Tigchelaar, "Evaluating the Discussions concerning the Original Order of Chapters 91–93 and Codicological Data Pertaining to 4Q212 and Chester Beatty XII Enoch," in *Enoch and Qumran Origins: New Light on a Forgotten Connection* (ed. G. Boccaccini; Grand Rapids: Eerdmans, 2005), 220–23.

53. In *EE*, Enoch consciously transmits revelation given to him in the production of books. Alex P. Jassen, "Sapiential Revelation in Apocalyptic Literature Preserved at Qumran," in *Mediating the Divine: Prophecy and Revelation in the Dead Sea Scrolls and Second Temple Judaism* (STDJ 68; Leiden: Brill, 2007), 260–78.

54. Nickelsburg, *1 Enoch 1*, 489.

55. Cf. "eternal judgment" (דין עלמא) (4Q212 1 IV, 23); cf. also "righteousness" and "right judgment" revealed in Week 9 (4Q212 1 IV, 19/*1 En.* 91:14).

in what may be the later compositions, the *Birth of Noah*, the remainder of the *Epistle*, or the *Parables*.[56]

Birth of Noah

The *Birth of Noah* records a suspected incident with the Watchers.[57] Was this remarkable-looking infant who praised God from the moment of birth Lamech's son or was he the son of a Watcher? Enoch instructs Methuselah to reassure Lamech that Noah is, indeed, his son and, furthermore, that the earth would be cleansed (ותתדכא) from great corruption (חבלא)[58] by means of a flood from which Noah and his children would be saved (יפלטון). Noah would be a "remnant from whom you will find rest," an interpretation of Noah's naming based on נו and not נחם (4Q204 5 II, 21–23/*1 En.* 106:16–18; cf. Gen 5:29).

In a Greek version of the *Birth of Noah*, the Chester Beatty Greek papyrus preserves "righteous"[59] as a descriptor of Noah in *1 En.* 106:18,[60] a word that neither the Ethiopic nor the Aramaic preserves. Nickelsburg reconstructs this verse as "this child will be righteous and blameless," appealing to the idiom, "righteous and pious [i.e., "blameless]," known from the *Epistle* and from Gen 6:9.[61]

Restoring "righteous" to Noah in 106:18 may be problematic on three counts. First, the Chester Beatty papyrus is not the most dependable source.[62] The most we may deduce from this variant is that at least *one* translator believed Noah's righteousness *should* be there; we cannot conclude that the term "righteous," describing Noah, was indeed in the Aramaic *Vorlage*.

Second, although the writers of the Enochic booklets would have known of Noah's righteousness from Genesis or from the *Book of Watchers*, "righteousness" is not unambiguously attributed to Noah in the remainder of the Enochic

---

56. In the *Community Rule*, the council of the Yaḥad appears to understand that they would have an active role in judgment, describing itself as "chosen by God's will to atone for the land and to recompense the wicked their due" (1QS VIII, 6–7).

57. For a brief discussion of sexual wrongdoing and the illicit sexual activity of the Watchers in *1 En.* 106–7 and the *Genesis Apocryphon*, see William Loader, *Enoch, Levi, and Jubilees on Sexuality: Attitudes Towards Sexuality in the Early Enoch Literature, the Aramaic Levi Document, and the Book of Jubilees* (Grand Rapids: Eerdmans, 2007), 71–77.

58. See also 4Q532 2 9 (4QEnGiants^d ar): "they [the Watchers] caused great corruption (חבל) in the [earth]."

59. Black, *Apocalypsis Henochi Graece*, 44.

60. קשוט does stand out clearly in the middle of this debated line: "[He is your son] in truth (בקשוט)." A play on words may have created an exegetical opening; the *Genesis Apocryphon* employs בקשוט eight times when retelling Noah's birth.

61. The Chester Beatty papyrus is a "notoriously corrupt and defective text" (Nickelsburg, *1 Enoch 1*, 547).

62. Nickelsburg's own assessment of the papyrus in "Response: Context, Text, and Social Setting," 238. On a further note, the Chester Beatty papyrus preserves "covenant," a reading that "may derive from a confusion between קומתא ('height', cf. Eth) and קימא ('covenant', cf. Gr^CB)" (so Knibb, *Ethiopic Book of Enoch*, 38–39, 245–46).

corpus and should not be restored to him without better textual evidence. Third, although "righteous" appears in a well-known idiom elsewhere in Enoch—in connection with Enoch and with the righteous "chosen"—this idiom should not be applied to Noah here when there is little evidence that it has been applied elsewhere to him. A more likely conclusion, based on the textual evidence, is that Noah's righteousness was deliberately transferred both backwards to Noah's great-grandfather, Enoch, and forward to Noah's righteous progeny.

According to the Qumran textual evidence, at least some of the Enochic books circulated in groupings. In 4Q203/204, the *Birth of Noah* is appended to *Dream Visions* following a two-line *vacat* in a text that also contains the *Book of Watchers* and the *Book of Giants*. The *Birth* surveys and interprets the plot and themes from other parts of the Enochic corpus: the Watchers transgress with women, the earth would be destroyed but some would be preserved as a remnant. The earth would rest, cleansed from corruption (4Q204 5 I-II/*1 En.* 106–7). Significantly, some of the technical terms describing righteousness and wickedness resurface as a group in the *Birth* as a supporting cast in this synopsis. There are the transgressors (עבר) and those who practice corruption (חבלא). Wickedness (רשא), evil (באישתה), and violence (חמסא) threaten to overwhelm those who would, however, be saved (פלט). In the eschaton, the generations of righteousness (דרי קושטא) would prevail, while all who opposed them would be wiped out together with everything they stood for (4Q204 5 II, 16–30/*1 En.* 106:13–107:2).

By positioning this suspected incident with the Watchers at the end of the corpus, the *Birth* comes full circle to Noah, whose character was originally recontextualized and subordinated into traditions more closely linked to the figure of Enoch in *BW*. The appended *Birth* not only summarizes the corpus but now also recontextualizes the Enoch traditions in terms of the *Birth*, reclaiming Noah and answering back to at least one kind of Judaism that had been shy about identifying too closely with "flood survivor Noah."

Book of Parables

Because *Parables* is not extant at Qumran, neither the digression on the flood (*1 En.* 54:7–55:2) nor what may be "Noachic" interpolations in *1 En.* 60 and 65:1–69:1 can be assumed to be part of the Enochic "base text" from which other Qumran interpretation of Noah traditions developed. However, *knowledge* of these or similar traditions by the authors of some Qumran texts cannot be precluded.

Where these traditions appear *only* in the *Parables* within the Enochic corpus, it is possible that they either represented later points in the overall trajectory of Noah traditions or that the narrator was influenced by other, possibly even Hebrew, sources. Therefore, it is important at this point to note the Noah traditions in the *Parables* that have parallels in the Aramaic and Hebrew Dead Sea Scrolls.

Michael Knibb has observed that, while the Noah passages in the *Parables* do not fit naturally into their context, they "have attracted secondary material to themselves."[63] The flood story serves a typological function, interrupting a sequence of four vision reports.[64] Noah is shown a vision of the angels who would release the waters (66:1-2) and is affirmed as "pure and blameless," and his name is confirmed among the holy ones (65:11-12). God speaks directly to Noah, assuring him that he is blameless and upright and that his seed would be preserved in his presence forever (67:1-3). Noah sees the future confinement and burning of the iniquitous angels (67:4-7). Finally, Enoch gathers the explanation of all of the secrets into a book for Noah (68:1). The role Noah plays in the *Parables* is heightened one, linking him even more closely to Enoch as Enoch's legitimate successor. The *Genesis Apocryphon*'s author was also familiar with traditions similar to these but, as we shall see in chapter 5, transfers Enochic characteristics to Noah, thus intensifying Noah's identification with Enoch.

Although Nickelsburg refutes the intentional creation of an Enochic Pentateuch proposed by Milik, he concedes that ch. 91 "does bear a significant resemblance to the last chapters of Deuteronomy" and that chs. 1-5 "with its allusions to Deuteronomy 33—interpreted the Enochic collection as a testament that paralleled the last words of Moses."[65] Furthermore, the very act of collecting the *Book of Watchers* together with the *Epistle of Enoch* may have reflected the origins of a trajectory of a heightened consciousness of Mosaic Torah within *1 Enoch* and a perception of its relationship to it, a trajectory that *Jubilees* followed and took in new directions. Just as Noah was subsumed to Enoch in *1 Enoch*, both Enoch and Noah would be subsumed to Moses and Mosaic Torah in *Jubilees*.

Finally, within the Enochic corpus, Noah is given "first person speech" only in the *Parables*, a development paralleled also in the *Genesis Apocryphon*. Unless both the *Genesis Apocryphon* and the *Parables* had access to another source that was not used in the earlier Enochic books, the lack of first person speech would tend to suggest that the "Book of the Words of Noah" (1Q20 V, 29) in the *Genesis Apocryphon* was a later literary creation by some who believed that such a book *must* have existed.

While Noah was given a heightened status and remembered in greater detail in the later Enochic traditions, the books were still framed within a revelation to Enoch, a strong indication that Enoch was still the figure with the most authority. This next section will explore why some Jews may have been uneasy with Noah as a "righteous flood survivor," choosing Enoch, instead, as a figure who did, after all, also survive the flood.

---

63. Michael A. Knibb, "The Structure and Composition of the Parables of Enoch," in *Enoch and the Messiah Son of Man: Revisiting the Book of Parables* (ed. G. Boccaccini; Grand Rapids: Eerdmans, 2007), 48-64, here 52.
64. Ibid., 57.
65. Nickelsburg, *1 Enoch 1*, 21-25.

Enoch: The Preferred Righteous Flood Survivor?

Intriguingly, while the Watchers and their progeny were presented as an archetype for contemporary wicked humanity, the extreme terseness concerning Noah hardly sets him up as a corresponding archetype for righteous survivors of judgment. The subdued presentation of Noah in *1 Enoch* contrasts sharply with the multidimensional multicultural figure of Enoch that dominates the corpus. We pause briefly here to pick up two questions. Why was the figure of Noah not idealized as a righteous flood survivor type? And why was Enoch preferred over Noah?

John Reeves suggests that the *Book of Giants* may have known of a flood survivor that resembled a giant. He identifies the Babylonian flood hero Utnapishtim with the giant "Atambish" from the Manichaean Book of Giants. According to Reeves, this view is supported by a polemic found in Noah's birth narratives in *1 En.* 106-7 and the *Genesis Apocryphon*. By pressing the point that Noah was the son of Lamech and not the son of the Watchers, the birth narratives were thus in dispute with the competing idea that Noah was a flood survivor of the giant variety.[66] The degree to which an archetypical Noah needed to be perceived as distinct from his Mesopotamian counterparts is likely directly related to the dispute over the degree to which the Jewish people should remain distinct from the foreign nations.

Loren Stuckenbruck suggests another link: Belos as a "giant who, unlike the other giants 'destroyed by the gods because of their impiety,' had been able to escape destruction and who dwelt in Babylon where he built a tower. . . . Belos thus seems at this point to correspond to the figure of Noah in the biblical tradition."[67] Stuckenbruck explains the rise of Enochic traditions as a response to a tradition preserved in the Pseudo-Eupolemus fragment that links Abraham *and* the giants to transmission of Babylonian astrological science and in which some giants escape the deluge.[68] Commenting on the fragment, Stuckenbruck hypothesizes how the biblical figure of Noah may have come to be associated as one of the giants:

---

66. John C. Reeves, "Utnapishtim in the Book of Giants," *JBL* 112 (1993): 110-15. Cf. Ronald V. Huggins, who relates Abraham's "gigantic pedigree" not to Noah but to Nimrod, whom LXX Gen 10:9 refers to as *gigas*; further, "it is better to regard 'Atambish' as an Enochic rather than an Noachic figure" (Huggins, "Noah and the Giants: A Response to John C. Reeves," *JBL* 114 [1995]: 103-10, here 109-10).

67. Loren T. Stuckenbruck, "The Origins of Evil in Jewish Apocalyptic Tradition: The Interpretation of Genesis 6:1-4 in the Second and Third Centuries B.C.E.," in *The Fall of the Angels* (ed. C. Auffarth and L. T. Stuckenbruck; Themes in Biblical Narrative 6; Leiden: Brill, 2004), 87-118, here 96.

68. Stuckenbruck, *Book of Giants*, 33-37. Traditions preserved by Eusebius of Caesarea in *Praep. ev.* 9.17.1-9 and 9.18.2 citing Alexander Polyhistor.

[the] giants' continued existence after the flood is taken for granted . . . if the great flood did indeed destroy "all flesh" and if giants did indeed survive this cataclysm, then the only survivors (i.e. Noah and his family) may have been "giants." In this way, the biblical giants have been made to function as an important link in the introduction and spread of culture, beginning in Babylonia. Significantly, the fragments draw no distinction between commendable and reprehensible knowledge.[69]

In conversation with and response to such ideas, those who composed and transmitted the *Giants* traditions were attempting to draw a clearer distinction, on the one hand, between the culpable giants and the flood survivor (Noah) and, on the other hand, between the *kind* of learning associated with the rebellious angels and the learning associated with Enoch in the Enochic traditions.[70] Therefore, although the *Book of Giants* seemed to *follow* Babylonian traditions, it was actually attempting to *refute* these traditions.

It is not difficult to imagine that some interpreters avoided Noah altogether because he was fraught with dangerous associations.[71] However, because Enoch "walked with האלהים" during the flood, he would have "survived" the flood without being one of the giants who, because of their height, were taller than the floodwaters. Therefore, Enoch avoided the dangerous connotations associated with an earthbound flood survivor like Noah. Furthermore, because both Noah and Enoch are said to have "walked with האלהים" in the Hebrew Bible, an observant interpreter could easily bestow other aspects of Noah's biblical character—including his righteousness and the revelation he received from God—upon Enoch, who consequently would become the one known as "righteous" (קשט) and who would receive greatly expanded visions as a revelation from God.

Enoch's dual biblical/Mesopotamian parentage within the Enochic books has been the subject of several important studies.[72] Enoch's name, his walk-about

---

69. Stuckenbruck, "Origins of Evil," 98.
70. Stuckenbruck, *Book of Giants*, 37; and idem, "Origins of Evil," 107–8.
71. For an excellent discussion on the subject, see Pieter W. van der Horst, "Antediluvian Knowledge: Graeco-Roman and Jewish Speculations about Wisdom from before the Flood," in *Japheth in the Tents of Shem: Studies on Jewish Hellenism in Antiquity* (CBET 32; Leuven: Peeters, 2002), 158: "The Jews . . . claiming antediluvian traditions in their wish to prove that Jewish culture is older than Greek culture, but since the biblical story ties the flood to the motif of the wickedness of mankind, some of these traditions tend to be regarded as very bad and connected with idolatry and violence. Others, however, having a less negative image of the 'sons of God' in Gen. 6:1-4, or of the giants, or of their cultural achievements – *i.e.*, by and large, the Hellenistic cultural achievements! – [sic] tend to see this antediluvian knowledge as worthwhile."
72. For discussions asserting dependence on the biblical text, see Devorah Dimant, "1 Enoch 6-11: A Fragment of a Parabiblical Work," *JJS* 8 (2002): 223–37, here 225. Philip S. Alexander allows for "strong external stimuli" that helped to realize the potential of the biblical narrative ("From Son of Adam to Second God," in *Biblical Figures Outside the Bible* [ed. M. E. Stone and T. A. Bergren; Harrisburg, Pa.: Trinity Press International, 1998], 90–91, 93).

in Genesis with אלהים, understood by the Enochic writers to be "angels,"[73] the fact that he lived 365 years, did not die, but was "taken" by God, together with his visions could all hang from the slender thread of the brief comment on Enoch in Gen 5.[74]

It could be argued that Enoch, like Noah, also carried potentially dangerous cultural baggage. His literary formation may have been influenced by the Mesopotamian Enmeduranki, by the seventh king in antediluvian lists, by the sun-god Shamash,[75] or by Atrahasis, who played the role not only of flood hero but also of "priest and diviner who acts as an intermediary between gods and the humans."[76]

Apparently, however, Enoch could be fearlessly associated with ancient traditions that existed outside Judaism but that were viewed as positive and desirable. Within the figure of Enoch and, by extension, within Jewish tradition, the new scientific knowledge of Babylonian origin could successfully be "domesticated within Jewish tradition."[77]

> The origin of these Enochic circles goes back to the Persian period in the fourth, or even possibly in the fifth century BCE. These circles first became interested in Enoch when they were looking for a patron for new scientific knowledge which they were importing to Israel. This knowledge, which was large astronomical and cosmographical in content, was ultimately Babylonian in origin, but it was transmitted to them in the medium of Aramaic.[78]

Alexander does not assume that "Enoch" and the "Bible" were fixed bodies of literature but rather sees that the close readings that the Enochic writers appear to be making of the biblical text are of the same kind that he is familiar with from his work on later rabbinic Midrash ("The Enochic Literature and the Bible: Intertextuality and Its Implications," in *The Bible as Book: The Hebrew Bible and the Judaean Desert Discoveries* (ed. E. D. Herbert and E. Tov; London: Library; New Castle, Del.: Oak Knoll Press, 2002], 57–69, here 64). For a case for the dependence of *1 En.* 6–11 on Gen 6:1–4 as "primary inspiration or at least the framework for the story" showing where the base text is expanded, nuanced, and where it clarifies it, see James C. VanderKam, "Biblical Interpretation in *1 Enoch* and *Jubilees*," in *The Pseudepigrapha and Early Biblical Interpretation* (ed. J. H. Charlesworth and C. A. Evans; JSPSup 14; Sheffield: Sheffield Academic Press, 1993), 96–125, here 103–7.

73. So VanderKam, "Interpretation of Genesis in *1 Enoch*," 134.

74. There may be up to two hundred parallels to "scripture" in *1 Enoch*. Alexander, "Enochic Literature and the Bible," 58.

75. This association is suggested by Enoch's life span and the number 365, the length of the solar year. John J. Collins, "The Place of Apocalypticism in the Religion of Ancient Israel," in *Ancient Israelite Religion: Essays in Honor of Frank Moore Cross* (ed. P.D. Miller, Jr., Paul D. Hanson, and S. Dean McBride; Philadelphia: Fortress, 1987), 539–58, here 542–43.

76. For a close resemblance to *1 En.* 12–13, in which Enoch makes petition, see Helge S. Kvanvig, "The Watchers Story, Genesis, and *Atra-hasis*, a Triangular Reading," *Hen* 24 (2002): 20.

77. Alexander, "Enochic Literature and the Bible," 66.

78. Ibid.; idem, "Enoch and the Beginnings of Jewish Interest in Natural Sciences," 232.

While Enoch's creators successfully domesticated Mesopotamian science within Judaism by means of Enoch, they strangely demonstrated little or no interest in creating a multicultural Noah. This wariness concerning Noah might well have originated in the concern of some Jews that Noah would be confused with flood survivor heroes and particularly giants outside of the Jewish tradition.

Whatever the reasons were behind the early selection of Enoch and the avoidance of Noah, it is reasonable to suppose that there was a movement in the corpus away from Noah and toward Enoch as the righteous primogenitor with the result that the righteous progeny were linked more directly to Enoch than to Noah. Therefore, Noah became merely a placeholder, a human who survived the flood by virtue of his righteous ancestor, Enoch.

An intriguing epilogue to this story reveals an interpretative dispute between groups. Apparently, one group was transferring Enochic characteristics to Noah in an attempt to "rehabilitate" him, but this was met with "fierce theological polemics against Noah" in the group represented by *2 Enoch*.[79] *2 Enoch* responded by systematically giving Noah's role to yet another character, Melchizedek. Noah is stripped of any priestly role, does not transmit priestly instruction, and is no longer the recipient of any divine or angelic revelation. Furthermore, Melchizedek is awarded the remarkable birth.[80]

The Ebb and Flow of Noah and his Righteousness in *1 Enoch*

The combinations and permutations of the Noah and Watchers traditions together with their ongoing recontextualizations and reinterpretations within the Enochic corpus make the task of mapping the development of Noah themes within the corpus a daunting enterprise. It is difficult to know when a theme is particularly Noachic; for example, sin and its effect on the land, past and future judgment, righteousness, and the survival of the remnant are all themes that are pervasive in the corpus and not restricted to the story of Noah.

The "righteousness of Noah" as established in Genesis and incorporated into the oldest part of the *Book of Watchers* appears to have been reinterpreted as early as the recontextualization of the Noah narrative (*1 En.* 6–11) within *1 En.* 1–36. Enoch is introduced as "righteous" in its earliest verses (*1 En.* 1:2), an attribution that remains with him throughout the compositional history of the books at the same time that the righteousness of Noah was ignored or even suppressed. "Righteousness" was an attribute, given to Noah both in Hebrew in the book of Genesis (צדיק) and in Aramaic in the *Book of Watchers* (קשט), that the exegetes

---

79. That *2 Enoch* may attest to "uncommon criticisms against Noah" in a writing that may also be responding to traditions in *Jubilees*, see Andrei A. Orlov, " 'Noah's Younger Brother': The Anti-Noachic Polemics in *2 Enoch*," *Hen* 22 (2000): 207–21.

80. For a comparison and contrast of *2 Enoch* with Hebrews in the New Testament and concerning the appropriation of Noah's priestly qualities to Melchizedek, see Andrei Orlov, "The Heir of Righteousness and the King of Righteousness: The Priestly Noachic Polemics in 2 Enoch and the Epistle to the Hebrews," *JTS* 58 (2007): 45–65.

of antiquity could variously choose to develop, polemicize, or simply ignore. It would be impossible to argue convincingly that they did *not* know about the righteousness of Noah either from *BW* or from Genesis. Therefore, at this point, the discoveries made particularly with respect to the Qumran evidence will be put to work in the tracing of the "righteousness of Noah" throughout the Enochic corpus.

In the books of Enoch, "righteousness" (קשט) is variously collocated with "plant," "way," "judgment," and "paradise," and associated with Noah's ancestor, Enoch, and his distant progeny. Even though, in its various forms and collocations, קשט had "virtually become a *terminus technicus* in Enoch,"[81] the word is only used once to describe Noah.

Among all of the Enochic books represented at Qumran, it is only in *BW* that Noah is unequivocally called "righteous." In chs. 6–11, which contain the oldest traditions in *BW*, God tells his angel to instruct the "righteous man" (קשטה) so that he would know what to do in order to preserve life. This man would carry the seed from which a plant would be planted. Only in *this* portion of the *BW*, which maintains the most recognizable affinities to Genesis and which contains no reference to the person of Enoch, does Noah survive with his righteousness intact (4Q201 1 V, 3–4/*1 En.* 10:3).

Whether later Enochic writers deliberately edited Noah's righteousness out of their received traditions, transferring this righteousness to the figure of Enoch, or whether they forgot about it, Noah as a righteous figure simply does not explicitly reappear in the Enochic books represented at Qumran. Unlike Enoch, Noah neither receives angelic revelation nor sees visions; he does not walk in a paradise of righteousness (*1 En.* 32:3) or proclaim woes or curses. The details of the Noah story are confined to his birth, to revelations of the coming flood, to building the ark, and to his survival of the flood.

Enoch takes on Noah's biblical characteristics and actions and, by also assimilating Babylonian knowledge of astronomical science, becomes a hybrid antediluvian super hero who survived the flood to "speak" to a postdiluvian world by means of the Enochic books. Noah is virtually forgotten.

In *Dream Visions*, the status of Noah was apparently debated at some point during the composition and/or translations of the Aramaic text. In the Ethiopic version, Noah becomes an angel but undergoes no such transformation in the Aramaic texts (4Q206 4 II, 4–5/*1 En.* 89:9; 4Q206 4 I, 13–14/*1 En.* 89:1). The status of Noah—whether human or angelic—was therefore in dispute.

In the *Dream Visions*, the credit for survival of humanity at all is attributed to the righteous prayer of Enoch and not that of Noah. Enoch recounts his first vision of the deluge in which all of humanity is obliterated, a prediction of what would have been the end of history entirely. However, Enoch intervenes, offer-

---

81. Black, *Apocalypsis Henochi Graecae*, 108. See 5:6; 25:4; 39:4; 60:2; 82:4; 95:3; 100:5.

ing an intercessory prayer, lifting his hands *in righteousness*, and supplicating God to raise up "the righteous and true flesh" as a "seed-bearing plant forever" (*1 En.* 84:1–6). What follows is a *second* dream vision of the history of humanity, a history that *now* continues beyond the deluge presumably as a direct result of Enoch's righteous prayer and not, as in Genesis, because of the righteousness of Noah.

In the *Apocalypse of Weeks*, "righteous" or "righteousness" (קשט) is repeatedly used—in Weeks 1, 3, 4, 7, 8, 9, and beyond—with respect to times or characters in Israel's history but is curiously absent with respect to the unnamed flood survivor. Because the Aramaic text breaks off at "deceit and violence will spring up," it is possible that this or another version recorded a "*righteous* man will be saved." However, Enoch's speech "until my time קשטא endured" makes a "righteous Noah" highly unlikely, for it would make the subsequent choosing of the plant of righteous judgment (Abraham) in Week 3 redundant (4Q212 1 III, 23–25/*1 En.* 93:3–5a). It is here, in the *Apocalypse of Weeks*, that Noah would appear to be most deliberately denuded of his righteousness.

While the term "righteousness" recurs frequently throughout the ten weeks, "deceit and violence" occur *only* in Weeks 2 and 7, the latter likely reflecting the "week" of the writer and the intended readers. For the author, then, the present days strongly resembled the days of Noah. The discovery of the Aramaic fragments of *AW* affirmed the presumed original order of the text, providing a more complete picture of the setting of "deceit and violence" within which the "eternal plant of righteousness" found itself in Week 7.

The time of violence and deceit in Week 7 had a well-developed archetypical time of violence and deceit in Week 2, the days of Noah. Also situated in Week 7 are the "chosen" ones from the "eternal plant of righteousness" (נצבת קשט), who would root out the implied "wicked weed" of violence and deceit. However, "a man who will be saved" in Week 2 is hardly an adequate corresponding righteous archetype for the "eternal plant of righteousness" in Week 7.[82] Rather, it would appear that Enoch had assumed the role of "righteous archetype" for the survivors of a coming cosmic judgment.

The preservation of "righteous" as a descriptor of Noah (*1 En.* 106:18) in the Greek Chester Beatty papyrus in contrast to its absence in the Ethiopic translation is evidence of the flux of Noah's status even in the *Birth of Noah* narrative. However, the *Birth* functions as an appendix to the collated *BW*, *BG*, and *DV* in 4Q203/204, recasting the collection in terms of Noah and the primordial judgment by flood.

This collation suggests an upsurge of interest in the figure of Noah. It may indicate the beginning of a dual trajectory that survives in later texts that either subdued or vilified Noah or, alternatively, rehabilitated and idealized Noah,

---

82. 4Q212 1 III, 24–25/*1 En.* 93:4.

reshaping him into a prophetic and visionary figure like Enoch. For the former, perhaps Noah continued to be too dangerous a figure, too loaded with cultural baggage to be successfully domesticated back into Judaism. For the latter, as we shall see in the next chapter, Noah was increasingly and successfully realigned not only with Genesis but also with the parts of Torah more easily associated with Moses. By so doing, he could legitimately be claimed and rehabilitated as a priestly Jewish ancestor.

The flatness and two-dimensionality of *1 Enoch*'s Noah (as a whole) has demanded other ways of reading these texts. It has been helpful to set Noah into the context of what he was *not*, thus filling in the negative spaces around him and bringing him into sharper focus. Noah was *not* a transgressor, not a murderer, he did not eat blood, and neither was he violent nor deceitful nor wicked, words that also became technical terms by which certain groups were labeled. He did *not* accept instruction from the wrong sort of angel. Therefore, he managed, perhaps by default and not necessarily because of his righteousness, to survive the flood. Even so, while Noah managed to escape being labeled by these villainous technical terms, neither was he consistently "righteous." That technical term was reserved for his righteous great-grandfather, Enoch, and also for his righteous progeny.

To conclude this section, once the figure of Enoch appeared in the Enochic corpus, "righteous Noah" faded away into the background, making a minor comeback much later by the time the *Birth of Noah* was appended to the corpus. Between these two points, Noah lingered in Enoch's shadow, as a mere *conduit* of קושטא, a seed-carrier linking his righteous ancestor, Enoch, to his righteous plant progeny, and to the "generations of righteousness" (קושטא) of the writers' day (4Q204 5 II, 28/*1 En.* 107:1).

Aramaic Levi Document: Noah as Ancestor of Priests

Noah and Enoch are hardly "priestly" in *1 Enoch* but there was another Aramaic tradition that had its origins as early as the 4th century B.C.E. and that adopted Noah as part of a continuous, unbroken line of priestly characters of which the visionary and wise Levi is the central one.[83] While Noah appears only briefly in the *Aramaic Levi Document* as a priestly ancestor, a study of the character of Levi in the *ALD* is critical to understanding a particular kind of "priestly Noah" who was also reformed and reshaped in the Aramaic and Hebrew compositions such as *Jubilees*, the *Genesis Apocryphon*, and the *Festival Prayers*.

---

83. On the high regard for Enoch, Jacob (and Bethel), Levi, and Moses and the "insistence that it is the prerogative of the Levites to interpret the Law," see George J. Brooke, "Levi and the Levites," in *The Dead Sea Scrolls and the New Testament* (Minneapolis: Fortress, 2005), 121.

The Text

"For thus my father Abraham commanded me for thus he found in the writing of the book of Noah concerning the blood" (*ALD* 10:10).[84] This is only one line within Isaac's instructions to Levi concerning various sacrifices in the *ALD*, and yet it links Noah to a lineage of priests that extends to Levi's son, Qahat, who is named to the high priesthood (11:5–6), and Amram, Qahat's son, whose marriage to Jochabed is reported (12:3), thus setting the stage for the birth of Moses.

ALD 10 survives only in the Greek Mount Athos text and is not extant in any of the seven Aramaic copies from Qumran[85] or in the Aramaic Genizah fragments. However, there are several good reasons to believe that Noah as a legitimate priestly ancestor to Levi existed even in the earliest "Aramaic Levi" traditions. First, based on other overlaps between the Aramaic texts and the observed reliability of the Greek text, Jonas C. Greenfield, Michael E. Stone, and Esther Eshel argue that the line mentioning Noah *was* originally in the Aramaic, for which they posit a third-century or very early second-century B.C.E. compositional date.[86]

A second argument for the inclusion of Noah within the original Aramaic version may be sought within the text itself. The *ALD* demonstrates a concern for the proper transmission of wisdom and priestly lore from antiquity, naming Abraham, Isaac, Jacob, and also Qahat and Amram within this lineage. Therefore, it is not unlikely that Noah would also have been included in the list.

Furthermore, the *Testament of Qahat* (4Q542) and the *Visions of Amram* (4Q543–548), also transmitted in Aramaic, continued in the tradition of the *ALD*, and their contents serve to "legitimate the continuity of the priestly line and its teaching."[87] Noah is named together with Levi and Moses as ones who offer up offerings, implying that either Noah did originally appear in the tradition or, alternatively, that later tradents saw his inclusion as a logical development in the trajectory. Noah's portrayal in the *Genesis Apocryphon*, as seen

---

84. Unless otherwise indicated, translation and numeration of the *ALD* follows Jonas C. Greenfield, Michael E. Stone, and Esther Eshel, *The Aramaic Levi Document: Edition, Translation, and Commentary* (SVTP 19; Leiden: Brill, 2004) (*TALD*). The authors base their reconstruction on the Genizah text and where neither the Genizah text nor the Qumran fragments exist, the authors follow the Greek Mount Athos text.

85. 1Q21, 4Q213, 4Q213a, 4Q213b, 4Q214, 4Q214a, and 4Q214b. See official editions: 1Q21 (DJD I); 4Q213–214b (M. E. Stone and J. C. Greenfield, DJD XXII).

86. The *ALD* is quoted in CD (2nd century B.C.E.), and something like it served as a source for *Jubilees*, dated to first third of the second century B.C.E. (*TALD*, 19–20).

87. *TALD*, 31. Noah's name does not survive in the extant text of *Qahat* but, as Stone argues, 4Q542 "stresses a cardinal point, the descent of priestly teaching from Abraham and eventually, according to Aramaic Levi, from Noah" ("The Axis of History at Qumran," in *Pseudepigraphic Perspectives: The Apocrypha and Pseudepigrapha in Light of the Dead Sea Scrolls. Proceedings of the International Symposium of the Orion Center for the Study of the Dead Sea Scrolls and Associated Literature, 12–14 January 1997* [ed. E. G. Chazon and M. E. Stone; STDJ 31; Leiden: Brill, 1999], 133–49, here 137).

below, bears a striking resemblance to the figure of Levi in the *ALD*, evidence that if Noah was not originally in the *ALD*, then that particular author made it clear that Noah did belong.

The dating of the *ALD* has evoked deep and passionate debate. As stated earlier, the official editors posit a third- or very early second-century B.C.E. compositional date. Others call for an earlier or later date. Appealing to Babylonian metrological lists and elements in a Babylonian scribal education, Henryk Drawnel compellingly argues for a *terminus a quo* for the *ALD* within the historical context of Ezra and Nehemiah's mission for "the formation of the Levitical tradition that eventually led to the composition of the *Document*,"[88] a dating that would be consistent with Milik's suggestion.[89] This could put the composition of the document as early as the end of the fourth century B.C.E., an Aramaic work being composed at the same time that the earliest Enochic books were being written but a document with a particularly *priestly* slant. Drawnel argues that Levi as an "ideal priest" is already observed as early as Mal 2:4–7, which attests religious reforms that led "to the reinterpretation of the biblical Levi and his life story in accordance with the new historical circumstances during the Persian dominion in the Trans-Euphrates province."[90] If Drawnel's dating is accepted, then early "priestly Levi" traditions that, at some point, attested a Noachic tradition were being transmitted during the same period that the earliest Aramaic Enochic traditions were set down in writing.

Making a case for a later dating is James L. Kugel, who argues that the *ALD*, in its final form, postdated even the second-century B.C.E. book of *Jubilees*. Kugel qualifies his conclusions by saying that "the sources on which it relied—an old elaboration of Mal 2:4–7 ('Levi's Apocalypse'); the Levi section of an ancient, priestly trilogy ('Levi's Priestly Initiation'); and the historical framework provided by *Jubilees*—must all belong to a somewhat earlier period."[91]

For this study, we accept that some form of an Aramaic Levi priestly tradition involving Noah as a priestly ancestor was foundational to subsequent various reinterpretations of a priestly Noah in texts such as the *Genesis Apocryphon* and in *Jubilees*. However, since this study is more about persistent and ongoing conversations involving Noah traditions in all of their diversity, across languages and over time, and in texts that continued to be copied and interpreted well past their compositional date, it is not necessary to insist on the priority of the Aramaic Levi Document.

---

88. Henryk Drawnel, *An Aramaic Wisdom Text from Qumran: A New Interpretation of the Levi Document* (JSJSup 86; Leiden: Brill, 2004), 66–68.

89. Milik suggests a Samaritan origin for the *ALD* (*BE*, 24).

90. Drawnel, *Aramaic Wisdom Text*, 71. Greenfield, Stone, and Eshel also observe the tendency to establish Levi "as an ideal priest from the past already in Malachi 2:4–9" (*TALD*, 36).

91. James L. Kugel, "How Old Is the *Aramaic Levi Document*?" *DSD* 14 (2007): 291–312, here 312.

The *Aramaic Levi Document* survives in seven Aramaic copies from Qumran (1Q21, 4Q213, 4Q213a, 4Q213b, 4Q214, 4Q214a, 4Q214b) ranging in date from the late second century B.C.E. in the Hasmonean period to the early Herodian period in the late first century B.C.E.[92] The Qumran fragments tell only a partial story, and their interpretation relies on how they are ordered and reconstructed. For example, whether or not Levi's calling as priest *preceded* or *followed* the retribution he brought against Shechem and the "workers of violence" in response to the sexual defilement of his sister, Dinah, could reveal how the narrator viewed the priesthood and whether the naming to the priesthood was contingent on an appropriate response to sexually defiling acts.[93]

The *Testament of Levi* cannot be trusted to reconstruct the Aramaic texts, as Robert A. Kugler has shown,[94] and even if it could, *T. Levi* contradicts itself with respect to the timing of Levi's visions, ordination to the priesthood, and the events at Shechem (see *T. Levi* 2:2–3; 5:2–3; 12:5–7). *Jubilees* would, however, clarify the matter, adding its perspective to the conversation or, more precisely, the dispute. Levi was chosen for the priesthood *because* of his righteous actions at Shechem (*Jub*. 30.18).

That Levi destroyed the "workers of violence" (*ALD* 12:6–7a) is an action that is nuanced by another Aramaic tradition in the *Genesis Apocryphon* in which Noah praises and blesses God for destroying the workers of violence, a subtle reinterpretation that may reflect a debate concerning whether vengeance upon the "workers of violence" belonged in human hands or in God's hands. The inclusion of at least two versions of the ordination to priesthood in the *ALD* and its chronological relationship to the Shechem incident may provide evidence of this internal tension and debate within the history of the tradition.

Levi as a Literary Ancestor of Noah?

Michael Stone aptly describes Noah's role in the *ALD* as an "initiator of sacrificial cult." The *ALD* "incorporates Noah into the priestly genealogy" and "draws attention to this pivotal role as a bridge over the Flood" so that Noah is "a second Adam for the new, postdiluvian world order."[95] In contrast to his role in

---

92. Dates obtained from DJD XXXIX.
93. For interpretations based on alternative reconstructions, see James L. Kugel, "Levi's Elevation to the Priesthood in Second Temple Writings," *HTR* 86 (1993): 1–64, here 8–9; and Marinus de Jonge, "Levi in Aramaic Levi and in the Testament of Levi," in *Pseudepigraphic Perspectives* (see n. 87 above), 84.
94. Kugler has demonstrated the unreliability of *T. Levi* for reconstruction and ordering of the Aramaic text. See Robert A. Kugler, *From Patriarch to Priest: The Levi-Priestly Tradition from* Aramaic Levi *to* Testament of Levi (SBLEJL; Atlanta: Scholars Press, 1996), 45–51; idem, *The Testaments of the Twelve Patriarchs* (Guides to Apocrypha and Pseudepigrapha; Sheffield: Sheffield Academic Press, 2001), 30. Kugler's reading would suggest a priesthood contingent on vengeance taken by humans.
95. Stone, "Axis of History at Qumran," 141.

Aramaic Enoch, Noah's role as a "second Adam" is enhanced as he is introduced also as a priestly progenitor. This raises the question of what *kind* of lineage is represented by the priests in the *ALD*.

First, there is what appears at first glance to be a prayer of repentance. Following his immersion and purification in water, Levi prays, "I made all my paths upright . . . grant me all the paths of truth. . . . Make far from me, my Lord, the unrighteous spirit, and evil thought and fornication" (*ALD* 2:5–3:5/4Q213a 1 6–13). However, Joseph Baumgarten aptly observes that "[o]ne might suppose that 'making his paths upright' denotes Levi's effort to repent," adding that it is odd that penitence follows and does not precede immersion. His alternative hypothesis is that Levi straightens the steps of his feet "thereby simulating the unswerving paths of the holy angels."[96] Furthermore, if repentance is not unambiguously associated with priesthood in the *ALD*, neither is the portion of Torah most obviously associated with Moses.

Greenfield, Stone, and Eshel argue that because of the emphasis on the "instructional function of the priesthood" by the "circles responsible for Aramaic Levi," the priesthood attracted sapiential motifs."[97] The *ALD* contains a prayer, a wisdom poem, and a teaching of Levi,[98] all of which are permeated with wisdom language. Marinus de Jonge has demonstrated that the *ALD* "stresses 'truth' and 'wisdom,' whereas in *T. Levi* the law of God and wisdom (subordinate to it) occupy a central position."[99] Such adaptation of the Aramaic Levi priestly tradition betrays only a *later* adjustment of wisdom traditions toward Mosaic Torah (outside of Genesis), a trajectory that is seen also in *Jubilees*.[100]

In the *ALD*, however, this alignment with "Moses" had not yet occurred and, in this, the *ALD* is similar to *1 Enoch*. The "Levi priest" of the *ALD*, like Enoch

---

96. Joseph M. Baumgarten, "Some 'Qumranic' Observations on the Aramaic Levi Document" in *Sefer Moshe: The Moshe Weinfeld Jubilee Volume* (ed. C. Cohen, A. Hurvitz, and S. M. Paul; Winona Lake, Ind.: Eisenbrauns, 2004), 393–401, 397–98.

97. *TALD*, 35.

98. Cf. "Blessed be every man who teaches wise discipline to his sons and he will not die in the days of wickedness" (4Q534 7 0–1). See also teaching of reading and writing in 4Q536 2 II,12. On "the sapiental characteristics of the priesthood" in the *ALD*, *T. Levi*, and Ben Sira, see Michael Stone, "Ideal Figures and Social Context: Priest and Sage in the Early Second Temple Age," in *Ancient Israelite Religion: Essays in Honor of Frank Moore Cross* (ed. P. D. Miller, Jr., P. D. Hanson, and S. D. McBride; Philadelphia: Fortress, 1987), 575–86.

99. De Jonge, "Levi in Aramaic Levi and in the Testament of Levi," 88–89. This example demonstrates the danger of reconstructing a theology of an earlier text based on a later one that contains similar traditions. Traditions are often reused from their sources but may be dramatically recontextualized and reinterpreted within their new context.

100. John Kampen has noted a similar decided shift from the vocabulary of "wisdom" (חכמה) to the vocabulary of "truth" (אמת) between the pre-sectarian and the sectarian texts at Qumran with a significant decline of חכמה in favor of אמת in the sectarian manuscripts ("Knowledge, Truth, and 'Wisdom' in the Cave 1 Texts?" [paper presented to the VIth Congress of the International Organization of Qumran Studies, Ljubljana, Slovenia, July 16, 2007]).

in *1 Enoch*, is not aligned strongly with Mosaic Torah (outside of Genesis) but inherits wisdom traditions that are taken up also by Noah in the *Genesis Apocryphon* (1Q20). A connection between the "priestly, wise, visionary Levi" in the *ALD* and the "priestly, wise, visionary Noah" in 1Q20 is evident through the sheer number of parallels between their characterizations.

TABLE: PRIESTLY LEVI AND PRIESTLY NOAH: A SYNOPTIC VIEW

Noah in the *Genesis Apocryphon*	Levi in the *Aramaic Levi Document*
Purports to be "The Book of the Words of Noah" (V, 29).	Abraham's teaching found in the "writing of the book of Noah concerning the blood" (10:10).
"I continued to walk in the paths (שביל) of eternal truth (אמת) ... righteousness (קשט) hastened on my paths (מסל)" (VI, 2–3).	"Grant me all the paths of righteousness (ארחת קשט)" (3:4); "You shall leave the ways of righteousness (קשטא) and the paths (שביל) of goodness" (4Q213 4 5–6).
Noah claims to have donned "wisdom (חכמתא) as a robe" (VI, 4).	"(Grant me) wisdom (חכמה)" (3:6/4Q213a 1 14); "do not be lax in the study of wisdom" (13:7; 4Q213 1 I, 13).
Noah married his sons to his brother's daughters, "in accordance with the law of the eternal statute" (VI, 8).	Levi is instructed with respect to endogamous marriage; marries from Abraham's family (6:4; 11:1).
Noah acts as priest, following the flood, making proper sacrifices and observing festivals (X, 13–17; XII, 13–17).	Levi is recognized as priest by Isaac and Jacob and is instructed in priestly activities and sexual purity (5:1–9:18).
Noah blesses God for destroying the workers of violence (עבדי חמסא), evil (רשעא), and deceit (שקרא) but rescuing a righteous one (צדיקא) (XI, 13–14).[101]	Levi destroys the workers of violence (עבדי חמסא) (12:6; cf. 2:1); Levi and Phinehas qualified for eternal priesthood after violent action.[102]
Noah is given dominion (שלט) over the earth (XI, 16).	"Let not any satan have dominion (שלט) over me" (3:9/4Q213a 1 17).
Noah's vision: "his [Shem's] seed (זרע) will call themselves by your [Noah's] name ... a righteous (קושט) planting ... existing forever (לעלמים)" (XIV, 11–14).	"You ... blessed Abraham ... you said (you would) give them a righteous seed (זרע דקשט) blessed forever (לעלם)" (3:15/4Q213a 2 6–7).

---

101. Cf. *AW*, in which Weeks 2 and 7 are marked by deceit and violence (שקרא וחמסא) (4Q212 1 III, 24/*1 En*. 93:4; 4Q212 1 IV, 12–14/*1 En*. 93:9–10; 91:11); cf. 4QApocryphon of Levi[b]? in which the priestly figure's days are marked by שקר וחמס; and cf. *Tg. Ps.-Jon.* Mal 2:6, in which no "deceit" is found in the mouth of the Levi priest.

102. See *TALD*, 145. Cf. 1QH XIX, 27; VII, 19; 1QS II, 4; Sir 45:24.

In the table above, the purported words of Noah are recorded from the "Book of Noah" in the *Genesis Apocryphon*; in the *ALD*, Levi is taught priestly instruction from his grandfather from the "book of Noah." Levi asks to be granted the paths of righteousness; Noah claims to have walked in paths of truth and righteousness. Levi asks for wisdom, but Noah has already donned wisdom. Levi is instructed regarding endogamous marriage and then takes a wife from Abraham's family; Noah has married his sons "in accordance with the law of the eternal statute." Levi destroys the "workers of violence,"[103] and Noah blesses God for having already destroyed the "workers of violence." Levi asks that a "satan" not have dominion over him;[104] Noah has dominion even over the earth. Abraham is promised a righteous seed;[105] Noah is told that Shem's seed would be "a righteous planting . . . existing forever." Both Noah and Levi act as priests.

The most noticeable difference is that the *ALD* emphasizes the beginning of Levi's priestly career; he supplicates God, receives vision(s) and priestly instruction. The *Genesis Apocryphon*, on the other hand, records the successes of a priestly Noah who claims to have been righteous from conception and whose prayer is one of thanksgiving rather than supplication. Therefore, Noah and Levi are situated at different points in their lifetimes but yet squarely in a similar tradition.[106] Although Noah's priesthood in the *ALD* and in the *Genesis Apocryphon* is conceived of differently than his priesthood would be in *Jubilees*, there can be little doubt of Noah's priestly character in the Aramaic Levi tradition.

Which came first, the *ALD* or the *Genesis Apocryphon*, or even the "Book of Noah" within the *Genesis Apocryphon*? Arguments surrounding the questions of literary dependence are not easy to solve. However, a more suitable question might be: Was it more likely that Noah was patterned after a "Levi priest" or that Levi was patterned after a "Noah priest"? Because the levitical priesthood was so well established throughout the Hebrew Bible and into the Second Temple period, it would seem much more likely that Levi was recognized as an archetypical priest before Noah was. Whereas the *ALD*'s portrayal of Levi is more tentative, the *Genesis Apocryphon*'s Noah is painted in bold strokes, as if the writer was basing a portrayal of Noah on traditions already familiar to the reader. Thus, perhaps even the "Book of Noah" was a literary creation formed out of a "silence," a "book" that someone decided really needed to be written!

---

103. Compare Gen 49:5 in which Simeon and Levi are cast as the violent ones.

104. Compare the Aramaic *Visions of Amram* texts (4Q543, 4Q544, 4Q547) in which Malki-resha, ruler of the children of darkness disputes with the ruler (Melchizedek?) of the children of light concerning who would rule (שלט) over Amram, Levi's grandson.

105. Compare *ALD* 6:4, in which Isaac teaches Levi, telling him not to defile his seed with harlots, adding "you are holy seed (זרע קדיש), and sanctify (קדיש) your seed like the holy place (קודשא)."

106. Parallels could also be drawn between Levi and Enoch. Enoch had visions of judgment, wrote books, was a purveyor of wisdom, counseled his children to walk in paths of righteousness (שבילי קושטא), and acted as a priest in Eden (4Q212 1 II, 19–20/*1 En.* 91:19).

How might have Noah and Levi become associated with each other as "priests" in the first place? Enoch, Noah, and Levi are the only figures in the Hebrew Bible who are said to have "walked with God" (Gen 5:22, 24; 6:9; Mal 2:6) but Malachi may also be the text that links Noah to Levi with respect to priestly matters. Kugler has pointed out that a synoptic reading of Gen 34; Exod 32:25–29; Num 25:6–13; and Deut 33:8–11 provided the "scriptural background for the priestly covenant" in Mal 2:4–7 that served to "reshape the biblical image of Levi." Malachi's reading of these texts set the groundwork necessary "for the development of the Levi-Priestly tradition."[107] If Noah and Levi were already linked as ones who "walked with God," then the inclusion of Noah as priest would have been only a small exegetical step. Therefore, the priestly, wise, and visionary characteristics attributed to Levi in the *ALD* could be expanded and justifiably transferred to Noah who was in the same priestly line, an archetypical idealized priest.

Continuing the Conversation

By adapting and recontextualizing flood traditions from literary sources originating in another time and written in other languages, the narrators and authors of the Aramaic Enochic writings and the *Aramaic Levi Document* did just what the narrators and authors of Genesis had done. These early tradents of Enoch and Levi traditions were at home in two cultures. While the characters are literarily set within Israelite history, the texts betray an intrinsic respect and familiarity with Mesopotamian science and story and language. The *ALD* knew of Babylonian metrological lists and Babylonian scribal practice, and the Enochic books knew of astronomical science and flood survivor stories. Furthermore, the Enochic books were written in an Aramaic of a high literary register, the language in which the Enochic circles received the Babylonian scientific traditions.[108] Therefore, the texts and their tradents were in some kind of conversation about "foreign" knowledge that concerned the extent to which foreign story and knowledge should become a part of the Jewish thought world.

However, the sources did not have equal weight or authority. The authors and narrators domesticated foreign science and story within the Jewish story, structuring new interpretations around an idealized figure in Genesis. In comparison to Noah, Genesis gives very little information on the characters of Enoch and Levi, leaving a rich field of gaps and silences, fertile ground for the imaginative creation of archetypes. For Levi, in particular, the prophetic tradition as preserved in Malachi 2:4–8 was a useful mantle in which to clothe the priestly figure of Levi. Therefore, while the characters *themselves* are presented as clearly and particularly "Jewish," the fact that the texts demonstrate such a

---

107. Kugler, *From Patriarch to Priest*, 22. On Deut 33:8–11 in Mal 2:4–7, see also *TALD*, 34. For Levi's vision in the *ALD* deriving from Mal 2:4–7, see Kugel, "Levi's Elevation," 31–32.

108. Alexander, "Enoch and the Beginnings," 238.

familiarity with foreign science and story and are written in Aramaic, indicates an openness on the part of the Jewish tradents to conversation with their Mesopotamian and Greek neighbors or about their relationship to them.

As an archetypical figure, Noah is very much in the shadow of his more famous great-grandfather, Enoch, and his priestly descendant, Levi, in the earliest Aramaic Enoch and Levi texts. The Noah narrative is integrally connected with the angel story (*1 En.* 6–11), but once it was recontextualized within the final form of the *Book of Watchers*, Enoch became the first righteous figure, rather than Noah, and the story of Noah was contained within a revelation given to Enoch. As we have argued, it could be that the Noah story as told in Genesis was too closely related to the flood survivor stories of the ancient Near East; Enoch, however, also "survived" the flood and, because little is said about him in Genesis, much could be said in the interpretative literature.

It has been particularly important to study the characterizations of the archetypical Enoch and Levi figures because, in the texts that we will be studying in the next chapters, these very characteristics are transferred (back?) to Noah. Indeed, it may be that biblical characters were easily interchangeable in the Dead Sea Scrolls because an interpretative text was deemed to be less of a character study of a particular figure than a "character study" of a particular line of priest or even a "character study" of God in relationship to his priests. Therefore, in the *Book of Watchers*, God could reveal wisdom to a righteous Enoch about past *and* future history, imminent *and* eschatological judgments in the earthly *and* heavenly realms but, in another narrative, he would just as easily reveal similar matters to Noah. Similarly, the Levi priest received visions, waged war against deceit and violence, and practiced the priesthood based on practices properly transmitted from his ancestors right from Noah. These characteristics, however, were just as easily applicable to another priest or an ancestor with priestly characteristics within that particular lineage.

While Noah is virtually sidelined in the Aramaic Enoch and Levi texts— after all, the books are not *about* him—he still makes small but significant gains toward archetypical status. Alternatively, if we move outside the linear model of development of traditions, we might say that the *Birth of Noah* is a brief nod, an acknowledgment as it were, to the conversation in process concerning Noah's full archetypical status as recorded elsewhere. His remarkable birth recorded in the *Birth of Noah* and appended to the collection at some point signifies a shift from preoccupation with the angel stories, Watchers, and the giants of Noah's day toward the archetypical righteous flood survivor and remnant, as distinguished from the Watchers. In the *Aramaic Levi Document*, we encounter Noah as an authoritative recorder of priestly tradition and transmitter of the implied revelation from God that he had received.

As we look ahead into the next chapters, the language a text was written in, whether Aramaic or Hebrew, reveals different stances toward the Mosaic Torah as the primary source of revelation from God.¹⁰⁹ The writings elevating Enoch, Noah, and Levi, for example, are in tension with Hebrew texts more oriented to Mosaic Torah. *1 Enoch* and the *ALD* say little, if anything, about sinful inclination, repentance, blessings and curses, and covenant¹¹⁰ in the texts represented at Qumran,¹¹¹ themes that are more at home in the interpretative texts more centered on Mosaic Torah.

As the conversation shifts into Hebrew while continuing in Aramaic, interest in Noah mounts. Whereas Adam had figured first in Genesis and Enoch had figured as the "first" figure of any importance in the Enochic tradition, Noah, who had appeared as a first priestly ancestor in the *Aramaic Levi Document*, will also be a first priestly ancestor in *Jubilees*, but with important conditions attached. *Jubilees*, written in Hebrew, would domesticate and subordinate the earliest Enochic traditions, distancing them even further from their foreign influences and grafting them much more securely to the Mosaic Torah exclusively belonging to Judaism.

---

109. For Enoch and Moses as rivals in *1 Enoch*, see Alexander, "From Son of Adam to Second God," 110. In later interpretation, Enoch-Metatron as "prince of Torah, dispensed the Law to Moses on Sinai" in *3 Enoch*. "Philo attributes to *Moses* many of the exalted characteristics of Enoch." Alexander further notes a "similar transference of Enochic roles to Ezra – as Moses redivivus – is implied in 4 Ezra 14:50" (ibid., 108–10).

110. Nickelsburg translates *šer'at* as "law" in *1 En.* 93:4 and "covenant" in 93:6; however, A. Bedenbender addresses the "anomaly of covenant" in 93:6 by arguing that *sherata* should be translated as "law" in both cases, that God gave Torah but not covenant in *AW* and neither Torah nor covenant in the *AA* ("Reflection on Ideology and Date of the Apocalypse of Weeks," in *Enoch and Qumran Origins: New Light on a Forgotten Connection* [Grand Rapids: Eerdmans, 2005], 200–203).

111. On absence of covenant in *1 Enoch* and differentiation of *DV* from Daniel 9, see Gabriele Boccaccini, "The Covenantal Theology of the Apocalyptic Book of Daniel," in *Enoch and Qumran Origins*, 39–44. Cf. Collins, "Place of Apocalypticism," 556: "The covenantal allusions . . . in *1 Enoch* 1–5 are placed in a new context of cosmic rather than Deuteronomic law."

CHAPTER FOUR

Noah in the Hebrew Pre-Sectarian Texts (1) Wisdom Texts and *Jubilees*

> *During this month he [Noah] made a covenant before the Lord God forever*
> *throughout all the history of the earth.*
> *For this reason he told you [Moses] too, to make a covenant—*
> *accompanied by an oath—*
> *with the Israelites during this month on the mountain.*
> Jubilees 6:10–11

Introduction

While traditions surrounding Enoch and Levi continued to be copied, reinterpreted, and transmitted in Aramaic, other tradents were preoccupied with adapting and reinterpreting Enoch, Levi, and Noah traditions in Hebrew. This chapter explores portrayals of Noah is wisdom traditions as diverse as 4QInstruction and Ben Sira together with the much fuller and highly nuanced characterization of Noah in the book of *Jubilees*.[1]

Two broadly defined types of wisdom are found in the Hebrew literature of the Dead Sea Scrolls. 4QInstruction contains Noah traditions familiar from Genesis and promotes a wisdom that had its source in the revelation of esoteric knowledge and mysteries made known to select individuals. This type of wisdom is found in the *Aramaic Levi Document* and *1 Enoch*. Ben Sira, on the other hand, acknowledges Noah and Enoch in the ancestral line but advocates a wisdom derived largely from Torah that would be, therefore, a wisdom available to all. *Jubilees* scarcely mentions wisdom at all,[2] but revelation from God, carefully restricted in both scope and timing, is centrally important to the book.

Jubilees offers a full and finely detailed portrayal of Noah. *Jubilees'* Noah lives during the days of Watchers but behaves in ways that prefigure Torah obedience,

---

1. All translations of *Jubilees*, unless otherwise noted, follow James C. VanderKam, *The Book of Jubilees* (CSCO 511, Tomus 88; Leuven: Peeters, 1989).
2. Enoch learns "wisdom" (*Jub.* 4:17) and the Egyptians declare Joseph to be "wise" (*Jub.* 40:5).

thus providing a "new Adam" archetype for Jews needing to understand their identity as Jews and how to be "rightly planted" in the land. He is a tradesman, a working ark-builder, agriculturalist, and vintner. Yet he is also the ancestor of priests, the first to enter into a covenant with God and offer up an atoning sacrifice. He ordains the timing of festivals on which a calendar was based, makes appropriate distinctions among his progeny by means of blessings and curses, and oversees the proper division of the land. While Noah does not have the same unrestricted access to angelic revelation that Enoch and Moses do in the book, he does receive and transmit God's instruction and successfully appeals to God concerning the demons that were harassing his grandchildren. In the midst of all of his other responsibilities, Noah finds time to write a book.

Jubilees appears, at first glance, to present a composite and harmonized portrait of Noah with characteristics conflated from Hebrew and Aramaic sources containing characterizations not only of Noah but also of Levi and Enoch. Yet this chapter will show that the narrator does not allow all traditions equal weight or authority. The study of the Noah traditions in *Jubilees* reveals a deliberate adaptation and recontextualization of both Aramaic and Hebrew traditions with the result that Noah comes to resemble Moses even more than he resembles Enoch or Levi.

Finally, the choice of *language* of transmission of a text might reveal something about an author's stance toward the "foreigner" or the extent to which the authors were oriented more inwardly within Judaism or outwardly toward the Gentiles. If Noah's characterizations are different in Hebrew traditions than in Aramaic traditions, we want to know *how* they are different and if these differences are consistent across the corpus of Hebrew texts and the corpus of Aramaic texts. This chapter and the next are particularly significant toward that end.

Texts and Observations

4QInstruction: Righteous ... Distinguishing between Good and Evil

For a seeker of Noah traditions, Torleif Elgvin's reconstruction of 4QInstruction would be an alluring addition to the growing gallery of portraits of Noah in the Dead Sea Scrolls. Elgvin's reading, if accepted, would contain another conversation point concerning the nature of the revelation of God to Noah. This trajectory had its origin in Gen 6:13 and in *Book of Watchers* 10:3, in which God speaks to Noah concerning imminent judgment.

> [He comes to convict (?)] all the spirit [of flesh for the works of wickedness which they have committed (?),] and establish His will [over all evil. He made known to Noah what was]to come, period upon period,] set time upon set time. [He will shut up all the sons of evil, and visit all flesh [?] according to their hosts. (from 4Q416; underlined portions from 4Q418 73, 201)[3]

---

3. Torleif Elgvin, "Wisdom With and Without Apocalyptic," in *Sapiential, Liturgical and*

As sensible a proposition as this might be in light of other potentially "Noachic" elements in the text, the official editors reject the reconstruction of "Noah" in 4Q418 201 1 as "orthographically very unlikely in this manuscript."[4] Noah is spelled defectively as נח, whereas elsewhere in the Dead Sea Scrolls it is spelled only in the *plene* form נוח.[5] Their reconstruction of 4Q418 201 1–2 follows:

] -- °[נהיה הודיע אל נח]לת --
] -- [ויסגר בעד כול בני ע]ולה -- [

[. . . by the mystery] that is to come God has made known the *inher[itance of . . .]*

[. . .] and *it* was shut upon all the sons of in[quity . . .]

The official editors struggle with the obscurity of the chronological reference of many of the verbs in 4Q416.[6] As an example of the challenges and complexity, their translation is given below with a suggested alternative translation in italics.

10 From heaven He will judge (ישפוט) the work of wickedness (רשעה), but all the sons of his truth (אמתו) will gain favor (ירצו) [. . .] 11 its time, and all who have indulged in wickedness will be terrified/*were terrified* (ויפחדו)[7] and shout aloud/*shouted aloud* (וירועו) for Heaven sees (יראו) [. . .] 12 seas and abysses were afraid

---

Poetical Texts from Qumran: Proceedings of the Third Meeting of the International Organization for Qumran Studies Oslo 1998 (ed. D. K. Falk, F. García Martínez, and E. M. Schuller; STDJ 35; Leiden: Brill, 2000), 15–38, here 24.

4. In a personal communication on May 5, 2008, Elgvin noted that he himself has since changed his views on the reconstruction of 4QInstruction and will be publishing a new synthesis of the fragments in a forthcoming study.

5. DJD XXXIV, 422–23. Italics are those of the editors. Eibert J. C. Tigchelaar also rejects Elgvin's ordering of the fragments of 4Q416 as problematic: "This implies that we would have in 4Q416 1 part of an eschatological discourse, with no clear indications why this discourse was situated at this specific place in the composition" (*To Increase Learning for the Understanding Ones: Reading and Reconstructing the Fragmentary Early Jewish Sapiential Text 4QInstruction* [STDJ 44; Leiden: Brill, 2001], 182).

6. The editors are confident that ישפוט and ירצו (line 10) are clearly "futures" as is תתם (line 13). However, they find ויפחדו וירועו to be semantically remote and, therefore, not necessarily a joined pair of verbs. Furthermore, these latter "might be converted past tenses or conjunctive futures." They add that "ויתערערו פחדו presents an even greater difficulty, unless one takes both the nominal and the *waw*-aorist to refer to the past. This is compounded by the fact that 4Q416 reads ויתערערו (with כל רוח בשר as its subject) while 4Q418 certainly reads a different verb, ויתר, with the sense of ויריעו 'cry out'" (DJD XXXIV, 86).

7. Compare Psalm 14 for the language of "terror" (פחד) of the evildoers, parallels to Gen 6, and language of wisdom and knowledge. This suggests one exegetical route by which flood traditions may have entered the wisdom genre.

(פחדו) and every spirit of flesh will be destroyed/*was destroyed?* (ויתערערו)[8] and the sons of heaven (בני השמים) [...] 13 [He ju]dges it (השפטה) and every iniquity (עולה) will perish (תתם) until the era (קץ) of truth is complete (ושלם) [...] 14 in all the eras of eternity, for He is the God of truth, and from of old the years of [...] 15 that the righteous may distinguish (להכון)[9] between good and evil [...] every judgm[ent...] 16 it is the inclination (יצר) and understanding. (4Q416 1 10–16)[10]

The editors attempt to make sense of verbs in frg. 1 11–12 as futures but it is possible that these perfects and *waw*-consecutives could, alternatively, simply denote past events. This results in a text that is not bound by chronology but instead moves freely through time, from a prediction of future judgment to a recounting of past judgment—most plausibly by flood—back to the assertion that, in the future, all iniquity will indeed perish.

This hypothesis of continuity between past, present, and future finds some support in several phrases from frg. 1 in lines 14–16. There is a "God" who was "from of old" (מקדם) and the inclination (יצר) of the flesh continues, presumably as it originated in Noah's day.[11] The phrase "righteous will distinguish between good and evil"[12] is also suggestive of a merging of past, present, and future. In her work on the *Damascus Document*, Maxine Grossman finds that the use of infinitives and participles "represses specific historical detail."[13] If this was also the practice in 4QInstruction, then the infinitive contained in "that the righteous may distinguish (להכון)" may be a deliberate indication of continuity, of a "distinguishing" that originated in the primeval narratives and that continued into the present. Throughout time, God would judge (השפטה) and the righteous would distinguish (להכון) between good and evil.

The phrase, "righteous may distinguish between good and evil" (4Q416 1 15), appears to be a conflation of Gen 3 and 6 and Mal 3:16–18. 4QInstruction casts

---

8. Compare Jer 51:58, in which the wall of Babylon is leveled (תתערער).
9. In line 15, the Hebrew reads להכון צדק בין טוב לרע. The editors support their reading by appealing to a variant reading in 4Q418 2 7 להבון צדיק בין טוב לרע (DJD XXXIV, 87).
10. Proposed tense changes are my own.
11. Jörg Frey argues that the יצר of Enosh patterned after the holy angels should be "conceived within a dualistic framework" that also contains the "spirits of flesh" who could not distinguish between good and evil (4Q417 1 I, 16–18) ("Flesh and Spirit in the Palestinian Jewish Sapiential Tradition and in the Qumran Texts: An Inquiry into the Background of Pauline Usage," in *The Wisdom Texts from Qumran and the Development of Sapiential Thought* [ed. C. Hempel, A. Lange, and H. Lichtenberger; BETL 159; Leuven: Peeters, 2002], 367–404, here 394–95).
12. In Genesis, Noah was righteous and it was God who made an implied distinction between the righteous and the wicked. The background of this text is possibly the "days of Noah" rather than the figure of Noah himself.
13. Maxine L. Grossman, *Reading for History in the Damascus Document: A Methodological Study* (STDJ 45; Leiden: Brill, 2002), 95. The infinitive constructs could be usefully employed to convey the timelessness of an action.

Adam and Eve's sin as a failure to distinguish between good and evil.[14] In Genesis, God implicitly makes the distinction between the righteous and the wicked by means of the flood and, in Malachi, humans are participants in the distinction between the righteous and the wicked, even if only as observers: "Then once more you shall see the difference between the righteous and the wicked" (Mal 3:18).[15]

Inscribed in the "book of remembrance" (cf. Mal 3:16)[16] was "every time of punishment"[17] including, it would seem, the primordial flood together with subsequent "punishments." This book is bequeathed to the children of Seth but *not* to the "spirit of flesh" for they "did not know the difference between good and evil" (4Q417 1 I, 14–18).[18]

Therefore, while the figure of Noah himself cannot be securely positioned in 4QInstruction, traditions associated with him can be. Wisdom, according to 4QInstruction, was passed along from the primeval ancestors in the form of a "book of remembrance" in which the "times of punishment" were inscribed. Past, present, and future times of judgments are linked, and wisdom concerning the past is also linked to esoteric wisdom about the future. An innovation concerning the righteous is that they are able to distinguish between good and evil, a concept that stands next to "every judgment" and "inclination of the flesh" in the text (4Q416 1 15–16) and which may, therefore, be an echo of the Noah story. Although this theme of "distinguishing" is not explicitly associated with the figure of Noah in this text, it will appear in other settings where it is more clearly so.[19] Therefore, even if Noah is not named in 4QInstruction[b] (4Q416), inheritors of this particular strand of wisdom tradition would have considered Noah a prime candidate for the role of archetypical recipient of esoteric knowledge,

---

14. John J. Collins comments on 4Q417 1 I, 16–18: "The knowledge of good and evil, it would appear, was not inherently off limits, but some people failed to master the distinction" ("Before the Fall: The Earliest Interpretation of Adam and Eve," in *The Idea of Biblical Interpretation: Essays in Honor of James L. Kugel* [ed. H. Najman and J. H. Newman; JSJSup 83; Leiden: Brill, 2004], 293–308, here 300).

15. Cf. Ben Sira, who draws the parallel between God's distinction between human beings at the time of their creation to the distinction made between days, seasons, and festivals (Sir 33:7–13/cf. SirE 1r:15–23).

16. George J. Brooke has also observed that, for the Qumran community and the larger movement of which it was a part, Mal 3:16–18 served to "distinguish between two kinds of people and takes the wisdom instruction from being general and universalistic to being particularly for an elect group" ("Biblical Interpretation in the Wisdom Texts from Qumran," in *The Wisdom Texts from Qumran and the Development of Sapiential Thought* [n. 11 above], 214).

17. Cf. *Jub.* 5:14 on ordained and inscribed judgments.

18. 4Q577, an enigmatic and highly fragmentary text, preserves "inscribed" (חקוקים) (1 3) and "he shall write" (יכתב) (2 1). "Destruction" (שחת) or "flood" (מבול) or a reconstructed "flames" (ל[הב) survive on four different fragments, suggesting that the flood is interpreted as only one of periodic times of judgment from which God would rescue (מלט) some.

19. Compare the discussions on 4Q508 and 4Q252–254a below.

especially when linked to the "inclination of the flesh," the "sons of heaven," and a coming judgment viewed through the lens of the primordial flood.

Michael Knibb has drawn out numerous parallels between 4QInstruction and *1 Enoch* as evidence for a "shared thought world" and a similar "theological perspective" between the two traditions.[20] Ben Sira, on the other hand, reinterprets wisdom differently from the interpretation of wisdom found in either the Aramaic Enoch and Aramaic Levi traditions or in 4QInstruction.[21]

BEN SIRA: "FOR HIS SAKE THERE WAS A REMNANT"

In Ben Sira's historical retelling, certain characters are emphasized at the expense of others. Noah appears first in a hymn of ancestors whose wisdom the assembly declares and whose "righteous deeds have not been forgotten" (Sir 44:1–50:21). Ben Sira's selective genealogy initially ignores Adam,[22] subdues Enoch, presents Noah as a survivor who kept the race alive but does not attribute to him any priestly or law-keeping role, exalts Abraham as the first one who keeps the law, ignores Levi and his immediate descendants, acknowledges Moses but highly praises Aaron, claims Phinehas for itself, and eventually honors the Maccabaean high priest, Simon II.[23] To complicate the issue, four antediluvian figures previously ignored are given their due near the end: "Shem and Seth and Enosh were honored, but above every other created living being, the glory of Adam"

---

20. Michael A. Knibb, "The Book of Enoch in Light of Qumran Wisdom Literature," in *Wisdom and Apocalypticism in the Dead Sea Scrolls and in the Biblical Tradition* (ed. F. García Martínez; BETL 168; Leuven: Leuven University Press, 2003), 193–210, here 210. See also Elgvin, who argues that "eternal planting" in 4QInstruction (4Q418 81+81a 13) reflects influence from the AW. However, compare Stuckenbruck, who argues that each text represented "alternative interpretative possibilities" with respect to the "planting" in Isaiah. *1 Enoch* more broadly identifies "planting" with "the men of Judah" (cf. Isa 5:7) and the narrower usage in 4QInstruction likely derived from Trito-Isaiah (Isa 60:21; 61:3). See Loren T. Stuckenbruck, "The Plant Metaphor in Its Inner-Enochic and Early Jewish Context," in *Enoch and Qumran Origins: New Light on a Forgotten Connection* (Grand Rapids: Eerdmans, 2005), 210–12. On the association of the planting in 4QInstruction with the priesthood, see Paul N. W. Swarup, "An Eternal Planting, a House of Holiness: The Self-Understanding of the Dead Sea Scrolls Community," *TynBul* 54 (2003): 151–56, here 153.

21. See Elgvin regarding a kind of wisdom instruction that is "different from Sirach 1 and 24, Bar 3:9–4:4, 4Q525 and 11QPs[a] 154, true wisdom and earthly blessings have their source in (studying) *raz nihyeh*, not in (following) the Torah" ("Wisdom With and Without Apocalyptic," 24). Furthermore, "[t]he eschatological understanding of history and its periods, which are among the mysteries of God revealed to the elect, unites *Sap. Work A* both with *1 Enoch* and sectarian literature" (Torleif Elgvin, "The Reconstruction of Sapiential Work A," *RevQ* 16 [1993–95]: 559–80, here 562).

22. Adam is listed in the final position in the final form of the text, "above every other created being" (Sir 49:16).

23. On the hymn as an encomium of the high priest Simon II, see Thomas R. Lee, *Studies in the Form of Sirach 44–50* (SBLDS 75; Atlanta: Scholars Press, 1986), 81–95.

(Sir 49:16/SirB 19r:6).[24] The exclusions and variations in emphasis strongly hint at a polemic against a differently interpreted priesthood that valued a particular "genealogy" contained in the *Aramaic Levi Document* and that honored Noah and Levi as prototypical priests.[25]

While the two Qumran fragments of Ben Sira do not attest the lines that refer to Noah (Sir 44:17-18), enough text survives from Masada[26] to reconstruct a text that is basically identical to the SirB Cairo Geniza manuscript.[27] The fact that a Hebrew manuscript existed at Masada of which the Cairo Geniza manuscripts appear to be faithful copies, suggests that the Qumran fragments might represent the larger text containing Noah traditions available to the sectarians during the first century B.C.E.[28] Their presence does not suggest that the sectarians subscribed to any or all of Ben Sira's ideologies, but it does make Ben Sira a potential partner in ancient disputes, perhaps even among the sectarians, concerning the origin of the priesthood, whether or not Noah was "priestly," and the means by which God could and did reveal wisdom.

First, we compare the two verses dealing explicitly with Noah in different versions and, second, we consider briefly Ben Sira's treatment of traditions associated with Noah. The following table, adapted from Milward D. Nelson, presents Sir 44:17 as it appears in the Cairo Genizah, Masada, Greek, and Syriac texts.[29]

---

24. For discussion of originality of this verse, see Lee, *Studies in the Form of Sirach 44–50*, 11.

25. "*1 Enoch* and *Aramaic Levi* are quite harsh in their critical stance vis-à-vis the priests who are in control in Jerusalem, precisely the people whom Ben Sira honors." So Benjamin G. Wright III, "'Fear the Lord and Honor the Priest': Ben Sira as Defender of the Jerusalem Priesthood," in *The Book of Ben Sira in Modern Research: Proceedings of the First International Ben Sira Conference, 28–31 July 1996*, (ed. P. C. Beentjes; Berlin/New York: de Gruyter, 1997), 189–222, here 201.

26. Mas 1h attests Sir 39:27–44:17 (early 1st c. B.C.E.); 2Q18 attests Sir 6:20–31 and possibly 6:14–15 (2nd half of 1st c. B.C.E.) and 11QPsª attests Sir 51:13–20, 30b (1st half of the 1st c. B.C.E.) (DJD III, 75–77).

27. Daniel J. Harrington, "Sirach Research Since 1965: Progress and Questions," in *Pursuing the Text: Studies in Honor of Ben Zion Wacholder on the Occasion of His Seventieth Birthday* (ed. J. C. Reeves and J. Kampen; JSOTSup 184; Sheffield: Sheffield Academic Press, 1994), 164–76, here 165.

28. Gabriele Boccaccini finds traces of successive Essene redactions in Hebrew recensions (*Middle Judaism: Jewish Thought, 300 B.C.E. to 200 C.E.* [Minneapolis: Fortress, 1991], 77).

29. Milward D. Nelson argues that the Syriac was translated directly from the Hebrew with affinities to M and B and influenced by the Greek (*The Syriac Version of the Wisdom of Ben Sira Compared to the Greek and Hebrew Materials* [SBLDS 107; Atlanta: Scholars Press, 1988], 111–12, 131). For more recent editions of the Hebrew manuscripts, see Pancratius C. Beentjes, *The Book of Ben Sira in Hebrew: A Text Edition of All Extant Hebrew Manuscripts and A Synopsis of All Parallel Hebrew Ben Sira Texts* (VTSup 68; Atlanta: Society of Biblical Literature, 2006); Benjamin H. Parker and Martin G. Abegg, Jr., "BENSIRA-E" (*Accordance Bible*

B (Ms. B) SirB 14r:1–3	M (Masada)	G (Ziegler Greek)	S (Mosul Syriac)
Noah the righteous (צדיק) was found blameless (תמים); for a time of destruction (כלה) he was the continuator (תחליף). For his sake there was a remnant (שארית) and by his covenant (ברית) the flood ceased.	Noah the righteous (צדיק) was found blameless (תמים); in [the time of destruction he was the continuator]. For [his sake there was a remnant and by his covenant the flood ceased.]	Noah was found perfect (τέλειος) and righteous (δίκαιος); in a time of wrath (ὀργῆς) he became the exchange (ἀντάλλαγμα). Because of this (man) there became a remnant (κατάλειμμα) for the earth when the cataclysm came.	Noah the righteous was found in his generation perfect; in the time of the flood he was the substitute (תחלפא) in the world and because of him there was deliverance and God swore that there would not again be a flood.

Very briefly, descriptors of Noah, such as "continuator" or "exchange" (תחליף or ἀντάλλαγμα) and as remnant (שארית), are likely interpretations of the Genesis text. The verbal root חלף in the hiphil could be translated variously as "to substitute (i.e., as a successor)," "to change (for better)," or "to renew." The Greek translator chose ἀντάλλαγμα ("exchange"); however, תחליף is translated elsewhere as διάδοχος or "successor" (Sir 48:8/SirB 17v:11). Most likely, תחליף in its various shades of meaning was understood to describe someone through whom humanity continued to exist, a second Adam representing the renewal of the world.

Noah as an archetypical "remnant" (שארית or κατάλειμμα) for all Israel could be derived from Genesis, in which "only Noah was left (ישאר)" (Gen 7:23). Yet Noah as "remnant" may also have been viewed through the contemporizing lenses of the prophets Isaiah, Jeremiah, and Micah, to name a few. In effect, the concept of "remnant" became layered with the experiences of another remnant that survived another kind of judgment, that of exile (e.g., Isa 46:3; Jer 23:3; Mic 4:7).[30]

"Covenant" is associated with Noah in SirB and is reconstructed in the Masada scrolls but does not appear in the Greek (Ziegler).[31] This might indicate that the association of "covenant" with Noah was problematic at some point in the

---

Software, 2007); Martin G. Abegg, Jr. with Casey A. Toews, "BENSIRA-C/M" (*Accordance Bible Software*, 2007).

30. "Remnant" occurs at key places in sectarian literature, describing both those of Israel who survived judgment (CD I, 4) and those against whom the angels of destruction come and who are left with "neither remnant nor survivor (שארית ופליטה)" (CD II, 6–7). Cf. 1QS IV, 14; V, 13; 4Q280 2 5; 1QM XIV, 5.

31. Nelson, *Syriac Version*, 112.

transmission and translation of the text,[32] a hint of another conversation or controversy being carried on in the background.

Elsewhere in the book, Ben Sira handles the angel traditions differently than the Enochic *Book of Watchers* did. In Ben Sira, a recounting of the "ancient giants" who "revolted in their might (גבור)" serves as a warning to the reader about the dangers of ungodly offspring and of God's certain wrath upon the sinner[33] (Sir 16:7/cf. SirA 6v:11). Whereas the *Book of Watchers* had attributed the origin of wickedness to the angels, the story of the ancient giants in Ben Sira becomes a cautionary tale concerning the rebellion of *free-willed* creatures, an example of how an Enochic story could be reinterpreted and recontextualized in a book at odds with the Enochic "thought world," serving vastly different interpretative ends.[34] Along a similar vein, Ben Sira extrapolates human "inclination" (Gen 6:5) back to creation when humans were given the power of their inclination (Sir 15:14/SirA 6r:25).[35] Angels could not, in Ben Sira, be blamed for human sin.

In his work on the social location of Ben Sira, the Enochic works, the *Aramaic Levi Document*, and their differently interpreted priesthoods, Benjamin Wright has identified passages in Sirach that address issues also found *1 Enoch* and in the *ALD*. Among these, Wright identifies polemics against dreams and visions (34:1-8) and against the mysteries of the sort revealed about the cosmos and eschaton to Enoch and Levi (3:21-24).[36] On this passage, he observes, "While it is true that ben Sira wants his readers to adhere closely to the precepts of Moses, I think this passage makes better sense when understood against the backdrop of the mysteries revealed to Enoch and Levi, especially cosmological speculation and eschatological realities."[37] Finally, the first lines of the Greek prologue added to Ben Sira orients the book even more consciously toward the Torah: "Many

---

32. The number and nature of the variants among the Hebrew, Greek, and Syriac witnesses also attest to the possible controversy over the figure of Enoch. The Genizah text states that Enoch was "found perfect" (תמים), walked with God, was taken up, and was a "sign of knowledge for generation to generation" (Sir 44:16). The verse is missing altogether in the Syriac and in the Masada scroll, possibly evidence of some uneasiness with the role and figure of Enoch.

33. See Boccaccini, *Middle Judaism*, 112, on Ben Sira's conceptual development of the law's role in human free will in opposition to the apocalyptic tradition that attributed the cause of evil to "angelic sin" that corrupted the human inclination.

34. See also the discussions of "false" dreams (Sir 34:5) and calendar disputes. God distinguishes (שפט) days, years, seasons, and festivals just as he distinguished (בדיל) humans from the time he created them (Sir 33:7-13/cf. SirE 1r:15-23), but the moon, not the sun, marks the seasons (Sir 43:6).

35. On "inclination" in Ben Sira as a positive gift, see Harrington "Sirach Research since 1965," 173.

36. Wright, "'Fear the Lord and Honor the Priest,'" 212.

37. Benjamin G. Wright III, "Putting the Puzzle Together: Some Suggestions Concerning the Social Location of the Wisdom of Ben Sira," in *SBL 1996 Seminar Papers* (SBLSP 35; Atlanta: Scholars Press, 1996), 133-49, here 138.

great teachings have been given to us through the Law and the Prophets and the others that followed them, and for these we should praise Israel for instruction and wisdom" (Sir prol.). If the readers had any doubt about the source of wisdom in the Hebrew version, the prologue in the Greek translation now made it abundantly clear.

In summary, Ben Sira is selective in its use of Genesis, specifically emphasizing that Noah was a remnant and successor to Adam. However, Noah is emphatically not a priest. Ben Sira reinterprets "inclination" and the Enochic Watchers story to develop a "free will" theology, an interpretation that adjusts the Enochic conception of the angelic origin of evil[38] and that insists on a reinterpreted wisdom that comes not from dreams, visions, and angels but, instead, from the Torah. At this point of our study, *Jubilees* contributes to the conversations and disputes on these issues, bringing its own interpretations to the big questions but in a narrative, a literary form that freshly characterizes Moses and biblical figures from Genesis, including Noah.

JUBILEES: TOWARD BECOMING AN ANCESTOR LIKE MOSES

THE TEXT[39]

Although the complete text of *Jubilees* is extant only in Ethiopic, the book was almost certainly originally composed in Hebrew, the language of the Qumran copies. Likely composed between 160 and 150 B.C.E.,[40] its fifteen or sixteen copies[41] represent a substantial portion of the text and range in date from last quarter

---

38. For further discussion of the differences between the wisdom contained in Ben Sira, Qumran wisdom and apocalyptic texts, and the polemic contained in Ben Sira against the *AB*, the *BW* and the *ALD*, see Randal A. Argall, *1 Enoch and Sirach: A Comparative Literary and Conceptual Analysis of the Themes of Revelation, Creation, and Judgment* (SBLEJL 8; Atlanta: Scholars Press, 1995), 250; Wright, "Putting the Puzzle Together," 133–49; Menahem Kister, "Wisdom Literature and Its Relation to Other Genres," in *Sapiential Perspectives: Wisdom Literature in Light of the Dead Sea Scrolls: Proceedings of the Sixth International Symposium of the Orion Center for the Study of the Dead Sea Scrolls and Associated Literature, 20-22 May, 2001* (ed. J. J. Collins, G. E. Sterling and R. A. Clements; STDJ 51; Leiden/Boston: Brill, 2004), 13–47, here 45. Compare also Daniel J. Harrington, "Two Early Jewish Approaches to Wisdom: Sirach and Qumran Sapiential Work A," in *SBL 1996 Seminar Papers* (SBLSP 35; Atlanta: Scholars Press, 1996), 123–32.

39. For a summary of nineteenth- and early-twentieth-century scholarship on *Jubilees* and questions of authorship, provenance, date of composition, language of the original, the biblical texts behind the book, and the religious doctrine of the book, see John C. Endres, *Biblical Interpretation in the Book of Jubilees* (CBQMS 18; Washington: Catholic Biblical Association of America, 1987), 7–17. See also VanderKam's literature review of *Jubilees* in James C. VanderKam, "The Origins and Purposes of the *Book of Jubilees*," in *Studies in the Book of Jubilees* (ed. M. Albani, J, Frey, and A. Lange; TSAJ 65; Tübingen: Mohr Siebeck, 1997), 3–24.

40. James C. Vanderkam, *The Book of Jubilees* (Guides to Apocrypha and Pseudepigrapha; Sheffield: Sheffield Academic Press: 2001), 21.

41. Editions of the texts include 1Q17–18 (DJD I); 2Q19–20, 3Q5 (DJD III); 4Q176a (Kis-

of the first century B.C.E. to the mid-first century C.E.[42] 4QJubilees[a] (4Q216), the oldest extant copy of *Jubilees*, was repaired and not discarded.[43] Therefore, the number, distribution, and longevity of the texts as well as the interest indicated by the type and variety of variants[44] all indicate that *Jubilees* and the Noah traditions continued to contribute to the conversation among the sectarians and their parent movements.

VanderKam has argued that *Jubilees*' author was a conservative Zadokite priest during 160/59–150/49,[45] a date that is largely accepted. He asserts that the writer presents Torah-abiding patriarchs in order to show that the Torah had not originated with Moses but that it was of far greater antiquity, reliably transmitted through a priestly line. This functioned as a rebuttal of those who were "wishing to live in the Hellenistic world, sought to do away with the commands of the Torah that separated Jew and non-Jew, arguing that such laws were not original. There was an ancient, better time, a golden age, when such separatist legislation was not in force."[46]

The corollary of VanderKam's compelling argument is that the writer of *Jubilees* was thus enhancing, rather than diminishing, the authority of the Mosaic Torah at a time when it was being challenged. If he is correct in his assessment of authorial intention and if the date of composition of *Jubilees* and its historical context can be pinpointed this closely, then *Jubilees* becomes a plausible vantage point from which to view what happened when earlier traditions characterizing Noah, Enoch, and Levi (in the Hebrew Bible, early Aramaic Enoch and Aramaic Levi traditions and, possibly, 4QInstruction) were confronted with a newly interpreted Moses and Mosaic Torah.

Would the revelation associated with Moses—the written Mosaic Torah—become more influential in the characterizations of figures such as Enoch and Levi, who were "accustomed" to hearing from God through visions, dreams, and angels? *Or* would Moses' characterization be influenced by earlier characterizations of a visionary Enoch and Levi? After whom would Noah be patterned? Finally, what might varying characterizations reveal about the authority of the

---

ter, *RevQ* 12 [1985–87]); 4Q216–224 (DJD XIII) and 11Q12 (DJD XXIII). Cf. 4Qpseudo-Jubilees[a-c] (4Q225–227) (DJD XIII).

42. DJD XIII, 2; DJD XXIII, 208.

43. DJD XIII, 1.

44. Variants include a longer Hebrew text (4Q216 VII, 6–7/*Jub.* 2:17; 4Q216 VII, 17/*Jub.* 2:23), a shorter Hebrew text (4Q221 5 5/*Jub.* 37:13; 4Q216 VII, 12–13/*Jub.* 2:20–22), differing word order (4Q216 VII, 13/*Jub.* 2:21–22), word substitution (4Q219 II, 35/*Jub.* 22:1; 4Q219 II, 31/*Jub.* 2:25; 4Q216 VII, 10–11/*Jub.* 2:19–20; 4Q218 1, 1–4/*Jub.* 2:26–27), different versions (Cf. 4Q219 II, 28–29 with 4Q221 1 5–7; cf. 4Q223–224 2 I, 49–50 with 1Q18 1–2, 3–4 where this line does not occur) and differences that parallel another known text (4Q221 7 10/*T. Jos.* 3:9).

45. James C. VanderKam, "2 Maccabees 6, 7a and Calendrical Change in Jerusalem," *JSJ* 12 (1981): 52–74, here 74.

46. VanderKam, "Origins and Purposes," in *Studies in the Book of Jubilees* (n. 39 above), 3–24, here 21–22. Cf. 1 Macc 1:11–13.

texts—Enochic, Levitic, Noachic, Mosaic—most closely associated with that particular revelatory figure?

Knibb's assessment of the "very strong links between Jubilees and the Qumran sectarian writings" and *Jubilees*' role in the origins of the Qumran community[47] further serves as an endorsement of the importance of the book for understanding not only the origin of the movement but, by extension, how *Jubilees*' adaptation of Noah traditions reflected the self-identity of the emerging Yaḥad sectarians.

Very few words of the Noah narrative are extant in the Hebrew copies of *Jubilees* in the Dead Sea Scrolls. Therefore, since we must work with the text in translation, we look for other ways to study the history of Noah traditions in this rich narrative. One strategy is to examine the rearrangement of the Noah material in the context of *Jubilees* as a whole and also in relationship to what might be its sources, Genesis and early Enoch and Levi traditions.

This brings with it immediate and obvious difficulties! The redactional histories of all of the literatures are complex, and so it is unwise to insist on direct dependencies, especially when the compositional dates of the supposed sources—Aramaic Enoch and Aramaic Levi traditions—are relatively close to the composition of *Jubilees*. As demonstrated in chapter 2, however, we are reasonably sure that a second-century exegete had a relatively stable text of Genesis available. Therefore, for the purpose of this study, although the possible influence of Aramaic Enoch and Aramaic Levi traditions on the composition of *Jubilees* must be acknowledged, we will use Genesis as the basis of comparison for the interpretative literary structure of *Jubilees*.

Noah first appears in a chapter that begins with the account of Cain, continues with Cain's murder of Abel, is followed by the birth of Seth, and concludes with the birth of Noah and the death of Adam and of Cain, in that order. The Watchers are introduced innocuously as ones who were sent to instruct humanity, and Enoch is introduced as one who learns directly from the "angels of God" (*Jub.* 4:7–33).

The next chapter moves between descriptions of primordial events and anticipation of eschatological ones. The flood is provoked by the transgression of boundaries between heaven and earth and ensuing evil. Future judgments are forecast for all transgressors except for righteous Noah; God would show mercy and pardon the transgressions of the children of Israel who would repent once a year (*Jub.* 5:1–32).

Jubilees 6:1–11:6 takes full advantage of the silence of Genesis concerning Noah's 350 post-flood years. Noah is identified with a lineage of the right kind of priests who offer proper sacrifices and operate under a reinterpreted covenant and calendar. As a "new Adam" in the "new creation," Noah witnesses the reestab-

---

47. Michael A. Knibb, "Jubilees and the Origins of the Qumran Community" (inaugural address delivered at King's College, London, Jan.17, 1989), 16.

lishment of seasons and the restatement of primeval blessings and prohibitions. He exemplifies the proper relationship of people to the land by participating in the division of land and by teaching his grandsons how to avoid the sins against each other—illicit sex, abuse of blood—that caused people to be cut off from the land by the flood in the first place. Furthermore, he achieves restraint of demonic power through prayer and receives and records remedies from angels against the demons that remained.

Flagrant disregard of the example and teaching of Noah accounts for the subsequent degeneration of humankind. The building of a tower that is to "reach into heavens" echoes the sins of the Watchers, who transgressed the proper boundaries, displacing God and his angels as the proper source of instruction. Canaan wrongfully occupies Shem's territory, and the sons of Noah begin to behave violently toward each other, shedding blood. In consequence, Mastemah and the spirits take control over humankind right until the time of Abram.

The Noah narrative in *Jubilees* is thus not easily detached from the narratives that precede it and follow it, posing challenges for discerning both the story's beginning and ending. Cain's violence toward Abel anticipates the violence among the Watchers' children and among Noah's grandchildren (*Jub.* 4:4). Later, the building of the Tower of Babel leads to bloodshed by the "children of Noah," harking back to the sins of the generation of Noah (*Jub.* 10–11). In telling a series of stories in this way, by utilizing both anticipation and echo, the narrative implicitly draws its characters into conversation with one another. For example, the covenant with Noah becomes a part of the covenant with Moses, Esau's sins are related to the Watchers' sins, and Abraham recalls and transmits the words of Noah to his son, Isaac.

Our examination below of *Jubilees* in comparison to Genesis will show that the interpreter took liberties particularly with the ordering of reported events and that, at the points of reordering, frequently interjected explanatory expansions. *Jubilees*' narrator listened well to the silences in the Genesis account, contributing to the conversation about Noah with both vigor and imagination.

SIGNPOSTS TO A NEW NOAH: REORDERING AND EXPANSION

Reordering of the narrative and accompanying expansions are apparent on a large scale as well as on a smaller scale. Most dramatically, and perhaps most significantly, *Jubilees* recontextualizes *all* of the book of Genesis together with pre-Sinai Exodus into an expansion of the revelation given to Moses on Mount Sinai on the sixteenth day of the third month,[48] at the time when God made his covenant with Israel (*Jub.* 1:1–5).[49] The importance of this reordering can hardly

---

48. Cf. *Jub.* 6:17–18. Shevuot had been celebrated in heaven from creation but was first celebrated by Noah on earth.

49. VanderKam explores *Jubilees*' scriptural setting in Exod 19; 24; and 23:10–22 and posits that the writer "wants his readers to situate the work at the historical point in which the Sinaitic covenant has just been concluded on the previous day (the festival of weeks) and when

be overemphasized. The book begins on Mount Sinai and ends on Mount Sinai. Therefore, everything in between, including revelation to Enoch and Noah is recontextualized within a revelation to *Moses*. This has significant implications for *Jubilees*' view of the nature, means, and extent of divine revelation.

Within this large-scale reordering are numerous other reorderings and expansions that occur regularly but on a smaller scale. These behave as signposts for interpretative developments of Noah traditions, points of departure from the origin of the tradition in Genesis. The italicized portions in the tables below represent material that is present in both Genesis and *Jubilees* but is reordered differently. Pertinent expansions in the narrative are noted in a smaller font.

Noah as "New Adam": Listening to the "Right" Source

Genesis	Jubilees
Cain kills Abel (4:8)	Cain kills Abel (4:3)
Cain's genealogy (4:17–24)	
Seth is born (4:25)	Seth is born (4:7)
No more mention of Cain	*Cain has one son, Enoch (4:9)*
Adam dies (5:5)	
Seth's genealogy: Jared and Enoch (5:6–27)	Seth's genealogy: Jared and Enoch (4:11–27) Expansion: Angels descend in Jared's day (15); Enoch learned writing, knowledge, wisdom and received dream visions concerning eschatological judgment; he recorded a testimony (16–19)
Noah is born (5:28–29)	Noah is born (4:28)
	Adam dies (4:29) Expansion: Cain is justly punished in his death; no record of other descendants (4:31)
Noah has Shem, Ham, and Japheth (5:32)	Noah has Shem, Ham, and Japheth (4:33) Expansion and interpretation: Angels, women, giants, everyone devouring one another (5:1–2)

A reordering of the reporting of Noah's birth appears more specifically as an "interlocked transition," a term coined by Bruce Longenecker to represent a nar-

---

Moses has ascended the mountain to receive additional information from God" ("The Scriptural Setting of the Book of Jubilees," *DSD* 13 [2006]: 61–72, here 64). If the writer has indeed located Moses and the entire book at this juncture, it follows that any "additional information" given at the time of *Shevuot* within the Noah narrative should receive special attention.

rative device that brings narrative units into an essential connection by means of overlapping elements.[50] By reporting Noah's birth immediately before Adam's death, the narrator is bringing both Noah and Adam into an "essential connection" that implies Noah's heightened status as a "new Adam."

Following the death of Adam, Cain dies without record of the descendants accorded him by Genesis.[51] It is possible that the narrator did this with no purpose beyond simply the need to omit the parts of Genesis that were not central to the story being carried forward in *Jubilees*. Yet the birth of Noah's sons in the lines immediately following does serve to contrast the recorded continuity of Noah's line with the discontinuity of Cain's line. The narrative about Cain and his violent action toward his brother anticipates the violent behavior of the Watchers' sons toward one another, and the "forgotten" lineage of Cain foreshadows the destruction of the sons of the angels (*Jub.* 5:7).

Violence among brothers and sexual defilement are themes signposted by further reorderings and expansions throughout *Jubilees*. For example, Esau is a double villain, guilty of the sins that brought about the flood. Not only does Esau have an evil inclination (יצר) (1Q18 1–2 3–4/*Jub.* 35:9; Gen 6:5; 8:21) but his ways are "violence and wickedness" (חמס ורשע) and he went after the "error of women" (4Q223–224 2 II, 5–8/*Jub.* 35:13–14; Gen 6:1–5; 11; 13).[52] With echoes of the Watcher story in the background, Isaac advises Jacob and Esau to practice brotherly love lest they be destroyed and uprooted from the land (*Jub.* 36:4–9).[53]

This threat of being uprooted from the land hung over a people who persisted in bickering and "devouring" one another, a prospect that clearly worried the writer of *Jubilees*. It is cast here as a revelation to Moses, "One group will struggle with another . . . regarding the law and the covenant. For they have forgotten commandment, covenant, festival, month, sabbath, jubilee, and every verdict. . . . He will deliver them to the sword, judgment, captivity, plundering and devouring" (*Jub.* 23:19, 23).

---

50. Longenecker bases his own study on the work of the second-century C.E. rhetorician Lucian of Samosata, who recognized "chain-link" interlock as a device that brought narrative units into "essential connection" through overlapping elements (Bruce W. Longenecker, "Lukan Aversion to Humps and Hollows: The Case of Acts 11:27–12:25," *NTS* 50 [2004]: 185–204, here 186–87).

51. "Enoch" is the sole descendant of Cain recorded earlier in the narrative (*Jub.* 4:9) in juxtaposition with the listing of Seth's descendants, one of whom is also named "Enoch."

52. See the reordering that highlights the contrast between Esau's intermarriages and Jacob's purity, thus justifying the blessing bestowed on Jacob (*Jub.* 25:1–27:11) and the reordering that contrasts the Judah and Tamar story with the attempted seduction of Joseph by Potiphar's wife (*Jub.* 38:1–42:57).

53. Noah (*Jub.* 7:20) and Abraham (*Jub.* 20:1–2) exhort their progeny to love their brother or neighbor. Israel prospered in Egypt partly because "each one loved his brother," and during the lifetime of Joseph "there was no Satan" (*Jub.* 46:1).

While it may not be possible to identify, with any certainty, the different groups struggling with one another, the text does indicate that the controversy, even if only one-sided in the text, was about "commandment, covenant, festival, month, sabbath and jubilee." The warning of the types of judgments to fall on them echoes the fate of those in the days of the Watchers (*Jub.* 5:2, 7-9).

Jubilees delays reporting the births of both Enoch and Noah until the Watchers are introduced, sent to teach uprightness to humans (*Jub.* 4:15-28). This early introduction anticipates the reintroduction of these "Nephilim" (הנפילים)[54] at the "expected" chronological position, following the birth of Noah.[55] An expansion at this point details the violence and sin on the earth that came as a consequence of the marriage between angels and women and the birth of their sons, the giants (*Jub.* 5:1-2).

While the reason for the introduction of the descent of the Watchers during the days of Jared may simply be in recognition of the wordplay on Jared's name (ירד), the result is that the instruction that the Watchers give to humans is highlighted in contrast to the instruction given by the angels to Enoch (*Jub.* 4:21). As James Scott has so effectively shown, the story of the Watchers is the antithesis of what he calls the "on earth as in heaven" theme, in which the "Watchers mingled the two spheres producing the opposite effect—'in heaven as on earth.'"[56]

The narrator has thus introduced two significant and interrelated themes: (1) the conception of systemic and cosmic evil resulting from *improper* mingling between angelic beings and humans; and (2) the beneficial results of a *proper* mingling so that Enoch was taught by the angels who transmitted the proper kind of teaching.[57] It is into this context that Noah, the "new Adam," is born.

Noah would also be the second recipient of supernatural instruction that was perceived to have positive consequences for the earth. The first man and woman had failed by ignoring God and by accepting their instruction from the wrong source (*Jub.* 3.17-20). The partnership, beginning with Enoch and Noah and typified by the right sort of interchange between supernatural beings and righteous human beings, made for a powerful relationship that could ultimately defeat evil.

---

54. Hebrew *Jubilees* attests the "Nephilim" (הנפילים), the "increase" (וירב) of something, presumably violence or wickedness, and the corruption of "their way" (השחיתו דרכם) (11Q12 7 1-3/*Jub.* 5:1-2; cf. Gen 6:1-13).

55. For a study of the exegetical techniques of rearrangement and anticipation in the another text, the *Genesis Apocryphon*, see Moshe J. Bernstein, "Rearrangement, Anticipation and Harmonization as Exegetical Features in the Genesis Apocryphon," *DJD* 3 (1996): 37-57.

56. James M. Scott, *On Earth as in Heaven: The Restoration of Sacred Time and Sacred Space in the Book of Jubilees* (JSJSup 91; Leiden: Brill, 2005), 5-6.

57. On *Jubilees*' effort to distinguish between these two tracks of learning, see Stuckenbruck, "The Origins of Evil in Jewish Apocalyptic Tradition: The Interpretation of Genesis 6:1-4 in the Second and Third Centuries B.C.E.," in *The Fall of the Angels* (ed. C. Auffarth and L. T. Stuckenbruck; Themes in Biblical Narrative 6; Leiden: Brill, 2004), 87-118.

Noah: The Repentant Righteous One Escapes Judgment

Genesis	**Jubilees**
God decides to blot out everything (6:7)	God decides to blot out everything (5:4)
Noah finds favor with God (6:8)	God is pleased with Noah alone (5:5) Expansion: judgment, repentance and Day of Atonement (5:6–18)
Noah called a "righteous man" (6:9)	God shows favor to Noah alone; Noah's mind is righteous (5:19)

Primordial judgment in *Jubilees* foreshadows future judgments provoked by other transgressions of boundaries, sexual defilement, and violence. *Jubilees* follows the *Book of Watchers* in linking the actions of the Watchers to the resulting rise of wickedness and violence upon the earth. God responds swiftly with the promise of annihilation of all flesh (*Jub.* 5.4). At this point of the narrative, an important expansion links primordial judgment to future judgments, repentance, atonement, and rescue. The expansion's point of departure and return are the words "Noah alone" (*Jub.* 5:5, 19).

> 5 *He was pleased with Noah alone.* 6 Against his angels whom he had sent to the earth he was angry enough to uproot them from all their (positions) of authority. He told us to tie them up in the depths of the earth; now they are tied within them and are alone. 7 Regarding their children there went out from his presence an order to strike them with the sword and to remove them from beneath the sky. 8 He said: "My spirit will not remain on people forever for they are flesh. Their lifespan is to be 120 years." . . . 12 He made a new and righteous nature for all his creatures so that they would not sin with their whole nature until eternity. Everyone will be righteous—each according to his kind—for all time. 13 The judgment of all has been ordained and written on the heavenly tablets; there is no injustice. (As for) all who transgress from their way in which it was ordained for them to go—if they do not go in it, judgment has been written down for each creature and for each kind. 17 Regarding the Israelites it has been written and ordained: "If they turn to him in the right way, he will forgive all their wickedness and will pardon all their sins." 18 It has been written and ordained that he will have mercy on all who turn from all their errors once each year. 19 To all who corrupted their ways and their plan(s) before the flood *no favor was shown except to Noah alone* because favor was shown to him for the sake of his children whom he saved from the flood waters for his sake because his mind was righteous in all his ways, as it had been commanded concerning him. He did not transgress anything that had been ordained for him. (*Jub.* 5:5–8, 12–19).[58]

---

58. Trans. Vanderkam, *Book of Jubilees* (1989). Italics are my own.

The beginning and the ending of this expansion marked by "Noah alone" are based on the characterization of Noah in Genesis: "But Noah found favor in the sight of the LORD. These are the descendants of Noah. Noah was a righteous man, blameless in his generation; Noah walked with God" (Gen 6:8–9). Contained within the expansion are descriptions of judgments against the angels and their children and for all humans who would transgress the way ordained for them but the expansion also makes provision for rescue through repentance and atonement (*Jub.* 5:6–16).

The readers are reminded that there was no escape from judgment for "all who transgress" *except* for those who would turn to God in the "right way," who would "turn from all their errors once each year," and upon whom God would have mercy (*Jub.* 5:13–18). Thus, the Day of Atonement as a festival of repentance is introduced as a means by which Israel could escape future judgments.

Therefore, *Jubilees* links Noah's righteousness to repentance, an element that did *not* define righteousness in the Enochic books, in the *ALD*, in most versions of Ben Sira, or in the extant text of 4QInstruction.[59] *Jubilees*' righteous Noah is not a sinless Noah.[60] He offers sacrifices on his own behalf (*Jub.* 7:3; cf. Lev. 16:11) and in his prayer concerning the demons, Noah does not appeal to his righteousness as the basis on which he was saved but instead acknowledges God's mercy (*Jub.* 10:1–3). Noah, as the subtly "repentant righteous one," stands in contrast to the Aramaic composite portrait in the *Genesis Apocryphon*, in which Noah claims to have been righteous from the womb (1Q20 VI, 1–2). Noah inhabits *Jubilees* as an archetype for a people for whom repentance was an integral component of covenant and atonement, embodying an explanation of the means by which the righteous might be distinguished from the wicked.[61]

Noah as Priest: Covenant Redefined

Genesis	Jubilees
Noah offers a sacrifice (8:20)	Noah offers a sacrifice (6:1–3) Expansion: atones for the land, all the sins of the land

---

59. Cf. Greek "Enoch . . . an example of repentance for generations" (Sir 44:16), which is missing from the Hebrew Masada text and from the Syriac.

60. Cf. Abraham's request that God give Jacob all the blessings that he had blessed Noah and Adam and that God would purify Jacob from "filthy pollution" and pardon him for all the guilt of his sins of ignorance (*Jub.* 22:13–14).

61. Noah makes one ambiguous reference to his own righteousness in *Jub.* 10:6.

Genesis	Jubilees
God promises never again to curse the ground; recognizes evil יצר of human heart; promises never again to destroy all living things as he had done. Seasons and day and night never to cease while the earth remained. God charges Noah's family to be fruitful; gives blood prohibitions (8:21–9:7)	
God establishes his covenant with Noah (6:18; 9:9, 11, 15)	God establishes his covenant with Noah (6:4)
God reiterates promise never again to destroy the earth; all flesh would never again be cut off (כרת) by a flood (9:8–17)	*God promises never again to send a flood that would destroy the earth; days and seasons would not change their prescribed pattern; Noah is charged to be fruitful; blood prohibitions are given (6:4–9)* Expansion: Noah and sons swear an oath during "this month" [third month] that Noah made a covenant before the Lord God (6:10) Expansion: Angels remind Moses that he made a covenant accompanied by an oath; that blood is not for eating but is to be reserved for sacrificial use so that Israel might not be uprooted (6:11–14)
Rainbow given as sign of covenant (9:13–14)	Rainbow given as a sign of the covenant (6:15–16) Expansion: commandment to keep the festival of weeks [oaths?] for all time (6:17–20)

In Genesis, Noah's first act after stepping onto the land after leaving the ark is to build an altar and offer a sacrifice to God (Gen 8:18–20; *Jub*. 6:1–4). In *Jubilees*, Noah had already sent out the animals, while in Genesis Noah heads the list of those leaving the ark. *Jubilees*' narrator appears to intensify and develop the "creation destroyed and renewed" theme from the creation and flood narratives in Genesis by more clearly fashioning Noah into a "second" or "new Adam" who then becomes, in effect, the "first" progenitor of humanity (*Jub*. 4:28–29).

The expansion at the point of reordering clarifies that Noah left the ark in the *third* month, an addition that anticipates the later discussion of *Shevuot*. Additionally, the narrator lists the animals offered and specifies that Noah's sacrifice atoned for the land. *Jubilees*' idea of a "priestly Noah"[62] may have been drawn

---

62. Moshe Bernstein provides an overview of the halakhic details that are added to the biblical story of Noah and that receive special emphasis in *Jubilees* ("Noah and the Flood at Qumran," in *The Provo International Conference on the Dead Sea Scrolls: Technological Innova-*

from Aramaic Levi traditions, but the details of *how* Noah fulfilled his priestly function were filled in by the narrator.[63]

Israel's Day of Atonement ceremony, in which the high priest atoned for the dwelling place of God (Lev 16:1–34),[64] is suggested by Noah's atoning sacrifice. Morally defiling actions[65] and resulting corruption had resulted in a wholesale judgment by destruction.[66] *Jubilees* specifies that Noah offered a kid goat, the same animal that atoned for the sanctuary on the Day of Atonement (Lev 16:15–16). However, goats were not sacrificed only on the Day of Atonement. More compelling is the interjection of lines observed earlier concerning the Day of Atonement into a litany of coming judgments (*Jub.* 5:17–18). Israel had sinned but, by means of repentance on the Day of Atonement, Israel alone was to be distinguished from all those who would suffer judgment.

That the land would require an atoning sacrifice is not easily deduced from the biblical text. In Num 35:33–34, the blood of the one who had shed blood would act as atonement for the land; however, in the case of the flood, anyone who had shed blood was already destroyed. Therefore, this judgment could, exegetically, have "atoned for the land." It would seem that *Jubilees*' interpretation of Noah's first postdiluvian act purposefully connects "atoning for the land" with judgment and with the Day of Atonement ritual as a means by which a righteously repentant Israel could be rescued from the judgment of God.

After Noah first drank the wine from the vine he had planted, he behaves as a high priest would on the Day of Atonement (*Jub.* 7:1–6),[67] making a high

---

tions, *New Texts, and Reformulated Issues* (ed. D. W. Parry and E. C. Ulrich; STDJ 30; Leiden: Brill, 1999), 205–6. On the priesthood of Noah, see James C. VanderKam, "The Righteousness of Noah," in *Ideal Figures in Ancient Judaism: Profiles and Paradigms* (ed. J. J. Collins and G. W. E. Nickelsburg; SBLSCS 12; Chico, Calif.: Scholars Press, 1980), 13–32; and Devorah Dimant, "Noah in Early Jewish Literature," in *Biblical Figures Outside the Bible* (ed. M. E. Stone and T. A. Bergren; Harrisburg, Pa.: Trinity Press International, 1998), 123–50.

63. But see VanderKam for the argument that the *ALD* is older than *Jubilees* and that there is "no strong evidence" that the author of *Jubilees* borrowed ideas from the *ALD* ("Isaac's Blessing of Levi and His Descendents in *Jubilees* 31," in *Provo International* [n. 62 above], 514, 518). This study may not ascertain proof of literary dependence but sees a strong suggestion of shared tradition.

64. Ezekiel 14:12 and Num 35:33–34 may form a part of the textual background against which Noah's "atoning-for-the-land sacrifice" may have developed.

65. These include illicit unions between Watchers and human women (*Jub.* 4:22), violence, bloodshed, and the increase of wickedness (*Jub.* 5:2).

66. The children of the Watchers were doomed to slay one another; the Watchers themselves were found for future judgment; and a flood blotted out all living beings (*Jub.* 5:9–11, 20).

67. William K. Gilders proposes that the Greek κέρατα (horns) and κρέατα (meat) could easily have been confused in translation and that *Jub.* 7:4 should read that Noah placed the blood of a sin offering on the *horns* of the altar and not on the "flesh of the altar," as the Ethiopic reads ("Where Did Noah Place the Blood? A Textual Note on *Jubilees* 7:4," *JBL* 124 [2005]: 745–49).

priestly sacrifice for himself and for his family (cf. Lev 16:11, 15). While Day of Atonement elements are compellingly associated with Noah's sacrifices, it is important to remember that Noah's atoning-for-the-land sacrifice in *Jub.* 6 is offered in the *third* month, the month for the renewal of covenants, and not in the seventh month, the month of the observance of the Day of Atonement (Lev 16). VanderKam has explored the literary and narrative setting of *Jubilees* at the particular point of Moses' second journey up Mount Sinai following his sacrifice and the observance of covenant renewal (Exod 24:1–8).[68] On Moses' second journey, he receives further instructions from God. Since Moses' sacrifice would have been understood in *Jubilees* to have occurred in the third month, it is possible that Noah's atoning sacrifice is meant to foreshadow the Mosaic one, a sacrifice that prompts the making of the covenant and prepares the way for further revelation from God.[69]

Rather than discard one interpretation in favor of the other, we might understand Noah's atoning sacrifice as containing elements of both the Day of Atonement and the covenant making that immediately followed God's acts of judgment.[70] Significantly, "atoning for the land" was also a descriptor and self-identity marker for the *Yaḥad* sectarians, who seemed to prefer a category of atonement that was inseparably bound with judgment (1QS VIII, 6, 10).[71] This raises a question. Was it more likely that a movement that already linked "atoning for the land" to covenant and judgment would create an archetype that embodied the connection, or is it more likely that the *Yaḥad* sectarians based their own statement of self-identity at least partially on the interpretation of Noah that they found in *Jubilees*? Perhaps the real story is that the emerging *Yaḥad* sectarian movement was in conversation with its variously constructed archetypes, each influencing the other. It is a conversation that we overhear only in small snatches contained in *Jubilees* and in the *Community Rule*, but in the next chapter Noah "atones for the land" in the *Genesis Apocryphon*, adding an Aramaic voice that sharpens the conversation into a dispute.

Another reordering in this section redefines the covenant with Noah to encompass priestly responsibilities In Genesis, Noah's sacrifice (Gen 8:20) is separated from the establishment of covenant (Gen 9:8) by nine verses containing God's promise never again to curse the ground, God's promise that the seasons and days would not cease, and God's renewal of the primeval blessings and the

---

68. VanderKam, "Scriptural Setting," 61–72.

69. Moses' sacrifice is featured in a copy of 4QVisions of Amram (4Q547), a document in the *ALD* tradition that places Noah into a hereditary priestly line.

70. Later sectarian interpretation imported elements of the Day of Atonement ceremony into its covenant renewal ceremony as expressed in 1QS I-II. See Dorothy M. Peters, "'Atoning for the Land' in the Dead Sea Scrolls: The Day of Atonement Revisited," in *Studies in Biblical Law* (ed. George J. Brooke; JSSSup 25; Oxford: Oxford University Press, forthcoming, 2008).

71. 1QS VIII, 6, 10; IX, 4; 1QSa III; 4Q265 7 9–10; 4Q508 30 1–2. This combination of themes appears also in a liturgical Day of Atonement prayer in *Festival Prayers* (4Q508).

prohibitions concerning the blood. In *Jubilees*, however, the narrator positions covenant making so that it fit neatly between Noah's atoning sacrifice and the aforementioned promises, blessings, and prohibitions, emphasizing all of these as priestly issues that were to be brought under the priestly covenant.

The reestablishment of seasons and days in *Jubilees* also expands to include memorial days, *Shevuot*, and the 364-day calendar[72] under the covenant with Noah.[73] Major milestones in the flood occurred in the first, fourth, seventh, and tenth months; therefore, Noah sets aside the first of each of these months as a memorial for all eternity (*Jub.* 6:28-29) and institutes *Shevuot* in the third month as a celebration of the covenant (*Jub.* 6:10-12),[74] an event utilized pedagogically by God, who says to Moses, "Now you command the Israelites" concerning blood and renewal of covenant during the third month (*Jub.* 6:13-17).

To covenant making, *Jubilees* adds the oath sworn by Noah.[75] Considering the play on words—oath (שבועה) and week (שבוע)—VanderKam comments that "[t]he oath sworn by Noah and his sons becomes the trigger for a discussion of the festival of weeks, the festival on which the covenant was made and renewed."[76] *Shevuot* resurfaces throughout *Jubilees*, while covenant renewal, new revelation, and new warnings followed a familiar calendrical pattern already established in the days of Noah.[77] Moses himself had ascended Mount Sinai on the sixteenth day of the third month (*Jub.* 1:1). Abraham offers sacrifices in the middle of the third month, and, in consequence, God gives to him the covenant of circumcision along with the requisite warning of uprooting from the land if this cov-

---

72. The affirmation of the 364-day calendar is clearly being presented here as one side of an ongoing debate in Judaism. Philip R. Davies does not find evidence in Qumran literature for any *recent* calendar dispute, dating the 364-day calendar to the Babylonian exile ("Calendrical Change and Qumran Origins: An Assessment of VanderKam's Theory," *CBQ* 45 [1983]: 80-89).

73. "The juxtaposition of sections about the festival of weeks and the calendar makes one wonder whether the author is trying to convey the idea that the correct dating of this festival was the cornerstone of the entire calendar and its festivals" (James C. VanderKam, "Covenant and Biblical Interpretation in Jubilees 6," in *The Dead Sea Scrolls Fifty Years after Their Discovery: Proceedings of the Jerusalem Congress, July 20-25, 1997* [ed. L. H. Schiffman, E. Tov, and J. C. VanderKam; Jerusalem: Israel Exploration Society, 2000], 92-104, here 99-100). For further discussion on the evolution of calendars in the Dead Sea Scrolls, see VanderKam, *Calendars in the Dead Sea Scrolls: Measuring Time* (London/New York: Routledge, 1998).

74. The first *mention* of the third month, however, is in *Jub.* 1:1, in which God called Moses up the mountain.

75. For oath taking in conjunction with covenant renewal, see CD XV, 12-XVI, 2; 1QS V, 8-10.

76. VanderKam, "Covenant and Biblical Interpretation in Jubilees 6," 96.

77. The Cave 4 Damascus documents, following *Jubilees*, instruct the community to convene in the third month but add that the Levites were to lead the inhabitants of the camps in cursing (ארר) the ones who strayed from the Torah (4Q266 11 16; 4Q269 16 14; 4Q270 7 II, 10). The additional curses would be a natural exegetical step when directed against those who would *not* keep Torah and therefore would not escape judgment.

enant is broken (*Jub.* 15:1–14). Near the end of his life, at the Well of the Oath (Beersheba)—another wordplay—Abraham celebrates *Shevuot* and the renewal of the covenant, remembering the blessing upon Noah (*Jub.* 22:1–15).

The proper use of blood in *Jubilees* is expanded from Genesis to include the sacrificial use of blood both at the time of covenant renewal (*Jub.* 6:11; cf. Exod 24:8) and for perpetual morning and evening sacrifices (*Jub.* 6:14). Later in *Jubilees*, Abraham instructs Isaac concerning sacrifice, concluding, "Because thus I have found written in the books of my forefathers and in the words of Enoch and in the words of Noah" (*Jub.* 21.10b) thus demonstrating a shared tradition with the *Aramaic Levi Document* that calls for accurate oral and written transmission of priestly practice from one generation to the next. Abraham further cautions Isaac concerning bloodshed (4Q219 II, 17–37/*Jub.* 21:18–22:1). Genesis has no record of this speech of Abraham but records similar words in connection with Noah. In this way, the narrator presses the point that teachings could be and had been accurately transmitted throughout the generations ever since the days of Noah.

Finally, by setting the covenant with Noah in the literary context within the Mosaic covenant at Mount Sinai, an intimate connection between the two is created.[78] As Jacques van Ruiten has demonstrated, the universalizing tendency of the covenant of Noah is extrapolated to the covenant of Moses so that the covenant applies to all humanity and for all time.[79]

Noah and Progeny: How to Be Rightly Planted in the Land

In Genesis, Noah blesses and curses his progeny, lives 350 years, and then dies, after which Genesis records the genealogies of Noah's sons and the division of the land. In *Jubilees*, Noah blesses Shem and Japheth and curses Canaan (*Jub.* 7:7–13) but then is kept very busy until his death is recorded three chapters later in *Jub.* 10:15–17. It is here that Noah most actively engages with his children and grandchildren, concerning himself with their future and demonstrating the accurate transmission of written and oral teaching that he had received from God and from the angels.

Genesis	Jubilees
Noah plants a vineyard (9:20)	Noah plants a vine, makes wine (7:1–2) Expansion: Noah makes high priestly atonement for himself and his sons (7:3–6)

---

78. Jacques T. A. G. M. van Ruiten has noted the parallels between the Noachic and Mosaic covenants in *Jubilees*, including blood prohibitions and oath-taking ("The Covenant of Noah in *Jubilees* 6.1–38," in *The Concept of the Covenant in the Second Temple Period* [ed. S. E. Porter and J. C. R. de Roo; JSJSup 71; Leiden: Brill, 2003], 167–90, here 188–90).

79. Ibid., 182, 190.

Genesis	Jubilees
Noah's drunkenness; blessings and curses upon progeny (9:21-27)	Noah's drunkenness; blessings and curses upon progeny (7:7-12); abbreviated *genealogies* of Noah's sons (7:13-19)
	Expansion: Noah exhorts his grandsons concerning sins that prompted the flood (fornication, uncleanness, injustice) and not to be led astray by demons lest they be cut off from the land (7:20-28), blood prohibitions (7:29-33), and how to be rightly planted (7:34-39)
	Division of land Expansion: Noah's children divide the land improperly after Peleg is born; proper division of the land by lot in Noah's presence (8:8-9:13); curses on those who would occupy another's share; future judgment by sword and fire (9:14-15)
	Expansion: Prayer against demons; Mastemah and 10 percent of demons to remain (10:1-9); Noah records antidotes against spirits and gives the books he has written to Shem (10:13-14)
Noah lives 350 years after the flood; Noah dies (9:28-29)	Noah dies (10:15-16)
Genealogies of Noah's sons and *division of land* (10:1-32); *earth divided in Peleg's day* (10:25); Shem's *genealogy* (2nd version) (11:10-26)	

Bookended between two accounts of curses (*Jub.* 7:10-13; 9:14-15) come the genealogies of Noah's sons, an abortive attempt to divide the land, and the proper division of the land in the presence of Noah. Noah warns his children against the sins of the flood generation so that they would not be blotted out from the land. Fornication, uncleanness, and injustice are given as reasons for the judgment by flood (*Jub.* 7:20-21).[80] Using the powerfully negative example of the children of

---

80. David Lambert argues that Noah's exhortations are derived exegetically from the Genesis text rather than originating from the writer's own concerns, as is the case in the testaments of Abraham, Isaac, and Rebekah ("Last Testaments in the Book of Jubilees," *DSD* 11 [2004]: 82-107). However, while we might agree that the exhortations could be derived exegetically from Genesis, the interpretative developments must have been, to some extent, informed by the author's concerns.

the Nephilim who "devoured one another," Noah shares his deep concern over the disunity that was arising among his progeny (*Jub.* 7:20-33).

Noah then exhorts his grandsons to "be rightly planted on the surface of the entire earth" (*Jub.* 7:34-39).[81] He warns them against walking in the paths of corruption and instructs them to offer proper sacrifices so that they will be "righteous" and that all of their "plants" will be upright (*Jub.* 7.37).[82] He emphasizes the ancestral line from which at least some of these commandments came, naming Lamech, Methuselah, and Enoch (*Jub.* 7:34-39).

Next, Cainan discovers inscriptions from the Watchers. Sin results and Noah's children began dividing the land in an "evil manner" (*Jub.* 8:1-9). Noah rectifies the mistake, divides the land by lot, and compels his sons to swear that they will curse anyone who occupies the portion of another (*Jub.* 8:10-9:15).

This section explicates the results of wrongful occupation of the land. The second "curse" intensifies this link and legitimates "cursing" for wrongful occupation, an interpretation of "curse" that may have been inspired by the Deuteronomic blessings and curses that the Israelites were to speak upon entrance to the land.[83]

In his intercessory prayer on behalf of his grandchildren, Noah demonstrates the efficacy of prayer against demonic power.[84] As a result, God allowed 10 percent of the demons to remain, but, against these, the angels give Noah the remedy. Noah writes the remedies in a book and bequeaths all of his books to his son,

---

81. See "righteous plant" in *1 En.* 10:16. *Jubilees* states concerning Israel: "I will transform them into a righteous plant" (1:16). Abraham blesses Isaac, saying: "He will raise from you a righteous plant in all the earth throughout all the history of the earth" (4Q219 II, 30/*Jub.* 21:24). Hebrew *Jubilees* reads, alternatively: "the [planting] of truth (מטעת האמת) on the earth for all the generations of the earth" (4Q219 II, 30). VanderKam notes that in the *Jubilees* fragments, אמת appears where the Ethiopic has *tsedq* ("The Jubilees Fragments from Qumran Cave 4," in *The Madrid Qumran Congress: Proceedings of the International Congress on the Dead Sea Scrolls, Madrid 18-21 March 1991* [ed. J. Trebolle Barrera and L. Vegas Montaner; STDJ 12; Leiden: Brill, 1992], 635-48, here 645). The only other place where a "planting of truth" (אמת למטעת) is found in the Hebrew Qumran corpus is in 1QHa XVI, 10-11, where the planting is "hidden and not esteemed." But cf. Aramaic *Testament of Jacob* (4Q537); 4Q500 1, 2-6; 1Q20 and the Enochic books, particularly 4Q204 and 4Q212 for the planting of truth/righteousness (נצבת קושט).

82. *OTP.*

83. Cf. Deut 11:29; 27:12-14. Cf. blessings and curses of Noah in 4Q252-254a and the liturgical blessings led by the priests and the curses led by the Levites in 1QS I, 18-II, 19. Cf. Deut 27:14-15, where the Levites led Israel in cursing.

84. See also the book of Tobit in which Tobias receives instructions from the angel Raphael against demons (Tob 6:6-7). Tobit survives in four Aramaic copies and one Hebrew copy from Qumran (4Q196-200) (DJD XIX, 1-76). In his instruction to his son, Tobias, Tobit appeals to Noah as an ancestor who took a wife from among his kindred (Tob 4:12). Compare *Jub.* 4:33, which also records the ancestry of Noah's wife, Emzara, the daughter of his uncle.

Shem (*Jub.* 10:1–14).[85] In a close study of the five prayers in *Jubilees*—the prayers of Moses, Noah, and the three prayers of Abraham—John Endres has identified a common theme of "God as creator." Within Noah's prayer is a confession of faith in God who shows mercy, and there is a reminder of the "God of creation in [sic] mentioned in Genesis 1: 'Now bless me and my sons, so we might increase and grow numerous and fill the earth.'"[86] Noah, covenant, and a remembrance of the mercies of God appear again in our study of 4QFestival Prayers.

The legitimacy of Noah's warnings is borne out as subsequent events echo the primordial story. Another interlock transition links the sons of Noah with Ur, thus creating the idolatrous context within which Abram was born (*Jub.* 10:18–11:6). Noah's progeny build the Tower of Babel for access to heaven, an implied attempt to transgress the set boundaries between earth and heaven, but God intervenes, destroying the tower and dispersing the people (*Jub.* 10:18–26). Conditions deteriorate on the earth once again. Canaan occupies Shem's land and his father, Ham, curses him (*Jub.* 10:27–34). Regew, one of Seth's descendants, marries the daughter of Ur and granddaughter of Kesed, the brother of Cainan, who had read the Watcher's writing (*Jub.* 11:1; cf. 8:1–4). The "sons of Noah" shed blood and eat blood (*Jub.* 11:2). Ur is built, idolatry takes hold, and Mastema and the spirits practice error and lead people astray into all manner of transgression (*Jub.* 11:3–6).

The postscript to the Noah narrative is that wrongful occupation of land, intermarriage, shedding and eating of blood, and the reception of Watchers' teachings—sins of the pre-flood generation and sins that Noah warned against—would once again lead to the control of the earth by evil forces. After Noah, none could stand against Mastemah until Abram, following Noah's example, prayed for salvation from the spirits and for protection for his own grandson, Jacob (*Jub.* 12:20; 19:28).

The Scope and Timing of Revelation to Noah

In *Jubilees*, Moses receives the book as fresh revelation from God and, in the midst of the revelation, encounters his legendary, visionary, revelatory ancestor Enoch. Both Enoch and Moses are clearly but differently honored idealized figures in *Jubilees*. Does this mean, however, that *Jubilees* was simply a melting pot of Enochic and Mosaic revelation, a book that spoke with conjoined Enochic-Mosaic authority or, rather, did *Jubilees* make a distinction between the types of revelation linked to the two? The question is complex. It is important to consider the relationship between the portrayal of the idealized figures of Enoch and

---

85. Noah is, therefore, associated with healing powers; cf. Abram's healing powers in 1Q20 XX, 21–22.

86. John Endres, "Prayers in Jubilees," in *Heavenly Tablets: Interpretation, Identity and Tradition in Ancient Judaism* (ed. L. LiDonnici and A. Lieber; JSJSup 119; Leiden: Brill, 2007), 31–47, here 40–41.

Moses as "revealers" and the authority accorded the revelatory texts traditionally associated with Moses and Enoch.[87]

This question may be explored through an examination of the scope and timing of divine revelation to Noah and how Noah, as portrayed in *Jubilees*, influenced Israel's future by his words and actions. This study suggests, first, that *Jubilees* imposed limits on Enoch—a figure who represented a certain *mode* of revelation in addition to a body of written revelation—and, second, that knowledge from heaven was accessible to Noah and his descendants especially during the third month but, unlike the revelation offered to Moses, was severely restricted in scope.[88]

Any kind of communication between the heavens and earth would require the crossing of a boundary. In the *Jubilees* narrative, this crossing of boundaries had results perceived to be beneficial, on one hand, but catastrophic, on the other. In a *proper* mingling, instruction from the right source was transmitted to Enoch and to Moses with beneficial results for humankind. However, an *improper* mingling and mating of Watchers and women had resulted in violence and disaster upon the earth (*Jub.* 4:15–22; 5:1–2). It was into this hotbed of unrestrained encounters between natural and supernatural beings, into difficult and dangerous times, that Noah was born (*Jub.* 4:28).[89]

Although *Jubilees* had inherited similar Enochic traditions, it did not share the enthusiasm for extrabiblical Noachic visions found in the "Enochic" trajectory that included *Parables* and the *Genesis Apocryphon*. *Jubilees* only selectively records divine speeches from Genesis. In *Jubilees*, God's expressed intention to destroy all flesh is embedded in the narrative as told to Moses but *not* revealed to Noah (*Jub.* 5:4; cf. Gen 6:13). *Jubilees* carefully restricts both the scope and timing of God's special revelation to Noah to the period following his post-flood atoning sacrifice and within the context of covenant making in the third month. *Jubilees* reorders the Genesis narrative so that covenant now includes the reestablishment

---

87. The *Astronomical Book*, *Book of Watchers*, and *Dream Visions* appear to be validated in *Jub.* 4:17–19.

88. Scott has already noted that "*Jubilees* adapts and reinterprets Enochic apocalyptic tradition, most notably the Apocalypse of Weeks, in order to assert that its own version of the revelation to Enoch (and to Moses after him) has the greater claim to authenticity and authority" (*On Earth as in Heaven*, 212). However, Nickelsburg aligns *Jubilees* more closely with the Enochic books: "[T]he book may also attest an ambivalence about the figure of Moses that is not at odds with the viewpoint of the Enochic authors" ("The Nature and Function of Revelation of 1 Enoch, Jubilees, and Some Qumranic Documents," in *Pseudepigraphic Perspectives: The Apocrypha and Pseudepigrapha in Light of the Dead Sea Scrolls: Proceedings of the International Symposium of the Orion Center for the Study of the Dead Sea Scrolls and Associated Literature, 12–14 January 1997* [ed. E. G. Chazon and M. E. Stone; STDJ 31; Leiden: Brill, 1999], 91–119, here 107).

89. The Enochic *Birth of Noah* and the *Genesis Apocryphon* both record Lamech's suspicion of Noah's angelic parentage (*1 En.* 106; 1Q20 II-V). In both texts, Enoch himself endorses Noah's legitimacy through Methuselah. *Jubilees* does not attest this story.

of seasons and days, a restatement of the primeval blessing, commandments concerning bloodshed, and God's promise never again to destroy the earth by floodwaters (*Jub.* 6:4–16; cf. Gen 8:22–9:17). The scope of revelation given to Moses as an "aside" is dramatically greater than that given to Noah. The angel offers a much fuller explanation for the proper use of sacrificial blood, the dire consequences should this new commandment be broken, the implementation of *Shevuot*, the Days of Remembrance, and the 364-day calendar (*Jub.* 6:11–38). It must be remembered, however, that within the narrative, even for Moses, the revelation is confined to the third month and takes place in the context of covenant renewal.

One key to understanding the transfer of authority from one revelatory figure to another may be found in a recontextualization of Noah traditions found in *Watchers*. In chs. 6–11, likely the oldest layer of the book, Noah learns of the imminent deluge from an angel (*1 En.* 10:1–3), but once this layer was recontextualized into chs. 1–36 and bookended by revelations to Enoch, the Noah narrative becomes merely part of Enoch's vision.[90] In the first set of *Dream Visions*, Enoch envisions a flood that leaves the earth survivorless. It is only because of Enoch's prayer offered in righteousness (84:1) (not Noah's righteousness!) that a remnant of humanity survived at all for Enoch to dream about in the *Animal Apocalypse*. In the *Apocalypse of Weeks*, the knowledge of the "first end" comes specifically to Enoch (93:4) and, in the appended *Birth of Noah*, Enoch informs Methuselah of coming judgment (106:15–17), an exegetical innovation that gave Enoch's descendants direct access to otherworldly revelation. The revelation to Noah had been superseded by the revelation to Enoch.

Just as *Watchers* used the literary device of recontextualizing and bookending the Noah narrative, thus elevating the authoritative status of the figure of Enoch, so *Jubilees* now bookended the entire Genesis and pre-Sinai narrative with the revelation to Moses on Mount Sinai. The literary and narrative setting of *Jubilees* follows Moses' first Mount Sinai journey during the third month.[91] Moses offers a sacrifice, reads from the book of the covenant, dashes the blood of covenant on the people, and then reclimbs the mountain for additional revelation (see Exod 24:1–8). Noah's atoning sacrifice in *Jub.* 6:1–3 and covenant making during the third month thus effectively foreshadow the more momentous—for the author—Mount Sinai event.

The recontextualization of Enoch and Noah stories within Mosaic bookends may have alerted the reader to the fact that Moses now superseded Enoch as the most authoritative revealer. Moses learns of the origin and proper implementa-

---

90. Cf. Helge Kvanvig's application of the literary categories of "master narrative," "counter story," and "alternative story." Utilizing these categories with respect to the displacement of the figure of Noah in favor of Enoch, *1 En.* 1–5 and 12–16 might function as "counter story" to 6–11 ("Enochic Judaism—A Judaism with the *Torah* and the Temple?" [paper presented to the Fourth Enoch Seminar, Camaldoli, Italy, July 8–12, 2007]).

91. VanderKam, "Scriptural Setting," 61–72.

tion of the Torah commandments, but, significantly, the scope of Enoch's revelation is now encompassed within the more extensive revelation to Moses. The figure to whom greater revelation is given is surely intended to be portrayed as the one possessing an elevated authoritative revelatory status.

Enoch, Noah, and others of Israel's ancestors also hear from God in *Jubilees*. However, the book delineates new restrictions and boundaries that reveal authorial concerns. How were humans to know when God—or the *right* kind of angel—was speaking or when a demon was leading them astray? Did God still speak in the same way as he had spoken previously to Enoch, Noah, and Moses? If so, how and when?

Even while *Jubilees* allows Enoch unrestricted access to the angels for "six jubilees of years," nowhere do humans, even Moses, have direct access to Enoch. This may indicate either a reduction of Enoch's *ongoing* authority as a revelatory figure who was now sequestered in Eden, or it may register a concern that, while the revelation to Enoch was still valid, Israel could no longer expect to receive safe and unrestricted "Enochic-style" revelation mediated by angels or in visions (*Jub.* 4:21–24).

Unlike his dreamer-writer ancestor, Enoch, *Jubilees'* Noah is a hard-working "down-to-earth" character, the epitome of a Mosaic-Torah-obedient priestly Jew.[92] Most significantly, Noah is the "first priest" to participate with God in the making of a covenant, a momentous and foundational festival occurring in the third month. Noah appears to be unaware of the far-reaching and cosmic implications of his actions in the third month. These are, however, revealed to Moses. Although *Shevuot* had been celebrated in heaven since creation, Noah is the first human to observe it and his action prompts the ordination of *Shevuot* in the heavenly tablets as a feast of covenant renewal to be celebrated annually (*Jub.* 6:17–18).

In *Jubilees*, the seventeenth day of the second month is especially troublesome for the intrusion of destructive forces into the land; the serpent deceives the woman and the destructive floodwaters enter the earth. Demons harass Noah's grandchildren, and humans become even more susceptible to the dangerous influences of supernatural beings (*Jub.* 10:1; 11:4–5).[93] The Enochic Watchers traditions are reinterpreted in *Jubilees* in a way that suggests that angelic revelation

---

92. Here, it is understood that Noah was obedient to the "first Torah" but also to *Jubilees*, both of which are partial representations of the heavenly tablets. For a discussion of the perception of "heavenly tablets" in *Jubilees*, see Gabriele Boccaccini, "From a Movement of Dissent to a Distinct Form of Judaism" (paper presented to the Fourth Enoch Seminar, Camaldoli, Italy, July 8–12, 2007).

93. However, see Annette Yoshiko Reed, who posits that "demonic influence diminishes as the narrative progresses" ("Angels, Demons, and the Dangerous Ones in Between: Reflections on Enochic and Mosaic Traditions in *Jubilees*" [paper presented to the Fourth Enoch Seminar, Camaldoli, Italy, July 8–12, 2007]).

was relatively trustworthy until Enoch's day.[94] In an unusual extrabiblical communication—for *Jubilees*—the angels teach Noah herbal remedies against demonic seductions and Noah records these, passing the book along to Shem (*Jub.* 10:12), thus implying the new susceptibility of humans, who must view with suspicion any communication from supernatural beings.

That said, the setting of the *Jubilees* itself in the third month confirms the long-lasting significance of the timing of Noah's celebration of *Shevuot* and its implication for ongoing revelation to Israel.[95] For example, during the third month, God promises land to Abram and tells him that Israel would suffer four hundred years (*Jub.* 14:1-4). He commands Abram concerning circumcision (*Jub.* 15:1-16), but it is Moses who receives the fuller explanation that circumcision was a sign differentiating the circumcised from those who would eventually come under God's wrath (*Jub.* 15:25-34). In the third month, Isaac is born, circumcised, and weaned (*Jub.* 16:13-19), the latter an occasion on which God speaks to Abraham and to Hagar (*Jub.* 17:1-14). Isaac and Ishmael celebrate *Shevuot* with Abraham (*Jub.* 22:1), and Abraham's blessing on Jacob at this feast verbalizes a hoped-for future for both Jacob's seed—that they would be forgiven their transgression and inherit the earth—and Canaan's seed, that they would be uprooted and blotted out (*Jub.* 22:11-23). This blessing is transformed from a "hoped-for future" into a more detailed and certain future in revelation given to Moses in the following chapter concerning future generations, exile, and healing (*Jub.* 23:11-31). Finally, in response to the celebration of the covenant on the third Monday, God appears also to Jacob (*Jub.* 44:5-6).

In conclusion, while the second month of the calendar was generally associated with the threat of destructive forces coming onto the earth, such as the floodwaters, during the *third* month there was a different kind of "open heavens," when the boundaries of communication between natural and supernatural could be safely navigated. Those who participated in sacrifice and renewal of the covenant established by Noah in the third month could expect that God was particularly attentive to their prayers and actions during this period and that what they

---

94. *Jubilees* does not blame misleading angelic instruction for the evil precipitating the deluge. Cf. *1 En.* 7:1-8:3. Ida Fröhlich argues that, in *Jubilees'* harmonization of Enochic and biblical traditions, the *deeds* of the angels became "unintentionally the source of evil" ("Enoch and Jubilees," in *Enoch and Qumran Origins: New Light on a Forgotten Connection* [Grand Rapids: Eerdmans, 2005], 141-47, here 144).

95. The seventh month is also a time of significant new beginnings in *Jubilees*. On the first day of this month, the waters begin to disappear into the abyss, reversing the destructive intrusion of floodwaters (*Jub.* 6:26). God calls Abram to a new land and gives him the Hebrew language (*Jub.* 12:16-26; cf. Gen 12: 1-3). Jacob erects an altar in Bethel, where Levi, later that month, dreams that he is ordained a priest and where Jacob reads the heavenly tablets (*Jub.* 31:3; 32:1, 20-26). Although God speaks at other specified and unspecified times, these occurrences are frequently either repetitions of previous revelation or do not have ongoing significance for Israel.

said and did at that time would have long-range and even cosmic implications.[96] Furthermore, if there was to be a fresh revelation, God's people could anticipate hearing from him during the covenant renewal celebration in the third month.

Enochic and Mosaic revelation, received and transmitted, was not simply melted and merged in *Jubilees* but rather placed into a definitive relationship. By recontextualizing and bookending the Enoch story within the Moses narrative, *Jubilees* effectively sequesters Enoch in Eden as an honorary emeritus revealer, transferring a fuller authority to Moses, recipient of the "first Torah" and the new revelation contained in *Jubilees*. The revelation to Enoch still stood, but accessibility to ongoing supernatural communication was now limited and restricted in both timing and scope. Moses and the written revelation represented by the "first Torah" and *Jubilees* were perceived to be sufficiently authoritative for Israel, for which Noah was the archetypal human obedient to a newly interpreted Torah.

Finally, while it is possible to differentiate successfully between the idealized figures of Enoch, Noah, and Moses as portrayed in the written texts associated with them, it is more challenging, but still possible, to differentiate the text-as-authoritative from the figure-as-authoritative. Revelations to Enoch, Noah, and all of Israel are distinct tesserae carefully restricted, defined, and bordered within a newly interpreted Mosaic Torah, given as a revelation to Moses and recorded in *Jubilees*.

Continuing the Conversation

The Hebrew texts under study in this chapter reflect intriguing growth and developments of Noah traditions. 4QInstruction does not mention Noah explicitly but develops traditions associated with Noah elsewhere in the Dead Sea Scrolls. The text appears to move without inhibition between past, present, and future so that what had happened in the distant past—the primordial flood—was inextricably linked to the more immediate past, to "every time of punishment," and also to future judgments. A conflation of Mal 3 and of the fall and flood narratives in Genesis yields the exegetical result that the righteous would (once again) distinguish between good and evil.

If Noah was not named in the original composition as one to whom mysteries were made known concerning the times of judgment, subsequent interpretation would find a place for him. Noah was at home within the wisdom-apocalyptic tradition that named specific biblical characters such as Noah, Enoch, and Levi as recipients of revelation concerning imminent and eschatological judgments.

Ben Sira's Noah is more exclusively an archetypal remnant and the "continuator" or successor of Adam. By resisting and even polemicizing revelation from dreams and visions and by emphasizing free will in its recounting of the

---

96. Cf. the *Yaḥad* sectarians, who pronounced blessings and curses during the third month in their covenant renewal ceremony (1QS I–II; 4Q266 11 16–17/4Q270 7 II, 11–12).

story of the Watchers, Ben Sira finds itself in dispute with *1 Enoch* and with the *Aramaic Levi Document*. If the naming of Noah and Levi as priestly ancestors is a marker for a movement of "Aramaic Levi" priests that advocated revelation from dream and visions, then the *omission* by Ben Sira of Noah and Levi as priestly ancestors could be a marker of the controversy between two differently interpreted priesthoods.

Unlike the Enochic books that mined the past in order to understand the future, Noah, the archetypical Torah-abiding Jew, reflects *Jubilees'* overall concern about the present, with details of *how* to be rightly planted and *how* to obey the Torah. Nevertheless, *Jubilees* strengthens the authority of Moses while embracing Enochic revelation,[97] and Noah is securely grafted back into *Jubilees'* adaptation and reinterpretation of Enochic tradition. To Enoch's insights into calendar and chronology are added festivals based on the chronology of the flood in *Jubilees* and, especially, the first celebration by a human of *Shevuot*.

Finally, for *Jubilees'* author, the time-honored Noah story, as presented in *Jubilees*, portrayed a microcosm of Israel's entire history that was prophetic. History was bracketed by two sequences of events, both comprised of the creation of a new or renewed earth and cosmic judgment. In between, familiar themes were replayed. Strife and sexual immorality intensified; wickedness and violence increased; and people fell away from the covenant. However, the "rightly planted," who would faithfully follow properly transmitted teachings, would always form a remnant that would possess the land and with whom God would renew his covenant.

For the writer of *Jubilees*, Noah must have been an exegetical windfall, perfectly suited as a magnetic archetype to whom would be attracted multiple themes of particular interest such as judgment and preservation, righteousness and wickedness, covenant and renewal of covenant, the right and wrong sort of instruction, proper and improper marriages, repentance and atonement, calendar and priesthood, possession of the land, division among brothers, appropriate blessings and curses, and, finally, the proper way to handle angels and demons.

The fortunate collocation of the flood story in Genesis with the encounter of the "sons of the gods" with humans in Genesis and ensuing wickedness lent itself well to the writer's purposes. *Jubilees'* view that history was instructive and even prophetic is illustrated in exhortations given by Noah and Israel's ancestors. It was not the figure of Noah alone, but the story as a whole, with all of its

---

97. So Nickelsburg; but he would align *Jubilees* more closely with the Enochic writings than this present study would allow: "[T]he author of Jubilees casts Moses as a figure like Enoch" and "the book may also attest an ambivalence about the figure of Moses that is not at odds with the viewpoint of the Enochic authors" (Nickelsburg, "Nature and Function of Revelation," 107). Scott, in his detailed study of *Jubilees'* reinterpretation of Enochic apocalyptic tradition, concludes that *Jubilees* asserted that "its own version of the revelation to Enoch (and to Moses after him) has the greater claim to authenticity and authority" (*On Earth as in Heaven*, 212).

accretions, that the writer found to be a sufficiently rich and variegated paradigm through which to view Israel's story.

Although *Jubilees* faithfully records the angelic visitations as they are found in the biblical text,[98] it is suspicious of "extrabiblical" accounts of angelic visitations. Revelation to Enoch, at least that which was acknowledged at the time of the composition of *Jubilees*, was "grandfathered" into *Jubilees*, but, beginning with Noah, revelation from heaven, whether directly from God or through the medium of angels, is severely restricted in content and timing. God does not reveal his eschatological plans to Noah in Genesis, and the times of new revelation in *Jubilees* are restricted to specific times, often in the third month, when metaphorical windows from heaven were opened for divine revelation in the context of covenant renewal.

This had contemporary implications for Israel: could God's people continue to expect the kind of revelation recorded in the Enochic books, or was the revelation from the heavenly tablets, as given to Moses in the "first Torah" and in *Jubilees*, all encompassing and all-sufficient? Finally, *Jubilees* neither adapts nor composes a remarkable birth narrative for Noah, a story that in *1 Enoch* and the *Genesis Apocryphon* implies freedom of movement between the earthly and quasi-heavenly spheres.

Simply put, the covenant that prefigured the Mosaic one is central to the Noah narrative. All characters in *Jubilees*, including Enoch and his visits with the angels and Noah with his limited revelation from God, are recontextualized within Mosaic bookends, within God's revelation to Moses. This raises an important question. By subordinating an archetypical Enoch to an archetypical Moses in this text, is *Jubilees* also subordinating the literature associated with Enoch (the Enochic books) to the literature associated with Moses (Torah and *Jubilees*)? If so, then the relative statuses of the archetypes may reflect the relative authority of their literatures. Furthermore, the author of *Jubilees* may be communicating a caution concerning the preferred mode of revelation, "Enochic" or "Mosaic."

Noah traditions that come together in *Jubilees* would tend to travel together in other Hebrew texts. Some are already known from Genesis, such as judgment of the wicked and rescue of the righteous, sacrifice, covenant, and blessings and curses. However, Noah as an archetypical priestly figure is more clearly drawn in *Jubilees*. Not only does he atone for the land, but now the covenant also includes the reestablishment of seasons (calendar), the proper use of blood, God's charge to Noah to be fruitful, and the specification of the third month for covenant renewal in perpetuity. Furthermore, Noah is an implied repentant archetype for future penitents on the Day of the Atonement who would escape judgment because of their repentance.

---

98. For example, Hagar (17:11); Jacob and the ladder (27:21); an angel brought Jacob heavenly tablets (32:21); Rebecca learned about Esau's threats in a dream but the text does not specifically mention "angels" (27:1).

Finally, *Jubilees* reserves some of its harshest polemic for sexual defilement and violence between brothers but accompanies it with a fatherly appeal for love and unity among brothers. The manner in which *Jubilees* so respectfully draws together various apocalyptic, wisdom, and priestly Noah traditions into a coherent whole under Moses conceivably reflects a drive to bring unity among movements that were in urgent conversation and debate but for whom there was still hope for a coherent unity.

CHAPTER FIVE

Noah in the *Genesis Apocryphon* and Other Aramaic Texts

*Again I blessed him because he had mercy upon the earth,
and because he removed and destroyed from upon it all
who work violence, evil and deceit,
but rescued a righteous man for . . . all creation, for his own sake.*
Genesis Apocryphon (1Q20 XI, 11–14)

Introduction

Noah, as he was presented in the Hebrew composition of *Jubilees*, was a righteous priest in a covenant with God that prefigured the Mosaic one, and he represented an exemplary, archetypical Torah-obedient Jew like Moses. It is Moses, however, who received the fullest revelation concerning Israel's past, present, and future both in the earthly and the heavenly realms. When the language of the conversation changes to Aramaic, however, Noah is transfigured into a figure much more like Enoch, a visionary figure and a dreamer and one in whom God confides.

In 4QTestament of Qahat and 4QVisions of Amram, texts in the Aramaic Levi tradition, Noah is situated in a line of a particular kind of priest who ably transmits priestly lore but finds himself outside of the land. 4Qpseudo-Daniel[a-c] ar includes Noah in a particular retelling of history recounted to a foreign king in Babylon and the highly enigmatic Naissance de Noé[a-c] attests a substantial number of characteristics shared by Noah and other noteworthy characters elsewhere in the Qumran writings.

Finally, the *Genesis Apocryphon* (1Q20) creates a "composite Noah" by selecting and adapting known traditions. However, the extant text does not attest covenant, sinful inclination, repentance, oaths, blessings, and curses as *Jubilees* does but, instead, recasts Noah in a way that is distinct from its Hebrew disputant. In 1Q20, Noah assumes the dual characters of the visionary Enoch and priestly Levi but in ways that are not accountable to or restrained by Mosaic Torah.

Texts and Observations

In the Aramaic Levi and Aramaic Daniel Traditions

The one extant copy of 4QTestament of Qahat (4Q542) is dated paleographically to the last quarter of the second century B.C.E.[1] and was, therefore, copied after *Jubilees* was composed but before the extant copy of the *Genesis Apocryphon*. In it, Qahat exhorts his son, Amram, to avoid intermingling and to be careful with the inheritance, teachings, and writings passed down from their ancestors Abraham, Isaac, Jacob, and Levi. Noah's name does not survive in the extant text but, as Michael Stone argues, 4Q542 "stresses a cardinal point, the descent of priestly teaching from Abraham and eventually, according to Aramaic Levi, from Noah."[2]

The visions and words of Amram, grandson of Levi, survive in six copies of 4QVisions of Amram (4Q543–548), attesting to a high level of interest in this document. The fragments follow the chronology of the Samaritan Pentateuch and copies range in date from the second part of the second century B.C.E. to the turn of the era.[3] Egypt figures largely in the texts as the literary setting for Levi's immediate descendants who lived outside the land"; intermarriage is a concern, as is the proper transmission of priestly practice.[4] In this text, Noah is one of a priestly line of which Levi and Moses are successors:

> [... o]ffering 2 [... that you] will offer thus 3 [... and af]ter him Noah 4 [...] f6.1 [...] he will be h[oly ...] 2 [...] burn incense up[on ...] 3 [... befo]re God and sins [they will forgive ...] 4 [... fo]rever and fore[ver ...] (4Q547 5 1–4; 6 1–4).

> [...] 2 [...]all that Levi his son offered up[on the altar ...] 3 [... which] I said to you, upon the altar of stone[s ...] (4Q547 8 1–3).

> [...] 2 [...]saved[...] 3 [... and Mos]es built [an altar ...] 4 [...] on Mount Sinai [...] 5 [... you shall sacrifice] your great [cattle] on the bronze altar [...] 6 [...] his son shall be exalted as priest over all the children of the world. Then [...] 7 [... he will be anoint]ed and his sons after him for all the eternal generations in righ[eousness] (א)[שט]דרי עלמין בקו). (4Q547 9 1–6)

---

1. DJD XXXI.

2. Michael E. Stone, "The Axis of History at Qumran," in *Pseudepigraphic Perspectives: The Apocrypha and Pseudepigrapha in Light of the Dead Sea Scrolls: Proceedings of the International Symposium of the Orion Center for the Study of the Dead Sea Scrolls and Associated Literature 12–14 January 1997* (ed. E. G. Chazon and M. E. Stone; STDJ 31; Leiden: Brill, 1999), 137.

3. DJD XXXI. Émile Puech posits a dependence of *Jubilees* on this text (DJD XXXI, 283–88).

4. 4Q547 1–2 III, 7–8; 4Q542 1 I, 5–9.

The priestly line continues for "eternal generations of righteousness," a phrase that roughly parallels *Qahat* (4Q542 1 I, 3–4) and echoes the *Birth of Noah* in which the דרי קושטא would arise in the eschaton (4Q204 5 II, 28/*1 En.* 107:1). This phrase or its equivalent, "generations (דור) of righteousness (צדיק/ צדק)," are not extant in Qumran Hebrew. In fact, the two words are found together in biblical Hebrew only in verses describing Noah as righteous (צדיק) in his generation (דור) (Gen 6:9; 7:1) and in Psalm 14, a psalm that has extensive linguistic and thematic parallels to the Genesis narrative.[5] The phrase "eternal generations of righteousness" therefore characterizes a concept preserved in Aramaic that visualizes generations of righteous ones that stretch not only far ahead into the future but also far back into the past before Mount Sinai, all the way to Noah, who was a "righteous one" in his generation.

For the writer, the figures of Qahat and Amram linked Levi genealogically to Moses and Aaron, priests of this ancient "priestly lineage" that authoritatively transmitted properly priestly practice at a time when Israel was in Egypt and not in the possession of "their" land. Already in the testamentary wisdom poem in the *Aramaic Levi Document*, the figure of Levi stressed reading, writing, and the teaching of wisdom so that his progeny would not be strangers in "every land and country" to which they would go (*ALD* 13:7–15).[6] Specifically now, in 4Q547, the claim to possess priestly authoritative teaching rested on an authority as ancient as Noah himself.

The Aramaic 4Qpseudo-Daniel texts (4Q243–245) name Enoch (4Q243 9 1), Noah (4Q244 8 2–3), and Qahat (4Q243 28 1; 4Q245 1 I, 5) together with references to a transmitted "writing"[7] and "paths of righteousness" (אורחת קושטא) (4Q243 7 3) in a literary setting outside of "the land." Daniel selectively recounts Israel's history to King Belshazzar in Babylon and mentions Noah: "after the flood [. . .N]oah from [Mount] Lubar" (4Q244 8 2–3).

The official editors decided to separate 4Q243–244 from 4Q245, reasoning that the latter recounts an "internal history of Israel" while 4Q243–244 view "Israel in the context of universal history."[8] However, although "internal history" and "universal history" may be appropriate terms for a movement that recounted its internal history beginning with Abraham (cf. CD III, 2), use of these terms

---

5. See parallels to Gen 6 in Ps 14 and also evidence that the psalm was read alongside Gen 6 in wisdom traditions (cf. 4Q416 1 10–16). The wise are contrasted to those who have "no knowledge" and who "eat up my people" (14:3). The fools are corrupt (שחת) (14:1); God looks down . . . to see (ראה) . . . if there are any who are wise (משכיל) (14:2); they [evildoers] shall be in terror (פחד) but God is "with the generation of the righteous (בדור צדיק)" (14:5).

6. On "writings" and "books," see 4Q545 1a I, 1; cf. 4Q543 1a-c 1; 4Q547 9 8; 4Q537 1+2+3 3 and 4Q542 1 II, 12.

7. "Daniel [. . .] a writing that was given [. . .] Qahat" (4Q245 1 I, 4–5).

8. J. Collins and P. Flint, DJD XXII, 133. 4Q243–245 are Herodian, dated to the early first century C.E. The composition can be no earlier that 142 B.C.E. and the *terminus ad quem* may be soon after Simon's death in 135 (DJD XXII, 158).

may create a false dichotomy for *other* groups that claimed Enoch and Noah as part of their "internal history." Those Qumran texts containing traditions about Enoch, Noah, Levi, Amram, and Qahat apparently did not differentiate between "Israel's history" and "primeval history."[9] Even so, the tradents must have recognized that Noah did not belong to Israel alone. In any case, a version of history that included Noah, ancestor of all humanity, was perceived by the author to be a suitable version to recount in Aramaic to a foreign king.

4QApocryphon of Levi (4Q540–541) presents a priestly teacher who suffers slander in times marked by deceit[10] and violence (שקר וחמס) and in which people go astray (טעה). This teacher transmits wisdom, teaches from and writes books, makes "atonement (יכפר) for all those of his generation," and his "teaching is like the will of God."[11] While Noah is not mentioned, Aramaic Levi priestly traditions that included Noah as a priestly ancestor undergo development in this text.

"Deceit and violence" echoes the Enochic *Apocalypse of Weeks* in which Weeks 2 and 7—the days of Noah and the days of the writer—are marked by "deceit and violence" (שקרא וחמסא).[12] It also parallels the *Genesis Apocryphon*, in which a priestly Noah, after offering an "atoning-for-the-land" sacrifice, thanks God for destroying all of the workers of "violence (חמסא), evil and deceit (שקרא)" (1Q20 XI, 13–14).

Beginning with Jean Starcky, the general scholarly consensus has identified the figure in 4Q541 as an eschatological high priest. Starcky dismisses an identification with the Teacher of Righteousness, "Mais nous n'avons pas relevé d'allusions convaincantes au Maître de Justice," asserting instead "que est certainement le grand prêtre de l'ère messianique."[13] Starcky understood 4Q541 to be "une recension du texte primitif" of *T. Levi*[14] with which it has close parallels and which clearly speaks of Levi as an eschatological messianic high priest (*T. Levi* 17:11–18:4). Émile Puech follows Starcky in reading 4Q541 anachronistically from the perspective of *T. Levi*, comparing 4Q541 9 1 with *T. Levi* 18:3–4.[15] Scholars continue to discuss the apocalyptic nature of the text and what *kind* of escha-

---

9. This is a term used by the editors (DJD XXII, 136). See also 1 Chr 1:4 and Ezek 14:14, 20, in which Noah is listed among Israel's ancestors.

10. For an Aramaic interpretation of a Levi tradition, see *Tg. Ps.-Jon.* Mal 2:6a: "The instruction of truth (תורת אמת) was in his [Levi's] mouth and no deceit (שקר) was found on his lips." False teaching also plagued the *Yaḥad* sectarians (1QH[a] XII, 5–27; CD I, 10–18; 4Q169 3–4 II, 8; 1QpHab X, 9–12; 4Q171 1–2 I, 17–28).

11. 4Q541 9 I, 1–7; 4Q540 1 1; 4Q541 2 II, 3; 4Q541 2 II, 8; 3 1; 4Q541 6 1, 3; 4Q541 2 I, 3; 7 4; 9 I, 2. 4QTJacob? ar (4Q537) shares vocabulary with other Aramaic texts that contain Enoch-Noah-Levi traditions: the righteous (צדיקיא), remnant (ישתארון), deceit (שקר), and oppression (עקה) (4Q537 1+2+3 2–4).

12. 4Q212 1 III, 25/*1 En.* 93:4 and 4Q212 1 IV, 14/*1 En.* 91:11.

13. Jean Starcky, "Les quatre étapes du messianisme," *RB* 70 (1963): 481–505, here 492.

14. Ibid., 490.

15. DJD XXXI.

tological high priest this figure was;[16] however, the question whether the priest was perceived to be eschatological at all in 4Q540–541 needs to be revisited.

As discussed in chapter 3, the *Aramaic Levi Document* cannot be considered an earlier recension of *T. Levi*. Furthermore, this study has already highlighted an ongoing hermeneutic of reinterpretation and recontextualizing of source materials in later texts that utilized them. Therefore, *T. Levi*, although possibly dependent on the *ALD*, may have recontextualized and reinterpreted its traditions with the addition of an eschatological insertion.[17] This hypothesis is strengthened when the context of the parallels is considered.

In *T. Levi*, a priest arises in Week 7, darkness is removed, and lawlessness ends, Beliar is bound and the people are returned to "Eden" (*T. Levi* 18). In 4Q541, while darkness vanishes, "deceit and violence" persist during the priest's term of office and he is attacked by slander and lies. In the extant text, 4Q541's priest has not been vindicated as has the Levi priest, who undergoes an eschatological transformation in *T. Levi*.

If times of "deceit and violence" in 4Q541 echo Week 7 of the *AW*, then the figure represented may not be an eschatological character at all. He would more likely be a teaching figure within a merged "Aramaic Enoch" and "Aramaic Levi" priestly lineage known to the writer, which named Noah and Levi as priestly ancestors. If so, the parallels between Levi traditions and Noah traditions could be sought and a common set of traits found that characterized a certain *line* of priests rather than only a particular individual. It might also be posited that Noah was re-created as an archetype with an ideal set of characteristics actually patterned after a known person or group. This next text attests numerous shared family traits attributed to an unnamed figure who was "related" to various other literary characters within this lineage.

4QNAISSANCE DE NOÉ AR[18]: CHOSEN ONE OF GOD

The figure in the so-called Naissance de Noé texts has been variously named Noah, Enoch, Enoch *redivivus*, Melchizedek, eschatological high priest, or a messiah, as scholars have struggled to match the descriptors in the text to a fig-

---

16. See John J. Collins, *Apocalypticism in the Dead Sea Scrolls* (London/New York: Routledge, 1997), 86–87, 157; George J. Brooke, "The *Apocryphon of Levi*ᵇ? and the Messianic Servant High Priest," in *The Dead Scrolls and the New Testament* (Minneapolis: Fortress, 2005), 150.

17. See discussion by Boccaccini on another eschatological insertion into the *Epistle* (*Beyond the Essene Hypothesis: The Parting of the Ways between Qumran and Enochic Judaism* [Grand Rapids: Eerdmans, 1998], 105–13).

18. Translations are adapted from Edward Cook in *The Dead Sea Scrolls Reader*, Part 3, *Parabiblical Texts* (ed. D. W. Parry and E. Tov; Leiden: Brill, 2005). Some readings are accepted from DJD XXXI.

ure that is known from other scrolls.[19] If a post-164 B.C.E. compositional date is accepted,[20] the writer may have had access to Levi, Noah, and Enoch traditions that had found their way into the *Aramaic Levi Document*, the earlier Enochic books, and *Jubilees*.

Joseph A. Fitzmyer was the first to identify the figure with Noah, noting the contemporary fascination with the birth of Noah.[21] Florentino García Martínez marshaled further support, citing the transmission of books and legacy from Enoch through to Noah in other texts (*Jub.* 4:17-22; *1 En.* 82:1; *Jub.* 7:38), Noah's longevity, (4Q534 1 I, 7), and knowledge of secrets.[22] Concerning Noah as the "elect," García Martínez notes that in the Enochic writings "the notion of justice and election are intimately bound together"[23] and that it is, therefore, "possible to understand the transition of Noah's traditional title from 'The Just' to 'The Elect.'" He goes on to say, "the identification of the mysterious personage with Noah rests on a series of indications" but that the "cumulative evidence seems convincing," adding the proviso that "none of these elements offers a final proof."[24]

VanderKam does not find the case for identifying Noah with "the chosen one" very compelling, cautioning "the text seems to be little more than a description of an extraordinary individual."[25] A closer examination of the characteristics of the figure in 4Q534-536 in parallel with characteristics of other figures in other texts may demonstrate that, while it would be hasty to make identification of the "chosen one" with any *one* figure, the extraordinary number of parallels between the characteristics of the unnamed person with characteristics of Noah as they appear elsewhere in the Dead Sea Scrolls is suggestive of at least kind of connection to Noah or to a lineage that named Noah.

---

19. For discussions on this question, see DJD XXXI, 118-20; Florentino García Martínez, "4QMess ar and the Book of Noah," in *Qumran and Apocalyptic: Studies on the Aramaic Texts from Qumran* (ed. R. Aguirre and F. García Martínez; STDJ 9; Leiden: Brill, 1992), 1-44, here 17-19; James R. Davila, "4QMess ar (4Q534) and Merkavah Mysticism," in *Qumran Studies Presented to Eugene Ulrich on His Sixtieth Birthday*, special issue, *DSD* 5 (1998): 367-81, here 367-68, 379.

20. DJD XXXI, 126, 131, 155, 162. That composition could be prior to Jubilees, possibly predating the *BW*, see García Martínez, "4QMess ar," 3 n. 9.

21. Joseph A. Fitzmyer, "The Aramaic 'Elect of God' Text from Qumran Cave 4" in *Essays on the Semitic Background of the New Testament* (ed. J. A. Fitzmyer; University of Montana: Scholars Press, 1974), 127-60, here 158-59. Starcky agreed ("Le Maitre de Justice et Jésus," in *Le Monde de la Bible* 4 (1978): 53-57. Cf. *1 En.* 106-8; *Jub.* 4-10; 1Q20 II; and 1Q19 3.

22. Regarding a "Noachic insertion" in *1 En.* 68:1, see García Martínez, "4QMess ar," 21.

23. Note *1 En.* 1:1; 93:10 and the reduction from the title "the Just and the Elect" (53:6) to simply "the Elect" (40:5; 45:3 and elsewhere).

24. García Martínez, 4QMess ar," 19, 24.

25. James C. VanderKam, "Mantic Wisdom in the Dead Sea Scrolls," *DSD* 4 (1997): 336-353 [345-46].

TABLE: PARALLELS TO NOAH IN 4Q534–536

4Q534–536	Linguistic/Thematic Parallels
Physical characteristics of unnamed man: red hair, "the mole on the man (גבר)," marks (4Q534 1 I, 1–3; 1 II + 2 1–5), weight of 35[1] shekels (4Q535 3 3)	**Physical characteristics noted?** Noah has white and red skin and white hair (*1 En.* 106 (cf. 1Q20 II)
"knowledge will be in his heart" (דעה בלבה) (4Q534 1 I, 3)	**Who has knowledge in his heart?** Noah knows and "makes known" (1Q20 V, 16)
	"Instructor" (1QS XI, 15)
"he will know the three books" (ינדע תלתת ספריא) (4Q534 1 I, 5)	**Who had knowledge of books?** Levi and descendants 4Q213 1 II, 8–12; 4Q542 1 II, 9–13; 4Q541 2 I, 6
	Who wrote books/was a writer? Noah (*ALD* 10:10; 1Q20 V, 29; *Jub.* 10:13) Enoch (11Q12 4 1–3/*Jub.* 4:16–24; 1Q20 XIX, 25) Qahat (4Q542 1 II, 9–13) Amram (4Q545 1a I, 1) Moses (*Jub.* 1:5)
"his wisdom (חכמה) shall come to all people" (4Q534 1 I, 7–8)	**Who is wise/possesses wisdom?** Noah (1Q20 VI, 4)
	Enoch (4Q212 1 II, 22–23/*1 En.* 92:1; 1Q20 XIX, 25)
	Levi; Joseph as an example of wisdom (4Q213 1 I, 9–21; 4Q213a 1 14)
	Amram (4Q543 2 a-b 2–4)
	The elect (בחיר) (4Q212 1 IV, 12–13/*1 En.* 93:10)
	Ones who observe priest's teaching: (4Q541 7 4–6)[26]
"he will know the paths (שבילי) of the sages—seers (חכמין חזין)" (4Q534 1 I, 6)	**Who follows/exhorts others to follow the right kind of paths (שביל)?** Noah (1Q20 VI, 2)
	Chosen of Israel (4Q275 1 1–3)

---

26. Cf. "wise one" in 4Q541 2 II, 6; 4QVisions of Amram[f]: "Indeed every fool and wicked man [is dark] and every [wise] and honest man is light" (4Q548 1 II-2 12).

4Q534-536	Linguistic/Thematic Parallels
"secrets (רז) of the brothers[27] will sadden him"; "he will know (ידע) the secrets of men…of living things (חי)" (4Q534 1 I, 7–8); perception (טעם) of secrets (4Q536 2 II + 3 9)	**Who knows (ידע) secrets/mysteries (רז)** Noah (1Q20 VI, 11–12) Enoch (4Q204 5 II, 26/*1 En.* 106:19)[28] The "son of understanding" (4Q417 1 I, 18–19) Teacher of Righteousness (1QpHab VII, 4–5); speaker in *Hodayot* (1QH IX, 23; XII, 28; XV, 30)
"he will reveal (גלה) secrets (רז)" (4Q536 2 I + 3 8–9)	**Who reveals mysteries/secrets?**[29] The Watchers to their wives (4Q201 1 IV, 5/4Q202 1 III, 5/*1 En.* 8:3) Those who reveal mysteries to the Gentiles (4Q270 2 II, 13) The Instructor (משכיל) to the ones who have chosen the "Way" (1QS IX, 17–19)
"the secret/knowledge which he transmitted (מסר) to me among the numbers (מנין) of the remnant (שאר)" (4Q536 2 II + 3 13)	**Who is the remnant?** Noah (Gen 7:23; *1 En.* 106) Isaac's seed (4Q219 II, 33/*Jub.* 21:2) Jacob's (?) upright and righteous progeny (4Q537 1+2+3 1) Community as remnant (CD I, 4; 4Q174 1–3 II, 2)
Chosen one of God (בחיר אלהא) (4Q534 1 I, 10)	**Who is the Chosen of God**[30] Noah(?) (בחירי כי אל); the one who is also glorified among the "sons of heaven" (1Q19 15 2)

---

27. Puech proposes ר[ז]י [אחין] rather than the alternative רז ו[אחין], remarking that these mysteries "concernant les frères, probablement en relation avec le déluge qui ne pourra pas ne pas affecter Noé" (DJD XXXI,139–40).

28. The occurrence is within the context of Noah's birth narrative and Enoch's prediction of the flood from which Noah will be saved.

29. Normally, God reveals mysteries (1QH XXIV, 27; XXVI, 15; 4Q416 2 III, 18).

30. Cf. 4Q212 1 II, 22–23/*1 En.* 92:1. Puech comments: "L'expression בחיר אלהא (4Q534 1 ii 10) est inconnue de l'Ancien Testament, la plus proche est בחיר יהוה en 2 S 21:6 mais le text n'est pas sans poser de problèmes (faute pour בהר?). La forme suffixée בחירי 'mon Élu' s'applique à Moïse (Ps 106:23), David (Ps 89:4), au Serviteur (Is 42:1), à Israël (Is 43:20; 45:4). L'hèbreu qumranien connaît le pluriel בחירי אל en 1QpHab X 13 désignant les membres de la

4Q534–536	Linguistic/Thematic Parallels
	Amram as [the chosen] of God (4Q543 2 a-b 2–4)
	Those blasphemed by Spreader of Lies (1QpHab X, 9–13); those under attack by the Man of the Lie (4Q171 3–10 IV,14)
	Instructor is "the chosen of mankind" (בחירי אדם)" (1QS XI, 16)
"all their designs against him will cease (סוף) and the dominion(?)[31] of all living things (ומסרת כול חייא) will be great" (4Q534 1 I, 9)	**Who will have dominion?** Noah (1Q20 XI, 3)
"write these words of mine in a book (כתב) that will not wear out" (536 2 II + 3 12)	**Whose words/acts recorded in a book?** Noah (1Q20 V, 29; XV, 20) Enoch (1Q20 XIX, 25; 4Q203 8 4; 4Q204 1 VI, 19) Jacob (4Q537 9 8) Levi (4Q541 14 3) Qahat (4Q542 1 II, 12) Amram (4Q543 1a-c 1) Michael (4Q529 1 1)

The figure in 4Q534–536 is of remarkable appearance at birth (4Q534 1 I, 1–3; 5Q535 3 3) although the physical description does not match Noah's appearance at birth in *1 En.* 106 (cf. 1Q20 II). He has knowledge of writing and the "three books"[32] (4Q534 1 I, 5; cf. 1Q20 V, 29) and his wisdom (חכמה) "shall come

---

Communauté (voir 1Q19 15 2: singulier/pluriel?) et l'araméen avec suffixe [הוא בחירה] en 4QSy 53 et l'expression תמיניא לבחיר en 4Q558 (une figure messianique?)" (DJD XXXI, 123). Enoch is chosen from among the sons of the earth. "Chosen of God" does not appear in HB but the "chosen" is variously the Servant of Yahweh (Isa 42:1), Moses (Ps 106:23), David (Ps 89:4), and the people of Israel (Isa 43:20; 45:4).

31. Concerning the *crux interpretum* ומסרת כול חייא, J. Carmignac proposes "dominion" (שרר) (DJD XXXI, 141).

32. To which "three books" does this writing refer? Puech plausibly suggests "d'y voir les trois livres d'Henoch connus de *Jub.* 4:16–24 qui seront source de science et de sagesse" and which include the *AB* (*1 En.* 72–82), *DV* (*1 En.* 83–90:40) and *BW* (*1 En.* 6–16 and 17–36) (DJD XXXI, 137–38). In *BE*, Milik notes that in the Samaritan *Kitâb al-'Asâtar*, three works of antediluvian wisdom ascribed to Enoch—the three Books of Creation—are learned by Noah, the "Book of the Signs," the "Book of Astronomy," and the "Book of the Wars which is the Book of the Generation of Adam." He concludes that "[w]e can recognize in these without much difficulty the earliest compositions attributed to Enoch: the sacred calendars...the astronomical treatise (En. 72–82), and the Visions of Enoch (En. 6–19)."

to all people" (4Q534 1 I, 7–8; 1Q20 VI, 4). He knows and walks in the right paths (שביל)³³ (4Q534 1 I, 6; cf. 1Q20 VI, 2). He knows and reveals (גלה) secrets (רז) to the remnant (שאר) (4Q534 1 I, 7–8; 4Q536 2 II + 3 9–13; 4Q536 2 I + 8–9; cf. Gen 7:23; *1 En.* 106; 1Q20 VI, 11–12). He is the "chosen one of God" (בחיר אלהא) (4Q534 1 I, 10; cf. 1Q19 15 2) who experiences opposition and lives in "days of wickedness" (רשעא) in which the works are compared to those of the "Watchers" (4Q536 2 II + 3 11–13; 4Q534 1 I, 9; 4Q534 1 II + 2 15–17). He instructs his listeners to "write these words of mine in a book" (536 2 II + 3 12). The word סוף links the "designs" of enemies to metaphorical floodwaters. "All their designs against him will cease (סוף)" (4Q534 1 I, 9) echoes or foreshadows—depending on the placement of the fragments—"water shall cease" (4Q534 1 II + 2 13–14).

Taken together and compared to other Noah interpretations in the Dead Sea Scrolls, if this personage is *not* Noah, he is at least related! Any one of these attributes may be found in connection with often multiple figures—including Enoch, Levi, Qahat, Amram, or even the Teacher of Righteousness—and it is difficult to identify any one characteristic exclusively with Noah. For example, Edward Cook notes the striking parallels between the "chosen one" in 4Q534–536 and the mighty priest in 4Q541, "There a prophecy is given of a mighty priest who will arise and 'reveal hidden mysteries' and whose 'teaching is like the will of God'— much like the 'chosen one' of this text who 'will reveal secrets like the Most High' . . . and whose 'wisdom shall come to all peoples.'"³⁴

Although Cook may not be correct in identifying this figure as a coming messiah, the parallels he draws out demonstrate that the texts and referents may be intimately connected. As in 4Q541, the personage in 4Q534–536 may be fashioned after someone known to the author, someone who shared a set of "ideal characteristics" with reinterpreted biblical characters in the Dead Sea Scrolls. This set of characteristics may not have been intended to be limited to any one character but may have applied to an entire lineage of exceptional people, chosen by God, through whom wisdom and esoteric knowledge were properly transmitted from Enoch to Noah, Levi, and through to the wise and inspired teachers of the writer's day.

The *Genesis Apocryphon*: An Enochic and Levitic Noah?

Text

Extant in one copy found in Cave 1, the Noah narrative in the *Genesis Apocryphon* (1Q20) reflects multiple "parents" and partners in conversation and dispute over, in particular, the nature and character of the priesthood as it was expressed

---

33. Puech reconstructs this as שב[י]לי חכ[מ]ין חזין appealing, in part, to parallels in Noah's speech in 1Q20: "paths (שבילי) of truth" and "paths of violence" (1Q20 VI, 2, 5) (DJD XXXI, 112).

34. WAC (2005), 539–40.

in Aramaic as opposed to Hebrew.³⁵ 1Q20 interacts with traditions transmitted in Hebrew found in Genesis,³⁶ *Jubilees*, wisdom texts, and the Hebrew prophets but also engages with traditions transmitted in Aramaic such as those found in the Aramaic Enoch books and the *Aramaic Levi Document*.

The text is fragmentary, and it would be tempting to read too much into the gaps and lacunae. Yet the words and phrases that are extant are high suggestive. Vocabulary and themes introduced in the earliest extant columns of 1Q20 and repeated in the Noah and Abram narratives betray a possible intentional unity; the adaptation and integration of themes introduced from sources also outside of Genesis indicate a particular "exegetical foresight" indicating that the author was a "careful reader as well as a careful composer."³⁷

Introduction of Themes? (0, 1 – I, 29)

5 [. . . in the da]y of your wrath (רגז) you will be strong (תקף) and will be established (קום). Who is he 6 [who . . .] the heat of your wrath? 7 [. . .] the humble and lowly quivering and trembling 8 [. . .] And now, as is clear, we are bound (אסר) (1Q20 0, 5–8). 13 [. . .] for we are bound [before] a fire that has been seen (1Q20 0, 13).

There is further reference to wrath (0, 10–11) and to coming obliteration (מחה) (0, 12; 0, 15). Women (נקבתא) are mentioned as are medicines (סמין), magicians (כשפין), diviners (חרש), and wickedness (רשעא) (I, 1–13). Finally, there is a curse on all flesh (קלל) (I, 25). Most obviously, "heat" and "fire" anticipate an eschatological fiery judgment, but the language of "women," the ones who are "bound," and the presence of evil and wickedness evoke the context within which Noah is introduced both in Genesis and in the *Book of Watchers*. "Obliteration" is later echoed in Noah's eschatological vision where the wicked are hurled onto the fire (X, 10–12).

More subtle is the use of תקף as an introduction of a leitmotif. In Noah's vision, the wind blows with destructive strength (תקוף) on the olive tree (1Q20 XIII, 16).³⁸ In the Abram portion of 1Q20, Pharaoh takes Sarah from Abram with force (תוקף) (1Q20 XX, 14), and God responds with afflictions that grow more

---

35. Editions of the text or portions of it include N. Avigad and Y. Yadin, *A Genesis Apocryphon: A Scroll from the Wilderness of Judaea* (Jerusalem: Magnes and Heikhal Ha-Sefer, 1956); DJD 1; Matthew Morgenstern, Elisha Qimron, and Daniel Sivan, "The Hitherto Unpublished Columns of the Genesis Apocryphon," *AbrN* 33 (1995): 30–54; Jonas C. Greenfield and Elisha Qimron, "The Genesis Apocryphon Col. XII," *AbrNSup* 3 (1992): 70–77.

36. The harmonizations found in 1Q20 are similar to those found in the Samaritan Pentateuch. See Moshe J. Bernstein, "Rearrangement, Anticipation and Harmonization as Exegetical Features in the Genesis Apocryphon," *DSD* 3 (1996): 38, 52.

37. Ibid., 38, 56–57.

38. Cf. the parallel wordplay in the Hebrew 1QBook of Noah. The wicked prevail (גבר) on the earth (1Q19 1 2), but God is the "Mightiest of the Mighty" (גבור גבורים) (1Q19bis 2 1).

severe (תקפו וגברו) (1Q20 XX, 18). Finally, God promises Abram, "I shall be your support, your strength (תקף)... against any foe mightier (לתקיף) than you" (1Q20 XXII, 31).[39] This persistent usage of תקף hints at a thematic unity acknowledging a battle between opponents of strength: "waters" and Watchers or enemies, on one hand, and God, together with his chosen, on the other.

This "curse (קלל) on all (כול) flesh (בשר)" (I, 25) follows mention of "women" and "diviners." It is an anomaly elsewhere within the Hebrew Bible and the Qumran corpus[40] but the expression "all flesh" (כל־בשר) does weave through the Genesis flood narrative. Corrupted "all flesh" is destroyed by God, but God preserves his covenant with those he preserves.[41] The Hebrew prophets envisioned judgment on כל־בשר by fire or sword.[42] The simplest explanation, in keeping with the imminent and eschatological judgment themes in the *Genesis Apocryphon*, is that the "curse on all flesh" is a phrase meant to refer to both types of judgments, primordial and eschatological.[43]

Therefore, whether or not other columns preceded the ones extant in 1Q20, cols. 0–I function well to anticipate Noah and his progeny, the ones who would be strong and prevail in the flood and heat of imminent and eschatological judgments. Next, cols. II-V introduce Noah, the first survivor of cosmic judgment.

Origin of Noah: Seed and True Planting (II, 1 – V, 27)

The similarities of the birth narrative in *1 En.* 106–107 to that in 1Q20 II-V are immediately obvious, but the differences are particularly noteworthy with respect to the "truth" about the origin of the seed and planting. Lamech, worried that this "seed" (זרעא) was from the Watchers, demanded Bitenosh to tell him all "in truth" (בקושטא) whether the conception was from the "sons of heaven" (בני שמין) (1Q20 II, 1–7). The "sons of heaven," who make their appearance in the birth narrative and then again in Noah's adulthood, are likely a synonym[44] for "sons of gods" (בני־האלהים) (Gen 6:2) already known in the Enochic corpus.[45]

---

39. Cf. Qahat's instruction to "Grasp tightly (אתקפו) the judgments of Abraham and the good deeds of Levi" and to avoid intermingling (4Q542 1 I, 8–9).

40. The *ground* is cursed (ארור) in Gen 3:17 (cf. 5:29); God promises Noah that he will never again curse (קלל) the ground in Gen 8:21.

41. See also Gen 6:12, 13, 17, 19; 7:15, 16, 21; 8:17; 9:11, 15, 16, 17.

42. For judgment on כל־בשר by fire or sword, see Isa 66:16; Jer 25:31; 45:5; Ezek 21:4–5. God's sword would come against כל־בשר in order to cut off both the righteous and the wicked from the land.

43. See Philip R. Davies on קלל in Gen 8:21 as a "counter-curse" to resolve the original, negative curse in Gen 3:17 and 4:11 ("Sons of Cain," in *A Word of Season: Essays in Honour of William McKane* [ed. James D. Martin and Philip R. Davies; JSOTSup 42; Sheffield: JSOT Press, 1986], 36–37).

44. The writer is generous with synonyms for the suspected father: Watchers, Holy Ones, Nephilim, or the "sons of heaven."

45. Cf. 4Q204 1 VI, 11b–12/*1 En.* 14:3; *1 En.* 106:5. Cf. the "wicked *Yaḥad*" and the uncleanness of the "sons of heaven" (4Q181 1 2). Not necessarily pejorative, the term is also

Bitenosh responds that the "planting of [this] fruit" (נצבת פריא) is Lamech's, appealing to her "heat" and "pleasure during lovemaking" (1Q20 II, 9–16), but Lamech, not satisfied, goes to Enoch through his father, Methuselah. Enoch affirms that the child is, in truth (בקשט), Lamech's son (1Q20 V, 3–10). If, within the narrative, Lamech was not going to believe his wife in the first place, then what was the purpose of including Bitenosh's speech? Were these just racy details added to spice up the narrative? Later, we will explore an intriguing possibility regarding the author's purpose for telling the story in just this way.

The deeds of the "sons of heaven" are revealed to Noah in a vision prior to judgment (1Q20 VI, 11)[46] but, in this early part of the narrative, 1Q20 confirms that Noah is not of their lineage. Rather, he is born as the true seed and true planting into a time when the deeds of the "sons of heaven" are provoking God's judgment.

"Seed" and "planting" are not expressions found in the accounts of Noah's birth in Genesis nor in the Enochic *Birth* but may be a development from the *Book of Watchers*, in which Noah is the one *from which* a plant (נצבה) would be planted that would be established (קום) forever.[47] The reference in col. II anticipates Noah's later claim that he himself was "planted for righteousness" (לקושט נציבת)" from conception (1Q20 VI, 1) as well as anticipating Noah's vision that his progeny or seed (זרע) would emerge as the righteous planting (לנצבת קושט) that would surely be established (קום)[48] for eternity (לעלמים) (1Q20 XIV, 9–14).[49]

One line from the Enochic *Birth*, "This boy is truly (בקשוט), and without deception (כדבין), his son" (4Q204 5 II, 20/*1 En.* 107:2) is emphasized in a leitmotif that wends its way through 1Q20's version of Noah's birth, setting up a reinterpretation of Noah's birth and a redefinition of his righteousness in col. VI. The root קשט preceded by preposition ב, imploring the listener to speak or know "in truth," appears fully eight times with respect to the parentage of Lamech's son.[50] Truth and deception are therefore set up as opposing values at the same time as the reader or hearer is being prepared to anticipate further development of קושט in the narrative to follow.

---

used synonymously in the Qumran corpus for "angels." Cf. 1Q19, where a figure is glorified among the sons of heaven (1Q19 13–14 3). See also 1QS IV, 22; 1QH[a] XI, 22.

46. Enoch also speaks of the "deeds of [the sons of heaven"] (1Q20 V, 22) and "great violence" (1Q20 V, 18).

47. 4Q201 1 V, 3–4/*1 En.*10:1–3. Once the angels were bound, the giants destroyed, and "perversity" destroyed from the earth, *then* the plant of righteousness (נצבת קושטא) would appear (4Q204 1 V, 3–4/*1 En.* 10:16).

48. This may be an echo of those would be established (קום) in the day of wrath (1Q20 0, 5).

49. Noah exhorts his grandsons to be planted in righteousness (*Jub.* 7:34). "Righteous planting" or "eternal planting" becomes a metaphor for the *Yaḥad* sectarians: 1QH XIV, 14–18; cf. Isa 60:21; 1QS VIII, 5. For "planting of truth" (מטעת האמת), cf. 4Q209 II 30/*Jub.* 21:24; for a planting of truth hidden and not esteemed, see 1QH XVI, 10–11.

50. 1Q20 II, 5, 7, 10, 18, 22; III, 13; V, 8, 9.

Noah, Righteous, Wise, Visionary Priest (V, 29 – XII, 17)

In chapter 3, we viewed the characterization of a priestly Levi in the *Aramaic Levi Document* alongside the characterization of Noah in the *Genesis Apocryphon*. This synoptic view revealed a priestly Noah who was likely patterned after a literary "Levi" archetype and fashioned into a newly interpreted priest like Levi in the *Genesis Apocryphon*.

Columns VI-VII establish Noah's righteousness as the writer re-creates a Noah who had priestly qualities even prior to his postdiluvian atoning sacrifice. This section is introduced by the phrase "Book of the Words of Noah" (V, 29) and contains the first-person speeches that a Second Temple Jew would expect to find in similar "books" such as those purporting to contain speeches by Enoch and Levi. García Martínez takes the heading at face value, claiming that the existence of the lost *Book of Noah* "is now completely certain thanks to the discovery of the heading of this book in a blackened fragment of 1QapGen V, 29."[51]

It must be observed, however, that in all other potential source texts for 1Q20, Noah always speaks or is spoken of in the third person.[52] As stated previously, in light of the lack of evidence elsewhere for first-person speech in the mouth of Noah, it is reasonable to consider that these speeches of Noah are literary innovations in 1Q20. Except in the *Birth of Noah*, the Enochic writers had been largely disinterested in creating expanded traditions surrounding Noah, and the *ALD* cared primarily for the antiquity that Noah lent to the line of priestly transmission.

In the first lines of the "Book of Noah," Noah summarizes his conception and life preceding the flood, making repeated claims to קשט:

> 1 from iniquity (עול), and in the crucible of she who bore me I took root (יעית) for righteousness (לקושט). So, when I emerged from my mother's womb, I was planted (נציבת) for righteousness (לקושט), 2 and it was righteousness (קושטא) that I practiced all of my days. I continued to walk (מהלך) in the paths (שבילי) of the eternal (עלמא) truth (אמת), accompanied by a holy [. . .] 3 righteousness (קושט) hastened (אוחת) on my paths (מסל), and to warn me about the [. . .] of falsehood/*deceit* (שקר) that leads to darkness (חשוך) and to [. . .] 4 [. . .] I bound (אסרת) my loins with a vision of righteousness (קושטא), and wisdom (חכמתא) as a robe [. . .] 5 [. . .] all the paths (שבילי) of violence (חמס). (vacat) 6 Th[e]n I, Noah, became a man; I laid hold of righteousness (בקושטא), and I prevailed (אתקפת) [. . .]. (1Q20 VI, 1–6)

---

51. Florentino García Martínez, "Interpretations of the Flood in the Dead Sea Scrolls," in *Interpretations of the Flood* (ed. F. García Martínez and G. P. Luttikhuizen; Themes in Biblical Narrative 1; Leiden: Brill, 1998), 86–108, here 88–89.

52. Devorah Dimant, "Two 'Scientific' Fictions: The So-Called *Book of Noah* and the Alleged Quotation of *Jubilees* in CD 16:3–4," in *Studies in the Hebrew Bible, Qumran, and the Septuagint Presented to Eugene Ulrich* (ed. P. W. Flint, E. Tov, and J. C. VanderKan; VTSup 101; Leiden/Boston: Brill, 2006), 234.

In col. VI, the meaning of קושט shifts from "in truth" as in the previous columns to "righteousness."[53] That the use of קושט is a deliberate decision on the part of the narrator may be substantiated by the fact that elsewhere in the text, the cognate for the biblical Hebrew term for "righteousness" (צדיקא) is used to describe Noah (1Q20 XI, 14; XV, 23; cf. Gen 6:9; 7:1).[54] Enochic traditions are thus adjusted, creating a bridge back into an enlarged understanding of the biblical language of righteousness.

Columns VI-VII develop themes contained in the birth narrative. Noah's righteousness is affirmed in VI, 1, as he himself is planted for righteousness, setting the stage for his seed (זרע), who would emerge as the righteous planting (לנצבת קושט) that would surely be established (קום)[55] for eternity (לעלמים) (1Q20 XIV, 9-14).[56]

Noah behaves in accordance with the law of the eternal statutes (דת חוק עלמא) (1Q20 VI, 8). He is not of the "sons of heaven" but does see their deeds in a vision (1Q20 VI, 11); in the midst of bloodshed and illegitimate matings, Noah finds great favor (חן) and righteousness (קושט) before the Most High (1Q20 VI, 19-23). Further, language used in col. VI betrays subtle priestly overtones that serve to set up Noah as an incipient priest, or, perhaps better, priest-in-waiting.

"Deceit" (שקר) is suggestive of Weeks 2 and 7 in the *Apocalypse of Weeks*, weeks that were characterized by "deceit (שקר) and violence (חמס)." A targum of Malachi, a later text in its final form but that may contain earlier traditions, locates "deceit" within an Aramaic tradition concerning Levi: "The instruction of truth (אוריתא דקשטא) was in his [Levi's] mouth and no deceit (שקר) was found on his lips; he walked (הליד) before me (קדמי) in integrity and in uprightness and he turned many away from sin (חובא)" (*Tg. Ps.-Jon.* Mal 2:6). קשטא appears here as the Aramaic equivalent of אמת.[57] Most interesting, however, is the interpretative substitution of שקר for the Hebrew עולה. In this targum, a priestly Levi walked before God[58] and there was "no deceit" on his lips.

The targum of Malachi preserves an Aramaic tradition contrasting "deceit" to "righteousness," linking the lack of "deceit" to a lineage of priests that named

---

53. Only the last of six occurrences is preceded by ב.

54. אמת is introduced at V, 2 representing "truth," reserving קושט for "righteousness."

55. This is possibly an echo of those who would be established (קום) in the day of wrath (1Q20 0, 5).

56. In 4QInstruction, an "eternal planting" is plausibly identified with a particular and chosen priesthood. Loren T. Stuckenbruck differentiates between the interpretation of plant in the AW and 4QInstruction ("The Plant Metaphor in Its Inner-Enochic and Early Jewish Context," in *Enoch and Qumran Origins: New Light on a Forgotten Connection* [Grand Rapids: Eerdmans, 2005], 210-12).

57. *Targum Onqelos* substitutes זכי for "righteous" as a descriptor of Noah at Gen 6:9 and 7:1. However, this substitution was commonly used elsewhere in the targums; for example, Zeph 3:5 translates righteous Yahweh as זכא.

58. That Enoch and Noah walked in the "fear of the Lord" (*Tg. Onq.* Gen 5:22; 6:9) is an interpretative step that removes what was probably a troubling anthropomorphism.

Levi. If such a tradition was early and was known to the narrator of 1Q20, then Noah's lack of deceit in 1Q20 may, indeed, credential him as the "right sort" of priest. Like Levi, Noah avoided deceit; like Levi, he had "walked with God" (Gen 6:9; cf. 1Q20 VI, 2–3).

Likewise, the phrase, "paths of eternal truth," was plausibly derived by conflating Malachi 2:6 and Genesis 6:9, thus enduing Noah with a priestly character re-created to resemble Levi as portrayed in Malachi.[59] 1Q20 continues by describing *how* Noah was obedient to "the law of eternal statutes" (דת חוק עלמא)" with respect to the marriages he arranged for his sons (1Q20 VI, 8).[60] To Noah's priestly character is added wisdom. Noah is robed in wisdom (VI, 4) and, following his contemplation of the "walk" of the earth-dwellers, he "knows" and "makes known" something (VI, 16).

Very little remains of cols. VII-IX and the narrative resumes when the ark comes to rest on Ararat: "12 [...] the ark came to rest upon one of the mountains of Ararat. And eternal fire [...] 13 [...] I atoned for all the earth (ועל כול ארעא כולהא כפרת); and a choice [...] 14 the [kid of the goat] first, and after it came [...] I burned the fat upon the fire" (1Q20 X, 12–14).

The context suggests that, because the land was morally defiled by the deeds of the "sons of heaven" (1Q20 VI, 11) and by the blood that the Nephilim had shed (1Q20 VI, 19), a flood had destroyed the earth and its inhabitants. When the text is read chronologically, Noah atones for the land *before* disembarking from the ark, an observation made by Daniel Falk, who further considers "the possibility that the author of *Genesis Apocryphon* regards it as essential that Noah built his altar on the ark specifically because of its *location*. Only one such location could be so compelling; that is, if the ark were seen to have come to rest directly on the rock where the later Temple altar would stand in Jerusalem."[61]

The order of the offerings in the atoning sacrifice may suggest 1Q20's chronological positioning in relation to sectarian texts. John C. Reeves argues that 1Q20 accepts the "ritual procedure and likewise envisions the offering of the חטאת prior to the עולה" as do *Jubilees* and the *Temple Scroll*, an order that differs from the pentateuchal ordinance. This, as Reeves puts it, "suggests that *Genesis*

---

59. See also Ezek 18:9, in which the "righteous" walk in God's statutes.
60. "Eternal statutes" or "perpetual ordinances" (חק-עולם) are largely connected to Aaron and his sons, most notably in the priestly texts of the Hebrew Bible (Exod 30:21; Lev 6:18, 22; 7:34; 10:15; 24:9; Num 18:8, 11, 19). Regarding the "purity of the chosen line" in 1Q20, see James C. VanderKam, "The Granddaughters and Grandsons of Noah," *RevQ* 16 (1993–94): 457–61. Shem has five sons and five daughters in contrast to *Jubilees*, where Japheth was a positive figure and intermarriage "did occur already in this generation between the families of Shem and Japheth" (ibid., 460).
61. Daniel K. Falk, "In the Door of the Ark: Noah's Prayer and Sacrifice in Genesis Apocryphon," (paper presented at the SBL Pacific Northwest regional meeting, Newport, Ore., May 3–5, 2002).

Apocryphon was a sectarian or proto-sectarian product."[62] 1Q20 does not contain elements of the typically sectarian texts, but this does not preclude the possibility that the text did engage with the emerging *Yaḥad* sectarian ideology.

After offering the sacrifice, Noah leaves the ark and walks upon a mountaintop, Eden-like (עדן) paradise that was separate from the land below to which Noah later descended and saw that "the devastation upon the earth was large-scale."[63] In *1 Enoch*, only Enoch sees the "Paradise of Righteousness," an equivalent term for Eden, in which the Tree of Knowledge stood.[64]

These next lines are, arguably, the theme of the entire Noah narrative in 1Q20, "13 Again I blessed him because he had mercy upon the earth, and because he removed and destroyed (אבד) from upon it 14 all who work violence (חמס), evil (רשע) and deceit (שקר), but rescued (פלט) a righteous (צדיקא) man for [. . .] for all creation, for his own sake" (1Q20 XI, 13–14). 1Q20 has, until now, employed קושטא for "righteousness," and so the appearance of the Aramaic cognate צדיקא of the Hebrew צדיק juxtaposed with "wickedness and violence" (רשע and חמס) brings to mind the Genesis text. Noah is now fully distinguished from the "workers of violence, evil, and deceit," and his righteousness is redefined to include characteristics both from Genesis and from the Enochic books. Noah and his seed are poised to inherit this renewed land.

"Covenant," does not appear in the extant text of 1Q20, a fact all the more noteworthy because it occurs fully eight times in connection with Noah in Genesis.[65] A "sign (את) in the cloud" appears (1Q20 XII, 1), which may have been intended to imply the "covenant" (Gen 9:13) or which may be more closely linked to one aspect of covenant, that of past and future judgment.[66] However, in light

---

62. Reeves also cites *Jub.* 2:2–3; 7:3–4; and 11QT XIV; see John C. Reeves, "What Does Noah Offer in 1QapGen X, 15?," *RevQ* 12 (1986): 415–19.

63. 1Q20 XI, 11–12; XII, 9. That עדן may be meant to recall the Garden of Eden, see Moshe J. Bernstein, "From the Watchers to the Flood: Story and Exegesis in the Early Columns of the *Genesis Apocryphon*," in *Reworking the Bible: Apocryphal and Related Texts at Qumran. Proceedings of a Joint Symposium by the Orion Center for the Study of the Dead Sea Scrolls and Associated Literature and the Hebrew University Institute for Advanced Studies Research Group on Qumran, 15–17 January, 2002* (ed. E. G. Chazon, D. Dimant, and R. A. Clements; STDJ 58; Leiden: Brill, 2005), 39–63, here 61.

64. 4Q206 1 XXVI, 21–XXVII, 10/*1 En.* 32:3–6. Cf. Ezek 36:24–36. Once Israel is cleansed by God from all her uncleanness, the desolated land would become like the garden of Eden.

65. Genesis 6:18; 9:9, 11, 12, 13, 15, 16, 17. For a view that the Noah and Abram narratives in 1Q20 included the promise of a specific land as a component of "covenant," see Daniel K. Falk, *The Parabiblical Texts: Strategies for Extending the Scriptures among the Dead Sea Scrolls* (Companion to the Qumran Scrolls 8; LSTS 63; New York: T&T Clark, 2007), 67. It may be that, although a particular and deliberate interpretation of "covenant" may have been in the mind of the author, the author may have had reason to avoid the term itself.

66. See discussion under 4QParaphrase of Genesis and Exodus (4Q422) and 4QAdmonition Based on the Flood (4Q370) regarding the rainbow both as "post-judgment" sign that hinted also at the possibility of future judgments upon later generations of the wicked and as linked to the reestablishment of days and seasons.

of the absence of "covenant" in most of the Enochic books, we might consider the possibility that the narrator also had reasons for avoiding the term in 1Q20. In the extant text, some of the elements normally associated at Qumran with covenant are not present, including confessions and blessings and curses (cf. 4Q508; 1QS I-II). Noah does offer a sacrifice, but it is of the highly specialized "atoning-for-the-land" variety, and God responds by giving Noah dominion over creation.

According to Falk's restoration of 1Q20 IX, 3,[67] Noah was given dominion (שלטנא) while in the ark and presumably over the animals, something he was not explicitly given in Gen 9:1-3, but which recalls the dominion over the animals given to the primeval couple in Gen 1:28-30.[68] This tradition emphasizes Noah's replacement of Adam; dominion that was lost to Adam was now restored to Noah.[69] In 1Q20 XI, 15-19, the "Lord of Heaven" gives Noah and his sons *who would be like him* dominion (שלט)[70] over the whole earth and everything for food, a further strengthening of Noah's role as a "new Adam" in a "new creation." Noah then descends the mountain, witnesses the devastation, plants a vineyard, celebrates a festival, and blesses God that he rescued (פלט) him from the destruction (אבדן) (XII, 7-17).[71]

Visions of Imminent and Eschatological Destinies (XIII, 8 - XVII, 19)

Briefly, Noah's vision of the past widespread destruction is in vegetative terms, unlike the animal metaphors of the Enochic *Animal Apocalypse*. Trees are cut down and olive trees are broken by winds of strength (תקף). Waters are released and then cease.[72] In the *Genesis Apocryphon*, Noah is not only "planted for righteousness," but he is described as a "great cedar" in contrast to the Enoch cycle, in which the righteous planting was *not* Noah but was to come *from* Noah.

---

67. Falk, *Parabiblical Texts*, 55.

68. Ibid., 59-60.

69. Ibid., 62.

70. Rulership is elsewhere expanded to include dominion over people. Cf. Melchizedek as ruler of lights and sons of light (4Q544 2, 16 - 3, 1); 4QLevi[b]ar (4Q213a) 1, 17 on "Satan's" rule; "I have been made ruler (אשלטת) [over all the sons of lig]ht" (4Q544 3 1); "Let no demonic adversary have power over me, [making me wander from Your path]" (4Q Aramaic Levi[b]/4Q213a 1 17-18).

71. אבדן is exclusively used elsewhere in Aramaic Enoch with respect to the destruction of the sons of the Watchers by war and by the sword (4Q201 1 VI, 17/*1 En.* 12:6; 4Q202 1 IV, 6, 10/*1 En.* 10:9, 12; 4Q204 1 VI, 17; *1 En.* 14:6), destruction of humans as a result of the violence being done to them (4Q202 1 III, 12/*1 En.* 9:3), and destruction by flood (4Q204 5 II, 20/*1 En.* 106:15; cf. 4Q203 8, 12). Cf. 4QNoah: "Woe to you O f[ool, for your mouth will throw (or: deceive) you into destruction]" (4Q534 7 2).

72. Daniel Machiela notes similarities of Noah's self-described dream and following explanation to the apocalyptic visions found in Daniel and *1 Enoch* ("Divinely Revealed History and Geography in the Genesis Apocryphon Columns 13-17," [paper presented at the annual meeting of SBL, Philadelphia, Nov. 22, 2005]).

Here, "eternal, righteous planting" also extends to Noah's progeny (1Q20 XIV, 13), echoing Noah's speech in 1Q20 VI, 1–2.

Daniel Machiela has argued that "the imagery is couched in a context which focuses largely on the progeny of Noah until the end of time, rather than only the flood and related plight of Shemihazai's two sons."[73] When read alongside *Jub.* 10, column XIV also anticipates the division of land and illegal occupation by Canaan through the metaphor of the Noachic shoots.[74] The dream then continues to the events of the eschaton.

Noah sees the imminent and eschatological destiny of those who would come from the shoot that was attached to the stump of the cedar—the righteous planting—but, in addition, he sees the destiny of the apostates who would be hurled upon the fire.[75] Noah awakes from his vision and reports having heard the angels say: "He has made all known to you in righteousness, and thus is it written about you[. . .] and do not [. . .] [Then] I, Noah, [awoke] from my sleep, and the sun. . .because I was blameless (זכי). . .the righteous man (צדיקא)" (1Q20 XV, 20–23).

Once again, as in VI, 23, Noah proclaims his righteousness subsequent to a vision of the wicked. In this vision, Noah foresees the fiery, eschatological judgment and calls himself a צדיקא.[76] Finally, the land is divided among his descendants as an everlasting inheritance (ירותת עלמים) (XVI, 1 – XVII, 19). We now turn to the contribution that the narrator of the *Genesis Apocryphon* made to the conversation or dispute concerning what was to constitute "righteousness" and a righteous priesthood.

Noah: A Different Kind of Righteous One

The emphasis on the "righteousness of Noah" in the *Genesis Apocryphon* is particularly noticeable in contrast to the ambivalence concerning Noah's righteousness in the Enochic texts. Other Hebraisms are present in Noah's speech, but the Aramaic word for "righteous" or "righteousness" (קשט) is retained even when the narrator also used the Aramaic cognate of the Hebrew צדיק in the same text. Therefore, it is worthwhile to explore whether the writer was purposefully contending with the language in *1 Enoch* in order to import the Enochic understanding of קושטא into Noah's "biblical" character and righteousness.

Noah claims to be a righteous planting endued with wisdom and knowledge, knowing how to avoid violence and deceit. Apparently re-created in the image of the righteous plant of Week 7 in the *AW*, Noah is admittedly more passive than the group in Week 7 that actively uproots violence and deceit and executes

---

73. Ibid.
74. Ibid.
75. Noah, as recipient of visions of the eschaton, effectively replaces Enoch in this role.
76. This is the second of only two occurrences of צדיקא in 1Q20.

judgment; however, he is a participant in judgment even if only as observer and witness.

In col. XI, 13–14 Noah blesses God for removing the workers of violence, wickedness,[77] and deceit and for rescuing a צדיקא. These lines introduce, for the first time in the extant text, Noah as a צדיקא who was saved in contrast to Week 2 in the *AW*, in which he was only a "*man* who was saved." By associating קושטא in col. VI with Noah's other biblical characteristics—his walk and his favor before God—the writer neatly forms a bridge into the biblical Hebrew vocabulary of righteousness in col. XI, thus not only reinstating the קושטא of the Enochic writings to Noah but adding to it his biblical character as a צדיק.

צדיקא is produced at a second significant juncture, in Noah's self description as a righteous one, immediately *after* he awakens from his vision of a fiery, eschatological judgment and immediately *prior* to the giving of land to his descendants as an everlasting inheritance (ירותת עלמים). The first occurrence of צדיקא had described Noah as a righteous man who would possess a renewed earth following the deluge that destroyed violence, wickedness, and deceit. It is possible that צדיקא is merely a Hebraicism seen as the equivalent of the קשטה, the righteous Noah in *1 En.* 10:3. It could be, however, that צדיקא was deliberately introduced at points in the story significant to the author. The author may have used this specific language at these particular points to highlight the identification of Noah as an archetype for the author and the group represented by the author. The progeny of the righteous one, the צדיקא, including the author's group, would be preserved while the "workers of violence, evil, and deceit" would be destroyed.

The *Genesis Apocryphon* thus engages with Enochic קושטא, transferring Enochic righteousness back to Noah, who had, after all, originally possessed it not only in Genesis but also in the most ancient traditions of the *Book of Watchers*. Noah becomes the legitimate successor of Enoch[78] by doing what Enoch had exhorted his descendants to do, choosing the paths of קושטא and keeping away from the paths of violence. Furthermore, Noah takes on attributes and experiences that were reserved for Enoch in the Enochic books, offering up prayers and receiving revelations of imminent *and* eschatological judgments.

Noah's portrayal also has roots in the Aramaic Levi tradition. As demonstrated in chapter 3, the figure of Levi in the *ALD* could well be the "literary prototype" of Noah in 1Q20. Levi destroys the "workers of violence," and Noah blesses God for destroying the "workers of violence." Levi and Noah are both concerned with the proper paths, dominion, righteous seed or planning, acting properly as a priest, the right kind of marriage, and the written transmission of tradition. In 1Q20, Noah is re-created not only as Enoch's legitimate successor

---

77. Cf. the language of wickedness (Gen 6:5, 11).

78. Enoch affirmed that Noah was, indeed, Lamech's son and, by extension, his great-grandson and legitimate heir (1Q20 V, 2–22), but Enoch then disappears from 1Q20 except for a sole reference to the "Book of the Words of Enoch" in the Abram portion (1Q20 XIX, 24–26). Noah makes no appeal to a "Book of Enoch" in the extant text.

(wise visionary) but also as Levi's legitimate prototype (priestly, wise visionary). He is a worthy archetype for the "righteous ones" of the narrator's day, an eternal righteous plant that possessed wisdom and knowledge and would witness the obliteration of deceit and violence.

The narrator has thus created a kind of a hybrid super-righteous Noah that expanded to include the character of Genesis's Noah, Enoch, and Levi. 1Q20 does in Aramaic for Noah what *Jubilees* had done in Hebrew; it brings together various wisdom, apocalyptic, priestly, and halakhic strands, fitting them onto the narrative structure from Genesis but creating a different sort of righteous archetypical Noah. Differently configured than the Noah of *Jubilees*, these two archetypes may well represent two priestly groups in conversation or dispute about the idealized characteristics of the priesthood.

Noah: Lamech's Son and Abraham's Ancestor

Legitimate parentage and lineage are highly important for the narrator of the *Genesis Apocryphon*. Yet elements of the story of Noah's birth and the parallels to be found with the Abram narrative suggest a purposeful linking of the two characters and a shared attitude toward knowledge originating outside of Judaism. We begin with Noah's birth.

Because of Noah's remarkable appearance at birth, Lamech is worried that Noah is not his son but, rather, that he is the child of the angelic Watchers, who were currently causing havoc on the earth by sleeping with women and fathering giants. What is particularly intriguing is the basis of his wife's response. Bitenosh bitterly protests that Lamech must know that Noah is indeed his son because of her "pleasure" in the "heat" of the moment, "Then Bitenosh, my wife, replied to me very passionately, we[eping . . .] she said, "O, my brother, my lord, remember my pleasure . . . in the heat of the time of lovemaking, and my ardent response" (1Q20 II, 8–10). However, Lamech is not satisfied. He appeals to Methuselah, who visits Enoch, who reveals the truth about Noah's parentage, "And to you Methuselah [my son . . .] this lad. 3 Behold, when I Enoch [. . . and not] from the sons of 4 Heaven, but by Lamech, your son" (1Q20 V, 2–4).

Two things are perplexing about this passage. First, why would it even have occurred to Bitenosh that her physical response during intercourse should be proof to Lamech that the child was his? Second, if she believed it should be accepted as proof, then why was Lamech not convinced? In a recent paper, Ida Fröhlich answered the first question, suggesting that by using the words for "heat" and "pleasure," the narrator was demonstrating knowledge of fourth century B.C.E. Greek medicine. In *On the Generating Seed and the Nature of the Child*, Hippocrates argues that female "pleasure" and "heat" during intercourse are offered as proofs of conception.[79] The woman's ardent physical response to her husband—

---

79. Ida Fröhlich, "Embryology and Healing in the Genesis Apocryphon" (paper pre-

pleasure and heat—told her that she has received and retained the male "seed" of her husband, Lamech.

Fröhlich suggests that the *Genesis Apocryphon*'s narrator had this knowledge, and so, in the narrative, Bitenosh was appealing to Greek science even for such a significant issue as proving the paternity of her son and his place in the succession. However, the second question still remains. Although Bitenosh has done her best to offer a compelling argument, Lamech is still not convinced. Therefore, it could be that by appealing to Methuselah and Enoch, Lamech implies that foreign knowledge and foreign science, while not necessarily flawed, are not a sufficient revelation. "True knowledge" or the "right kind of knowledge" could be confirmed only through revelation reliably transmitted from generation to generation and from a reliable source, Enoch, who had originally received his instruction directly from the angels.

Furthermore, the fact that the narrator even included such a birth story suggests a refutation of the Mesopotamian flood story of giant flood survivors, an interpretation that argues, in essence, that the Jewish Noah was not a giant. Therefore this text, like the *Book of Watchers*, demonstrates knowledge of, deliberate engagement with, and adaptation of Mesopotamian and Greek science and story, bringing these into a proper relationship under Judaism.

The *Genesis Apocryphon* was oriented toward Greece in yet another way. Authors of antiquity utilized the Table of Nations in Gen. 10 together with existing *mapa mundi* in their constructions of the inhabited world in order to interpret the division of the world among Noah's children and grandchildren.[80] While the author of *Jubilees* was aware of Greek geography and used the framework of the Ionian world map, Zion is transformed into the *omphalos* of the earth instead of Delphi.[81] In her analysis of the role of the map in *Jubilees*, Cana Werman argues that *Jubilees* "utilized its familiarity with Hellenizing trends in order

---

sented at the VIth Congress of the International Organization for Qumran Studies, Ljubljana, July 17, 2007).

80. This has been well explored by scholars who may also share cartographical interests with their ancient counterparts: Esther Eshel, "The *Imago Mundi* of the *Genesis Apocryphon*," in *Heavenly Tablets: Interpretation, Identity and Tradition in Ancient Judaism* (ed. L. LiDonnici and A. Lieber; JSJSup 119; Leiden: Brill, 2007), 111-31; Jacques T. van Ruiten, "The Division of the Earth," in *Primaeval History Interpreted: The Rewriting of Genesis 1-11 in the Book of Jubilees* (JSJSup 66; Leiden: Brill, 2000), 307-63. Philip S. Alexander, "Notes on the 'Imago Mundi' of the Book of Jubilees," *JJS* 33 (1982): 197-213; idem, "Jerusalem as the *Omphalos* of the World: On the History of a Geographical Concept," in *Jerusalem: Its Sanctity and Centrality to Judaism, Christianity, and Islam* (ed. L. I. Levine; New York: Continuum, 1999), 104-19; Cana Werman, "*Jubilees* in the Hellenistic Context," in *Heavenly Tablets*, 133-58; James C. VanderKam, "Putting Them in Their Place: Geography as an Evaluative Tool," in idem, *From Revelation to Canon: Studies in the Hebrew Bible and Second Temple Literature* (JSJSup 62; Leiden: Brill, 2000), 476-99; James M. Scott, "*Jubilees* 8-9," in *Geography in Early Judaism and Christianity: The Book of Jubilees* (Cambridge: Cambridge University Press, 2002), 23-43.

81. Alexander, "Notes," 198-99.

to rebut them" and was "[s]eeking to erect a barrier between the Jewish people and a foreign (in his view, idolatrous) culture, and to combat that culture, *Jubilees* borrowed a weapon from Hellenistic culture itself."[82]

Concerning the fragmentary account of the division of the world among Noah's sons in the *Genesis Apocryphon*, Esther Eshel has demonstrated that the author preserves the focus of the original Ionian map, which is oriented to Delphi in Greece, a focus that it shares with Josephus.[83] Eshel suggests that the significance of the differences in the way the Ionian map is used in 1Q20 and in *Jubilees* is that *Jubilees* links the map to its particular worldview, "namely, Shem's priority, the importance of ethnographic divisions, and above all, the centrality of Jerusalem as the navel of the world, in contrast to the *Genesis Apocryphon*'s greater interest in the geographical aspects of the division of the world."[84]

Whether or not a map with its center adjusted to Jerusalem from Delphi, as it was in *Jubilees*, was previously *known* by the author of the *Genesis Apocryphon* is really not of importance here. What *is* significant is that the *Genesis Apocryphon*'s reinterpretation of the division of the land among Noah's sons and grandsons obviously did not require that the center of its map be similarly adjusted away from Delphi and toward Jerusalem.

The Abram narrative also displays an orientation to regions outside of the "land." The survival of the Noah and Abram stories in the *Genesis Apocryphon* attest "to a well-constructed narrative with specific goals."[85] Certainly the congruencies between the narratives and the language used to evoke certain themes are suggestive of a literary unity.

Noah Narrative	**Abram Narrative**
God obliterates (0, 12; 0, 15) in the day of wrath. Cf. Gen 6:7; 7:4; 7:23.	Kings kill and threaten to obliterate (מחה); Abram defeats them (XXI, 23 – XXII, 11)
Sexual misalliances between Watchers and women (I, 1); Noah *not* a product of sexual misalliance (I, 1; II, 1 – V, 25)	Sexual alliance between Pharaoh and Sarah threatened but not consummated (XX, 8–31)
Deliverance from primordial destruction of the righteous one; deliverance from eschatological destruction anticipated.	Deliverance from Egypt of the righteous; deliverance of "Israel out of Egypt" anticipated (XX, 31–33)

---

82. Werman, "*Jubilees* in the Hellenistic Context," 135, 140.
83. Eshel, "*Imago Mundi*," 123, 129.
84. Ibid., 131.
85. For the earth's division in 1Q20 XVI-XVII as background for the geographic descriptions in the Abram section that speak "to a well-constructed narrative with specific goals," see Machiela, "Divinely Revealed History."

Noah Narrative	Abram Narrative
Noah's legitimate birth confirmed by Enoch (V, 2–4)	Abram appeals to the Book of the Words of Enoch (XIX, 25)
Noah's righteousness and wisdom (VI, 4)	Abram's wisdom and righteousness (XIX, 25)
Noah marries his sons to his nephews; first shoot from Noah emerges as the "righteous, eternal planting"; proper lineage (VI, 8; XIV, 11–13)	Both cedar and date palm (Sarah) are from a single root: Proper marriage; proper lineage (XIX, 14–15)
Noah sacrifices and atones for the land (X, 13–17; XII, 16–17)	Abram builds altar and sacrifices (XIX, 7; XXI 21–22). (However, no need for a sacrifice that atoned for the land; no defilement of the land had occurred)
Noah walks about mountaintop, Eden-like land; temple parallels (XI, 11–12)	"holy mountain" (XIX, 8)
Noah descends from the mountaintop to the devastated land below (XII, 8–9)	Abram returns from walking about the promised land to the Oaks of Mamre (XXI, 15–19)
Noah dreams of destructive forces against trees (XIII, 8–17)	Abram dreams that he—the cedar—would be murdered (cut-down) (XIX, 15–17)
The "strong" who would survive the wrath (0, 5); Noah sees winds blow with destructive strength (תקף) on the trees (XIII, 16); Noah grasped or prevailed (תקף) (VI, 6).	Pharaoh takes Sarah by force (תקף) (XX, 14); God responds with severe (תקף) plagues (XX, 18) and promises to Abram that he himself would be his strength (תקף) against a foe mightier (תקף) than he (XXII, 31)
Noah is a cedar (XIV, 9)	Abram is a cedar (XIX, 14)
Noah walks about (הלך) the length (אורך) and breadth (פותי) of the mountaintop land (XI, 11); Noah's sons receive land as an everlasting inheritance (ירת) (XVI, 12, 14)	Abram surveys the promised land and is told to walk (הלך) the length (אורך) and breadth (פותי) of it; God promises that Abram's seed (זרע) would inherit (ירת) the land (XXI, 8–14)
"The portion of the sons of Ham" (XVII, 19)	Abram travels to the "land of the children of Ham" (XIX, 12–15)
Noah material ends with description of the everlasting inheritance (ירת) belonging to Noah's sons (XVI, 8 - XVII, 19)	Abram material ends with the God's promise that Abram's legitimate heir would inherit (ירת) (XXII, 34)

Abram possesses wisdom (חמכה) and righteousness (קושטא) (XIX, 25), offers sacrifices (XIX 7; XXI 21–22), and is endogamously married to Sarah (XIX, 14–15). Foreign powers threaten, but Abram and Sarah are delivered. The sexual misalliance between Pharaoh and Sarah is threatened but not consummated (XX, 8–31), and kings seek to obliterate (מחה) Abram but are unable to (XXI, 23–XX, 11). Deliverance of the righteous out of Egypt is anticipated (XX, 31–33). Abram walks about the promised land (XXI, 15–19), and the extant account ends with God's promise to Abram that his legitimate heir would inherit (XXII, 34).

The Noah and Abram narratives, together with the themes in cols. 0–1—sexual misalliances, deliverance of the "strong" and obliteration of the wicked—attest a plausible thematic cohesion in 1Q20 even within the fragmentary remains of the extant text. The nature and extent of the similarities suggest that, even if the narrator was not responsible for the writing of every part of the composition, some deliberate choices were made especially with respect to aligning the Noah narrative with that of Abram, so that both represented righteous archetypes who were delivered from outside threats, behaved as priests, and inherited the land.

Noah as "Writer": Was There a "Book of Noah"?

The question of whether a physical text was "known" as the *Book of Noah* by the tradents of tradition in even the earliest Aramaic Enoch and Levi texts is a much different question than whether the tradents "knew" that Noah was a writer. While "Noah as writer" is known in *Jubilees* as the preserver of remedies against demons—knowledge not "preserved" in the "first Torah"—this role may not have been as critical for the tradents of texts in closest agreement with *Jubilees*. In *Jubilees*, all was revealed to Moses, so if anything important from God had been "missed" or "lost" in translation or transmission, it was ultimately revealed to Moses, who then wrote it down. In *Jubilees*, Moses was the recorder of the most comprehensive revelation.

However, especially in the Aramaic traditions that did not make Moses solely responsible for the reception and transmission of revelation but rather gave more weight to the revelation given to individual ancestors beginning with Enoch and Noah, *how* revelation from God was kept from being lost across the generations and in times of trouble was of utmost concern. Within this particular construction of the world, when the tradents came to think about it, Noah would have "had" to write a book containing all of the important bits and pieces of revelation given to him by God in order for that revelation to be preserved. A body of instruction that depended on oral transmission was vulnerable to being lost in the course of a single generation such as was experienced in the days of the "sons of Noah" in Mesopotamia or in the days of Jacob's descendants in Egypt up until the time of Moses.

Therefore, within the context of this study and for this author, the "Noah as writer" tradition as it relates to the reception and reliable transmission of the revelation of God, is of much more interest than the question of the existence of a *Book of Noah* that may have existed as a literary source text for other texts such as the *Books of Watchers* and the *ALD*. When asked by one's friends, however, one must contribute to the latter conversation. What follows, therefore, are a few tentative sketches of an argument that remains to be properly tested and constructed but that offers another explanation for the fragments and traces of a book attributed to Noah.

Jack Lewis was the first to differentiate between the *Book of Noah* and "Noah as writer," in his assertion that "the idea of Noah as a writer belongs to a cycle of material which pictured the patriarchs as transmitters of esoteric materials."[86] Along a similar vein, James C. VanderKam marshaled evidence of Noah's writings or words from the *Book of Asaph*, the *ALD*, and *Jubilees*, suggesting that, according to these texts, Noah was perceived to have engaged in writing[87] even if he did not write a "book" that the Enochic authors, for example, held in their hands.

Because Noah's purported writings or words address diverse topics in a variety of contexts, some scholars have argued that one cannot meaningfully speak of a single, coherent *Book of Noah*.[88] As already noted in chapter 3, Devorah Dimant observed that, since the Noah narrative in the *Book of Watchers* is written in third-person style and not in first-person style as would be expected of a "book," this is evidence that the *Book of Watchers*, at least, did not have a *Book of Noah* as a literary source."[89]

For Michael Stone, however, "the burden of proof falls on scholars who would deny the authenticity of the Book of Noah titles and sections *a priori* and not on those who would assert it." Stone accepts the attributions made to Noachic writings in the *ALD*, *Jubilees*, 1Q20, and the *Similitudes*, arguing for a Noachic work dating, at the latest, to the third century B.C.E., which then fell out of use, surviving only in citations.[90] He correctly observes that "the relationship between

---

86. Jack P. Lewis, *A Study of the Interpretation of Noah and the Flood in Jewish and Christian Literature* (Leiden: Brill, 1968), 14–15.

87. James C. VanderKam, *The Book of Jubilees* (Guides to Apocrypha and Pseudepigrapha; Sheffield: Sheffield Academic Press, 2001), 137–38.

88. James M. Scott concludes that many books of Noah may have been in circulation but that it might not be possible to reconstruct a single *Book of Noah* ("Geographic Aspects of Noachic Materials in the Scrolls at Qumran," in *The Scrolls and the Scriptures: Qumran Fifty Years After* [JSPSup 26; ed. S. E. Porter and C. A. Evans; Sheffield: Sheffield Academic Press, 1997], 368–81, here 368).

89. Dimant, "Two 'Scientific' Fictions," 234. On the idea of two cosmic judgments demonstrating a unity between the Enoch and Noah portions so that the "Noah apocalypses" are not to be treated as a "foreign body" within the Enoch saga, see Matthew Black, *The Book of Enoch, or, 1 Enoch: A New English Edition with Commentary and Textual Notes* (SVTP 7; Leiden: Brill, 1985), 8.

90. See also García Martínez who has construed from 4Q534 that this text preserves a part of the lost *Book of Noah* that is attested in *Jubilees* and in the Mt. Athos Greek manuscript of the *T. Levi* and that has parallels to the *ALD*. García Martínez, "4QMess ar and the Book of Noah," 24. He also catalogues candidates for excerpts from the *Book* in other known literature and has offered an ordered outline of the book; however he does not state why the order

both the figures and the writings of Enoch and Noah" needs to be determined as well as the potential social correlative *if* the "Noah material was taken over by the Enochic material."[91]

Concerning the "interpolations" of Noah material into the *Book of Parables*, Michael A. Knibb appropriately concludes that some material may have been "interpolated or added at a secondary stage, but it seems likely that this was done on an ad hoc basis over a period of time, and the absence of alternative versions of the Parables makes it difficult to make dogmatic statements about the extent of the additions or the stages at which the additions were made."[92]

What is certain is that *Jubilees*, the *Genesis Apocryphon*, and the *Aramaic Levi Document* all refer to either the book or writings of Noah.[93] For example, in the *ALD*, Levi received oral teaching from his grandfather, Isaac, who in turn had received it from Abraham, who had found it in a "writing of the book of Noah."[94] Other authors that are acknowledged in the Dead Sea Scrolls include Enoch (11Q12 4 1–3/*Jub.* 4.16–24; 1Q20 XIX, 25.), Qahat (4Q542 1 II, 9–13), Amram (4Q545 1a I, 1),[95] and Moses (*Jub.* 1:5). Enoch is instructed by the angel to write for his children (*1 En.* 81:6) and then charges Methuselah to preserve these books (*1 En.* 82:1). Concerning *1 En.* 104:11–13 and the importance of written transmission, Alex Jassen observes that teaching accessible in written books was perceived to "serve as the core element of the sapiential curriculum."[96]

It is not surprising, then, that pseudepigraphic writings appear also in the name of Kohath and Amram, son and grandson of Levi: "Now, to you, Amram my son, I command [. . .] 10 [. . .] you, and to their descendants I command [. . . to guard the sacred writings that they left behind] 11 and gave to my father Levi, and that my father Levi gave to me. [. . .] 12 all my writings as a testimony that you should be careful with [. . .] 13 to you. In them is great merit when you carry them along with you" (4Q542 1 II, 9–13).

Clearly, written as well as oral transmission along a selected priestly bloodline is a common factor in these texts. However, the *Genesis Apocryphon* is the

---

he suggests is chronological and not topical as the variant contents of the hypothetical book would suggest.

91. Michael E. Stone, "The Book(s) Attributed to Noah," *DSD* 13 (2006): 4–23 [17–18].

92. Michael A. Knibb, "The Structure and Composition of the Parables of Enoch," in *Enoch and the Messiah Son of Man: Revisiting the Book of Parables* (ed. G. Boccaccini; Grand Rapids: Wm. B. Eerdmans, 2007), 48–64 [64].

93. *Jub.* 10.13; 1Q20 V, 29; *ALD* 10:10. Cf. 4Q536 2 II, 12–13; and 4Q534 7, 3–4.

94. *ALD* 10:10. This text only claims that Abraham had seen the Book of Noah; neither Isaac nor Levi claimed to have seen it.

95. On other "writings" and "books" in the "Aramaic Levi" trajectory of tradition, see 4Q545 1a I, 1; cf. 4Q543 1a-c 1; 4Q547 9 8; 4Q537 1+2+3 3; 4Q542 1 II, 12, and 4Q541 7, 2.

96. Alex P. Jassen, "Sapiential Revelation in Apocalyptic Literature Preserved at Qumran," in *Mediating the Divine: Prophecy and Revelation in the Dead Sea Scrolls and Second Temple Judaism* (STDJ 68; Leiden: Brill, 2007), 260–78, here 270.

only text that explicitly purports to *contain* the writings of Noah. That Noah was reinterpreted as a "writer" in the Dead Sea Scrolls and that there was a trajectory and history of traditions of Noah as writer and author of a "book" is certain. The corollary is, at the very least, that the authors intentionally created an archetype of Noah as a writer and author of a book that contained teachings that were purportedly reliably preserved and transmitted.

Furthermore, the author of the *Genesis Apocryphon* seemed to believe that such a book *should* contain first-person speech as a written account recording and substantiating a message orally delivered. If we look backwards through the lens of the "archetype," we may catch a glimpse of the types of conversations and debates in which the authors of these traditions were participating. How teachings were to be preserved in times of threat of a break in the chain of oral transmission from one generation to the next may have been a matter of concern and for discussion.

Noah was perfectly suited for his role as an archetypical writer and author. He and his family were the sole survivors of a catastrophic event and, between Noah and Abraham, there was a perceived break in the teachings and traditions that some of the "sons of Noah" failed to transmit. The only hope for the survival of these teachings and traditions was that they be written down so that God's revealed wisdom would not be lost.

In conclusion, the mere existence of traditions naming a "Book of Noah" and of references to the writings of Noah in the Dead Sea Scrolls does not require the existence of the physical remains of a *Book of Noah* as a literary source that was cited and excerpted by later writers. These references and allusions could be explained by a drive to create an archetype that added "writer" to Noah's credentials in the Second Temple Period and also "book" to his resume. When it came time for the ghostwriters to write the "book" for Noah, the pattern of the books of Enoch, in which the characters spoke in the first person as they were meant to, was readily at hand. This falls far short of saying that a *Book of Noah* did not exist from the time before the books of Enoch. However, it does offer another explanation of the exceptionally keen interest, especially in the Aramaic traditions, in bestowing suitably credentialed characters prior to Moses—Enoch, Noah, and Levi, to name a few—with the capacity to receive and reliably transmit revelation from God in writing.

Continuing the Conversation

The Aramaic texts in the tradition of the *Aramaic Levi Document* opened the discussion and offered fresh readings of the portrayal of Noah as a "literary prototype" for Levi in the *Genesis Apocryphon* and, perhaps, as one in a line of figures to whom esoteric knowledge was revealed in the 4QNaissance de Noé texts. Noah as an idealized archetype reaches new heights in these Aramaic texts in greatly expanded roles, hearing from God in ways that he had not elsewhere.

In texts following the "Aramaic Levi" tradition, such as 4QTestament of Qahat and 4QVisions of Amram, Noah is perceived as one of a priestly line that includes Levi and Moses and that would continue for "eternal generations of righteousness." This retelling appears to validate an ancient lineage of priests who authoritatively transmitted tradition even while they were outside of the land and stands in contrast to Ben Sira or the *Damascus Document*, which acknowledged the priesthood as originating only during Moses' and Aaron's time. The 4QpseudoDaniel texts point to a movement that either accepted Noah as part of its "internal history" in contrast to other retellings of Israel's history that began with Abraham or simply included Noah in its recounting of history as an accommodation toward the Babylonian king. Either way, Noah as a common ancestor of all humanity and not exclusively of Israel, was gladly claimed by this group.

In the priestly Aramaic Levi texts and their literary successors, Noah figures strongly as a progenitor. Enoch's presence is still felt, but he had already been removed from the earthly realm. Noah is the priestly flood survivor who is "on the ground," the first of a priestly line who was working out obedience to God's revelation on the renewed earth.

In the *Genesis Apocryphon*, Noah is characterized by wisdom *and* truth and avoids deceit. He recovers both his biblical "righteousness" and inherits the righteousness that had been his great-grandfather Enoch's in the Enochic books. In contrast to *Jubilees*, there is no "righteous repentant" Noah in the extant text of the *Genesis Apocryphon*. Instead, Noah proclaims himself righteous right from the womb. In contrast to the Watchers, Noah arranges the proper (endogamous) marriages for his sons. He observes the destruction of deceit and violence, atones for the land in a sacrifice, and walks on an Eden-like renewed land over which he was given the dominion in his role as a new Adam. Noah is the recipient of a full revelation, seeing visions of imminent *and* eschatological judgment and observing the destiny of wicked and righteous in both earthly and cosmic realms.

In the extant text, Noah does not celebrate covenant, bless, or curse, and there is no mention of human inclination or of the opportunity for repentance, implied or otherwise. Because of the fragmentary text, the absence of one or two might be expected, but the absence of all of them is surprising. In 4QCommentary on Genesis A – D, written in Hebrew, mention of Noachic curses in connection with "land" is predominant in even the smallest and most fragmentary text. An argument for intentional exclusion of this terminology and these themes in 1Q20 is an argument from silence but one that at least needs to be heard together with other evidence as we move through this study.

The *Genesis Apocryphon* sets Noah into a context between Enoch and Abram. Whereas the Noah story is cosmic in scope, the Abram narrative plays out in a much smaller earth-bound sphere and could have served for its readers as an archetype of the righteous, who could effectively escape the defilements of the land and eventually inherit a land not yet fully possessed.

While Noah was the person of primary interest in the extant text of the

Genesis Apocryphon, Enoch also had an important role. Methuselah's appeal to Enoch for legitimating Noah's birth and Abram's use of the books of Enoch in Egypt indicate that the revelation from Enoch was absolutely necessary. As in *Jubilees*, both Noah and Abram are figures "on the ground," while Enoch is in another world. The difference in 1Q20 is that Enoch's descendants still have access to them. In *Jubilees*, that access is denied. When one takes this together with the evidence from the *Aramaic Levi Document*, that Noah's "book" was the one consulted on priestly practice and that the earliest figure mentioned in the extant fragments of *Amram* is Noah, it does seem that Noah appears prominently as at least one of the first characters of interest in Aramaic retellings of history.

The re-creation of Noah in 1Q20 also differs particularly from that in *Jubilees*, most dramatically in its attitudes toward the books of "Mosaic" Torah. *Jubilees* demonstrates its dependence on Genesis by the systematic way it reorders it, borrowing from but subordinating at least the earlier Aramaic Enoch and Aramaic Levi traditions, but then viewing the whole through a Mosaic, even Deuteronomic lens. On the other hand, the *Genesis Apocryphon* converses freely with its Hebrew and Aramaic sources but is much less oriented toward the Torah associated with Moses, omitting discussion of covenant, inclination, repentance, blessings, and curses in the extant texts. This Aramaic text, loaded with Hebraisms,[97] even hints at points of contact with Qumran sectarian theology and praxis in its creation of its ideal archetype.

There is a keen interest, in the texts examined in this chapter, in biblical figures who, at some point, lived outside of the land: Enoch, Noah, Levi, Qahat, Amram, and Daniel. This particular line also shares characteristics with the unnamed figure in the 4QNaissance de Noé texts and in 4QApocryphon of Levi. A possibility suggested by the evidence is that an idealized Noah in the *Genesis Apocryphon* may have been created retroactively as an archetypical figure whose literary character was fashioned after a known, wise, teaching, priestly, and possibly suffering figure or group. Such a retrofit would have been shaped quite differently in the hands of those interpreters who were more focused on Moses and the Mosaic Torah, as the portrayal in *Jubilees* reveals. Might the two competing archetypes represent two differing conceptions and perceptions of a particular known character claimed by the groups that the authors represented? This remains an enticing possibility.

The *Genesis Apocryphon* has also revealed what appears to be a deliberate and intentional engagement with Greek science, story, and geography. The birth story of Noah betrays awareness of Greek medical knowledge concerning the proofs of conception, a familiarity with the stories of flood survivor giants, a respect for the wisdom of Egypt, and a willingness to base the division of the land among Noah's sons and grandsons on a map with its center in Delphi. However,

---

97. The many grammatical and lexical Hebraisms are noted by Morgenstern, Qimron, and Sivan, "Hitherto Unpublished Columns," 30–54.

for the author, foreign knowledge was not sufficient. It had to be legitimated by and subordinated to the revelation from its proper source, Enoch. In the next two chapters, Noah will feature in Hebrew texts across the genres in which he is noticeable by his absence in some texts but in others is a worthy ancestor of first and primary importance.

CHAPTER SIX

NOAH IN THE HEBREW PRE-SECTARIAN TEXTS (2)

[Prayer for the Day of Atonemen]t:
Remember, Lord, the festival of Your mercies (compassions?)
and the time of return [. . .]
for You established it for us as a festival of fasting, and ever[lasting] statute [. . .]
and You know the things hidden and revea[led . . .] You [kn]ow our inclination
[. . . ou]r [rising] and our lying down [. . .] we have done wickedly [. . .]
[. . .] and because they were more in number.
[Then] You established [Your covenant] for Noah
4QFestival Prayers[b] 1 2–6; 3 1–2

INTRODUCTION

Traditions associated with Noah were not genre-bound nor language-bound, and liturgists, poets, and storytellers continued to work and rework their source materials into new narratives, admonitions, prayers, and rule books. At times, the "Noah" who appeared in a Hebrew text looked much different from the "Noah" in an Aramaic text, even when the narrators would have had access to similar source materials. At other times, however, the crossover of a tradition could have been as simple as translating the text.

For example, 1QBook of Noah has more elements in common with Aramaic texts than it does with Hebrew ones, while others, such as 4QFestival Prayers and 4QAdmonition Based on the Flood, exhibit certain characteristics that appear primarily in other Hebrew texts. 4QTanḥumim excerpts and interprets biblical texts, contemporizing the prophetic words. 4QText Mentioning the Flood and 4QParaphrase of Genesis and Exodus both exhibit wisdom and apocalyptic tendencies that speak to multiple "times of judgment."

As we make the transition from the Aramaic texts to the Hebrew pre-sectarian and sectarian texts at Qumran, we begin with a brief study of 4QExposition on the Patriarchs, a scroll that may reveal the musings of a group in the thick of the debate concerning the choice of language for contexts in which languages other than the "holy tongue" were known and used.

Texts and Observations

4QExposition on the Patriarchs (4Q464): A Confusion of Languages

Once the Hasmoneans came to power in the second century B.C.E., Hebrew became "the language of national independence" and was increasingly popular as the language of choice in which texts with authoritative status were written.[1] Yet the practice of copying and collecting Aramaic texts continued even after the Hebrew sectarian texts were being composed and copied, a fact that needs to be accounted for if, as is commonly believed, the Aramaic texts belonged in the sect's prehistory.[2] 4Q464 appears to mention the flood, but it may also present hints of one side of a controversy between those who advocated Aramaic for certain purposes and those who advocated Hebrew.

Written in Hebrew in a Herodian hand (30 B.C.E.–70 C.E.), the eleven fragments of 4Q464 are arranged by the editors according to a biblical chronology that appears to include mention of the flood.[3] Based on the quotation from Zephaniah and the use of the term *pesher* (פשר), the editors subscribe to the "expository character" of this text and its "sustained eschatological interest."[4]

The editors have tried to make sense of what is a highly fragmentary and difficult text: "*1* . . .outside (חֹוץ) and [. . .] *2* and he placed water (וישם מים). [. . .] *3* shall be there, the water in the [flood] shall come to an end (יכלון מֹי).[5] [. . .] *4* to destroy (להשחית) the earth because [their] wa[y . . .] (דר[כם) *5* they [were] open[ed and (נ]פתחֹו). . . " (4Q464 5 II, 1–5).[6] They support their reconstruction ויסגור מחוץ by appealing to Gen 7:16 (LXX) and *Jub.* 5:23. The exact expression וישם מים does

---

1. George J. Brooke, "Between Authority and Canon: The Significance of Reworking the Bible for Understanding the Canonical Process," in *Reworking the Bible: Apocryphal and Related Texts at Qumran: Proceedings of a Joint Symposium by the Orion Center for the Study of the Dead Sea Scrolls and Associated Literature and the Hebrew University Institute for Advanced Studies Research Group* (ed. E. G. Chazon, D. Dimant, and R. A. Clements; STDJ 58; Leiden/Boston: Brill, 2005), 85–104, here 91–92.

2. On 4Q464 demonstrating that the use of Hebrew was "part of the covenanters' apocalyptic ideology" and reiterating the statement that "there are no indications that the sectarian covenanters . . . used Aramaic for any of their writings," see Matthew Morgenstern, "Language and Literature of the Second Temple Period," *JJS* 48 (1997): 130–45, here 144.

3. The editors acknowledge that "it is not certain that in fact the fragments did occur in this order" (E. Eshel and M. Stone, DJD XIX, 215).

4. Michael E. Stone and Esther Eshel, "An Exposition on the Patriarchs (4Q464) and Two Other Documents (4Q464ᵃ and 4Q464ᵇ)," *Muséon* 105 (1992): 243–64, here 246. In the same article, Stone and Eshel point to *Midrash Tanḥuma* on Zeph 3:9, where "the connection between the Tower of Babel, the Hebrew language, and the eschatological reunification of human speech (as Hebrew) is explicit" (252). Although this midrash could preserve an earlier tradition, 4Q464 itself is not clearly eschatological.

5. "This is probably to be reconstructed as [מי ה]מבול" (DJD XIX, 224).

6. Trans. DJD XIX.

not appear in the Hebrew Bible or in Qumran writings,[7] nor is מי יכלון attested in the Hebrew Bible or in Qumran literature. However, the editors note a variant of the Hebrew in Gen 8:2, which reads ויכל (the rain) was gone instead of ויכלא (MT). Finally, "they were opened," as reconstructed, echoes Gen 7:11.

The biblical flood template was likely useful in creating the reconstruction, but if it is set aside other reconstructions could be considered as alternatives. For example, the infinitive construct of שחת with the object הארץ is found only in Isa 36:10, in which representatives of Sennacherib claim that God sent them up against the land to destroy it. Hezekiah's representatives respond, "Please speak to your servants in Aramaic, since we understand it. Don't speak to us in Hebrew in the hearing of the people on the wall" (Isa 36:11). With or without the presence of "flood" in frg. 5, however, a common element between the narratives might be that of people among foreign peoples and languages.

Israel's other patriarchs are mentioned more explicitly. Reference to "Abraham the son of Terah" in "Haran" (4Q464 1 1–2)[8] is followed by a quotation of Zeph 3:9: "[. . .] confused (נבלת) . . . to Abraham [. . . re]ad the holy language (לשון הקודש).[9] [. . . "For I will change] the speech of the peoples to a pure speech" (excerpted from 4Q464 3 I, 5–9). "Confusion" brings to mind Babel (Gen 11:7, 9) and may set the context within which Abraham is said to "read the holy language." The prophetic lens borrowed from Zephaniah may have contemporized the text, implying to the reader that the "holy language" would once again be spoken amid the contemporary babble of languages.[10] The writer of 4Q464 could also have perceived Zephaniah's prophecy as applicable to his own day,[11] speaking to a debate occurring in real time concerning the use of Hebrew.

The author quotes Genesis, "[Indeed you know that your offspring shall be strangers in a land that is not their own] and they shall serve them and they shall oppress [them for four hundred years]" (4Q464 3 II, 3–4; cf. Gen 15:13). Jacob

---

7. But cf. Exod 14:21: "he turned the *sea* into dry land . . . divided waters."

8. This is puzzling. The renamed "Abraham" was not known as a son of Terah in the Hebrew Bible except in Joshua's farewell address to Israel, in which he reviews Israel's history and in which Terah and his sons Abraham and Nahor "lived beyond the Euphrates and served other gods" (Josh 24:2). In 4Q464, the phrase, "Abraham the son of Terah," may create an association between the use of other languages in the land "beyond the Euphrates," on one hand, and serving other gods, on the other hand.

9. לשון is one of the few recognizable words in frg. 2.

10. Ishodad of Merv, commenting on Gen 1:11, writes that Abraham spoke the language of the region of his father when he was in Babylonia and also when his father was in Haran. After he crossed the Euphrates and had spent some time in Canaan, his language was mingled with Canaanite, hence the resemblance of Hebrew to Syriac. See J. M. Vosté and C. Van den Eynde, eds., *Commentaire d'Isodad de Merv sur l'Ancien Testament: Genèse* (CSCO 126; Scriptores Syri 67; Louvain: Peeters, 1950), 134–35.

11. For the citation of Zeph 3:9 in 4Q464 as not eschatological but rather a proof text to justify *Jubilees'* expansion of the Abram story, see John C. Poirier, "4Q464: Not Eschatological," *RevQ* 20 (2002): 583–87, here 586–87.

travels to Haran (4Q464 7 2). Fragment 10 contains "Asshur" (שׁוּר[)[12] and "they sold him" (4Q464 10 1-2), a possible reference to Joseph being sold into Egypt (Gen 36:26).

"Do not lay your hand on the lad" (4Q464 6 3) is likely a quotation of the angel's speech to Abraham at the time of the near sacrifice of Isaac (Gen 22:12). In *Jubilees*, an angel reveals Hebrew to Abram prior to his departure from Haran (*Jub.* 12:25-27); however, it is possible that 4Q464 interprets its angelic speech as the time in which Abraham's ears were opened to Hebrew. Both *Jubilees* and 4Q464 portray Abraham/Abram as one who learned Hebrew. Which language Noah was perceived to have spoken is not spelled out in either text. In *Jubilees*, Hebrew as a language was lost "from the day of the Fall" (*Jub.* 12:25-27).

1QBOOK OF NOAH (1Q19): GLORIFIED AMONG THE SONS OF HEAVEN

Dated to the late first century B.C.E., this Hebrew text has striking similarities to the Aramaic traditions of the birth of Noah but describes a figure that is even more exalted.[13]

> [... the gian]ts prevailed (גברו] ם[גברי]) on the earth and [...] *3* [for all flesh had corrupted] its way upon the earth (דרכו על הארץ) [...] *4* [therefore they cried out, and] their [cry ascended] to God[14] (1Q19 1 2-4)

> [the Holy One]s of hea[ven...] *2* [Saying, "Make] our [ca]se befo[re the Most High..."] *3* [...] and not instead of you [...] *4* [Michael and Uriel, Raph]ael and Gabriel [...] *5* [Lord] of Lords and Might[iest of the Mighty...] ([-- (וגב]ור גבורים). (1Q19bis 2 1-5)

> *2* [his] expression chang[ed...] *3* [the fi]rst-born had been born, for the Glorious Ones (נכבדים) [...] *4* his father. And when Lamech saw [the baby...] *5* [light filled] the rooms of the house like shafts of sunlight [...]. (1Q19 3 1-5)

> *1* [...] because glory [...] to glorify God in [...] *2* he shall be lifted up in glorious honor, and glory [...] *3* he shall be glorified among [the Sons of H]eaven and [....]. (1Q19 13-14 1-3)

> My [ch]osen one[15] (ב]חירי), for a God who establishes (כונן). (1Q19 15 2)

---

12. Cf. *Jub.* 10:26 and the Tower of Babel's location between Asshur and Babylon.

13. Translation adapted from Michael Wise, Martin G. Abegg, and Edward Cook with N. Gordon, in *DSSR 3*, 581-84.

14. "Les ff. 1 et 2 correspondent à I Hénoch, ch. 6-10, et plus précisement 8⁴-9⁴... le 3ᵉ à I Hénoch, ch. 106... le 12ᵉ et les suivv. semblent n'avoir pas été repris dan le livre d'Hénoch" (DJD I, 84).

15. Translated as "my chosen ones" in *DSSR 3*.

Certain antecedents are ambiguous or missing, which raises the following questions: Who or what prevails on the earth? Who is glorified among the Sons of Heaven? Who is the chosen one? If the "mighty ones" are reconstructed here as the ones who prevailed (ג[ברי]ם גברו) rather than the "wicked" (ר[שעי]ם),[16] the reconstruction would take into account the possibility that the author noticed one or two powerful wordplays. First, the prevailing "mighty ones" bring to mind the oft-repeated "the waters prevailed (גברו)" in Genesis (7:18, 19, 20, 24). In Genesis, this phrase is reiterated with increasing intensity and suspense until "only Noah was left and those that were with him in the ark" (Gen 7:23). Then, again, the waters prevailed for 150 days (Gen 7:24). The reader of antiquity (or the child hearing this as a bedtime story!) might wonder, "Could God, indeed, prevail against these waters that were prevailing over the earth so mightily?" Genesis does not keep its readers in suspense long, continuing with "But God remembered Noah . . . and the waters subsided" (Gen 8:1-2).

The waters did not, in the end, prevail forever, and neither would the "mighty ones" of this text. Second, "the mighty ones" (cf. Gen 6:4) would serve as a poetic counterfoil in apposition to "the Lord of Lords and the Mightiest of the mighty ones ([אדון] אדונים וגב[ור גבורים])" in another part of the same text (1Q19bis 2 5).

Another possibility, though only the final *mem* is extant, is the reconstruction of "waters" (ה[מי]ם גברו) (cf. Gen 7:18, 19, 20, 24). However, this would pose difficulties chronologically because the "cry" *follows* "waters" in 1QBook of Noah. In the *Book of Watchers*, the giants (גברין) acted violently, the cry of humankind ascended to heaven, and *then* the flood came (4Q202 1 II, 20–1 III, 6/*1 En.* 7:2–8:4). If, however, "the waters prevailed" was in the text originally, even these likely functioned as a metaphor for "mighty ones" representing Israel's enemies, an interpretation already hinted at in Isa 54:1-10.

Fragment 3 alludes to the remarkable birth narrative of Noah. The "glorious ones" (נכבדים) in the form of the *niphal* participle could describe either angelic beings or honored human beings (4Q400 2 2; 4Q509 16 4), but the context would suggest that angels are meant. The term "sons of heaven" in frgs. 13–14 is normally a descriptive rather than a pejorative expression in the Qumran corpus, variously describing a wicked "Yaḥad" (4Q181 1 2), those who accompany those initiated into the (true) Yaḥad (1QH^a XI, 23/4Q427 7 II, 18), those who possess inheritance of eternal life (4Q418 69 II, 2–13), or those who come under suspicion of fathering Noah (1Q20 II, 4, 15; V, 3–4).

The antecedent of the third masculine singular "he" of "he shall be glorified (יכבד) among the sons of heaven" (1Q19 13–14 3) is missing. If the verb had been plural, the antecedent could have been those "who enter the Yaḥad with the congregation of the sons of heaven" (1QH^a XI, 23/4Q427 7 II, 18). But a singular pronoun requires a singular antecedent and the most promising candidate in the extant text, by default, is Noah. It is tempting to hypothesize that the writer had

---

16. Reconstructed as "wicked" (ר[שעי]ם) in the *DSSR 3*.

a sense of poetic justice; that the one wrongfully suspected of being illegitimately fathered by one of the "sons of heaven" would one day be glorified among them.

It is fairly safe to say that on the basis of the mere juxtaposition of the phrases, "my chosen one"[17] refers to either Noah himself or to a chosen line for which Noah is an archetypical ancestor. For example, 4QNaissance de Noé[a] (4Q534) attests a "chosen one of God" (בחיר אלהא)" (4Q534 1 I, 10) in a text shown to contain many parallels to Noah or to the lineage to which he belonged.

1QBook of Noah expands Noah's already exalted portrayal in the *Genesis Apocryphon*, but it is a small stretch and not an unreasonable one. If the glorified and chosen figure in 1Q19 was intended to be Noah, this text would preserve a logical continuation of a trajectory already observable in the *Genesis Apocryphon*.

4QTanḥumim (4Q176): The Name of Noah and Consoling Words[18]

4QTanḥumim incorporates Isa 54:4–10a—the "days of Noah . . . waters of Noah"[19] text—into other biblical "words of comfort" in which God speaks in the first person[20] (4Q176 8–11), but it stops short of quoting v. 10b: "Neither will my covenant of peace be removed, says the Lord God who has compassion on you."[21] It would be difficult to prove that the exclusion was exegetically motivated unless evidence was found in the text that the exegete believed that the covenant of peace had been or could be removed from at least some of Israel. Most likely the final line of the quotation satisfactorily communicated the thrust of the message: "My steadfast love (חסד) will not depart from you" (4Q176 8–11 12/Isa 54:10a).

Interpretation of the quotation follows immediately: "*13* [. . . one could not] grow tired of these words of comfort (תנחומים), for great honor is written in [. . .] *14* [. . .] for those who love [. . .] will never again [. . .] *15* [Beli]al to oppress (לענות) His servants [. . .]" (4Q176 8–11 13–15). The juxtaposition of תנחומים with "days of Noah" suggests a wordplay dually based on Noah's naming (ינחמנו) in Gen 5:29 and on Deutero-Isaiah. In his supplication to God that he would do "righteousness" (הצדק) and would see the "corpses of your priests," the author of 4Q176 appeals first to Isa 40:1–5, beginning with "Comfort (נחמו), comfort my people" (1Q176 1–2 I, 1–4).[22] The "days of Noah" and, possibly, the naming of Noah are,

---

17. This word could be translated either as "my chosen ones" or "one" (cf. Isa 45:4; 65:9). In 1Q19, there is little to support the translation as plural.

18. On 4Q176, see DJD V and John Strugnell, "Notes en marge du volume V des Discoveries in the Judaean Desert of Jordan," *RevQ* 7 (1970): 163–276, here 229–36.

19. See discussion of Isa 54 in chapter 2 above.

20. Christopher D. Stanley, "The Importance of *Tanḥumim* (4Q176)," *RevQ* 15 (1991–92): 569–82, here 576.

21. Variations between 4Q176's quotation of Isa 54 are primarily orthographic. However, עוד is lacking where the MT preserves it (עוד על הארץ) and includes it (נשבעתי מקצוף עליך עד) where it is lacking in the MT but present in 1QIsa[a] (*DSSB*, 361).

22. This reading is based on the ordering of the fragments in DJD V, 60–67.

therefore, linked to times of catastrophic destruction but also to the remembrance and comforting promise of "never again."

God's "never again" promise to Noah (see Gen 8:21, 22; 9:8–17), interpreted in Isa 54:9 to apply to the exile, is here reinterpreted and contemporized by the author of 4Q176 as "consoling words" for those oppressed by Belial in the writer's own day. Therefore, the "days of Noah" act as a foundational story that continued to have relevance into the present; throughout time, God had turned and would continue to turn toward his people with great and eternal compassions (רחם/רחמים) (4Q176 8–11 9–10).[23]

4QFestival Prayers[B]: Covenant, Atonement, and Judgment

In 4QFestival Prayers, God's compassion (רחם) is celebrated annually in a ceremony that also remembered God's covenant with Noah and that shared a number of Noah traditions with *Jubilees*.[24] Noah appears, somewhat unexpectedly, in the middle of this set of prayers for the Day of Atonement:[25]

> 1 [of the earth in order to dis]tinguish between the righteous (צדיק) and the wicked (לרשע). And You have appointed [the wicked as our ransom and by the upright] 2 [You shall execute destruction] upon all of our oppressors. (4Q508 1 1–2/1Q34bis 3 I, 4–5)

> 2 [Prayer for the Day of Atonemen]t: Remember, Lord, the festival (מועד) of your compassions (רחמיך) and the time of return (שוב) 3 [. . .] for You established it for us as a festival of fasting, and ever[lasting] statute (חוק עולם) [. . .] 4 [. . .] and You know the things hidden (הנסתרות) and revea[led (הנגלות). . .] 5 [. . .] You [kn]ow our inclination (יצר) [. . .] 6 [. . . ou]r [rising] and our lying down [. . ..] (4Q508 2 2–6)

> 1 [. . .] we have done wickedly (הרשענו) [. . .] 2 [. . .] and because they were more in number. [Then] You established (תקם) [Your covenant] for Noah [. . .] 3 [. . . You]r faithfulness with [Is]aac and Jacob [. . .]. (4Q508 3 1–3)

> [. . . the God of Israel] who chose us, and His covenant [. . .]. (4Q508 4 2)

---

23. For "great compassions," see 4Q417 1 II, 8.
24. See "Return (שובי), Jerusalem" from a quotation of Isa 52:1–3 preceding that of Isa 54:4–10a in 4Q176 8–11 3. The juxtaposition of the two quotations hints at a subsidiary theme whereby "return" is interpreted also as "repentance."
25. 4Q508 2–3 has "points of contact with the Confession for the Day of Atonement in the conventional Jewish liturgy": "you have known things hidden and revealed" (2 4) and its proximity to "we have done wickedly" (3 1) (Moshe Weinfeld, "Prayer and Liturgical Practice in the Qumran Sect," in *The Dead Sea Scrolls: Forty Years of Research* [ed. D. Dimant and U. Rappaport; STDJ 10; Leiden: Brill, 1992], 241–58, here 246–47.

4Q508 is one of likely four copies of *Festival Prayers* (4Q507–509; 1Q34–34[bis]) dating from the late Hasmonean to the Herodian period.[26] As a potentially relatively stable liturgical text, 4Q508 could be an early composition, influencing Noah interpretation across the genres, including the narrative of *Jubilees*.[27]

Daniel Falk categorizes *Festival Prayers* as "communal confessions," and his approach frees the prayers from calendrical constraints, providing room for his alternative categorization of "confessions." His reconstruction results in a set of prayers that are "definitely out of calendrical order," in contrast to James Davila, who uses chronology as an organizing principle.[28] The Day of Atonement and the Feast of Weeks feature prominently in *Festival Prayers*, and, according to Falk, only these are certain.[29]

The covenant with Noah is not associated with confession in the Hebrew Bible, and while a subtly "repentant Noah" is linked to the Day of Atonement in *Jubilees*, the direction of dependence, if any, is difficult to ascertain. However, there may be hints of the exegetical basis for linking covenant, atonement, and judgment to Noah in other phrases in the prayer.

"TO DISTINGUISH BETWEEN THE RIGHTEOUS AND THE WICKED" (4Q508 1 1)

"To distinguish between the righteous and the wicked (לדעת בין צדיק לרשע)"[30] appears in what is likely another Day of Atonement prayer[31] in the same text, preceding the penitent's acknowledgment that God would execute destruction upon oppressors. בין צדיק לרשע is preserved in the Hebrew Bible only in Malachi in a verse quoted or alluded to and variously interpreted at Qumran in a variety of texts.[32] "Once more you shall see the difference between the righteous and the

---

26. 4Q509 (ca. 70 B.C.E.) to 4Q507–509 (early first c. C.E.). See James H. Charlesworth and D. T. Olson, "Prayers for the Festivals," in *The Dead Sea Scrolls: Hebrew, Aramaic, and Greek Texts with English Translations*, vol. 4A (ed. J. H. Charlesworth; Princeton Theological Seminary Dead Sea Scrolls Project; Tübingen: Mohr Siebeck, 1997), 46–105, here 47.

27. Regarding the distinction between nonsectarian and sectarian liturgical texts, see Eileen M. Schuller, "Prayer, Hymnic, and Liturgical Texts," in *The Community of the Renewed Covenant: The Notre Dame Symposium on the Dead Sea Scrolls* (ed. E. Ulrich and J. VanderKam; Notre Dame, Ind.: University of Notre Dame Press, 1994), 153–71, here 170: "The very essence of prayer/hymnic discourse, whether sectarian or non-sectarian, is its dependence on a common stock of stereotypical and formulaic, biblically-based phraseology."

28. James R. Davila, *Liturgical Works* (Eerdmans Commentaries on the Dead Sea Scrolls; Grand Rapids: Eerdmans, 2000), 34. Cf. M. Baillet's allocations that also include New Year and Omer in 4Q508 (DJD VII, 177) and Tabernacles and Second Passover in 4Q509 (DJD VII, 185).

29. Daniel Falk, *Daily, Sabbath and Festival Prayers in the Dead Sea Scrolls* (STDJ 27; Leiden: Brill, 1998), 159–62. Cf. Charlesworth and Olson: "strong emphasis on the covenant relationship between God and the Community permeates the prayers ("Prayers," 47–48).

30. See parallel in 1Q34[bis] 3 I, 4–5.

31. WAC (2005), 206.

32. See CD XX, 20–21; 4Q253a 1 I, 4–5; 1QH[a] XV, 15; 4Q521 14 2.

wicked" (Mal 3:18) implies that God had already once made such a distinction in the past, most notably in the days of Noah.

The penitents thus hoped to be included among the "righteous" who would be distinguished from the "wicked" in a future judgment. The *Genesis Apocryphon* later makes the distinction explicit in connection with Noah; Noah blesses God for destroying the workers of violence, wickedness (רשע), and deceit and for rescuing the righteous one (צדיק) (1Q20 XI, 13–14).

"You know our inclination" (4Q508 2 5)

In this prayer, which remembers the covenant with Noah, the liturgist is selective concerning God's response to human inclination (יצר). "You know our inclination (ידעת יצרנו)" and the "festival of compassions" (4Q508 2 2–5) allude to Ps 103, in which God removes transgressions and bestows compassion (רחם)[33] on those who fear him as a response to his knowledge of human inclination: "for he knows (ידע) our inclination (יצרנו)" (Ps 103:12–14). The liturgist of the *Festival Prayers* apparently accepts the psalmist's reading of human inclination as derived from Gen 8:21, in which human inclination prompts God's compassion, instead of Gen 6:5, in which human inclination prompts God's judgment.

"We have done wickedly" (4Q508 3 1)

The need for a confession as part of the Day of Atonement is implied already in Lev 16:21, but the form in 4Q508 more closely resembles other Hebrew Bible penitential prayers. Daniel prays to his covenant-keeping God, "We have sinned, we have committed iniquity, we have acted wickedly (הרשענו), we have rebelled" (Dan 9:4–5; cf. Neh 9:33; Ps 106:6; Lev 26:40).

Notably, the initiates into the Qumran community make confession during the sectarian covenant renewal ceremony in the *Community Rule*, saying, "We have committed iniquity, we have transgressed, we have sinned, we have acted wickedly (הרשענו), we and our fathers before us" (1QS I, 24–25; cf. also CD XX, 28–29).[34] It is significant that a Day of Atonement prayer (4Q508) shares elements with and is possibly subordinated to the covenant renewal ceremony confes-

---

33. Cf. *Jubilees*, where God would forgive transgressions and show mercy to those who turned to him in righteousness (5:17–18).

34. A first-person confessional prayer spoken by the high priest on the Day of Atonement is preserved in a later tradition: "I have committed iniquity, I have transgressed, I have sinned before you, I and my household" (*m. Yoma* 3:8). The connection between these verbs and those of 1QS I, 24–25 was noted already by J. Licht, מגילת הסרכים [*The Rule of the Community*] (Jerusalem: Bialik Institute, 1965), 66–67. Regarding a further parallel between *m. Yoma* 5:4 and 11QT XXVI, 5–7, in which the blood from the goat is collected in a golden basin, see Lawrence H. Schiffman, "The Case of the Day of Atonement Ritual," in *Biblical Perspectives: Early Use and Interpretation of the Bible in Light of the Dead Sea Scrolls: Proceedings of the First International Symposium of the Orion Center for the Study of the Dead Sea Scrolls and Associated Literature, 12–14 May 1996* (ed. M. E. Stone and E. G. Chazon; STDJ 28; Leiden: Brill, 1998), 181–88, here 186–87.

sional prayer in the *Community Rule*. A possible harmonization and conflation of elements of these two festivals may already be anticipated in the collection of predominately Day of Atonement and *Shevuot* prayers in 4Q508, which associates atonement with covenant, oath taking, and judgment. 5QRule, to be studied in the next chapter, appears to attest another version of the covenant renewal ceremony that, unlike the ceremony in 1QS, explicitly maintains its historical connection with Noah.

"You established your covenant for Noah" (4Q508 3 2)

4Q508 selects a particular kind of historical remembrance that begins with Noah, remembering him as the first one with whom God makes a covenant. A lacuna follows "Noah" where "Abraham" would be expected, after which God's faithfulness to Isaac and Jacob is remembered. Thus far, this study indicates that texts in the priestly Aramaic Levi traditions tend to begin their retellings and remembrances with Noah. In contrast, the sectarian *Damascus Document* will skip over Noah to the "sons of Noah" who went astray, listing Abraham as the first positive figure and associating covenant first with Abraham rather than with Noah (CD III, 1-2; XII, 11).

A liturgist of 4QFestival Prayers wishing to introduce "covenant," could have chosen from an array of biblical figures. However, the covenant with Noah in Genesis was already conveniently associated with the judgment of the wicked and the preservation of the righteous. Read alongside Malachi's "distinguishing between the righteous and the wicked," the text thus essentially reinterpreted the Day of Atonement as a remembrance of the covenant with Noah in which past distinctions between the righteous and the wicked (cf. Mal 3:18) were remembered, and present and future distinctions hoped for.

The liturgy continues with "who chose us and his covenant." It is not said of Noah that he was "chosen" in 4Q508. However, writers familiar with the liturgy may have later fashioned Noah into an archetype for a "chosen" group, also attributing this "chosenness" to Noah.[35]

We might ask by what exegetical pathway Noah appeared in a confessional prayer. There are several possibilities. Righteousness could be reinterpreted as a "repentant" righteousness, and so what distinguished the righteous from the wicked (רשע) (4Q508 1 1/cf. Mal 3:18; Gen 6:5, 9) was not that the righteous ones had never been wicked. It was that they had repented of their wickedness (הרשענו) (4Q508 3 1). Noah as an implied repentant righteous figure also emerged in the narrative genre in *Jub.* 5:5-19.

Human "inclination" in the Noah narrative in Genesis is read through Ps 103, in which God knew and understood human inclination and was prepared

---

35. Cf. 4Q534 1 I, 10, "chosen one of God," and 1Q19 15 2, a text that relates the remarkable appearance of Noah at birth and in which God chooses someone to establish what is likely a covenant.

to be compassionate and forgiving, a foundational understanding of prayers of confession. Finally, a remembrance of the "covenant with Noah" in the liturgy following the confession may have been designed to remind God once again to distinguish the penitent righteous from the unrepentant wicked.

1QFestival Prayers specifically mentions covenant renewal (1Q34^{bis} 3 II, 5–6), a theme fully developed throughout the *Jubilees* narrative, in which the original covenant with Noah is renewed and celebrated by Noah's descendants. All of these Noah traditions, in particular, point to a strong, shared tradition that possibly stands behind both *Festival Prayers* and *Jubilees*. Although 4Q508 is more explicit in linking repentance to Noah's covenant and judgment than *Jubilees* is, this does not entail the literary dependence of the liturgy on the narrative. *Jubilees* was constrained by the limitation of the narrative genre, and the shaping of traditions likely needed to be more subtly achieved.

4QFestival Prayers salvages the covenant with Noah from its relative obscurity in the Hebrew Bible apart from Genesis, placing Noah first and foremost in a remembrance of the covenant in arguably the most important festival of the liturgical calendar, the Day of Atonement. It includes Noah in the list of ancestors, a marker notably of texts of priestly "Aramaic Levi" traditions, but here, too, as in *Jubilees*, Noah is found in a priestly context as transmitted in the Hebrew language.

It may well be that, even in the Aramaic priestly traditions, prayers for designated festivals—Day of Atonement and First Fruits (*Shevuot*)—and certain words, such as blessings and curses, had to be spoken in Hebrew. A rabbinic tradition preserved in *m. Sotah* 7:2 specifies eight occasions when Hebrew (לשון קודש) must be spoken, including the "verses of the firstfruits" (Deut 26:3–10), blessings and curses (Deut 27:15–26), and the blessing of the high priest on the Day of Atonement (Lev 16).[36] It is interesting that Noah was priestly in an early *Aramaic* tradition, but he made the transition successfully to Hebrew, becoming a bilingual priest. Not all Aramaic Noah traditions transferred into Hebrew texts as easily. While *m. Sotah* cannot be dated, it does stand as another witness to a trajectory of conversations about language, a discussion about the uses of Hebrew and languages other than Hebrew within the life and the praxis of a movement.

4QPARAPHRASE OF GENESIS AND EXODUS (4Q422):
CREATION AND RE-CREATION

4Q422 also incorporates judgment into its definition of covenant. Identifiable in this fragmentary copy, dated to the Hasmonean period, are some lines on

---

36. For a study of the categorization of liturgical and hymnic texts based on the particular shape of the blessing and curse formula and their correlation to this list in *m. Sotah* 7:2, see Martin G. Abegg, Jr., "'And He Shall Answer and Say...'—A Little Backlighting," in *Studies in the Hebrew Bible, Qumran, and the Septuagint Presented to Eugene Ulrich* (ed. P. W. Flint, E. Tov and J. C. VanderKam; VTSup 101; Leiden: Brill, 2006), 203–11.

creation, the Egyptian plagues, and strong hints of the flood narrative. The title given by the official editors[37] is misleading, for it is not known whether any other stories from Genesis and Exodus were a part of this text.[38] The flood narrative, if actually extant in the way the editors envision it to be in frgs. 2–7, is more complex and exegetically developed than a simple paraphrase would allow. Of the additional twenty-three unassigned or "unidentified" fragments, seven contain language related to Noah traditions that could be either interpretative comments on the Noah narrative or even variant, duplicate retellings.[39]

The study of 4Q422 is further complicated by the number and the small size of some of the fragments and by the high level of uncertainty of reconstructed words and the placement of fragments.[40] Six of the fragments have been reconstructed, although sometimes on the basis of doubtful readings, to form col. II, an interpreted narrative about Noah and the flood.

The first narrative retold in 4Q422, as reconstructed, is preserved in frg. 1 and recounts that "he made" (עשה) the heavens and earth and caused Adam/humankind (reconstructed) to rule (המשילו) with the instruction that he not eat from the tree that gives knowledge of good and evil. "Evil inclination" (ביוצר רע) and "work[s of wickedness]" (למעשי רשעה) follow immediately after reference to the tree of knowledge (4Q422 I, 6–12) and act as "a bridge to the Flood narrative."[41] "Inclination" in 4Q422, then, prompts acts of judgment (cf. Gen 6:5) and not God's compassion, as in *Festival Prayers*.

The Noah story is recounted in frgs. 2–7 (discussed below) followed by the plagues narrative. Its very juxtaposition with the creation and flood narratives highlights a thematic reversal of creation: waters turn to blood; darkness is "appointed" instead of light;[42] food meant for eating is destroyed;[43] locusts consume the green plants; and the firstborn are destroyed.

---

37. DJD XIII.
38. On the selective use of biblical themes in 4Q422, see DJD XIII, 426.
39. These include "into the ark" (4Q422 7); "cut off" (כרת) and a partially reconstructed "the deeps" (תהומות) (4Q422 8); "his way" (דרכו) (frg. C); "fountains of the great" (frg. D), "they shouted" ... "they cry" (frg. G); "his righteousness" (צדקתו) (frg. L); "his inclination" (יצרו) and "waters" or, perhaps, "waters will cease" (frg. P).
40. Very shortly before this study went to press, Ariel Feldman kindly sent me his fresh edition and commentary on 4Q422, a masterful study that I only regret I did not have before me as I was struggling with the interpretation of the text. Thankfully, it is soon to be published as Ariel Feldman, "The Story of the Flood in 4Q422," in *Proceedings of the Symposium 'The Dynamics of Exegesis and Language at Qumran' held on May 14–16, 2007 at Göttingen* (ed. D. Dimant and R. Kratz; forthcoming).
41. So DJD XIII, 423; Torleif Elgvin, "The Genesis Section of 4Q422 (4QParaGenExod)," *DSD* 1 (1994): 180–96, here 187. "The fact that the use of יצר in 4Q422 seems to be related to Genesis 3–4 and not to the flood generation indicates a conscious reflection on the beginning of sin on earth with Adam" (DJD XIII, 423). Cf. Rom 5:12–18.
42. Cf. 1QS X, 1–2; Ps 18:12 [18:11]; 2 Sam 22:12.
43. In Eden, mankind was set in charge "to eat the fruit" (לאכול פרי) (4Q422 I, 9). Cf. Exod 10:15; Gen 3:2–6.

Almost all of the language in col. III may be accounted for either by the Exodus plagues narrative and Pss 78 and 105,[44] psalms that pass over the creation and flood narratives but include the plagues in their historical retellings. It appears that the author felt that, in order to be comprehensive, Israel's primeval stories needed to be included as part of Israel's "internal history."[45] However, another compelling reason is discernible.

One phrase (here italicized) is an exegetical development not found precisely in Exodus, Ps 78, or Ps 105. "[And] he hardened [his] heart [so that he would] sin *in order that the pe[ople of Isra]el would know* (למען דעת) <*it*> *for eternal gene[rations]* (דורות עולם). He turned their [water] to blood" (4Q422 III, 7).

The phrase may have been derived exegetically from a conflation of the biblical accounts of the flood and the plagues. God proclaims that he will harden Pharaoh's heart and so gain glory for himself over Pharaoh and that the *Egyptians* will know that he is the Lord (Exod 14:4). The rainbow, the "sign of the covenant" is given by God not only for Noah and all living creatures but also for "eternal generations" (Gen 9:12). Components of the phrase are paralleled in the Noah section. The waters prevailed upon the earth so that there would be those who would "know (למען דעת) the glory of the Most High" and "he illumined the heavens" is also a sign for eternal generations (דורות עולם) (4Q422 II, 8–11).

The rainbow is thus a sign of God's covenant but with new layers of meaning. In Genesis, the rainbow was a sign of God's promise that he would never again destroy the world by a flood. It also becomes a "post-judgment sign" announcing to "eternal generations" that God had the power to destroy his enemies because he had done so already in the past. The force of "never again" (Gen 9:15) is blunted and becomes a subtle threat and even a promise of judgments to come. God could still and would still carry out his judgments as he had done upon the Egyptians by means of the plagues.

We turn now to col. II and the reconstruction of frgs. 2–7.[46]

1 [and God saw that ?] great and [was the evil of mankind on the earth?] 2 [ ] the [ ] 2a [righteous in] his generation o[n the earth] to the living God [ ] 3 [ ] they were saved (נצל) o[n the earth] on the earth because[ ] 4 [to save]the[animals, Noah] and his sons, [his] wi[fe and his sons' wives from]the waters of the flood and from [ ] 5 and the [They entered] the ar[k and] God [sh]ut (סגר) behind them [ ]and on it[47] he will put[ ] 6 whom/*which* Go[d] chose (בחר) *it*[48] [ ]the sluices of heav[en] were op[en]ed [and] they [pou]red out [rain] on the earth 7 under the heave[ns to] raise water upon the ear[th forty] days and for[ty] 8 nights there was r[ain]o[n the earth the water]s were mig[ht]y (גבר) on[the earth] (?) in order to 9 know (למען דעת) the glory

---

44. DJD XIII, 429.
45. Cf. 4Q243–244, which also include primeval stories in Israel's history.
46. Suggested alternative readings are shown in italics.
47. עליו, "on" or "against it," could refer to the door. Cf. תרע 1Q20 XI, 1.
48. No antecedent is apparent in the extant text.

(כבוד) of the High[est] (עליון) the[The bow/*sacrifice?*] he set/*brought* before him *10* and it shone on [the] heave[ns and it became a sign between God and the ea]rth and man[ki]nd [on the earth]a fut[ure] sign for generation[s] *11* of eternity. Greatly [and never more] will a flood[destroy the earth] *12* [the s]et times/*appointed times?* of day and night [the lights to shine o]n heaven and ear[th   ] *13* [the earth and]its [fu]ll[ne]ss   [everythi]ng He gave [to mankind] (4Q422 II, 2–7).⁴⁹

Before proceeding with the text as reconstructed, one strong caution is in order. Fragment 2 has been pieced together by the editors with frgs. 3–7 to form a flood narrative, but no word in frg. 2 is explicitly or exclusively Noachic: neither "whom/which God chose it (בחר בה)," "under all the heaven," "night," "to know the glory of the Most High," "he illumined the heavens," "eternity," "appointed times of day and night," nor "fullness." Even a cursory examination of the language suggests that the fragment could belong to a parallel creation narrative. These fragments require further examination; however, we proceed for the moment according to the editors' reconstruction and ordering.

Partly because the text is so fragmentary, any recurrence of a word is noteworthy and invites the suggestion of wordplay. For example, that God closed (qal of סגר) the door of the ark implies deliverance *from* an act of judgment (4Q422 II, 5), whereas God delivered (hiphil of סגר) the Egyptians *to* death (III, 9).⁵⁰

"Whom/what God chose (it) (אשר בחר בה אל)"? (4Q422 II, 6)
Of particular interest is the unknown antecedent of "whom/what God chose (it) (אשר בחר בה אל)?" (4Q422 II, 6). There is a third feminine singular ending with no obvious antecedent, an object that automatically excludes Noah or any group of people. The editors are aware of the difficulty, translating as "God elected her" in the official edition⁵¹ but modifying their translation in the *Dead Sea Scrolls Reader* to "whom God chose."

The shape of the phrase is remarkably similar to 4Q508 4 2: "Who chose us and his covenant (אשר בחר בנו ובריתו)," a *Festival Prayer* that also remembers God's covenant with Noah (4Q508 3 2).⁵² While caution must be exercised in attributing any of the language of frg. 2 of 4Q422 to the Noah narrative, the unusual shape of the phrase as it appears in both the liturgy and in 4Q422 does suggest that remembrance of covenant is intended in both texts, in which times

---

49. Torleif Elgvin and Emanuel Tov, *DSSR 3*, 570–73. A comparison of this translation with DJD reveals that the editors present a "corrected" edition in *DSSR 3* but have neglected to signify that the "correction" is actually an incorporation of frg. 7. The edition and translation are headed with "Col. II (fragments 2–6)," and frg. 7 appears independently on the next page.

50. The language is derived from Ps 78:50.

51. DJD XIII, 426.

52. אשר followed by בחר and ב is found elsewhere only in 1QSb III, 22–23: "God chose the sons of Zadok," and 4Q503 24–25 4: "The God of Israel who chose us."

of judgment are remembered and deliverance from judgment hoped for. Furthermore, significant congruencies between 4Q422 and the community hymn in 1QH^a IX with respect to creation language would suggest that 4Q422 derives its language from hymn and liturgy[53] and that 4Q422 itself has overtones of creation throughout the fragments.

"To raise water upon the earth (לעלות מים על הארץ)" (4Q422 II, 7)

"Waters on the earth" is a familiar phrase from the Genesis account, as are the "waters of Noah" (Isa 54:9). But the verb עלה is rarely used in the Hebrew Bible in collocation with and describing מים upon ארץ and *never* in connection with the creation or flood accounts.[54]

Where they do appear, "waters" that rise up "on the earth" become a metaphor for the nations such as Egypt (Jer 46:8) and the Philistines (Jer 47:1–2). Furthermore, the presence of "cover" (כסה), the verb describing the plague of locusts that covered the earth (4Q422 III, 10) and describes the action of the floodwaters covering the earth in Gen 7:19–20, is found *also* in Jer 46:8. From the little that remains of the text, there are hints that the writer read Jeremiah alongside Genesis (and perhaps Exodus), interpreting Noah's floodwaters metaphorically as "nations" or enemies from which God's people would be protected.[55]

"It shone on the heavens ... the earth ... as a sign for future generations of eternity" (4Q422 II, 9–11)

The rainbow shines (אור) on the heavens and the earth. This hiphil verb is collocated with "heavens" only in Gen 1:15, 17—lights in the sky—and in the reconstructed 4QJub^a (4Q216) describing the sun, moon, and stars.[56] The use here may indicate a harmonization of Gen 9:11 with Gen 1:14. The covenant with Noah included God's "never again" promise and was accompanied by the reestablishment of days and seasons in Gen 8:22. In the creation account in Genesis, God put lights in the sky as signs (לאתת) and to mark seasons (למועדים).

According to this reading, the writer imports creation language from Gen 1 into the illumination by the rainbow to emphasize that the seasons (מועדים) had

---

53. 1QH^a IX: "eternal" (IX, 5; cf. 4Q422 II, 11); "counsel" (IX, 7; cf. 4Q422 frg. M); lengthening of anger in judgment (IX, 8; cf. 4Q422 frg. Q); "before you made them" (IX, 9; cf. 4Q422 9); "you formed all their hosts" (IX, 12; cf. 4Q422 I, 6); creation of angels as luminaries (אורות מ) for mysteries (IX, 13; cf. II, 10 "he illumined"); "you created seas and deeps" (IX, 15–16; cf. 4Q422 8 partially reconstructed as "the deeps"); "appointed times ... generation to generation ... punishment for retribution" (IX, 19; cf. 4Q422 II, 12; I, 13).

54. *Jubilees* recounts the second day of creation, where some waters went up (עלו) above and others went down over the earth (4Q216 V, 12–14/*Jub.* 2:3b).

55. The biblical prophets are read alongside Genesis narratives also in 4Q176 and 4Q252—254.

56. See also Ezek 32:7 as an example of "de-creation": "When I blot you out, I will cover the heavens and make their stars dark. I will cover the sun with a cloud and the moon shall not give its light (יאיר)."

ceased during the flood and were *also* reestablished following Noah's post-flood sacrifice, evidence that the two narratives were viewed as two parts of the same story. This telling implies that the beginning of the calendar began post-flood and suggests a priestly interest within 4Q422.

In conclusion, 4Q422 intensifies the connection in the biblical narrative of creation, undoing of creation, and re-creation by juxtaposing the creation, flood, and plagues narratives and by incorporating harmonizing elements with a possible unifying theme.[57] Serious difficulties do still remain with regard to the reconstruction and ordering of the 4Q422 fragments, and any present conclusions about the function of the Noah story within the work should not be based on any particular *ordering* of the fragments.[58] Even so, the presence of one or more versions of the creation, flood, and plague narratives permits an attempt to discern an exegetical purpose of the piece. "Evil inclination" and misappropriation of knowledge prompt judgment—exemplified by flood and plagues—but what was established at creation would ultimately be preserved, including human and animal life, heavenly lights, and "appointed times." The "reversal of creation" that the plagues demonstrated affected the Egyptians and not Israel. For eternal generations, the glory of the Most High would be demonstrated by the deliverance *to* death of those who acted out of an evil inclination and the deliverance of the righteous *from* death.

4QAdmonition Based on the Flood (4Q370): Survival of the "Made Righteous"

4Q370 is written in a late Hasmonean hand, and the editor notes that the text probably was not composed by the Qumran community, for it contains none of Qumran's distinctive theological terminology.[59] Divergences from the Genesis text do not appear to be exegetically motivated and may be explained as if the writer was citing Genesis from memory.[60] Column I tells the biblical flood story, electing to narrate the events of destruction by flood while remaining silent about

---

57. Esther G. Chazon has observed that both 4Q422 and the *Dibre Hamme'orot* draw together Adam and the flood "with sin and its punishment providing the unifying theme" ("The Creation and Fall of Adam in the Dead Sea Scrolls," in *The Book of Genesis in Jewish and Oriental Christian Interpretation: A Collection of Essays* [ed. J. Frishman and L. Van Rompey; Traditio exegetica Graeca 5; Leuven: Peeters, 1997], 13–24, here 2). Michael E. Stone notes that the Adam traditions themselves lack legendary expansion and reworking ("The Axis of History at Qumran," in *Pseudepigraphic Perspectives: The Apocrypha and Pseudepigrapha in Light of the Dead Sea Scrolls: Proceedings of the International Symposium of the Orion Center for the Study of the Dead Sea Scrolls and Associated Literature, 12–14 January 1997* [ed. E. G. Chazon and M. E. Stone; STDJ 31; Leiden: Brill, 1999], 145).

58. See, however, Ariel Feldman's forthcoming study, "The Story of the Flood in 4Q422."

59. C. A. Newsom, DJD XIX, 86.

60. DJD XIX, 87.

Noah, the ark, and the preservation of life. Column II cautions the writer's contemporaries regarding iniquity and rebellion but promises God's compassionate response toward those who would seek him.

Carol Newsom has observed that "[t]he author of 4Q370 does not mention Noah. In 4Q370 there is only the statement of divine judgment as the response to human evil and rebellion. This selection and omission of detail suggests that the author is interested in the flood as a story of disobedience and punishment rather than, e.g., as a story of the deliverance of the righteous."[61]

4Q370 may not mention Noah, but this omission does not necessarily require that the author was *not* interested in deliverance of the *contemporary* righteous. The narrative in col. I is told within a framework of *waw* consecutive and perfect verbs, but col. II signals a shift from the past to the future with a *waw* + perfect verb, "they will seek" (ודרשו), and an imperfect verb: God would "declare righteous" (יצדיק). Column II thus effectively contemporized the primordial story of destruction and deliverance, containing instructions for how to be delivered from future judgment based on an implied understanding of how and why the primordial Noah was delivered.[62]

> *1* From iniquity (עון), they will seek (ודרשו) [. . .] *2* The LORD will make righteous (יצדיק) [. . .] *3* And he will purify (טהר) them of their iniquity (עון) [. . .] *4* their evil (רעתם), in their knowing (בדעתם) (how to distinguish) bet[ween (בין) good and evil] [. . .] *5* they spring up (צמח), but like a shadow (צל) are their days o[n the earth][. . .] *6* and forevermore he will have compassion (רחם) [. . .] *7* the mighty acts (גבורת) of the LORD, remember the won[ders] [. . .] *8* on account of the dread (פחד) of him; and [your] sou[l] will rejoice [. . .] *9* those who follow you. Do not rebel (מרה) against the word[s of the LORD]. (4Q370 1 II, 1–9)

Column I begins with a comment on the bestowal of great abundance and the subsequent rebellion (מרה) of the people that brought God's judgment on those with "evil inclination" (I, 1–3a). The Qumran corpus as a whole exhibits heightened interest in the deluge as punishment for sin, whereas interpretation of the expulsion from Eden is virtually unscripted. Even though Newsom suspects that the author of 4Q370 is describing creation in the first lines of the text, she concludes, "One has to ask . . . for the homiletical purposes of the author of 4Q370, the entire primeval history of Genesis 1–5 has been radically telescoped, so that the pattern of creation-punishment is focused on the events of the deluge rather than on the expulsion from Eden, the first murder, etc."[63]

Creation and the expulsion from Eden may have been perceived by the writer as merely the prelude to the main flood event, which had cosmic implica-

---

61. Carol A. Newsom, "4Q370: An Admonition Based on the Flood," *RevQ* 13 (1988): 23–43, here 35. Cf. DJD XIX, 88.
62. Trans. adapted from DJD XIX, 91, 96.
63. DJD XIX, 92. For rabbinic parallels, see DJD XIX, 92–93.

tions, and it was the antediluvian evil and rebellion in the Noah narrative that led directly to the flood. The verbs "eat, be satisfied, bless" (4Q370 1 I, 1–2) resonate with Deut 8:19, "the single instance in which all three verbs ('eat, be satisfied, and bless') occur in uninterrupted sequence."[64] Israel is brought into a "good land" and is warned not to forget God or to fail to keep his commandments lest they perish as the nations that God destroys (Deut 8:7–20). The threat intrinsic in this allusion to Deut in 4Q370 subtly warned the readers of a judgment to come.

"He judged them ... according to their ... inclination" (1 I, 3a)

This derives from Genesis (וכל־יצר מחשבת לבו רק רע) (Gen 6:5). Inclination (יצר), here, in contrast to the approach in 4QFestival Prayers, prompts God's judgment rather than his compassion (cf. Gen 8:21). The *Damascus Document* is similar to 4Q370 in its treatment of "inclination"; both texts neglect to mention Noah in their historical recounting. Notably, 4QInstruction nuances יצר so that those of certain "inclinations" receive punishment (4Q416 1 16), but other "formations" are patterned after the holy angels (4Q417 1 I, 17).[65]

God "thunders" and the earth "trembles" (1 I, 3b–4)

Not seen in the Genesis account, this language occurs when God wars against the nations (Isa 29:6; Joel 4:15–16).[66] "The windows of heaven are opened, and the foundations of the earth tremble" is a judgment foretold to come upon transgressing Israel when she broke the "everlasting covenant" (Isa 24:5–18).

"Giants (הגבורים), too, did not escape (מלט)" (1 I, 5–9)

The text continues to recount the extermination of everything. The subtext of this interpretative interjection, that the giants did *not* escape, reveals a polemic within the text against a tradition holding that the giants *did* escape.[67] Finally, God sets a rainbow in the cloud so that he would remember the covenant (1 I, 7–9). Within the column, the language used has already seeded hints of other periodic judgments instead of a simple *Urzeit-Endzeit* model and, therefore, also the continuous relevance of the covenant for those who would hope to be the "righteous survivors."[68]

---

64. DJD XIX, 92.
65. Cf. CD, which nuances "inclination" by its association with two kinds of hearts.
66. Ariel Feldman, "*Mikra* and *Haggada* in the Flood Story According to 4Q370" (paper presented to the Graduate Enoch Seminar, Ann Arbor, Mich., May 2–4, 2006), 13.
67. See discussion in chapter 3 of traditions concerning giants that did escape the flood.
68. For "rainbow" integrally connected to judgment, see the discussions above on the *Genesis Apocryphon* and 4QParaphrase of Genesis and Exodus.

God "makes righteous (יצדיק)" (1 II, 1–4)

In col. II, God would make righteous (יצדיק) those who would seek (God). He would "purify (טהר) them of their iniquity (עון) [...] their evil (רעתם), in their knowing (בדעתם) (how to distinguish) bet[ween (בין) good and evil"[69] (4Q370 1 II, 1–4). What remains of col. II implies that God would "make righteous" those who turned from iniquity.[70]

Purification (טהר) of iniquity (עון) echoes "on the day I will cleanse (טהר) you from your iniquities (עון)" (Ezek 36:33). This was a purification following exile as the divine response to land-defiling bloodshed and idolatry (Ezek 36:16–18). Newsom has noted "striking parallels" throughout 4Q370 and Ezek 36:19–33, adding that "Ezekiel itself alludes to such an *Urzeit/Endzeit* typology in the eschatological prophecy recalling Israel's history of defiling the land and God's intention to purify the people and restore the desolate land like the garden of Eden (Ezek 36:35)."[71] Even if Ezekiel alludes to *Urzeit/Endzeit* typology, it would appear that the exegete behind 4Q370, by utilizing Genesis *and* Ezekiel, subscribes to an expanded view of periodic times of judgment, of which the biblical flood was the first.

"Forevermore (עולם) he will have compassion (רחם)" (4Q370 1 II, 6)

The terms עולם and רחם occur in collocation only in Isa 54:8, "with everlasting love I will have compassion on you." Isaiah continues, with the by-now-familiar "This is like the days of Noah to me" (Isa 54:9), a quotation cited in 4QTanḥumim and in which floodwaters are compared to exile. Compassion and deliverance are further linked to the Day of Atonement, a connection already made by the writer of *Jubilees* (5:17–18) in the context of the narrative of Noah and the flood and further developed in Qumran's *Festival Prayers*.[72] Of pressing concern for the writer was how people could become the righteous survivors of the future destruction.

4Q370 telescopes the creation and flood narratives and works with a variety of sources but with particular attention to Ezekiel. The text follows closely in the tradition of *Jubilees* and 4Q508 with one small surprise. The abundance upon the earth at creation is given as a reason for the rise of wickedness, and the text demonstrates an active resistance to the Enochic view of the origin of evil.

---

69. Cf. Gen 2:9, 17; 3:5, 22, and Solomon's prayer in 1 Kgs 3:9. Note especially Deut 1:39; 1QSa I, 10–11 (DJD XIX, 96).

70. Cf. God "makes righteous" the "Sons of Zadok, the priests" (1QSb III, 22–23), the only other occurrence of יצדיק in the Qumran writings.

71. DJD XIX, 88–89.

72. God's compassion also is linked with the Day of Atonement with reference to the inclination, confession of wickedness, repentance, and return, the covenant with Noah, and the God of Israel "who chose us" in 4QFestival Prayers[b] (4Q508 2 2–6; 3 1–2; 4 2). See also 4Q509 17 2–3, "He had compassion on us ... forever."

Repentance in the context of covenant is the only way to escape implied future judgment.

Continuing the Conversation

Worthy of remark is that all of the texts in this chapter exhibit the interpreters' recognition that their authoritative texts were already in conversation with each other. Genesis "converses" with Aramaic "Enochic" traditions in 1QNoah; 4QParaphrase of Genesis and Exodus conflates the judgments of flood and plagues; a quotation of Zephaniah is applied to the confusion of languages in 4QExposition on the Patriarchs; the naming of Noah is brought to bear on the "words of comfort" in 4QTanḥumim; and Ps 103 is applied alongside Genesis to the understanding of "inclination" in 4QFestival Prayers[b]. In addition, multiple allusions to the biblical prophets are found in 4QAdmonition Based on the Flood. In all of these, some authoritative texts were utilized as lenses to view other parts of their authoritative texts and without visible consideration for dating, provenance, or literary dependencies! In their own time, perhaps, interpreters simply viewed themselves as continuing a noble tradition, already observable in the psalms and prophets, of contemporizing the Noah and the flood story for a new day.

The Hebrew texts in this chapter and the next are specific and selective in their use of Noah traditions, at times even detaching the figure of Noah from traditions elsewhere associated with him. 4QTanḥumim plausibly plays on Noah's naming so that the "days of Noah" are remembered as part of a parcel of "comforting words" offered to those suffering oppression under Belial.

4QParaphrase of Genesis and Exodus (4Q422) and 4QAdmonition Based on the Flood take a retrospective look at the biblical flood as the first judgment story in a series of periodic judgments. They do not, in the extant text, recognize or require the archetypical flood survivor; however, both conflate the creation story with the flood story, thus implicating Noah as a "new Adam." There are new voices, however, that find new roles for Noah in the life of the community—4QFestival Prayers[b]—and also in the life of the imagination of the narrator or translator telling another rendition of the birth of Noah but this time in Hebrew.

The fragmentary 1QBook of Noah is "Enoch-like" in that it records the remarkable birth of Noah and possibly continues the trajectory of idealizing Noah. He is born into a time when the "mighty ones" prevailed just as the waters had prevailed during the flood. Light filled the room when he was born and Noah becomes the most promising candidate for a "chosen one" who is also "glorified among the sons of heaven." This *type* of idealization is unexpected in Hebrew. If Noah is indeed visualized as being among the "sons of heaven," then he would have access to revelation from the angels, and if this narrative parallels the Aramaic versions, then Lamech would have access to Enoch through Methuselah.

The choice of language for the transmission of at least certain types of traditions appears to have been a matter of live debate within the Dead Sea Scrolls. 4QExposition on the Patriarchs seems to mention the flood, but its importance here is for the reference to the "holy tongue" and what may be an argument, paralleled in *Jubilees*, that Abraham spoke Hebrew.

A comparison of the Noah traditions transmitted in the liturgical 4QFestival Prayers[b]—the covenant with Noah, the "first" named ancestor, atonement, inclination, destruction of the oppressors, confession, atonement, and distinguishing between the righteous and the wicked—with the Noah traditions transmitted in some Aramaic texts, points to the preservation of an early differentiation between what was usually transmitted in Hebrew from what was transmitted in Aramaic. In *Aramaic Levi Document*, in which Noah was named as "first priest," the Levi-priest was more oriented to "wisdom" than to Torah. However, as the movement developed and engaged more thoroughly with concepts of covenant, repentance, and priestly atonement drawn from the Mosaic Torah, Noah successfully made the transition from "first priest" in the Aramaic traditions to a newly interpreted "first priest" in the Hebrew traditions as preserved in *Jubilees* and 4QFestival Prayers[b].

In the next chapter, Noah traditions in Hebrew sectarian texts are studied. The *Damascus Document* and 4Ages of Creation, like 4QAdmonition Based on the Flood, detach Noah from the flood, whereas the *Commentaries on Genesis* and 5QRule remember and honor Noah as their "first priest."

CHAPTER SEVEN

Noah in the Hebrew Sectarian Texts

[In the] four hundred and eightieth year of Noah's life,
their end came to Noah
4QCommentary on Genesis B I, 1

You chose from among the he[ave]nly beings [. . .]
and You were pleased with Noah
5QRule13 1 6–7

Introduction

Dead Sea Scrolls that were more obviously composed or copied outside of the *Yaḥad* sectarian movement contained often quite different portrayals of Noah representing different positions on some of the most important questions of the day. In the scrolls that are more obviously sectarian and in which we might expect a more unified portrayal of Noah, the controversy actually sharpens and intensifies to the brink of polemic.

Each of the four texts under study in this chapter contains elements of its own version of the Noah and Watchers stories, its own cast of Israel's protagonists and antagonists with their own particular sets of characteristics tailored to the contexts within which they find themselves. In two of the scrolls—the *Damascus Document* and 4QAges of Creation—Noah is not named in the extant text, but the Watchers, Azazel, and progeny are developed as archetypical commandment breakers and lovers of iniquity, compared to the vilified "sons of Noah."

Noah appears as the first figure in 4QCommentary on Genesis A–D (4Q252–254a) and 5QRule (5Q13) and in the latter is even a likely candidate for the one who was "chosen from among the sons of gods." In all of these sectarian texts, the writers reach back into Aramaic and Hebrew traditions to newly reinterpret and recontextualize the stories of Noah and/or the Watchers. This chapter identifies Noah's role in each historical retelling and suggests affinities based on that role with pre-sectarian Hebrew and Aramaic Qumran texts.

Texts and Observations

The *Damascus Document*: The Missing Noah

In her insightful study of historical surveys in the Dead Sea Scrolls, Ida Fröhlich has identified significant themes shared among the *Genesis Apocryphon* (1Q20), the *Damascus Document* (CD), and "Pesher Genesis,"[1] renamed 4QCommentary on Genesis A (4Q252) in the *editio princeps*.[2] These historical surveys begin with the foundational story of the Watchers and antediluvian humanity and, according to Fröhlich, contain the common theme of the sins of זנות that defile the land.

The *Damascus Document* (CD) is extant in two medieval manuscripts discovered in the Cairo Genizah. Early versions of the document were also found in Caves 4 (4Q266–270), 5, and 6 at Qumran, but most significant for the present study is col. II of the *Damascus Document* and its 4QD Qumran parallels in 4Q266 and 4Q270, copies of which range in date from the mid-first century B.C.E. (4Q266) to the first half of the first century C.E. (4Q270). Although the part of CD that relates to the antediluvian period is not extant in the Qumran text, Joseph M. Baumgarten has established the essential reliability of the CD text for reconstruction.[3]

In the historical survey contained in CD II, 2–III, 12, figures from biblical and Enochic sources are divided between those who followed their inclination or willful heart and those who did not. The Watchers and their sons fell (נפלו), "ensnared by their willful heart," as did the "sons of Noah," who also followed their collective "willful heart" (CD II, 14–III, 1). The fallen angels, together with the "sons of Noah," are said to possess "eyes of adultery" and "guilty inclination" (יצר); the periods of sin are related to the violation of sexual taboos, the transgression of Noachic laws, and idolatry.[4] The phrase "thoughts (במחשבות) caused by sinful inclination (יצר אשמה)" (CD II, 16/4Q270 1 I, 1), is likely drawn from "inclination of thoughts" (יצר מחשבת) (Gen 6:5), calling to mind the flood and judgment.

4Q266 attests a preamble not extant in the Genizah copy that, according to Ben Zion Wacholder, presents "a new vision of the *Damascus Document*."[5]

---

1. Ida Fröhlich, "'Narrative Exegesis' in the Dead Sea Scrolls,' in *Biblical Perspectives: Early Use and Interpretation of the Bible in Light of the Dead Sea Scrolls: Proceedings of the First International Symposium of the Orion Center for the Study of the Dead Sea Scrolls and Associated Literature, 12–14 May 1996* (ed. M. E. Stone and E. G. Chazon; STDJ 28; Leiden: Brill, 1998), 96.

2. DJD XXII, 185–236.

3. In 326 complete or partial lines that parallel the Genizah text, there are fewer than thirty significant variants (Baumgarten, DJD XVIII, 6).

4. Fröhlich, "Narrative Exegesis," 83–86.

5. Ben Zion Wacholder, "The Preamble to the Damascus Document: A Composite Edition of 4Q266–4Q268," *HUCA* 69 (1998): 31–47, here 31.

3 [... and h]e inscribed periods of wrath (חקוק קץ חרון) for a people who know him not 4 [and he established times of favor for those who see]k His commandments and to those who walk blamelessly in the proper way (להולכים בתמים דרך) 5 [and he opened their eyes to the hidden things and] opened their [ea]rs that they might hear deep things and understand 6 [future events before they come upon them (4Q266 2 I, 3–6).

The language of inscribed "times of punishment" and "wrath in every period" prepares the reader to anticipate mention of the biblical flood as one of the times of wrath. Furthermore, להולכים בתמים prepares the reader to expect an exemplary archetypical Noah as an example of a "blameless walk" (cf. Gen 6:8–9). Instead, the author detaches both Enoch and Noah[6] from the Watchers traditions and from any allusion to the flood.

"Flames of fire" and "angels of destruction" come against those who "despise the law (חק) until they are without remnant (שרת) or survivor (פליטה) for God had not chosen (בחר) them from ancient eternity (מקדם עולם)" (4Q266 2 II, 5–7/ CD II, 7–9). Conversely, in all times "there would always be survivors (פליטה) on the earth, replenishing (למלא) the surface of the earth with their descendants (מזרעם)" (4Q266 2 II, 11–12/CD II, 12–13). This use of "re-creation" language— the filling of the earth with seed—assured the readers that "in all of these times" there would be survivors to fill the earth. Here, at least, may be an allusion to the survivors of the Genesis flood.[7]

Throughout the whole retelling and development of traditions elsewhere associated with Noah—the Watchers, sinful inclination, the righteous among the wicked, the "perfect walk," covenant, and the survival of a remnant—Noah himself is not named except as the progenitor of his sons—the "sons of Noah"— who are identified closely with the Watchers. Noah himself is barely in the background of the text as an unnamed primordial seed carrier.

In contrast, *Jubilees* had greatly elevated Noah's status, re-creating Noah as an implicit "second Adam," "first priest," and first participant in covenant making who instituted the celebration of *Shevuot* during the third month, the same month in CD in which the Levites and those in the camps convened to curse those who strayed.[8] In *Jubilees*, the foundational covenant is not the covenant with Abraham, Moses, or David but the annually renewed covenant with Noah. Unlike CD, *Jubilees* valued and upheld a priestly genealogy along which priestly

---

6. Cf. Ben Sira's detachment of the Watchers tradition from Enoch in his creation of a cautionary tale of the rebellion of free-willed creatures (Sir 16:18–19/cf. SirA 6v:11).

7. Maxine L. Grossman argues that in the third admonition there is a regular use of expressions within a repetitive narrative structure and that CD presents "a series of historical events as repetitions of one another" (*Reading for History in the Damascus Document: A Methodological Study* [STDJ 45; Leiden: Brill, 2002], 122–23).

8. Such a liturgy of cursing is even more intimately connected to repentance and covenant renewal in CD (4Q266 11 16–17/4Q270 7 II, 11–12; cf. 1QS II, 4–18).

lore was transmitted in written and oral traditions from named early ancestors, including Noah and Levi.

CD focuses instead on Abraham, Isaac, and Jacob as Israel's true progenitors and does not include Noah as the one with whom God first made a covenant in Genesis (CD III, 2-4; XII, 11).[9] Clearly, CD did not need to reach back into primordial or even pre-Sinai history to create an archetypical priest for its Levites; its covenant does not extend back to Noah. If CD was dependent on *Jubilees*, it was selectively dependent with respect to the Noah traditions to the point of rejecting Noah's status with God, his priesthood, and the primacy of the Noachic covenant.

This dramatic departure from *Jubilees*, this detachment of a priestly genealogy incorporating Noah may reveal a differing understanding of the levitical priesthood in CD from that contained in *Jubilees* and 4QCommentary on Genesis A-D.[10] Although the writer rehabilitates Ezekiel's Levites (CD III, 21-IV, 4),[11] the origin of the priesthood is not to be found in a single biblical figure or in single foundational story of the priesthood. Apparently, the Levites of the *Damascus Document* did not require further authentication by their earliest ancestors for their priestly role.[12]

4QAges of Creation (4Q180-181)[13]: The Serek of the Sons of Noah

4QAges of Creation A and B (4Q180-181) are two sectarian texts[14] described as "thematic pesher" by Armin Lange.[15] In both texts, the instruction of Azazel

---

9. "Eternal covenant" (ברית לעולם) may be the phrase that links Abraham, Isaac, and Jacob to the ברית לעולם made with the priesthood in the Hebrew Bible (Lev 24:8; Num 25:13; Sir 45:15; cf. Mal 2:4-5). Grossman would link Noah together with Abraham, Isaac, and Jacob as participants in the "covenant of the forefathers" (CD I, 4) because "he is not mentioned negatively" (*Reading for History*, 111 n. 63). However, because Noah's sons are mentioned in this third admonition, whereas Noah is not, his exclusion from the list is all the more noteworthy.

10. Sirach, which also emphasizes covenant and inclination, emphasizes priests in its historical retelling but does not accord priesthood to any figure before Aaron (Sir 45:6-7).

11. In Ezek 48:11 the priests *are* the sons of Zadok and are favored over the Levites who went astray. CD interprets these as three separate groups: the priests are the repentant of Israel, the Levites accompany them, and the sons of Zadok are the chosen of Israel (CD III, 21-IV, 4).

12. Grossman has observed that the priesthood of CD is metaphorical and that the writers of this text "lay claim to the authority of the priesthood, without actually claiming to *be* hereditary priests" ("Priesthood as Authority: Interpretive Competition in First-Century Judaism and Christianity," in *The Dead Sea Scrolls as Background to Postbiblical Judaism and Early Christianity: Papers from an International Conference at St. Andrews in 2001* [ed. J. R. Davila; STDJ 46; Leiden: Brill, 2003], 117-31, here 127).

13. See DJD V and also the better readings by John Strugnell in "Notes en marge du volume V des Discoveries in the Judaean Desert of Jordan," *RevQ* 7 (1970): 163-276.

14. For 4Q180 and 4Q181 as "deux copies d'un même ouvrage," see Jozef T. Milik, "Milkî-ṣedeq et Milkî-rešaʿ dans les anciens écrits juifs et chrétiens," *JJS* 23 (1972): 95-144.

15. Armin Lange, "Wisdom and Predestination in the Dead Sea Scrolls," *DSD* 2 (1995): 340-54, here 352 n. 27.

predominates in the period beginning with the "sons of Noah" and ending with the birth of Isaac.¹⁶ In neither work is Noah mentioned in the extant text,¹⁷ and so these texts join others that potentially treat the Watchers traditions as detached from the figure of Noah. While these are not likely copies of the same text, the content is similar enough to permit the use of one to interpret other.¹⁸

"This is the rule/order of the sons of Noah" (4Q180 1 4)

The first five lines of 4QAges of Creation A (4Q180) function as what Lange calls a "theological introduction."¹⁹

> *1* The prophetic interpretation (פשר) concerning the ages (הקצים) which God made: an age to terminate²⁰ (להתם) [all that is]²¹ *2* and shall be. Before He created them, He established [their] rewards/punishments (פעולותיהם)²² [...] *3* age by age. And it was engraved (חרות)²³ upon [eternal] tablets [...] *4* [...] ages of their dominion (קצי ממשלותם). This is the rule/order (סרך) of the so[ns of Noah to]²⁴ *5* [Abraham un]til he bore Isaac, ten [generations]²⁵ (4Q180 1 1–5).

Punishments "engraved" on tablets are echoed dually in 4QInstruction, where "engraved" (חרות) is found in parallel with "inscribed" (חקק) (4Q417 1 I, 14) and also in the preamble to CD in inscribed "times of wrath" (חקוק קץ חרון). All three texts interpret periods of judgment in reference to the primordial judgment but, in the extant text, do so without reference to an archetypical righteous flood survivor.

J. T. Milik reconstructs this fragmentary section as "This is the order of (generations after) the creation [of Adam; and from Noah to] Abraham," restoring בריאת אדם in line 4, creating an expression that imitates "this is the book of the descendants of Adam, זה ספר תולדת אדם in Gen 5:1.²⁶ Devorah Dimant,

---

16. See Devorah Dimant, who adds that the exposition on Azazel is the "first significant event in the Period in question" ("The 'Pesher on the Periods'[4Q180] and 4Q181," *IOS* 9 [1979]: 77–102, here 95).

17. However, the text is fragmentary and 4Q180 2–4 I, 1–2, 6–9 are "undecipherable" (Dimant, "Pesher," 82).

18. Dimant argues for separate sectarian texts but concedes their similar "general atmosphere" and terminology and the possibility that one may cite the other ("Pesher," 89–91, 96).

19. Lange, "Wisdom and Predestination," 353.

20. Dimant, "Pesher," 78. Cf. [להתה]לך, DJD V, 78.

21. Reconstructed by Strugnell in parallel to 1QS III, 15 ("Notes en marge," 252).

22. Cf. 4Q417 1 I, 14: "your reward (פעלתכה) is in the (book of) remembrance of [... for] the decree is engraved (חרות) and inscribed (חקוק) is every time of punishment."

23. Their rewards/punishments are engraved upon tablets (חרות in parallel with חקק in 4Q417 1 I, 14).

24. Dimant restores ב[ני נוח following Strugnell's suggestion in a private communication with her ("Pesher," 80).

25. Milik reconstructs "weeks" (*BE*, 251).

26. Milik, *BE*, 250.

unconvinced by the reconstruction, argues that סרך indicates the "succession of generations" and not creation and offers instead "the so[ns of Noah from Shem to Abraham]."[27] Both of these reconstructions, however, assume a relatively positive view of that "order," an assumption that might be reexamined.

Serek (סרך) is most obviously found in the so-called S documents of the *Community Rule* as סרך היחד, the "rule/order of the *Yaḥad*" (1QS I, 16). 4Q180, on the other hand, introduces an "order" (סרך) quite different from the סרך היחד with which the sectarians were familiar. This counterorder or "anti-order" is that of the "sons of Noah," who inherited the iniquity and wickedness passed along as an inheritance from Azazel. The case for סרך as an "anti-order" as a self-conscious imitation of a sectarian term of self-identity would not be compelling on its own; however, other intriguing examples of wordplays on sectarian technical terms in both 4Q180 and 4Q181 strengthen the possibility.

4QAges of Creation A continues with a *pesher* (פשר) "concerning Azazel," who passed on wickedness (רשעה) as an inheritance (להנחיל) and a "judgment of the council" (סוד) (4Q180 1 7–10). "Sodom and Gomorrah" (2–4 II, 1–10) and "Pharaoh" (5–6 5) are the subjects of other fragments of the text. The final extant line of the Sodom pericope echoes the biblical flood narrative, "before He created them He knew [their] designs (מחשבותיהם)" (cf. Gen 6:5), a phrase that does not occur in the Genesis account of Sodom and Gomorrah but serves here to link the judgment by flood in the distant past to the judgment upon Sodom and Gomorrah in the most recent past. 4Q181 2 contains a similar *pesher* on Azazel;[28] however, it is frg. 1 that sets a contemporary context for this selective retelling of Israel's stories.

4QAges of Creation B (4Q181) opens with "guilt in the *Yaḥad*" (לאשמה ביחד) and, uniquely among the sectarian texts, introduces the provocative title "*Yaḥad* of wickedness" (ליחד רשאה) (4Q181 1 1–2). The "council (סוד) of the sons of heaven and earth" is implicitly contrasted with the "council (סוד) of the gods as a holy congregation" into which some of the "sons of the world" (מבני תבל) are brought (4Q181 1 3–4).

> [. . .] for guilt in the *Yaḥad* (ביחד) with the coun[cil ([ד]סו)[29] of shamef[ulness] ([ער]וה)[30] to wa[l]low in the sin of humankind (בני אדם), and for great judgments and severe diseases 2 in their flesh, according to the mighty deeds of God, and corresponding to their wickedness, according to their uncleanness caused by the council (סוד) of the sons of h[eaven] and earth, as a wicked *Yaḥad* (ליחד רשעה) until 3 the end. Corresponding to the compassion of God, according to His goodness, and the wonder of His glory, He brings some of the sons of

---

27. Dimant, "Pesher," 80, 78.
28. By implication, Dimant reorders the fragments, commenting first on frg. 2 ("Pesher," 86).
29. So Milik, "Milkî-ṣedeq," 114.
30. Dimant restores [ער]וה ("Pesher," 88).

the world near, to be reckoned with Him in [the council] 4 [of the g]ods as a holy congregation, destined for eternal life and in the lot with His holy ones [...] 5 [...] each one [acco]mplishes according to the lot which falls t[o him...] 6 [...] for e[te]rn[al] life [....] (4Q181 1 1–6)

"Council of the sons of heaven and earth" (4Q181 1 2)

In 4Q181, the guilt in the *Yaḥad* is a direct outcome of wickedness and uncleanness "caused by the council (סוד) of the sons of heaven and earth" (4Q181 1 1–2).[31] This particular council of angels and humans is cast into sharp relief against another council in the following lines, the "council (סוד) of the gods as a holy congregation which is destined for eternal life" to which "some of the sons of the world are brought near" (4Q181 1 3–4).[32] Thus, there are two opposing "councils" made up of angels and humans. The "judgment of the council" (סוד) in 4Q180 1 10 follows a description of Azazel and his wicked inheritance, implying that this council would pass judgment on the deeds of Azazel and his followers.

"Guilt in the Yaḥad ... a wicked Yaḥad" (4Q181 1 1–2)

That "guilt in the *Yaḥad*" (אשמה ביחד) and the "wicked *Yaḥad*" (יחד רשעה) appear to be an innovative and creative wordplay on the sectarian self-designation of *Yaḥad* is reinforced by what appear to be the dual dueling "councils" and "rules/orders" in 4Q180. The *Community Rule* states, "He has made them heirs (וינחילם) in the legacy (גורל) of the holy ones (קדושים); with the sons of heaven (בני שמים) has he united their assembly (סודם), a *Yaḥad* council (לעצת יחד)" (1QS XI, 7–8). In contrast to this, the "council of the sons of heaven and earth" and the "wicked *Yaḥad*" (4Q181 1 2) are a suitable counterfoil.

The use of three sets of sectarian terms—"order," "council," and "*Yaḥad*"—as potential wordplays describing two opposing groups suggest that the choice of these particular words is more than coincidence. To whom are the authors referring in these texts? One possibility is this. The author deliberately sets the members of the "guilty (אשמה) *Yaḥad*" within the line of succession that originated from Azazel and his ilk, who had subsequently passed on "guilt (אשמה) as an inheritance." This "anti-*Yaḥad*" is implicitly accused of not subscribing to the legitimate *Serek ha-Yaḥad* but instead to the illegitimate *serek* (order) of the wicked "sons of Noah." Their deeds were seen to originate not from the "council of the gods as a holy congregation" (4Q181 1 3–4) but from the "council (סוד) of the sons of heaven and earth" (4Q181 1 1–2).

In this scenario, the author is in harsh dispute with a group within the sectarians; the *Yaḥad* sectarians were dealing with "guilt" and "wickedness" in their own ranks. The author employs both sectarian terminology and a foundational story treasured by the rebellious faction. The Watchers were initially sent to

---

31. See also partially reconstructed "council."
32. Cf. also the "council of the people" (סוד עם), CD XIX, 35 and 1QS II, 25.

teach justice and uprightness (*Jub.* 4:15) but then turned aside from their original purpose, offering false instruction with catastrophic results. Now this story is adapted and reused against a rebellious group within the *Yaḥad*. The contemporary guilty ones belonged to the *Serek ha-Yaḥad* and had been privy to its council but now, as inheritors of Azazel, are condemned for receiving and giving wicked instruction.

4QCOMMENTARY ON GENESIS A–D (4Q252–254A): DISTINGUISHING BETWEEN THE RIGHTEOUS AND THE WICKED [33]

While Noah is not explicitly named "priest" in 4QCommentary on Genesis A–D (4Q252–254a), priestly concerns are associated with him, and it is clear is that he is a "first" priestly ancestor of no little importance. The sheer massive primacy of Noah, even where there are only a few extant lines, as in 4Q253–254a, stands in contrast to his brief or allusive appearances in other indisputably sectarian texts. In 4Q252, where much more is extant, the Noah story stands at the beginning of the commentary and occupies fully one and a half columns (twenty-two lines in col. I and seven of thirteen lines in col. II) of a six-column text.[34] In all that survives of the *Commentaries*, Noah, in comparison to other characters in Genesis, plays an unexpectedly primary and highly disproportionate role.

Apart from the official edition, most scholarly attention has been focused on the lengthy and exegetically diverse 4Q252. The texts of 4Q253–254a have appeared primarily as parallels and footnotes in the discussion of their more substantial cousin. This study, however, begins with the role of the Noah traditions within each of the smaller commentaries before moving to Noah's complex role in 4Q252 and the trajectory of tradition he represents.

4Q253 AND 4Q253A: NOAH UNDERSTOOD ALONGSIDE MALACHI?

Four fragments were originally assigned to 4QCommGen B (4Q253).[35] One of them, a quotation and interpretation of Mal 3:16–18, was subsequently separated from the others and titled 4QCommentary on Malachi (4Q253a).[36] The quotation from Malachi, "[. . . you shall once again see the difference] between the righteous and the wicked" (4Q253a 1 I, 4), echoes *Festival Prayers* "[to distinguish between the righ]teous and the wicked" in a set of Day of Atonement prayers that also remembers the covenant with Noah (4Q508 1 1; 3 2).

---

33. Quotations from 4Q252–254a follow G. J. Brooke, DJD XXII, 185–236.

34. "The physical evidence of the scroll indicates—apparent remnants of the tie and discoloration on the reverse of frg. 1—that the text of 4Q252 does indeed begin with the extant col. I" (DJD XXII, 190).

35. Ben Zion Wacholder and Martin G. Abegg, Jr. [based on the work of J. T. Milik and others], *A Preliminary Edition of the Unpublished Dead Sea Scrolls: The Hebrew and Aramaic Texts from Cave Four, Fascicle Two* (Washington: Biblical Archaeology Society, 1992), 216–17.

36. DJD XXII, 213–15.

This parallel provides an impetus to investigate the possibility of the recombination of 4Q253 and 4Q253a. The fragments, of similar physical description and paleography, pale tan in color and written in late Hasmonean or early Herodian formal script,[37] were originally assigned to one text.

Fragments 1 and 3 of 4Q253 do not show visible line rulings, whereas 4Q253a and 4Q253 2 do. 4Q253a preserves an upper margin and the right margin of one column (II) and the left margin of another (I). 4Q253 2 preserves a bottom margin and a right margin. Therefore, 4Q253 2 may be positioned tentatively under col. II of 4Q253a. There is not enough physical evidence to locate frgs. 1 and 3 of 4Q253 with any precision. Both have bottom margins (1.6 cm. and 1.4 cm. respectively), but the absence of line rulings suggests that these fragments are not parts of the columns already reconstructed. The contents, however, do suggest a potential ordering.[38]

4Q253 1 contains "from the ark" and "to make known to Noah" (להודיע לנוח) and may be placed before the quotation of Malachi (4Q253a 1 I).[39] 4Q253 3 makes reference to "the sea," to "Belial," and "he will forsake," terminology that may represent the writer's present or future and therefore may be placed after 4Q253 2.[40] The resultant ordering of fragments (4Q253 1, 4Q253a 1 I, 4Q253a 1 II, 4Q253 2, and 4Q253 3) presents a possible interpretation of the Noah story that has parallels in other texts that exhibit wisdom and "Aramaic Levi" traditions.

According to this suggested order, something is "made known" to Noah,[41] possibly the coming judgment,[42] in the first fragment (4Q253 1). While possibly derived from Genesis, this "mystical Noah" who received esoteric knowledge may plausibly be located in a wisdom/apocalyptic tradition of those who received such knowledge.[43]

Second, the quotation from Mal 3:16–18 is followed by the key phrases "book of remembrance," "on that day," and "once more you shall see the difference between the righteous (הצדיק) and the wicked"[44] (4Q253a 1 I, 1–5). This "book

---

37. DJD XXII, 213.

38. The recombination of 4Q253 and 4Q253a is more closely argued in a paper to be presented later this year at the annual meeting of the Society of Biblical Literature in Boston, 2008. Dorothy M. Peters, "'Once Again You Shall See the Difference between the Righteous and the Wicked': A Proposed Reunification of 4QCommentary on Malachi and 4QCommentary on Genesis B."

39. Cf. 4Q254, where fragments containing Noah's curse reference to Hagar and to Isaac are positioned before the quotation of Zech 4:14 (DJD XXII, 217–32).

40. A majority of the occurrences of הים are in the *pesharim*; cf. also ויעזוב את אל, a description of the actions of the Wicked Priest (1QpHab VIII, 8–10) (DJD XXII, 212).

41. Alternatively, ק[להודיע לכו]ל (Wacholder and Abegg, *Preliminary Edition*, 216, based on Milik's transcription).

42. See discussion on 4Q252 below.

43. See Noah's dreams in 1Q20; cf. revelation of knowledge to (possibly) Noah in 5Q13 1 7, 11 and in 4Q534.

44. Concerning הצדק "[t]he term, its synonyms and its opposites feature thematically in

of remembrance" appears also in 4QInstruction, in which "every time of punishment" is inscribed and which is bequeathed to those whose inclination (יצר) is like that of the "holy ones" (קדושים) (4Q417 1 I, 14–17). "Once more" brings Noah the righteous (צדיק) to mind (Gen 6:9), the one who was effectively distinguished by God from the wicked (רעה/רע) (Gen 6:5) by means of the flood.

The third fragment in this reordering is suggestive of sacrifice and a "distinguishing" role of priests and Levites, containing the phrases "a man of Israel who" and "brings (נגש) its blood" (4Q253a 1 II, 1–4). The only other collocation of "bring" and "blood" in Qumran texts is a modified quotation of Ezek 44:15 in which the "priests and Levites and sons of Zadok" bring fat and blood (CD III, 21–IV, 2/4Q270 1a II, 1).

The fourth fragment (4Q253 2 1–5) mentions "the impurity" (הטמאה), "his burnt offering (עולתו) for acceptance (לרצון)" and "the gates of the heights." הטמאה appears with the definite article only in Zech 13:2 with respect to the future "on that day" when the prophets and "unclean spirit" would be removed from the land, and in 2 Chr 29:16, where the descendants of Levi cleanse the house of the God of uncleanness. Therefore, this text, as recombined, could be tentatively placed into the trajectory of an "Aramaic Levi" tradition that named Noah as a priestly ancestor.

There could be multiple candidates for the one who offers the burnt offering, including Noah,[45] but the significance of the language in this text may be its portability throughout time, that any one priest of this particular interpretation of the lineage of the priesthood could potentially offer acceptable sacrifices. As recombined (4Q253/253a), the text has moved from the exegete's historical distant past (Genesis) to mine the more recent past (Malachi) for a prophecy concerning the exegete's present.

Finally, "the sea," "Belial," and "he will forsake" (4Q253 3) may refer to a time either contemporary to or future to the writer. Parallels are found in many places, including one with Noah. In 4QTanḥumim, the "days of Noah" are interpreted as an example of how Belial has oppressed and, presumably, continues to oppress his servants (4Q176 8–11 11–15).

Therefore, in conclusion, the physical evidence may allow for a recombination, and the text and commentary thus rearranged result in an interpretation of the Noah story that is consistent with and has parallels to similar exegesis in other texts. The Malachi quotation is excerpted from a chapter concerning the purification of the descendants of Levi so that they would present offerings in righteousness (בצדקה) that would please God as in days of old (Mal 3:3–4). Again, Noah stands in this interpretative tradition.

The use of prophets in 4QCommentary on Genesis A–D to contemporize the

---

CD XX. Perhaps in light of CD XX, 4Q253a 1 5 should be restored in such a way as to mention the Teacher of Righteousness" (DJD XXII, 215).

45. *Jub.* 6:1–3; cf. 1Q20 X, 13–17; 1QS IX, 4–5; 4Q512 29–32 10.

Genesis narrative is not unknown. Thus, 4QCommentary on Genesis C (4Q254 4 2) appeals to Zech 4:14 and 4QCommentary on Genesis A (4Q252 V, 2) appeals to Jer 33:17. Just as *Jubilees* pointed to Israel's foundational stories in order to make the present and the future understood, in this recombination Malachi effectively contemporizes the Noah story, confirming that, "once again," the difference between the righteous and the wicked would be seen.

4Q254: More Blessings and Curses

Noah's curse upon Canaan opens the extant text of 4Q254 and is followed by a possible reference to Hagar (4Q254 2), the near sacrifice of Isaac (4Q254 3), a quotation of Zech 4:14, "the two sons of oil,"[46] a reference to the "keepers of the commandments of God," and "men of the community" (היחד) (4Q254 4). Also appearing are Jacob's patriarchal blessings and curses upon Issachar and Dan (4Q254 5-6), Jacob's blessing on Joseph (4Q254 7), and the phrase "he distinguished between" (הבדיל בין) (4Q254 8 7). The official editor notes the "overall theme of the interpretation of blessings and curses which seem to be a feature of this commentary as also of 4Q252"[47] and it is noteworthy that the cursing of Canaan by Noah is extant in the little that remains of the Noah narrative in this commentary.

"He distinguished between" (הבדל בין) (4Q254 8 7) is found in the creation account in Genesis where God separates light from darkness, waters from waters, and day from night (Gen 1:4, 6, 7, 14, 18). Six of the remaining eight collocations in the Hebrew Bible denote priestly concerns and occur in Leviticus and Ezekiel with reference to distinguishing between holy and common and/or clean and unclean (Lev 10:10; 11:47; 20:25; Ezek 22:26; 42:20). Perhaps an allusion to Gen 1 is being used metaphorically in 4Q254 alongside priestly texts as a dual lens concerning the different kinds of distinction that must be made by God's people. In comparison, the "light and darkness" metaphor in sectarian texts appears to be employed in the distinction made between those initiated with unrepentant heart—implied sons of darkness—and the sons of light (cf. 1QS I, 10; II, 11-16).

In the context of 4Q254, Noah was the first human to bless or curse, effectively distinguishing among his descendants. Jacob does the same, and Hagar and Isaac may be mentioned with respect to the exclusion or inclusion in the blessing. The selective re-presentation of Noah and other characters in Genesis could have served, therefore, as an exegetical apologetic for the blessings and curses performed by the priestly community itself. Simply put, Noah was an archetype for cursing priests.

---

46. 4Q254 demonstrates, as do 4Q253 and 4Q253a, that the writer freely appealed to a prophet (in this case, Zech 4:14 with "two sons of oil") in order to contemporize the Genesis text.

47. DJD XXII, 223.

4Q254A: "AT THEIR APPOINTED TIME"[48]

The details that the writer selected for this commentary include reference to the dove (4Q254a 1–2 1), measurements of the ark (4Q254a 1–2 2–4), Noah's disembarkation "at the appointed time year by year" (למועד ימים ימימה) (4Q254a 3 1–2), and a raven who makes something known (להודיע) to the "latter generations" (לדורות האחרונים) (4Q254a 3 4–5). Two points are of particular interest.

The birds appear in an odd order chronologically: the dove appears *before* the measurements of the ark and the raven *after* Noah leaves the ark. In Hebrew tradition, doves and ravens were known to have the ability to see into the future.[49] This knowledge-giving raven is anomalous at Qumran, but other subjects have messages to the "latter generations" in Hebrew literature. In the Qumran writings,[50] the message is normally judgment—wrath of God, desolation of the land—and, in the Hebrew Bible,[51] it is either judgment or the recounting to the next (latter) generations of the mighty deeds of God, including God's judgments upon Israel's enemies and Israel itself.

Especially suggestive of a theme that recurs in the *Commentaries* is a "latter generation" found in Deuteronomy where the addressees are the ones entering the covenant (לעברך בברית). With respect to those who would follow "their stubborn ways," God would "separate/distinguish them" (הבדילו) from the tribes of Israel in "accordance with the curses of the covenant" and the next or latter generation would see the devastation of the land (Deut 29:10–20 [29:11–21]). It is reasonable to suggest that the raven's message to the latter generations revealed that those in the covenant would be distinguished from those who would suffer impending judgment.

The second noteworthy phrase is "at their appointed time year by year," a phrase that differs from its approximate counterpart in 4Q252: למועד שנה תמימה (4Q252 II, 4–5). George J. Brooke has observed: "The temporal idiom ימים ימימה occurs in a similar phrase in Exod 13:10. . . . This implies that the content of 4Q254a 3 1–2 concerns the yearly celebration of the disembarkation of Noah from the ark, the time of the establishment of Shavuot, according to *Jubilees* 6.17."[52]

This resonates with the liturgical *Festival Prayers* in which Noah was remembered annually. Furthermore, 5QRule adapted the remembrance of Noah into what might be a liturgy for the covenant renewal ceremony, and this elliptical reference in 4Q252 may refer briefly to such an observance. In such a scenario, the community viewed itself as living within this "latter generation," when they

---

48. 4Q254 and 4Q254a, although originally treated as one text, were subsequently divided because of the distinctive shape of the some of the letters (DJD XXII, 223).

49. B. *Giṭ.* 45a; Philo, *Quaestiones in Genesis* 2.35 (DJD XXII, 235–36).

50. See 1QpHab II, 6–8; CD I, 12–13/4Q266 2 I, 15–16; 1Q14 17–19 3–5. The one exception is 4Q177 9 8.

51. See Deut 29:21 [29:22]; Isa 41:4; Pss 48:14 [48:13]; 78:4, 6; 102:19 [102:18].

52. DJD XII, 236.

would, during the covenant renewal ceremony, curse those whom God had already separated out from "Israel" for judgment.

4Q252: Another "First" for Noah

A hint of Noah's priestly role in 4Q252 may be found in the systematic linking between the events of his life and the flood to specific days of the week and month as well as Noah's ability to make proper distinctions by means of the appropriate blessings and curses. 4Q252 has prompted considerable interest because of the types of exegesis found in the text.[53] The search for a thematic coherence ranges from Moshe Bernstein's assertion that there is "no overt principle governing the choice of passages on which to comment"[54] to Robert Eisenman and Michael Wise's labeling of 4Q252 as a "Genesis Florilegium" with ideological goals.[55]

Scholarly response to Bernstein's statement that "[i]f 4Q252 is a commentary, addressing only whatever problematic issues its author saw fit, then it is unproductive and inappropriate to search for artificial unifiers,"[56] has been to search for just such a thematic unity. Suggestions include "interpretation of blessings and curses,"[57] the elected and rejected,[58] and contrasting traditions in which sin connected with sex is punished with destruction but the righteous are rewarded with the possession of the land.[59]

4Q252 begins with "[In] the four hundred and eightieth year of Noah's life their end came to[60] Noah (בא קצם לנוח)" (4Q252 I, 1). There is no preserved antecedent for "their."[61] Timothy Lim identifies the antecedent as "all flesh" from Gen

---

53. Moshe J. Bernstein, "4Q252: From Re-written Bible to Biblical Commentary," *JJS* 45 (1994): 1–27; George J. Brooke, "4Q252 as Early Jewish Commentary," *RevQ* 17 (1996): 385–401; Esther Eshel, "Hermeneutical Approaches to Genesis in the Dead Sea Scrolls," in *The Book of Genesis in Jewish and Oriental Christian Interpretation: A Collection of Essays* (ed. J. Frishman and L. van Rompay; Traditio exegetica Graeca 5; Leuven: Peeters, 1997), 1–12; Moshe J. Bernstein, "Pentateuchal Interpretation at Qumran," in vol. 1 of *The Dead Sea Scrolls after Fifty Years: A Comprehensive Assessment* (ed. P. W. Flint and J. C. VanderKam; Leiden: Brill, 1998), 128–59; Fröhlich, "Narrative Exegesis," 67–90.

54. Bernstein, "4Q252: From Re-written Bible," 5.

55. For these texts as containing "escape and salvation stories" and demonstrating a "collateral interest in sexual matters," see Robert H. Eisenman and Michael Wise, *The Dead Sea Scrolls Uncovered* (Shaftesbury: Element, 1992), 80–81.

56. Bernstein, "4Q252: From Rewritten Bible," 26.

57. DJD XXII, 223.

58. Juhanna Saukkonen, "From the Flood to the Messiah: Is 4Q252 a History Book?" (paper presented at the annual meeting of the SBL, San Antonio, Tex., Nov. 21, 2004).

59. Fröhlich, "Narrative Exegesis," 87–88.

60. Translated as "for Noah" in DJD XXII.

61. Brooke notes that the lack of a preserved antecedent "is the first indication that the compiler of this text may be quoting from a source and may have considered that his audience would be sufficiently familiar with the subject not to have the source altered" (DJD XXII, 197).

6:13 so that בא קצם לנוח has "the sense of 'having come to Noah's knowledge,'"[62] resembling what was "made known to Noah" (4Q253 1 4; cf. Gen 6:13, 17; 5Q13 1).

Although "their end" had already been determined, there was an interim period of 120 years before the floodwaters of destruction actually came and so "their days" are determined at 120 years, and the flood begins in Noah's six hundredth year. As Bernstein has noted, 4Q252 stands apart from other ancient sources in "not assigning this span as a period within which mankind could repent."[63] "Repentance," in fact, does not appear in the extant text.

The narrative continues by linking events of the flood year and Noah's actions in a highly specific chronology. The days marked include the beginning of the flood, the duration of the rainfall, the length of time that water prevailed on the earth, the decreasing of water, the ark's descent onto the mountain, the appearance of mountaintops, the opening of the ark's window, the dove's forays over the earth, the drying of ground, and Noah's disembarkation from the ark (4Q252 I, 3–II, 4).

Lim notes: "First, the dates of the flood narrative in Genesis correspond to the chronology of the solar calendar. Second, the Qumran commentator has succeeded in resolving the long-standing anomaly of 150 days of mighty waters and the 17/VII date of the ark's coming to rest on Ararat (Turarat): they are two distinct events!"[64] The 364–day idealized solar calendar, also featured in *Jubilees* (5:21–32; cf. 6.23–32), is thus supported, and the writer has simultaneously resolved the anomaly of 150 days, dating the origin of the establishment of the solar calendar back to Noah himself. Thus, as Falk has stated, 4Q252 is "even more meticulous" in its working out of the 364–day calendar than *Jubilees* was in both explicit and implicit ways.[65] Like *Jubilees*, 4Q252 emphasizes that the all-important calendar was based on the flood events, thereby heightening the importance of the Noah narrative as a foundation story for at least part of the community.[66]

In 4Q252, as in the *Aramaic Levi Document*, Noah appears as the "first priest" in a selective retelling of Israel's early history, and now the priestly Noah becomes even more intimately connected with a calendar of 364 days. The priestly interest does not extend to sacrifice in 4Q252 as it does in 4Q253, however. Lim observes, "[I]t is noteworthy that the entire episode of post-diluvian sacrifice and Noachic commandments (especially the prohibition to eat flesh with blood), which

---

62. Timothy Lim, "The Chronology of the Flood Story in a Qumran Text (4Q252)," *JJS* 43 (1992): 288–98, here 291.

63. Bernstein, "4Q252: From Re-Written Bible," 6.

64. Lim, "Chronology," 297–98.

65. Daniel K. Falk, *The Parabiblical Texts: Strategies for Extending the Scriptures among the Dead Sea Scrolls* (CQS 8; LSTS 63; New York: T&T Calrk, 2007), 129. See *Jub.* 5:21–32; cf. 6:23–32.

66. Genesis 8:22 itself with its post-flood reestablishment of seasons already suggested to later exegetes that the new calendar began with Noah.

became the legal precedent of later cultic practices and religious observances (e.g. in Leviticus, book of Noah, Aramaic Levi Document, etc.), were passed over in silence."[67]

While *Jubilees* had painstakingly linked Noah to the first celebration of covenant, a tradition also followed in *Festival Prayers* (4Q508) and in 5Q13, 4Q252 makes no mention of covenant except with respect to the one made with David (4Q252 V, 2). If 4Q252 reflects the Deuteronomic curses, then the silence of "covenant," so integral to Deuteronomy, is somewhat surprising.[68]

Noah's disembarkation from the ark and subsequent cursing of Canaan are, perhaps, foundational acts in a narrative that concerns itself with distinguishing between who *would* and who would *not* possess the land. This emphasis on curses is reflected also in the covenant renewal ceremony in the *Community Rule* (1QS II, 4–5), in which the Levites curse those foreordained to Belial. Noah did not curse (קלל) Ham because God had already blessed him, but Canaan *was* cursed (ארור) (4Q252 II, 6–7). In the *Community Rule*, the Levites—the cursers (מקללים)—are responsible for cursing (קלל) those foreordained to Belial: "May you be damned (ארור)" (1QS II, 4–10). The sectarians themselves lived in the interim between announcement of judgment and the final judgment and possession of the land. In the meantime, while they waited, they could curse.

Noah's cursing of Canaan is an archetypical act in this set of commentaries on Genesis that contains, as a subtheme, the making of distinctions between who *would* and who would *not* possess the land. Noah curses Canaan[69] in 4Q252 and also in 4Q254, a text that contains "he distinguished between" (4Q254 1 3–4; 8 7). If 4Q253 and 4Q253a, indeed, originally belonged together, then the quote from Mal 3:16–18, "[you shall once again see the difference] between the righteous (צדיק) and the wicked (רשע)," may signify a retrospective view of the flood in Genesis to a time when the first differentiation was made between the righteous and the wicked. Noah, in his act of pronouncing the appropriate curses and differentiating properly among his sons, was plausibly credentialed in 4Q252–254a as a worthy archetypical ancestor for a line of Levites who knew how to differentiate between those who should be cursed and those who should be blessed.[70] In summary, 4Q252–254a develops Noah traditions already familiar from Genesis and *Jubilees* and maintains their connection to the figure of Noah, most notably,

---

67. Lim, "Chronology," 298.
68. Language from Deuteronomy is brought to bear on the recountings of Japheth, Sodom and Gomorrah and Amalek. So George J. Brooke, "The Deuteronomic Character of 4Q252," in *Pursuing the Text: Studies in Honor of Ben Zion Wacholder on the Occasion of his Seventieth Birthday* (ed. J.C. Reeves and J. Kampen; JSOT Sup. 184; Sheffield Academic Press, 1994), 121–135.
69. Noah did not curse (קלל) Ham because God had already blessed, him but Canaan *was* cursed (ארור) (4Q252 II, 6–7).
70. See Deut 27:14–26; cf. 4QDamascus Document A (4Q266 11 17).

the refinement of chronology and calendar, emphasis on curses, and the portrayal of Noah as the first priestly ancestor.

5QRULE (5Q13): THE LEVITES REMEMBER NOAH

Whereas Noah is either well disguised or ignored in the *Damascus Document* and 4QAges of Creation, the exceptional fragments of 5QRule (5Q13) give Noah "star status" as a priestly progenitor.[71] The text has points of contact with the *Community Rule* (1QS) but is nevertheless a historical retelling in a "liturgical framework"[72] that also has similarities to *Festival Prayers*, containing, as it does, a historical retelling that extends back to Noah.

As Menahem Kister has observed, frg. 4 has similarities to the *Community Rule* and CD, but "the precise relations between the fragments and the Serekh material is likewise obscure."[73] This text may represent a differently interpreted covenant renewal ceremony that is plausibly connected with a particular priestly lineage that honored Noah and Levi as priestly ancestors. Familiar Noah traditions are woven together in 5Q13.

> 6 [. . .] You chose (בחרתה) from among the son of g[o]ds (מבני אלים) and [. . .] 7 [. . .] and You were pleased (רצה) with Noah [. . .] 8 [. . .] of the death and [. . .] 9 [. . .] God, to understand the works [of . . .] 10 [. . .] the service of [. . .] 11 [. . . to make k]nown the hidden [things . . .] (להודיע נסתרות]) 12 [. . .] in the year you shall command (צוה) him to [. . .] 13 [. . .] to all the Israelites (לכול איש ישראל) [. . .]. (5Q13 1 6–13)
>
> 4 [. . .] forever 5 [. . .] with Abraham 6 [. . .] You made [kn]own to Jacob at Bethel 7 [. . .] and Levi You [. . .] and You appointed him to bind 8 [. . .] You chose [the sons of] Levi to go out 9 [. . .] by their spirit before You. (5Q13 2 4–9)

Fragment 3 preserves only "Enoch,"[74] and frg. 4 may quote from the *Community Rule* or, alternatively, be a "strongly variant form."[75] The parallels to 1QS are in brackets:

---

71. On the importance of Bethel as a place and on the figures of Enoch, Noah, Abraham, Jacob and Levi and in texts that feature the Levites, see George J. Brooke, "Levi and the Levites," in *The Dead Sea Scrolls and the New Testament* (Minneapolis: Fortress, 2005), 115–39, here 121. DJD III is the official edition for 5Q13.

72. Brooke, "Levi and the Levites," 121.

73. Menahem Kister, "5Q13 and the 'Avodah: A Historical Survey and Its Significance," *DSD* 8 (2001): 136–48, here 136.

74. Kister has attempted a reconstruction of frgs. 1–3 that incorporates Enoch as the one who is chosen "from among the sons of A[da]m"—instead of "sons of god," which includes a reconstructed "Isaac" and "Aaron" ("5Q13," 137). While this reconstruction is materially possible, it is based on one fragment containing only the one word establishing no wider context.

75. WAC (2005), 570.

[... he shall st]and before the Overseer [....] 2 [... (1QS III, 4) ...] And ceremonies of atonement cannot restore his innocence, [neither cultic waters his purity. He cannot be sanctified by baptism in seas (1QS III, 5) and rivers] 3 [nor purified by mere ritual bathing.] Unclean, unclean shall he be [all the] d[ays that he rejects the laws (1QS III, 6) of God] 4 [...] (1QS II, 19) These they shall do annually, a[ll the days of Belial's dominion ...]. (5Q13 4 1–4)

Fragment 5 contains a reference to the "hand of Belial"; frg. 6 "to exterminate them (לבלותמה); while frgs. 7–21 preserve only scattered letters and words.

The only statement that may be made with certainty about Noah in 5Q13 is that God was pleased with him (5Q13 1 7). However, a "chosen" one appears in the previous line, and the near proximity suggests, at the very least, that Noah was positioned within the lineage of the one who was "chosen" from among the sons of gods (5Q13 1 6).[76]

Neither the subject of this sentence nor the recipient of the knowledge of the "hidden things" is clearly stated. In the Qumran corpus, the subject could be divine, human, or even a raven.[77] However, the juxtaposition of "to make known" in 5QRule with mention of Noah would suggest that Noah was perceived to have at least a role—even as an archetype—with respect to the transmission of hidden things. That Noah would be either the giver of or receiver of knowledge is not inconsistent with other Qumran texts.[78]

The fragmentary sentence "... in the year you shall command (צוה) him to [...] to all the Israelites (לבול איש ישראל)" (5Q13 1 12–13), is strongly suggestive of the occasion when Moses commanded (צוה) the tribes of Israel, in the future, to assemble on Mount Gerizim and on Mount Ebal, and the Levites to "declare in a loud voice to all the Israelites (אל־כל־איש ישראל)" (Deut 27:13–14) a litany of curses that Moses gave them.

5QRule may simply have been a variant version of the covenant renewal ceremony; however, it could also represent a *fuller* version of what is only summarized in the *Community Rule*. The chart below is constructed in such a way as to highlight the "missing" pieces of the *Community Rule*. The *Rule* only referred to elements of the covenant renewal ceremony such as prayers and recitals of Israel's history but did not include them; therefore, 5QRule might represent a more fully expanded version of the covenant renewal ceremony.

---

76. Cf. 11Q13: "Melchizedek" holds judgment "in the midst of gods (אלוהים)" on an eschatological Day of Atonement (11Q13 II, 10). At that time, Melchizedek would prosecute Belial and all those predestined to him (11Q13 II, 11–13).

77. 1QH^a IX, 31; 4Q491 11 I, 20–23; cf. 11Q5 XVIII, 10–12; 4Q254a 3 4; CD II, 12–13/4Q266 2 II, 12; 1QpHab VII, 4–5.

78. Cf. 4Q252 I, 1 translating קצם לנוח as "their end was made known to Noah."

The *Community Rule*	5QRule and Parallels
While the initiates are being inducted into the covenant... "The priests and Levites shall continually bless the God of deliverance and all of his veritable deeds" (1QS I, 18–19)	
Contents of prayer or blessing concerning God's "veritable deeds" are not included in the Community Rule.	A prayer and blessing to God "You chose... you were pleased with Noah... to understand the works of" (5Q13 1 1–13) Compare 4QFestival Prayers' containing prayers for *Shevuot* and the Day of Atonement. 4Q508 includes reference to the covenant with Noah, confession, and a reminder to God that he would execute destruction and the "Amen, amen."
The initiates respond: "Amen Amen" (1QS I, 20)	
The priests recount God's acts of justice and his mighty deeds; Levites recount the wicked acts (עוונות), guilty transgressions (פשעי אשמתם) and sins (חטאת) of the children of Israel during the dominion of Belial (1QS I, 21–24)	
Details of God's acts of justice and mighty deeds are not included in the Community Rule.	A recounting of Israel's history: "Abraham... Jacob at Bethel... Levi... you appointed him to bind... you chose the sons of Levi to go out" (5Q13 2 4–11); "Enoch" (5Q13 3 2)
Priests bless the "lot of God" (1QS II, 1–4)	
Levites curse the "lot of Belial" (וענו ואמרו) (1QS II, 4–9)	"to all the Israelites (לכול איש ישראל)" (5Q13 1 13; cf. the instructions in the Levites to curse given in Deut 27:13–14); "to exterminate them (לכלותמה)" (5Q13 6 2)
The initiates respond: "Amen, Amen" (1QS II, 10, 18)	
"They shall do as follows annually, all the days of Belial's dominion" (1QS II, 19)	"These they shall do annually, a[ll the days of Belial's dominion" (5Q13 4 4)

The *Community Rule*	5QRule and Parallels
Those who do not enter the Covenant ... "ceremonies of atonement (כפורים) cannot restore his innocence..." (1QS II, 25–III, 6).	Those who reject God's laws: "... ceremonies of atonement cannot restore his innocence" (5Q13 4 2–3)

In the *Community Rule* edition of the covenant renewal ceremony, neither the blessing of God, the recounting of God's acts, nor the specific details of the recital of Israel's history are included. 5QRule's remembrance of Noah, however, may have formed part of the prayer, blessing, or the historical remembrance within the covenant renewal ceremony that the sectarians were to recite annually (5Q13 4 4; cf. 1QS II, 12, 19). With respect to Noah, 5QRule followed *Jubilees* more closely than the *Damascus Document*. While CD refused to acknowledge Noah's covenant, 5QRule remembered Noah at the time of covenant renewal, thus, implicitly, crediting him with the making of the first covenant upon which all subsequent covenant renewals were based.

Continuing the Conversation

In the extant texts of the *Damascus Document* (CD) and in 4QAges of Creation A and B (4Q180–181), "Noah themes" are detached from the figure of Noah himself and Noah is most noticeably denuded of his archetypical status. In the *Damascus Document*, if Noah is remembered at all, it is as the father to the sons who are compared to Azazel, archetypical commandment breakers and lovers of iniquity.

In CD, human inclination incurs God's wrath rather than God's compassion as it did in 4QFestival Prayers[b]. "Noah traditions" or traditions normally associated with Noah are found in CD—the Watchers, sinful inclination, the righteous among the wicked, the "perfect walk," covenant, and the survival of a remnant—but, at the very most, Noah is assumed to be in the deep background as the primordial seed carrier necessary for the survival of the remnant.

Perhaps Noah was simply extraneous to the CD narrative, which concentrated on the Watchers as archetypical sinners. However, at least two troubling omissions in CD would speak for a deliberate exclusion of Noah in favor of his descendants.

First, while CD's authors may not have had a text of *Jubilees* in front of them, it is likely that they would have known of the traditions naming Noah as a priest and first participant in the covenant. The caves at Qumran boasted plenty of witnesses! Yet, in CD, Noah is completely passed over; there is no claim to a pre-Sinai priestly genealogy, and Abraham is the first covenant partner. Philip Davies has highlighted the exclusivity demanded by the *new* covenant in CD, which was based on the "dismal failure of the 'covenant of the first [people] (הברית הראשנים)'" (CD III, 10–13). Excluded from the new covenant are "those outside the group who do not 'return' or 'repent.'"[79] Davies's view that the Admonitions were directed to people at the point of joining the community who were familiar with another history of Israel and who held another view of God's dealings[80] might explain CD's expressed exclusivity. At least some of the initiates may have been accustomed to a history that included also the figures of Enoch, Noah, and Levi and who were entering a new covenant that now replaced the old. Perhaps these initiates joining the community claimed Aramaic Enoch and Aramaic Levi traditions as part of their interpretative heritage.

The *Damascus Document* clarified the boundaries of the community and defined it in more exclusive terms. The CD Admonitions (CD I, 11–12; XX, 13–14) represented a solidifying and categorization of selected teachings of the Teacher of Righteousness that no longer needed to acknowledge the parent traditions of *Jubilees* that had included Noah in a priestly genealogy.

The virulence of 4QAges of Creation A and B (180–181) is directed against a group within the *Yaḥad* that remembered the traditions surrounding the Watchers. The writer implies that this rebel group descended from Azazel, who passed on "wickedness as an inheritance." Therefore, its members did not belong to the legitimate line. Here the conversation becomes a bitter dispute as the author attacks "rebellious" members of the sectarian community itself. This text knows Noah only by his sons and, like 4QInstruction and CD, does not require the naming of the archetypical righteous flood survivor. The more pressing need is to identify the contemporary "guilty ones," ones who had received and accepted illegitimate instruction and thus belonged to the line of Azazel.[81]

In the 4QCommentary on Genesis A–D (252–254a) and 5QRule (5Q13), the figure of Noah is of first importance. In 4QCommentary on Genesis B, the adjustment to calendar and chronology with respect to the flood narrative creates a particular kind of "priestly Noah" who also has "mystical" characteristics in his role as recipient of esoteric knowledge concerning imminent judgments. By beginning with "their end came to Noah" during his 480th year even when the flood does not come until Noah's 600th year, the author seems to locate the *Yaḥad* somewhere between the time when the "end" of the sinful ones was made known to the *Yaḥad* sectarians and the time when judgment was realized. The recurring dual Noah traditions of "curses" and making distinctions in 4Q252–254a may indicate that Noah was created as the archetype for the sectarians who also recited appropriate blessings and curses especially during the ceremony of

---

79. Philip R. Davies, "'The Torah at Qumran," in *Judaism in Late Antiquity*, part 5, *The Judaism of Qumran: A Systematic Reading of the Dead Sea Scrolls* (ed. A. J. Avery-Peck, J. Neusner, and B. D. Chilton; 2 vols.; Leiden: Brill, 2001), 2:23–44, here 34–35.

80. Philip R. Davies, *The Damascus Covenant: An Interpretation of the "Damascus Document"* (JSOTSup 25; Sheffield: University of Sheffield, 1983), 61, 77.

81. An important implication is that the Enochic stories were still talked about and mined for illustrative examples by the sectarians even if they did not subscribe to the full range of ideologies conveyed in the Enochic books.

covenant renewal (1QS I–II).[82] According to this interpretation, by uttering curses as Noah had, the sectarians understood that they were making the coming judgment known to a "latter generation" whose end God had already announced.

The "overall interest in blessings and curses" in 4Q252 and the Levites' role of cursing in 1QS I–II strongly indicate that Levites were responsible for the "interpretative traditions in 4Q252."[83] Perhaps this position may be nuanced slightly. The *particular* Levites responsible for the Noah portion of 4Q252 were the ones who claimed Noah as a priestly ancestor. They inherited and transmitted "Aramaic Levi" traditions that were also influential in the formation of the *Genesis Apocryphon, Jubilees, Festival Prayers*, and 5QRule.

"Covenant" is not mentioned in the extant text of the Noah portion of 4QCommentary on Genesis A–D. "Covenant" is also missing from the Enochic books represented at Qumran and is, indeed, not present in any of the Qumran Aramaic texts, so the possibility may be considered that some movements, during some points of their existence may have, either deliberately or without intent, set aside the term. "Covenant" does appear in connection with Noah in *Jubilees* and in the liturgical *Festival Prayers*, and it is implied in 5QRule. All of these texts appear to incorporate "Aramaic Levi" traditions, naming Noah as a priestly ancestor. Therefore, while the covenant with Noah is not mentioned in the *Commentaries*, the focus on "blessings and curses" and "distinguishing between the righteous and the wicked" is strongly suggestive that "covenant" was, indeed, understood (cf. Deut 29:10–20 [11–21]).

5QRule may preserve what was once a version of the *Yaḥad*'s covenant renewal ceremony that contained a fuller version of the blessing to God (1QS I, 18–19) and the recounting of God's mighty deeds (1QS I, 22–24), remembering Noah in the remnants of a prayer and in a recounting of history. 5QRule follows an "Aramaic Levi" tradition, naming Noah as essential to the origin and transmission of priestly lore. The liturgy in 4QFestival Prayers also recognized Noah in the priestly Day of Atonement prayer, and the narrative of 4Q252 linked Noah to the priestly calendar. This suggests, at least, a persistent tradition of Levites who honored Noah and who may have been at odds with another view of the priesthood represented by the *Damascus Document* and Ben Sira that denied priesthood to their the pre-Sinai ancestors.

A Deuteronomic-style "covenant" was introduced as part of new interpretations of source traditions—such as those contained in the Aramaic Levi and Aramaic Enoch texts—that had, to that point, overlooked or neglected it. The *Damascus Document* developed its concept of "covenant" but severed any connection with Noah, whereas *Festival Prayers* remembered the covenant with Noah regularly.

On the whole, the diverse and selective ways that the Noah traditions were

---

82. See 1QS II, 16. God separates (בדל) out the one set aside for destruction.
83. So Brooke, "Deuteronomic Character of 4Q252," 135.

handled in the sectarian literature indicates that the *Commentaries* and 5QRule held to a definition of priesthood different from either CD or 4Q180–181. Certainly, CD also "rehabilitated" Ezekiel's Levites (CD III, 21–IV, 4/cf. Ezek 48:11) but its understanding of the Levites did not extend to an acknowledgment of Noah or the early priestly line, as did the *Commentaries* and 5QRule.

Traditions associated with Noah within the sectarian texts were utilized in very different ways that may reflect controversies within the conversations even among the sectarians of the *Yaḥad*. This "conversation" may have, indeed, become a dispute among the sectarians with Noah at its very center.

CHAPTER EIGHT

Conclusions

The Book of the Words of Noah...

*So I considered all the activity of those who dwell upon the earth;
I knew and I made known...*
Genesis Apocryphon (1Q20 V, 29; VI, 16)

Conversations among Traditions and Tradents of Noah

Inside Cave 1, just two kilometers from the Qumran settlement on the west shore of the Dead Sea, a community of sectarian Jews gathered and preserved its scrolls and on some of these were inscribed interpretations of Noah and the traditions associated with him. That copies of Genesis, Isaiah, Ezekiel, *Book of Giants*, *Aramaic Levi Document*, *Jubilees*, the *Genesis Apocryphon*, *Festival Prayers*, the so-called 1QBook of Noah, and the *Community Rule* actually resided in the same cave for about two thousand years before their rediscovery in 1946/1947 does invite the metaphor of "texts in conversation."[1] The widely diverse portrayals of Noah, such as those found in *Jubilees* and in the *Genesis Apocryphon*, demand the recognition that a singular, composite "Noah of the Dead Sea Scrolls" cannot be found even within this one cave, much less within the entire collection housed in all eleven caves.

In this study, each text has been given a turn to speak with its own voice, but, along the way, we have caught snatches of texts, people, and movements in

---

1. 1QGenesis, 1QIsaiah[a-b], 1QEzekiel, 1QEnochGiants[a-b], 1QTestament of Levi, *Genesis Apocryphon* (1Q20), 1QBook of Noah, 1QJubilees[a-b], 1QFestival Prayers, 1QRule of the Community (1QS). Cave 4, discovered in 1952, also housed a richly diverse collection of scrolls containing Noah traditions that included copies of Genesis, Isaiah, Ezekiel, Tobit, *Book of Watchers*, *Dream Visions*, *Apocalypse of Weeks*, the *Birth of Noah*, *Book of Giants*, *Aramaic Levi Document*, *Jubilees*, 4QTanḥumim, 4QAges of Creation A and B, 4QInstruction, 4QExhortation Based on the Flood, 4QPseudo-Daniel[b], 4QNaissance de Noé(?), 4QText Mentioning the Flood, 4QFestival Prayers[b], 4QCommentary on Genesis A – D, 4QParaphrase of Genesis and Exodus, 4QVisions of Amram[e], the *Damascus Document*, and Cave 4 copies of the *Community Rule*.

bilingual conversation with their predecessors and with their contemporaries, with friends but also, it would seem, with rivals. The conversations and disputes reflected in the portrayals of Noah were not merely literary exercises; they reflected the deep questions and concerns of real authors living in real communities.

This concluding chapter is more streamlined and less weighted with footnotes, referring the reader back to the more thorough analyses and nuanced text-by-text studies that have gone before. In this chapter, we step back from evaluating the more intricate details of the construction in order to assess the overall shape of Noah and the traditions that traveled with him in the Dead Sea Scrolls. We also step into the story to test its seaworthiness and to ready ourselves for further spirited dialogue on enhancing the design. The first part of this chapter summarizes the discoveries in the body of this work, and the second part distinguishes the Noah traditions as they appear in the Hebrew and Aramaic texts, so that the similarities and the differences might be more clearly seen and evaluated for their potential significance.

The three underlying questions introduced in chapter 1 resurface periodically in the guise of interpretations that seemed to have addressed them. How and to what extent is Noah portrayed as an archetype for a particular interpretation of what it meant to be Jewish? What does God reveal to Noah and how does he do it? To what extent is Noah claimed as a "distinctly Jewish" ancestor or, alternatively, claimed as a common ancestor of all humanity shared by the Gentiles?

Noah in the Earlier Hebrew and Aramaic Sources

Genesis, Ezekiel, and Isaiah

Genesis is the earliest of texts represented at Qumran that took flood survivor stories from other cultures and languages—traditions of the flood survivor heroes Utnapishtim, Atrahasis, Belos, the gigantic Atambish—and invested them with new theological meanings within the context of Israel's God in relationship with Israel's earliest ancestors. That the Noah narrative appeared to be virtually missing from the Genesis scrolls of the Qumran caves is puzzling, but since Noah's interpreters demonstrated such an obvious familiarity with the narrative, it would be difficult to argue for deliberate selection against its preservation. At the very least, Noah's interpreters knew a stable oral tradition that was substantially similar to the written tradition that eventually found its way into the Hebrew Bible.

The Noah narrative, as told in Genesis, explicitly associates a rich diversity of traditions with Noah but is also sufficiently enigmatic at strategic points to stimulate creative freedom in its interpreters working in Hebrew and Aramaic, across time, within different movements, and across genres. The structure proposed for the Noah narrative makes a case for its literary integrity. Repetition and deliberate adjustments of words and phrases, wordplays, and development of themes anticipated by the language in earlier sections all serve the coherency of the text not only within the flood narrative but also within the context of the entire primeval history that links the creation and Tower of Babel narratives to the Noah story. Exegetes of antiquity seemed to have noticed this literary unity, and Noah became, variously, a new "Adam" on a renewed earth as well as a "first priest," the first participant with God in a series of "times of punishment," and the first protagonist in a retelling of Israel's history.

Although the intermarriage of the "sons of gods" with women was not explicitly connected to the Noah narrative in Genesis except by juxtaposition, some interpreters of antiquity read the stories alongside each other, formulating a theology of the origin and the continuation of wickedness in the world, subsequent primordial judgment, and an *Urzeit* and *Endzeit* model of binary judgments. Still others detached the figure of Noah entirely from the "Watchers and the giants" traditions while maintaining the connection to the primordial judgment.

The book of Genesis is not intrinsically "Mosaic" as are the other books of the biblical Pentateuch; however, *Jubilees* would claim Genesis for Moses. The "authority" of the book of Genesis in Second Temple Judaism has not been questioned here. However, the precise relationship of Genesis to the books of the Torah more closely associated with Moses could well have been ambiguous right up until the second century B.C.E., when *Jubilees* pointedly included Genesis, and pre-Sinai Exodus under the revelation to Moses on Mount Sinai.

The exilic prophet Ezekiel listed Noah first in a group including Job and Daniel, righteous figures who, nonetheless, would have been unable to save any except for themselves in a future judgment. Abraham and Moses had been successful petitioners against judgments in other biblical accounts of Israel's history, so it is significant that Ezekiel features those who have points of contact with culture *outside* the land of Israel and whose stories are preserved in the Aramaic narratives, testamentary literature, and targums at Qumran.

Ezekiel's spiritual successors seem to have consciously claimed Noah—an ancestor who was "cut off" from the land—as a righteous and worthy ancestor, a natural archetype for a people in exile. Like Ezekiel, they included Noah in their retellings of history, possibly as a counterstory and a response to those who would not include Noah in an "internal" history. Noah's appearance in a recounting of a priestly tradition may mark an interpretation of the priesthood that was not restricted to Ezra and Nehemiah's attempts to reconstruct the priesthood in postexilic Jerusalem according to a more narrowly defined Zadokite Judaism.

The phrase "waters of Noah" in Deutero-Isaiah (Isa 54) recalled God's initiative during periodic times of judgment and his remembrance of a people he had temporarily abandoned. Specifically, the primordial flood is represented as a prototypical "time of judgment" for which the Babylonian exile was a later one. The prevailing "waters of Noah" were and would continue to be cast as a metaphor for continually redefined "enemies," but, as in the days of Noah, the "waters" would not prevail forever. The tension between the power of the "waters" and God as felt already in the Genesis narrative is intensified in Isaiah. The enemies, like the waters, would not be able to prevail against God.

The Books of Aramaic Enoch

The final redaction of Genesis emerged out of an interaction with ancient Near Eastern stories, but the striking similarities between the Noah of Genesis and the ancient Near Eastern stories of flood survivors could have been troublesome for some Second Temple Jews who knew of these stories from the exile in Babylon. Even for those who esteemed and hoped to "domesticate" Mesopotamian science and culture into a Jewish idealized figure, Noah carried too much "cultural baggage" and was too easily confused with the gigantic flood survivors in Mesopotamian literary culture.

Enoch, however, was a candidate better suited for the domestication of Babylonian science and culture, and the sparing mention of Enoch in Genesis allowed for much fertile ground and vast exegetical freedom. Furthermore, Enoch's "walk" with God/the gods (האלהים) (Gen 5:24) so resembled Noah's walk with God or the gods, that the exegetes could also transfer and adapt Noah's biblical characteristics and experiences to a more acceptable "flood survivor," Enoch.

Just as Genesis had recontextualized and reinterpreted flood survivor traditions into Hebrew, so now the *Book of Watchers* recontextualized the Genesis Noah traditions into the story of Enoch. Enoch was re-created into the first "righteous man" and the idealized "flood survivor." Throughout much of the remainder of the Enochic corpus represented at Qumran, Noah is apparently submerged or suppressed and, it would seem, even denuded of his righteousness.

Only in the *Birth of Noah* are found the beginnings of the rehabilitation of Noah; Enoch acknowledges Noah's status as his legitimate great-grandson and, implicitly, as his potential successor. This trajectory culminates in a heightened and exalted status for Noah, as earlier Enochic traditions travel into the *Parables*, the *Genesis Apocryphon*, 1QNoah, and, possibly, 4QNaissance de Noé (4Q534). That trend, however, reverses, and Noah is dramatically renounced in *2 Enoch's* scathing and explicit polemic.

Although Noah plays a modest role in *1 Enoch*, the study of Enoch's character in the Enochic books has proved to be important for understanding Noah's characterization in other texts in which Noah bears a strong resemblance to Enoch. Revelation and wisdom come to Enoch directly from the angels. Therefore, Enoch appears to have required neither the Torah to know God nor the contemporary temple establishment to meet God. Once the "Enochic Noah" met "Levi" and "Moses" traditions, new portrayals of Noah resulted that revealed something of the interaction among the people and movements who gave rise to these writings.

The *Aramaic Levi Document*

While only a single reference to Noah as the originator of priestly lore in the "Book of Noah" survives in a Greek version of the *Aramaic Levi Document*, a synoptic view of "Levi" as idealized priest in the *ALD* and "Noah" in the *Genesis Apocryphon* reveals the importance of this text for tracing the origins of a "priestly Noah." More obviously "priestly" than the representations in the Enochic corpus, the *ALD*'s idealized Levi is nonetheless also visited by angels and exemplifies oral and written transmission along a hereditary pre-Mosaic line. The composition of subsequent Aramaic texts in the same tradition continued well after the time of the composition of the Hebrew Yaḥad sectarian texts, hinting at the possibility that Aramaic traditions influenced by the *ALD* may have continued to develop independently even after earlier Aramaic traditions were domesticated into *Jubilees*.

The *Aramaic Levi Document* picked Noah as the bridge from an antediluvian world to the postdiluvian world, in which he was the first to offer a sacrifice. The *ALD* draws its characterization of Levi from Genesis and from the prophets, specifically Malachi, but does not appear to be similarly oriented to Sinai and post-Sinai Torah. Although the *Testament of Levi*—a text that subsequently recontextualized and reinterpreted the *ALD*—would stress a wisdom subordinated to Torah, the *ALD* stressed wisdom and truth without making the same explicit connection to Torah. Additionally, while Levi prays in *ALD*, there is no clear indication in the extant text of repentance, confession, or atonement for this particular type of "Levi-priest."

The *ALD*'s genealogy of priests that names Noah as a priestly ancestor is shared by *Jubilees*, 4QFestival Prayers, and 5QRule but not by Ben Sira or the *Damascus Document*. The implication of this genealogy is that, as early as the early postexilic period, there were priests who understood themselves to be the true hereditary priesthood, claiming their descent not only from Levi but also from Noah, who first acted as priest. These traditions stand in a trajectory of priestly texts that maintained a focus on characters that lived for at least part of their lives outside the land; therefore, we might speculate that priestly traditions that named Noah originated among priests who counted themselves as priests even though they were not a part of the Jerusalem establishment. For them, a literature constructed around ancestral archetypes, such as Noah and Levi, who could be priests and accurately transmit priestly lore even while outside the land, would have been crucial for their own validation.

Ongoing Aramaic Conversations about Noah

A Trajectory of Noah in "Levi Priestly" Traditions

Oral and written transmission along a priestly line that named Noah and Levi is clearly a key thrust in the testamentary material of 4QVisions of Amram and 4QTestament of Qahat. Whereas the *ALD* simply mentioned the "Book of

Noah," the text of 4QVisions of Amram^e (4Q547) describes Noah's sacrifices, also mentioning Abraham, Isaac, Jacob, Levi, and Moses, people who lived or journeyed outside of "the land." These texts following in an "Aramaic Levi" tradition strongly hint at the challenges facing the priestly movement composing and transmitting them. Its chosen archetypes, living as they did before Moses and outside of the land, are portrayed as notable representatives of a particular priestly line that could accurately transmit knowledge of the proper practices of priesthood. These texts, therefore, possibly reflected a dispute of these priests with the dominant priestly establishment in Jerusalem concerning the validity of their priesthood.

The unnamed "chosen" figure of remarkable birth in 4QNaissance de Noé (4Q534) who received and transmitted esoteric knowledge but who experienced opposition was likely a member of the hereditary line that claimed Noah as an ancestor and of which each member shared ideal characteristics. It is not unreasonable to expect that a trajectory of tradition that was elevating a "wise Noah" could also have called him "chosen" in 4Q534, chosen to survive and flourish in times of oppression and wickedness. An interesting footnote to this study involves the identity of the priestly figure in 4QApocryphon of Levi who shared some of the family traits of this priestly line and who lived in times of "deceit and violence" during the time of the author.

The *Genesis Apocryphon*

The *Genesis Apocryphon* (1Q20) did for Noah within an Aramaic tradition what *Jubilees* did differently in Hebrew. It pulled together wisdom, apocalyptic, and priestly traditions from a variety of Hebrew and Aramaic sources, creating a collage consisting of a "wise Noah" who receives esoteric knowledge and walks in the truth, a "priestly Noah" patterned after Levi from the *ALD*, and a "visionary Noah" patterned after Enoch and whose words were "collected" and reliably transmitted in the era before Moses. Noah's conflated righteousness is expressed as both the Aramaic קשוט characterizing Enoch and as the cognate to the Hebrew צדיק accorded Noah in Genesis. In 1Q20, he takes on the characteristics of Enoch, including his righteousness, his visions of imminent and eschatological judgment, and his sojourn in paradise as a new Adam.

In contrast to Noah's fraternal twin in *Jubilees,* who is "priestly" and who also offers a sacrifice that atones for the land, 1Q20 does not introduce sinful inclination, repentance, covenant, blessings and curses, or the "Day of Atonement" in the extant text. Noah is painted onto an Enochic and Levi-priestly canvas—the parallels are too numerous to be accidental—rather than the Mosaic or, more specifically, Deuteronomic canvas that *Jubilees* presents. Therefore, the topic of this conversation is represented by these two portrayals of Noah, presenting two separate understandings of priesthood with differing orientations toward Moses and Enoch and, by extension, differing stances concerning the relative authority of the books associated with Enoch and Moses.

The *Genesis Apocryphon* reveals, in explicit and implicit ways, the narrator's engagement with foreign science and wisdom and a willingness to locate the text geographically within the Hellenistic world with Delphi at its center. However, the authority of the character of Enoch would supersede the wisdom and science of Egypt and Greece. When asked to teach wisdom to the king of Egypt, Abram reads from the "Book of Enoch." When Bitenosh, Lamech's wife, offers proof of conception obtained from Greek medical science, Lamech still appeals to Enoch through Methuselah to legitimize Noah's birth and to assure him that the child, indeed, belonged to him.

Noah functions as differently interpreted archetypical priests "atoning for the land" in *Jubilees* and the *Genesis Apocryphon*. Because he is the only character to "atone for the land" anywhere in the Dead Sea Scrolls, this particular function links him most closely to the Yaḥad sectarians for whom "atoning for the land" described their role in a particular way. In the *Community Rule*, those who "atoned for the land" belonged to a community of covenant keepers[2] situated in a period of purification prior to its possession of and atonement for the sanctuary and in connection with acts of judgment upon those who had committed iniquity. Therefore, in the *Community Rule* (1QS), "atoning for the land" had achieved the status of a technical term that carried powerful associations of catastrophic judgment upon all of the wicked ones at the hands of a people living in covenant with God.

> *1* In the Council of the Yaḥad there shall be twelve laymen and three priests who are without blemish (תמימים) in everything which is revealed from the entire *2* Torah, in order to[3] practice truth (אמת), righteousness (צדקה) and justice/judgment (משפט) ... *5* then shall the Council of the Yaḥad be established in truth as an "eternal planting" (מטעת עולם), as a holy house for Israel, and as an assembly of utter *6* holiness for Aaron; witnesses of truth for judgment, and chosen ones of God's favor in order to atone for the land and to recompense *7* the wicked their retribution. (*vacat*) *9* In all of their knowledge (דעת) with respect to[4] a covenant of judgment (ברית משפט), they must bring a soothing aroma (ריח ניחוח) and be a blameless and true house in Israel, *10* in order to establish a covenant (ברית) of eternal (עולם) statutes (חוקות). They will be an acceptable sacrifice in

---

2. For example, see other sectarian texts describing those who atoned for the land: "who kept his covenant in the midst of wickedness, in order to atone for the land" (4Q249ᵍ 1–2 3); "[These must l]ive by the law of the sons of Zadok, the priests, and the men of their covenant, they who ce[ased to walk in the w]ay of the people. These same are the men of his Council who kept his covenant in the midst of wickedness, in order to aton[e for the lan]d (1QSa I, 1–3). See also 4Q265 7, 7–14, a text that cites Mal 2:10: "Why then are we faithless to one another, profaning the covenant of our ancestors?" (4Q265 3 1–3); cf. also 1QS IX, 3–5.

3. *Lamed* of purpose. See Ronald J. Williams, *Hebrew Syntax: An Outline* (2nd ed.; Toronto: University of Toronto Press, 1976), §277. This construction serves to subordinate the actions of the Yaḥad to the Torah.

4. *Lamed* of specification. See Williams, *Hebrew Syntax*, §273.

order to atone for the land (לכפר בעד) and to decide judgment (משפט) of wickedness (רשעה) so there will no longer be iniquity. (excerpted from 1QS VIII, 1–10a)[5]

This expression of the *Yaḥad*'s self-identity in the *Community Rule*, though so clearly aligned with "Torah," still appears to retain the historical memory of Noah in the plethora of "Noah" traditions here detached from the figure of Noah but which the group adopted for itself. The traditions of "atoning for the land," "truth and righteousness," an "eternal planting," and obedience to "eternal statutes" accompany Noah in the *Genesis Apocryphon*. *Jubilees*, on the other hand, gives priority to the covenant, and both texts link "atoning for the land" to the judgment of the wicked. However, while Noah is a passive observer of judgment in the texts that name him, the sectarians were more self-consciously active participants in a covenant that included judgment for which they would be God's active agents of retribution upon the wicked.

Noah may be understood in the *Genesis Apocryphon*, therefore, as the representation of an archetype for a known righteous figure or as the hoped-for ideal of a contemporary group or movement who lived in a time of "violence, evil, and deceit" (1Q20 XI, 13–14). In addition to retaining his biblical character as drawn from Genesis, he inherited character traits from Enoch and Levi obtained from the Aramaic Enoch and Aramaic Levi texts. He becomes, therefore, a super-righteous pattern for a uniquely "Aramaic" understanding of an idealized righteous, wise, and visionary priesthood.

Ongoing Hebrew Conversations about Noah

Hebrew Pre-sectarian Texts

Wisdom in 4QInstruction was obtained by a supernatural revelation of secrets and mysteries and not, at least explicitly, from the Torah of Moses. These wisdom traditions seem to have influenced the characterizations of Noah, Enoch, and Levi in the Aramaic traditions from the earliest Enochic books and the *ALD* through to the composition of 1Q20. They were closely associated with periods of judgment and appear to be at home within an "Aramaic Levi" priesthood that looked to the figure of Levi as an archetype. The interpretation of wisdom as found in 4QInstruction coheres well with the type of priesthood that embraced esoteric knowledge and valued oral transmission of priestly lore rather than sole dependence on the written Torah as a source of revelation.

Ben Sira also was grounded in Genesis but appealed to Torah as the source of wisdom. The author was suspicious of revelation by angels and dreams and, in the narrative, restricted angelic visitations to those characters that had received such visitations in the Hebrew Bible. The Watchers story is recontextualized,

---

5. Translation is that of the author.

becoming an example of how free-willed creatures rebelled, which served to emphasize Ben Sira's view of human rather than angelic responsibility for sin. Ben Sira's genealogy of ancestors attributes the beginning of wisdom to Enoch and mentions Noah, but it omits Levi and does not attribute priesthood to anyone until Aaron. Therefore, in view of Ben Sira's positive stance toward Torah, the way it recontextualized the Watchers traditions, and its retelling of a history that excluded Noah and Levi from the priesthood, Ben Sira appears to be in engaged in a polemical conversation with movements much like those that gave rise to the Aramaic Enoch and Aramaic Levi texts.

Jubilees, like Ben Sira, represents a movement that was oriented toward the Mosaic Torah but, unlike Ben Sira, was much more accommodating of Enochic traditions. It shows itself to be strongly influenced by the priestly movement behind the Aramaic Levi traditions. Thus, *Jubilees* may reflect or have been influential upon a developing unity among those of diverse backgrounds—priests from the Aramaic Levi tradition, Jews who held to Enochic traditions, and Jews from the "back-to-Torah" and "back-to-Hebrew" movement.

Rather than exclude Enoch and Noah as the *Damascus Document* would do, *Jubilees* "grandfathers" Enoch as a revelatory figure into the narrative, and Noah's status is enhanced as he becomes an archetype for Moses himself. Noah orally transmits instruction to his progeny; he successfully intercedes on behalf of his grandchildren; he receives limited revelation from God; and he records in a book the remedies against demons supplied to him by the angels. In this way, as in the *Genesis Apocryphon*, selected characteristics of Enoch are transferred to Noah. Noah, however, did not need to be legitimized by Enoch; his behavior as a Torah-obedient priestly figure that prefigured Moses was sufficient.

Noah as painted onto the "Mosaic canvas" had a profoundly new look. The Genesis flood chronology was now fashioned into a priestly calendar featuring Noah as the originator and celebrator of its festivals known from the Torah. Noah was the first to participate in the making of a covenant that Moses was told to renew every year. Elements of the Day of Atonement and *Shevuot* were linked in *Jubilees*, in *Festival Prayers*, and, more explicitly, in the sectarian covenant renewal ceremony itself, which incorporated covenant making with repentance and curses.

The so-called 1QBook of Noah (1Q19) strongly resembles 1Q20 and is one of best examples of a free interchange in a bilingual conversation between Noah texts. Both contain versions of Noah's remarkable birth narrative that also mention Lamech and Methuselah, but 1Q19 exhibits the logical terminus of a trajectory that increasingly exalted Noah. 1Q19 mentions a "chosen" male figure, one who is "glorified among the sons of heaven." If this figure is, indeed, Noah, it would be an ironic yet fitting destiny for one who was suspected of being a son of the Watchers and who, for so long, was under suspicion in the Enochic corpus of being confused with the giants. A text that is oddly shaped, interpretatively speaking, among the Hebrew scrolls, 1Q19 appears to have reached back into an Enochic tradition that was unmediated by *Jubilees*, retelling the tradition in Hebrew and, in so doing, creating an archetype for those who hoped also to be "chosen" and to be "glorified" among the angels.

4QTanḥumim continued the trajectory begun in Isa 54 by expanding the Noachic element in the analogies between the foundational primordial story and the days of the author. While Isaiah used the "waters of Noah" as a metaphor for enemies and exile, the exegete responsible for 4Q176, by means of strategic juxtaposition of certain passages, has linked the promised consolation of Israel to the naming of Noah. The primordial flood in this text thus becomes a foundational story that focused also on God's remembrance and comfort of his people even in the midst of the most catastrophic events that had cut them off from the land.

The historical remembrance of the covenant with Noah in 4QFestival Prayers[b] has, in this study, called to mind Noah's celebration of *Shevuot* in *Jubilees*. Included in the Day of Atonement prayers is a group of Noah traditions, some of which tended to travel together in Hebrew texts—covenant and "inclination," and a confession for repentance addressed to God who knows things "hidden and revealed," who would execute judgment and who would "distinguish between the righteous and the wicked."

Mishnah Sotah preserves what may be an early tradition that specifies that certain prayers for *Shevuot* and the Day of Atonement were to be spoken in Hebrew. Even in the Second Temple period, then, liturgists may have continued to compose and copy narrative texts in Aramaic while transmitting liturgies in Hebrew. The inclusion of Noah's name in the liturgy meant that Noah's place in the priestly line was still important for this group or movement. That would change for at least some interpreters within the *Yaḥad* as the sect became oriented more toward Moses and less toward Enoch, Noah, and Levi as foundational figures.

4QParaphrase of Genesis and Exodus (4Q422) draws from the historical retellings in Pss 78 and 105, but, by adding the creation and the flood narratives to the plagues narrative already in the Psalms, the author implies that the primeval narratives were also a part of Israel's history inextricably linked to what would follow. The flood and the plagues narratives were likely viewed as reversals of creation, a theme already hinted at in Genesis and Exodus, carried forward in *Jubilees* and 1Q20, which resonated with 4QInstruction. Covenant and past judgment, linked only by juxtaposition to Noah in Genesis, come into a powerful relationship in *Jubilees*, *Festival Prayers*, and now, also, 4Q422.

4QAdmonition Based on the Flood (4Q370) acknowledges Enochic themes—that the giants were destroyed in the flood is selected for particular mention—but the author, although interested in how people would escape future judgments, does not mention Noah explicitly. Perhaps the genre did not demand it; however, 4Q370 is representative of a group of texts that detached the figure of Noah from themes of judgment, covenant, and atoning for the land.

Hebrew Sectarian Texts

The Admonitions in the *Damascus Document* (CD) did not include Noah in the historical retelling but rather skipped over to the "sons of Noah" who, like the Watchers and their sons, followed their sinful inclination. CD preferentially introduced Abraham as the first figure with whom God made a covenant. No priestly prototypes, including Levi, are offered within CD's interpretation of Ezekiel's "priest, Levites, and sons of Zadok."

While detached from the Watchers and flood traditions, Noah may still be in the background as a "survivor figure," echoing the emphasis of much of the Enochic corpus and of Ben Sira. Like *Jubilees*, CD discredits the sons of Noah, attributing to them the sins of the human and angelic generation of the flood. The confessional formula echoed also in 4QFestival Prayers and 5QRule appears in CD but without reference to Noah.

4QAges of Creation A and B (4Q180-181) relates a periodization of history that recounts the second period of ten generations beginning with the "sons of Noah" and ending with Abram. As in CD, Noah does not figure in this retelling. Uniquely among the extant sectarian texts, 4Q181 introduces a "*Yaḥad* of wickedness," an "order (*serek*) of the sons of Noah," together with the negatively termed "council of the sons of heaven and earth."

This text reaches back, therefore, for the story of Azazel to address the "guilt" and "wickedness" that were likely now within the ranks of the sectarians themselves. While claiming to be part of the true *Yaḥad*, this "*anti-Yaḥad*" was consorting with the wrong sort of angels. Rather than being true progeny of Noah, its "rule" or order was more like the "sons of Noah," and the rebels resembled the archetypical enemies found in the group's foundational story of the Watchers.

Noah is the character who appears "first" in 4QCommentary on Genesis A (4Q252). The preoccupation with the 364-day calendar and the explicit links to the flood chronology confirm the priestly interests behind the text and suggest similar calendar interests to those in *Jubilees*. Esoteric knowledge revealed to Noah, most likely about coming judgments, indicates a 4QInstruction-like wisdom strand that had earlier coalesced with the priestly tradition. References to the annual remembrance of Noah's disembarkation from the ark brings to mind liturgies that may have given rise to the *Yaḥad*'s covenant renewal ceremony.

Blessings and curses in connection with Noah appear even on the fragmentary smaller commentaries in connection with possession of the land. Covenant and repentance are features connected with Noah in the *Jubilees* narrative and also in the *Festival Prayers*, yet there is no explicit mention of covenant or repentance in the extant text of 4QCommentary on Genesis A-D.

Finally, 5QRule (5Q13) remembers Noah in what could be a variant rendition of a fragmentary covenant renewal ceremony. Someone, possibly Noah, is chosen "from among the heavenly beings," an echo of wisdom and apocalyptic traditions resident in 1QNoah and 4QNaissance de Noé, language that does not derive from *Jubilees*. The fact that both Aramaic and Hebrew Noah traditions unmediated by *Jubilees* were still accessible and, possibly, adapted into a sectarian document suggests that the Aramaic texts were still a part of the conversation among the sectarians even while a parallel trajectory of Aramaic traditions mediated through *Jubilees* and *Festival Prayers*, for example, was influential in the forming of the covenant renewal ceremony for the community.

The ceremony that was to be carried out "annually, all the days of Belial's dominion" is most reasonably the ceremony celebrating the renewal of the Mosaic covenant. The mention of "Belial" also reflects the interpretation of the "days of Noah" in 4QTanḥumim—which, incidentally, may indicate that this text had a liturgical function—and in 4Q253, in which Belial appears in the same text as a "priestly Noah" who offers up a burnt offering.

5QRule (5Q13) stands in a tradition similar to that behind 4QFestival Prayers[b], which also remembered the covenant with Noah. While the *Community Rule* preserved in 1QS did not include a rehearsal of history in the recorded ceremony, it is not necessary to posit that 5QRule was the creation of a separate group. Rather, it may preserve the remnant of a larger version of the covenant renewal ceremony recorded by those in the emerging sect who were more loyal about remembering Noah, more insistent about rehearsing a specialized "Aramaic Levi" version of their history.

Bilingual and Bicultural Noah: Noah Traditions in Hebrew and Aramaic

The two tables below arrange the traditions of Noah within Hebrew and Aramaic categories in order to clarify the similarities and differences.

NOAH TRADITIONS SHARED IN ARAMAIC AND HEBREW

Noah Tradition	Tradition appears in Aramaic and Hebrew
Angelic origin of wickedness and violence	Throughout *1 Enoch*, 1Q20, *Jubilees*, CD, 4Q180–181 (pervasive in Hebrew and Aramaic texts)
Deluge and eschatological judgment as twin events or periodic times of judgment beginning with flood and including exile	*1 Enoch* (pervasive), 1Q20, Ezekiel, Isaiah, 4Q176, 4Q180–181, 4Q577, 4QInstruction, *Jubilees*
Endogamous marriage	1Q20, Tobit, *Jubilees*
Survivorship: remnant, chosen	BW, DV, AW, BN, 1Q20, Genesis, Ben Sira, *Jubilees*, CD, 4Q534(?), 5Q13
Noah as first named priestly ancestor; e.g., sacrifices specifically for atonement, blood prohibitions, calendar/chronology, division of land	ALD, 1Q20, 4Q547, *Jubilees*, 4Q508, 4Q252–254a

CONCLUSIONS

Noah Tradition	Tradition appears in Aramaic and Hebrew
Noah as "new Adam"; e.g., dominion over the earth, reestablishment of seasons; reentry into and walking upon renewed land; "new Adam" implied by conflation of elements of biblical creation and flood narratives	1Q20, Genesis, *Jubilees*, 4Q422
Noah as writer and teacher: transmission of teaching orally and/or in writing (i.e., "Book of Noah")	ALD, 1Q20, *Jubilees*,
Righteous plant	BW (comes *from* Noah), 1Q20, *Jubilees*
Remarkable birth narrative	BN, 1Q20, 4Q534 (?), 1Q19

NOAH TRADITIONS EXCLUSIVE TO ARAMAIC OR HEBREW

Noah Tradition	Aramaic Dead Sea Scrolls[6]	Hebrew Dead Sea Scrolls[7]
Covenant (קים/ברית); also in collocation with confession	Not in Aramaic corpus	*Jubilees*, 4Q508, 5Q13[8]
Sinful inclination (יצר)	Not in Aramaic corpus	4Q508, 4Q370, 4Q180–181, CD, *Jubilees* (Esau)
Noah blesses/curses (ארר/קלל)	Not in Aramaic corpus	*Jubilees*, 4Q252, 4Q254, 5Q13[9]
Distinguishing between the righteous and the wicked (בין צדיק לרשע)	Not in Aramaic corpus	4Q508, 4Q253a,[10] cf. 4Q254 8 7: (. . . והבדיל בי[ן).
Implied penitent Noah	Not in Aramaic corpus	*Jubilees*; cf. 4Q508
"Wise Noah" (חכמה/חכם)	1Q20, (4Q534)(?)	Only Enoch and Joseph "wise" in *Jubilees*.
"Mystic Noah": recipient of otherworldly revelation	Visions of imminent *and* eschatological judgment on humanity *and* angelic world	No revelation to Noah about eschatological judgment and the fate of the angelic world. Reserved for Moses.

---

6. See chapter 1 for a listing of the Aramaic texts that contain Noah traditions.
7. See chapter 1 for a listing of Hebrew texts that contain Noah traditions.
8. Noah remembered in what may be a variant covenant renewal ceremony.
9. See parallels to 1QS II, 16–III, 6 and the "curses of the covenant."
10. See chapter 7 for an argument for the recombination of 4Q253a and 4Q253.

Noah Tradition	Aramaic Dead Sea Scrolls	Hebrew Dead Sea Scrolls
Direct speech recorded for …	Only the giants, angels, Enoch, Methuselah, Lamech, Bitenosh, Noah, Abram, Jacob, Judah, Joseph, Levi, Qahat, Amram and Daniel "speak" in Aramaic.	Moses and Joshua speak only in Hebrew. *Jubilees*, like Genesis, records direct speech for Noah and others in Hebrew.

Briefly and in summary, Hebrew Noah traditions that are completely missing from the extant Aramaic portrayals include covenant, repentance, sinful inclination, blessings and curses, and the explicit distinction between the righteous and the wicked. Because the Aramaic evidence for Noah, in particular, represents a small part of the corpus and is very fragmentary, it is reasonable to ask whether too much is being read into a slender corpus of exclusively Noah traditions. However, the case is strengthened considerably when we expand the search for these words and themes into the entire Aramaic corpus. Not only are these themes and traditions absent in connection with *Noah*, but they are missing from virtually *all* Aramaic texts, including those characterizing Enoch, Noah, Abram, Jacob, Judah, Levi, Amram, Qahat, Daniel, or Job.

Some tentative conclusions may be offered as a basis for more conversation. The language and themes found exclusively in Hebrew texts and not in the extant Aramaic texts may be more oriented to a worldview that needed to clarify the distinctions between the "group" and those outside the group. For example, in *Jubilees* and 4QCommentary on Genesis A–D, the archetypical blessings and curses that Noah speaks may represent the archetypical proper kinds of "distinction."[11]

4QFestival Prayers[b] (4Q508) incorporates the "distinction between the righteous and the wicked," assurance of coming judgment upon the oppressors, acknowledgment of human inclination, a confession, *and* remembrance of the covenant with Noah all within one text. It really is a small exegetical step from the primordial distinction between the righteous and wicked by God during the flood to a redefined latter-day hoped-for distinction between the "righteous and the wicked." In the meantime, a "Hebrew Noah" could be an archetype for those who perceived themselves to be participants with God in making proper distinctions between the righteous and the wicked by knowing whom to bless and whom to curse.

In the Aramaic texts, Noah is a wise and mystic figure, given to visions of the eschatological judgment and knowledgeable about what was occurring in the world of the supernatural. However, while *Jubilees* does allow Noah's great-grandfather Enoch to maintain his wise, visionary role (*Jub.* 4:17), Noah himself

---

11. Perhaps not incidentally, Noah's curse and blessing in Gen 9:25–27 is Noah's first and only speech in the entire Hebrew narrative.

is *not* called wise, and neither are Israel's other ancestors except Joseph, who is recognized as "wise" only by the foreign Egyptians (*Jub.* 40:5; cf. Gen 41:39).

Generally speaking, *Jubilees* appears to replace the generalized wisdom (חכמה) found in the Aramaic texts with the revelation to Moses as repository of all revelation. The term חכמה may have had unsatisfactory risky associations with ongoing Enochic-style apocalyptic revelation, from which the sectarians deliberately moved away as they became more oriented toward a newly interpreted Torah of Moses, in which the fullest revelation came to and through Moses.

There is still one more intriguing observation. At the risk of stating what is all too obvious, in Aramaic texts that record direct speech, the characters speak Aramaic, and in Hebrew texts, they speak Hebrew. Within the larger Aramaic corpus, as would be expected, King Nabonidus of the Neo-Babylonian empire of Israel's exile speaks Aramaic[12] as does Daniel when retelling Israel's history for King Belshazzar.[13] Other Aramaic speakers in the Dead Sea Scrolls include Enoch,[14] Methuselah, Lamech, Bitenosh, Noah,[15] Abram,[16] Jacob,[17] Judah,[18] Joseph,[19] Levi, Qahat, and Amram.[20] However, after Amram, no characters "speak" in Aramaic until Daniel of the exile.

The "Aramaic speakers"—Enoch through Amram and then exilic characters such as Daniel—all had something in common; within the biblical narrative, all spent significant periods, if not their whole lives, outside of the land.[21] These were characters who, for various reasons were "cut off" from the land and were outside the land of Israel. They had to know how to survive successfully among the nations, and they obviously would "need" to communicate in a language shared by their neighbors.

In conclusion, there appears to have been, in general, a "Hebrew Noah" archetype and an "Aramaic Noah" archetype participating in a bilingual conversation even among the sectarians at Qumran. Noah, as transmitted in Aramaic, actively contended with foreign wisdom, science, story, and philosophy while reframing

---

12. 4Q Prayer of Nabonidus (4Q242); 4Q Proto-Esther[a-e] (4Q550, 4Q550[a-e]).
13. 4QPseudo-Daniel[a-c] (4Q243–245).
14. 4Q201–202, 204–207, 4Q212.
15. Noah's recorded words in the "Words of the Book of Noah" in the *Genesis Apocryphon* are, naturally, in Aramaic.
16. In 1Q20, which focuses its attention on the journeys of Abram in Mesopotamia and in Egypt.
17. 4Q537.
18. 4Q538 recounts the events in Egypt between Joseph and his brothers.
19. 4QApocryphon of Joseph B (4Q539).
20. Spoken while he was in Egypt (4Q543). He recounts the time he was in Haran and Egypt.
21. Cf. Deut 26:5 spoken at the offering of firstfruits, "My father was a wandering Aramean and he went down to Egypt and sojourned there." Obviously, Moses was never in the land, but books of Torah associated with Moses have much to do with the land.

the foreign elements and subordinating them within a particular interpretation of Judaism.

Hebrew texts, in turn, recontextualized some Aramaic traditions but also turned the Jewish gaze inward so that the Hebrew Noah became much more distinct from that which was foreign. The traditions transmitted in Hebrew centered more self-consciously on the things that distinguished Jews from their foreign neighbors: liturgy and prayer, curses separating out one group from another, and the renewal of the covenant made specifically with Israel. Therefore, while a bilingual Noah was permitted to dream in Aramaic, he definitely cursed in Hebrew!

For all their differences from the Hebrew sectarian scrolls, the Aramaic texts continued to be collected at Qumran long after the Hebrew sectarian rule books and commentaries were written, hinting at the possibility that there was ongoing discussion concerning the extent to which the community—or some of the sectarians—could and should still contend with foreign science and story in a language *other* than Hebrew. Alternatively, perhaps it was simply that the Noah traditions most closely associated with the sectarian's *distinctive* identity—study and reinterpretation of the Mosaic Torah, prayers for the Day of Atonement, curses, and the covenant renewal liturgy—required the use of Hebrew but that the sectarians were free, in other moments, to remember and enjoy, to copy, and to transmit their favorite stories about their pre-Mosaic ancestors in Aramaic.

The Conversation: To Be Continued

In conclusion, there is great diversity in the use of Noah traditions by different movements that were, at different times, in friendly or in adversarial relationships. The texts still stand as independent entities, as individual snapshots of Noah traditions. However, suggestions of certain patterns and relationships between the various trajectories are discernible and have, I hope, prepared the ground for future fruitful inquiry and discussion.

From their beginnings in Genesis, Noah traditions were lifted out of their texts, set into new contexts and, in this way, were freshly reinterpreted for a new time and for a people finding themselves in new and different circumstances. The appearance of Noah with a particular associated tradition, such as that of the Watchers, hardly guarantees that one text followed the ideology of the earlier one from which it was borrowing. Indeed, the opposite was frequently true, making Noah a complex and intriguing figure to follow through the conversations that spilled over boundaries among the movements and groups represented by the texts at Qumran.

While the texts written in Aramaic oriented themselves more closely toward the pre-Sinai figures of Noah, Enoch, and Levi and the literatures associated with them, Noah was also at home in the Hebrew texts that oriented themselves more specifically toward Moses and his Torah. Noah possesses multiple personalities in the Dead Sea Scrolls, and his characterizations provide clues to the self-identities and worldviews of the developing movements within the community that created them. Even the *Yaḥad* sectarians, within the language of their liturgy, commentaries, and the foundational documents expressing their self-identity, continued to remember Noah.

Bibliography

Reference Works and Primary Sources

Abegg, Martin G., Jr. "QUMRAN." *Accordance Bible Software.* Altamonte Springs, Fl.: Oaktree Software Specialists, 2006.

Abegg, Martin G., Jr., James E. Bowley, and Edward M. Cook. "QUMENG." *Accordance Bible Software.* Altamonte Springs, Fl.: Oaktree Software Specialists, 2006.

Abegg, Martin G., Jr., James E. Bowley, and Edward M. Cook, with Casey Toews. "QUMBIB-M/C." *Accordance Bible Software.* Altamonte Springs, Fl.: Oaktree Software Specialists, 2006.

Abegg, Martin G., Jr., with James E. Bowley and Edward M. Cook, in consultation with Emanuel Tov. *The Dead Sea Scrolls Concordance.* Vol. 1, *The Non-Biblical Texts from Qumran.* Leiden/Boston: Brill, 2003.

Abegg, Martin G., Jr., Peter Flint, and Eugene Ulrich. *The Dead Sea Scrolls Bible.* New York: HarperSanFrancisco, 1999.

Abegg, Martin G., Jr., with Casey A. Toews. "BENSIRA-C/M." *Accordance Bible Software.* Altamonte Springs, Fl.: Oaktree Software Specialists, 2007.

Aberbach, Moses, and Bernard Grossfeld. *Targum Onkelos to Genesis.* New York: Ktav, 1982.

Allegro, John Marco. *Qumran Cave 4.I (4Q158–186).* Discoveries in the Judaean Desert V. Oxford: Clarendon, 1968.

Alter, Robert. *The Five Books of Moses: A Translation with Commentary.* New York: W. W. Norton, 2004.

———. *Genesis: Translation and Commentary.* New York: W. W. Norton, 1997.

Attridge, H. W., T. Elgvin, J. Milik, S. Olyan, J. Strugnell, E. Tov, J. VanderKam, and S. White in consultation with J. C. VanderKam. *Qumran Cave 4.VIII: Parabiblical Texts, Part I.* Discoveries in the Judaean Desert XIII. Oxford: Clarendon, 1994.

Avigad, N., and Y. Yadin. *A Genesis Apocryphon: A Scroll from the Wilderness of Judaea.* Jerusalem: Magnes and Heikhal Ha-Sefer, 1956.

Baillet, M. *Qumrân Grotte 4.III (4Q282–5Q520).* Discoveries in the Judaean Desert VII. Oxford, Clarendon, 1982.

Baillet, M., J. T. Milik and R. de Vaux. *Les "petites grottes" de Qumrân.* Discoveries in the Judaean Desert III. Oxford: Clarendon, 1962.

Barthélemy, D., and J. T. Milik. *Qumran Cave 1*. Discoveries in the Judaean Desert I. Oxford: Clarendon, 1955.

Baumgarten, J. M. *Qumran Cave 4.XIII*. Discoveries in the Judaean Desert XVIII. Oxford: Clarendon, 1996.

Beentjes, Pancratius C. *The Book of Ben Sira in Hebrew: A Text Edition of All Extant Hebrew Manuscripts and A Synopsis of All Parallel Hebrew Ben Sira Texts*. Supplements to Vetus Testamentum 68. Atlanta: Society of Biblical Literature, 2006.

Black, Matthew. *Apocalypsis Henochi Graecae*. Pseudepigrapha Veteris Testamenti Graece 3. Leiden: Brill, 1970.

Black, Matthew, in consultation with James C. VanderKam, with an appendix on the 'Astronomical' chapters (72–82) by Otto Neugebauer. *The Book of Enoch, or, 1 Enoch: A New English Edition with Commentary and Textual Notes*. Studia in Veteris Testamenti pseudepigraphica 7. Leiden: Brill, 1985.

Blackman, Philip. *Mishnayoth*. Gateshead: Judaica, 1977.

Botterweck, G. Johannes, Helmer Ringgren, and Heinz-Josef Fabry, eds. *Theological Dictionary of the Old Testament*. Translated by John T. Willis, G. W. Bromiley, and D. E. Green. 9 vols. Grand Rapids: Eerdmans, 1974–.

Brooke, G. J., J. Collins, P. Flint, J. Greenfield, E. Larson, C. Newsom, É. Puech, L. H. Schiffman, M. Stone, and J. Trebolle Barrera, in consultation with J. VanderKam, partially based on earlier transcriptions by J. T. Milik and J. Strugnell. *Qumran Cave 4.XVII: Parabiblical Texts, Part 3*. Discoveries in the Judaean Desert XXII. Oxford: Clarendon, 1996.

Broshi, M., E. Eshel, J. Fitzmyer, E. Larson, C. Newsom, L. Schiffman, M. Smith, M. Stone, J. Strugnell, and A. Yardeni, in consultation with J. C. VanderKam. *Qumran Cave 4.XIV: Parabiblical Texts, Part 2*. Discoveries in the Judaean Desert XIX. Oxford: Clarendon, 1995.

Brown, F., S. Driver, and C. Briggs. *The Brown-Driver-Briggs Hebrew and English Lexicon*. 1906. Repr., Peabody, Mass.: Hendrickson, 1997.

Cassuto, Umberto. *A Commentary on the Book of Genesis*. Translated by I. Abrahams. 2 vols. Jerusalem: Magnes, 1978.

Cathcart, Kevin, and Michael Maher. *Targum Neofiti: Genesis*. The Aramaic Bible 1A. Translated by Martin McNamara. Collegeville, Minn.: Liturgical Press, 1992.

———. *Targum Pseudo-Jonathan*. The Aramaic Bible 1B. Translated by Michael Maher. Collegeville, Minn.: Liturgical Press, 1992.

Cathcart, Kevin, Michael Maher, and Martin McNamara. *Targum Onqelos to Genesis*. The Aramaic Bible 6. Translated by Bernard Grossfeld. Wilmington, Del.: Michael Glazier, 1988.

Charles, R. H. *The Apocrypha and Pseudepigrapha of the Old Testament*. Oxford: Clarendon, 1913.

———. *The Book of Enoch*. Oxford: Clarendon, 1893.

———. *The Book of Enoch or 1 Enoch*. 2nd ed.; Oxford: Clarendon, 1912.
———. *The Book of Jubilees or the Little Genesis*. London: SPCK, 1902.
Charlesworth, James H., ed. *The Old Testament Pseudepigrapha*. 2 vols. Garden City, N.Y.: Doubleday, 1983, 1985.
Charlesworth, James H., and D. T. Olson. "Prayers for the Festivals." Pages 46–105 in vol. 4A of *The Dead Sea Scrolls: Hebrew, Aramaic, and Greek Texts with English Translations*. Edited by J. H. Charlesworth. Princeton Theological Seminary Dead Sea Scrolls Project. Tübingen: Mohr Siebeck, 1997.
Chazon, E., T. Elgvin, E. Eshel, D. Falk, B. Nitzan, E. Qimron, E. Schuller, D. Seely, E. Tigchelaar, and M. Weinfeld, in consultation with J. VanderKam and M. Brady. *Qumran Cave 4.XX: Poetical and Liturgical Texts, Part 2*. Discoveries in the Judaean Desert XXIX. Oxford: Clarendon, 1999.
Clarke, E. G. *Targum Pseudo-Jonathan of the Pentateuch*. Hoboken, N.J.: Ktav, 1984.
Danby, Herbert. *The Mishnah*. Oxford: Oxford University Press, 1933.
Delamarter, Steve. *A Scripture Index to Charlesworth's Old Testament Pseudepigrapha*. Sheffield: Sheffield Academic Press, 2002.
Elliger, K., and W. Rudolph. *Biblia Hebraica Stuttgartensia*. Stuttgart: Deutsche Bibelstiftung, 1966–77.
Evans, Craig A., and Stanley E. Porter, eds. *Dictionary of New Testament Background*. Downers Grove, Ill.: Intervarsity, 2000.
Fleming, Johannes, and Ludwig Radermacher. *Das Buch Henoch*. Die griechische christliche Schriftsteller der ersten [drei] Jahrhunderte 5. Leipzig: Hinrichs, 1901.
García Martínez, Florentino, and Eibert J. C. Tigchelaar. *The Dead Sea Scrolls Study Edition*. 2 vols. Leiden: Brill, 1997–2000.
García Martínez, Florentino. E. J. C. Tigchelaar, and A. S. van der Woude. *Manuscripts from Qumran Cave 11 (11Q2–18, 11Q20–30)*. Discoveries in the Judaean Desert XXIII. Oxford: Clarendon, 1997.
Greenfield, Jonas C., Michael E. Stone, and Esther Eshel. *The Aramaic Levi Document: Edition, Translation, and Commentary*. Studia in Veteris Testamenti pseudepigrapha. Leiden: Brill, 2004.
Grossfeld, Bernard. *Targum Neofiti I: An Exegetical Commentary with Full Rabbinic Parallels*. New York: Sepher-Hermon, 2000.
Gunkel, Hermann. *Genesis*. Translated by M. E. Biddle. Macon, Ga.: Mercer University Press, 1997.
Gunn, David M. "Deutero-Isaiah and the Flood." *Journal of Biblical Literature* 94 (1975): 493–508.
Hamilton, Victor P. *The Book of Genesis Chapters 1–17*. New International Commentary on the Old Testament. Grand Rapids: Eerdmans, 1990.
Harris, R. Laird, Gleason L. Archer, and Bruce K. Waltke. *The Theological Wordbook of the Old Testament*. Chicago: Moody, 1980.

Hartley, John E. *Leviticus*. Word Biblical Commentary 4. Dallas: Word Books, 1992.

Hatch, Edwin, and Henry A. Redpath. *A Concordance to the Septuagint*. 2nd ed. Grand Rapids: Baker, 1978.

Hiebert, Robert J. V. "Genesis." Pages 1–42 in *A New English Translation of the Septuagint and Other Greek Translations Traditionally Included under That Title*. Edited by Albert Pietersma and Benjamin G. Wright. New York/Oxford: Oxford University Press, 2007.

Hoffmann, Andreas Gottlieb. *Das Buch Henoch in vollständiger Uebersetzung mit fortlaufendem Commentar, ausführlicher Einleitung und erläuternden Excursen*. 2 vols. Jena: Croeker'schen Buchhandlung, 1833–38.

Isaac, E. "(Ethiopic Apocalypse of) Enoch (Second Century B.C.–First Century A.D.)." Pages 5–89 in *Apocalyptic Literature and Testaments*. Vol. 1 of *The Old Testament Pseudepigrapha*. Edited by James H. Charlesworth. New York: Doubleday, 1983.

Jastrow, Marcus. *A Dictionary of the Targumim, the Talmud Babli and Yerushalmi, and the Midrashic Literature*. 2nd ed. New York: Pardes, 1903.

Jenni, Ernst, and Claus Westermann. *Theological Lexicon of the Old Testament*. 3 vols. Translated by Mark E. Biddle. Peabody, Mass.: Hendrickson, 1997.

Knibb, Michael A. *The Ethiopic Book of Enoch: A New Edition in the Light of the Aramaic Dead Sea Fragments*. Oxford: Clarendon, 1978.

Koehler, Ludwig, Walter Baumgartner, M. E. J. Richardson, and Johann Stamm. *The Hebrew and Aramaic Lexicon of the Old Testament*. 5 vols. Leiden: Brill, 1994–2000.

Kugel, James L. *Traditions of the Bible: A Guide to the Bible As It Was at the Start of the Common Era*. Cambridge, Mass./London: Harvard University Press, 1998.

Leaney, A. R. C. *The Rule of Qumran and Its Meaning: Introduction, Translation, and Commentary*. London: SCM, 1966.

Martin, Françoise. *Le livre d'Henoch*. Documents pour l'étude de la Bible: Les Apocryphes de l'Ancien Testament. Paris: Letouzey et Ané, 1906.

McCarter, P. Kyle, Jr. *Textual Criticism: Recovering the Text of the Hebrew Bible*. Philadelphia: Fortress, 1986.

Milik, Jozef T. *The Books of Enoch: Aramaic Fragments of Qumran Cave 4*. Oxford: Clarendon, 1976.

Nelson, Milward Douglas. *The Syriac Version of the Wisdom of Ben Sira Compared to the Greek and Hebrew Materials*. Society of Biblical Literature Dissertation Series 107. Atlanta: Scholars Press, 1988.

Neusner, Jacob. *Genesis Rabbah: The Judaic Commentary to the Book of Genesis: A New American Translation*. 3 vols. Atlanta: Scholars Press, 1985.

Nickelsburg, George W. E. *1 Enoch 1: A Commentary on the Book of 1 Enoch: Chapters 1–36; 81–108*. Hermeneia. Minneapolis: Fortress, 2001.

Nickelsburg, George W. E., and James C. VanderKam. *1 Enoch: A New Translation*. Minneapolis: Fortress, 2004.

Parker, Benjamin H., and Martin G. Abegg, Jr. "BENSIRA-E." *Accordance Bible Software*. Altamonte Springs, Fl.: Oaktree Software Specialists, 2007.

Parry, Donald W., and Emanuel Tov, eds. *The Dead Sea Scrolls Reader. Part 3, Parabiblical Texts*. Leiden: Brill, 2005.

Pfann, S. J., P. Alexander, M. Broshi, E. Chazon, H. Cotton, F. M. Cross, T. Elgvin, D. Ernst, E. Eshel, H. Eshel, J. Fitzmyer, F.García Martínez, J. C. Greenfield, M. Kister, A. Lange, E. Larson, A. Lamaire, T. Lim, J. Naveh, D. Pike, M. Sokoloff, H. Stegemann, A. Steudel, M. Stone, L. Stuckenbruck, S. Talmon, S. Tanzer, E. J. C. Tigchelaar, E. Tov, G. Vermes, and A. Yardeni. *Qumran Cave 4. XXVI: Cryptic Texts and Miscellanea, Part 1*. Discoveries in the Judaean Desert XXXVI. Oxford: Clarendon, 2000.

Puech, É. *Qumrân Grotte 4.XXII: Textes Araméen, Première Partie, 4Q529–549*. Discoveries in the Judaean Desert XXXI. Oxford, Clarendon, 2001.

———. *Textes Hebreux (4Q521–4Q528, 4Q576–579): Qumran Cave 4.XVIII*. Discoveries in the Judaean Desert XXV. Oxford: Clarendon, 1997.

Rabin, Chaim. *The Development of the Syntax of Post-Biblical Hebrew*. Studies in Semitic Languages and Linguistics 29. Edited by T. Muraoka and C. H. M. Versteegh. Leiden: Brill, 2000.

Rad, Gerhard von. *Genesis: A Commentary*. Old Testament Library. Philadelphia: Westminster, 1972.

Sarna, Nahum M. *Genesis*. The JPS Torah Commentary. Philadelphia: Jewish Publication Society, 1989.

Schiffman, Lawrence H., and James C. VanderKam, eds. *Encyclopedia of the Dead Sea Scrolls*. 2 vols. Oxford: Oxford University Press, 2000.

Schodde, George H. *The Book of Enoch: Translated from the Ethiopic with Introduction and Notes*. Andover: Draper, 1882.

Scott, William R. *A Simplified Guide to BHS: Critical Apparatus, Masora, Accents, Unusual Letters and Other Markings*. Berkeley: BIBAL, 1987.

Skehan, Patrick W., and Alexander A. De Lella. *The Wisdom of Ben Sira*. Anchor Bible. New York: Doubleday, 1987.

Skehan, P[atrick] W., E. Ulrich, and J. E. Sanderson. *Qumran Cave IV.4: Palaeo-Hebrew and Greek Biblical Manuscripts*. Discoveries in the Judaean Desert IX. Oxford: Clarendon, 1992.

Snaith, J. G. *Ecclesiasticus, or, the Wisdom of Jesus son of Sirach*. Cambridge Bible Commentary. London: Cambridge University Press, 1974.

Speiser, E. A. *Genesis: Introduction, Translation and Notes*. Anchor Bible 1. New York: Doubleday, 1964.

Strugnell, J., D. J. Harrington, and T. Elgvin, in consultation with J.A. Fitzmyer. *Qumran Cave 4.XXIV: Sapiential Texts, Part 2, 4QInstruction: 4Q415ff*. Discoveries in the Judaean Desert XXXIV. Oxford: Clarendon, 1999.

Stuckenbruck, Loren. *The Book of Giants from Qumran: Texts, Translation, and Commentary.* Tübingen: Mohr Siebeck, 1997.

Tiller, Patrick A. *A Commentary on the Animal Apocalypse of I Enoch.* Society of Biblical Literature Early Judaism and Its Literature 4. Atlanta: Scholars Press, 1993.

Tov, E., with contributions by M. G. Abegg, Jr., A. Lange, U. Mittmann-Richert, S. J. Pfann, E. J. C. Tigchelaar, E. Ulrich, and B. Webster. *The Texts from the Judaean Desert: Indices and an Introduction to the Discoveries in the Judaean Desert Series.* Oxford: Clarendon, 2002.

Townsend, John T. *Midrash Tanhuma.* Hoboken, N.J.: Ktav, 1989.

Ulrich, E., F. M. Cross, S. W. Crawford, J. A. Duncan, P. W. Skehan, E. Tov, and J. Trebolle Barrera. *Qumran Cave 4.IX: Deuteronomy to Kings.* Discoveries in the Judaean Desert XIV. Oxford: Clarendon, 1995.

Ulrich, E., F. M. Cross, J. R. Davila, J. Jastram, J. E. Sanderson, E. Tov, and J. Strugnell. *Qumran Cave 4.VII: Genesis to Numbers.* Discoveries in the Judaean Desert XII. Oxford: Clarendon, 1994.

Ulrich, E., F. M. Cross, J. A. Fitzmyer, P. W. Flint, S. Metso, C. M. Murphy, C. Niccum, P. W. Skehan, E. Tov, and J. Trebolle Barrera. *Qumran Cave 4.XI: Psalms to Chronicles.* Discoveries in the Judaean Desert XVI. Oxford: Clarendon, 2000.

VanderKam, James C. *The Book of Jubilees: A Critical Text.* 2 vols. Corpus scriptorum christianorum orientalium 510-11. Scriptores Aethiopici 87-88. Leuven: Peeters. 1989.

VanGemeren, Willem A. *A New International Dictionary of Old Theology and Exegesis.* Grand Rapids: Zondervan, 1997.

Vermes, Geza. *An Introduction to the Complete Dead Sea Scrolls.* Minneapolis: Fortress, 1999.

Vosté, J. M., and C. Van den Eynde, eds. *Commentaire d'Isodad de Merv sur l'Ancien Testament: Genèse.* Corpus scriptorum christianorum orientalium 126. Scriptores Syri 67. Leuven: Peeters, 1950.

Wacholder, Ben Zion, and Martin G. Abegg, Jr. *A Preliminary Edition of the Unpublished Dead Sea Scrolls: The Hebrew and Aramaic Texts from Cave Four, Fascicle Two.* Washington: Biblical Archaeology Society, 1992.

Watts, John D. W. *Isaiah 34-66.* Word Biblical Commentary 25. Waco: Word Books, 1987.

Wenham, Gordon J. *Genesis 1-15.* Word Biblical Commentary 1. Nashville: Thomas Nelson, 1987.

Westermann, Claus. *Genesis 1-11: A Commentary.* Translated by J. J. Scullion. Minneapolis: Augsburg, 1984.

Wevers, John William. *Septuaginta.* Göttingen: Vandenhoeck and Ruprecht, 1976.

Williams, Ronald J. *Hebrew Syntax: An Outline.* Toronto: University of Toronto Press, 1976.

Wise, Michael, Martin Abegg, Jr., and Edward Cook. *The Dead Sea Scrolls: A New Translation*. New York: HarperCollins, 1996, 2005.

SECONDARY SOURCES

Abegg, Martin G., Jr. "1QM 10-19 and 4QBerakhot: Lest We Be Speechless in the Day of Strife." Paper presented at the annual meeting of the Society of Biblical Literature. Philadelphia, November 1995.

———. "'And He Shall Answer and Say . . .'—A Little Backlighting." Pages 203-11 in *Studies in the Hebrew Bible, Qumran, and the Septuagint Presented to Eugene Ulrich*. Edited by Peter W. Flint, Emanuel Tov, and James C. VanderKam. Supplements to Vetus Testamentum 101. Leiden: Brill, 2006.

———. "The Covenant of the Qumran Sectarians." Pages 81-97 in *The Concept of the Covenant in the Second Temple Period*. Edited by Stanley E. Porter and Jacqueline C. R. de Roo. Supplements to the Journal for the Study of Judaism 71. Leiden: Brill, 2003.

———. "Exile and the Dead Sea Scrolls." Pages 111-25 in *Exile: Old Testament, Jewish, and Christian Conceptions*. Edited by James M. Scott. Supplements to the Journal for the Study of Judaism 56. Leiden: Brill, 1997.

———. "Hebrew 2." Pages 459-63 in *Dictionary of New Testament Background*. Edited by Craig A. Evans and Stanley E. Porter. Downers Grove, Ill.: InterVarsity, 2000.

———. "Messianic Hope and 4Q285: A Reassessment." *Journal of Biblical Literature* 113 (1994): 81-91.

Aitken, James K. "Apocalyptic, Revelation, and Early Jewish Wisdom Literature." Pages 181-93 in *New Heaven and New Earth: Prophecy and the Millennium. Essays in Honour of Anthony Gelson*. Edited by P. J. Harland and C. T. R. Hayward. Supplements to Vetus Testamentum 77. Leiden: Brill, 1999.

Albeck, Ch. "Das Buch der Jubilaen und die Halacha." In *Lehranstalt Berichte* 47 (1921-25). Hochschule für die Wissenschaft des Judentums in Berlin, 1930.

Alexander, Philip S. "Enoch and the Beginnings of Jewish Interest in Natural Science." Pages 223-43 in *The Wisdom Texts from Qumran and the Development of Sapiential Thought*. Edited by Charlotte Hempel, Armin Lange, and Hermann Lichtenberger. Bibliotheca Ephemeridum Theologicarum Lovaniensium 159. Leuven: Leuven University Press, 2002.

———. "The Enochic Literature and the Bible: Intertextuality and Its Implications." Pages 57-69 in *The Bible as Book: The Hebrew Bible and the Judaean Desert Discoveries*. Edited by Edward D. Herbert and Emanuel Tov. London: British Library; New Castle, Del.: Oak Knoll Press, 2002.

———. "From Son of Adam to Second God." Pages 87-122 in *Biblical Figures Outside the Bible*. Edited by Michael E. Stone and Theodore A. Bergren. Harrisburg, Pa.: Trinity Press International. 1998.

———. "Jewish Aramaic Translations of Hebrew Scriptures." Pages 217-53 in

Mikra: Text, Translation, Reading and Interpretation of the Hebrew Bible in Ancient Judaism and Early Christianity. Edited by Martin J. Mulder. Assen/Maastricht: Van Gorcum, 1988.

———. "Notes on the 'Imago Mundi' of the Book of Jubilees." *Journal of Jewish Studies* 33 (1982): 197–213

———. "The Redaction History of *Serekh Ha-Yahad*: A Proposal." *Revue de Qumran* 17 (1996): 437–56.

Alter, Robert. *The Art of Biblical Narrative*. New York: Basic Books, 1981.

Anderson, Gary A. "The Status of the Torah before Sinai." *Dead Sea Discoveries* 1 (1994): 1–29.

———. "The Status of the Torah in the Pre-Sinaitic Period: St. Paul's Epistle to the Romans." Pages 1–23 in *Biblical Perspectives: Early Use and Interpretation of the Bible in Light of the Dead Sea Scrolls. Proceedings of the First International Symposium of the Orion Center for the Study of the Dead Sea Scrolls and Associated Literature, 12–14 May 1996*. Edited by Michael E. Stone and Esther G. Chazon. Studies on the Texts of the Desert of Judah 28. Leiden: Brill, 1998.

Argall, Randal A. *1 Enoch and Sirach: A Comparative Literary and Conceptual Analysis of the Themes of Revelation, Creation, and Judgment*. Society of Biblical Literature Early Judaism and Its Literature 8. Atlanta: Scholars Press, 1995.

Aune, David E., with Eric Stewart. "From the Idealized Past to the Imaginary Future: Eschatological Restoration in Jewish Apocalyptic Literature." Pages 147–77 in *Restoration: Old Testament, Jewish, and Christian Perspectives*. Edited by James M. Scott. Leiden: Brill, 2001.

Barker, Margaret. *The Older Testament: The Survival of Themes from the Ancient Royal Cult in Sectarian Judaism and Early Christianity*. London: SPCK, 1987.

Barr, James. "Reflections on the Covenant with Noah." Pages 11–22 in *Covenant as Context: Essays in Honour of E. W. Nicholson*. Edited by A. D. H. Mayes and R. B. Salters. Oxford: Oxford University Press, 2003.

Baumgarten, Albert I. "The Perception of the Past in the Damascus Document." Pages 1–15 in *The Damascus Document: A Centennial of Discovery. Proceedings of the Third International Symposium of the Orion Center for the Study of the Dead Sea Scrolls and Associated Literature, 4–8 February 1998*. Edited by Joseph M. Baumgarten, Esther G. Chazon, and Avital Pinnick. Studies on the Texts of the Desert of Judah 34. Leiden: Brill, 2000

Baumgarten, Joseph M. "Purification after Childbirth and the Sacred Garden in 4Q265 and Jubilees." Pages 3–10 in *New Qumran Texts and Studies*. Edited by George J. Brooke and Florentino García Martínez. Studies on the Texts of the Desert of Judah 15. Leiden: Brill, 1994.

———. "Some 'Qumranic' Observations on the Aramaic Levi Document." Pages 393–401 in *Sefer Moshe: The Moshe Weinfeld Jubilee Volume*. Edited by Chaim Cohen, Avi Hurvitz, and Shalom M. Paul. Winona Lake, Ind.: Eisenbrauns, 2004.

———. "Yom Kippur in the Qumran Scrolls and Second Temple Sources." *Dead Sea Discoveries* 6 (1999): 184-91.

Becker, H. *Das Heil Gottes: Heil-und-Sündenbegriffe in den Qumrantexten und im Neuen Testament*. Studien zur Umwelt des Neuen Testaments 3. Göttingen: Vandenhoeck & Ruprecht, 1964.

Beckwith, Roger T. "The Earliest Enoch Literature and Its Calendar: Marks of Their Origin, Date, and Motivation." *Revue de Qumran* 10/3 (1981): 365-403.

———. "Formation of the Hebrew Bible." Pages 39-87 in *Mikra: Text, Translation, Reading and Interpretation of the Hebrew Bible in Ancient Judaism and Early Christianity*. Edited by Martin J. Mulder. Assen/Maastricht: Van Gorcum, 1988.

Bedenbender, Andreas. "Reflection on Ideology and Date of the Apocalypse of Weeks." Pages 200-204 in *Enoch and Qumran Origins: New Light on a Forgotten Connection*. Edited by Gabriele Boccaccini. Grand Rapids: Eerdmans, 2005.

Bekkum, Wout J. van. "The Lesson of the Flood: מבול in Rabbinic Tradition." Pages 124-33 in *Interpretations of the Flood*. Edited by Florentino García Martínez and Gerard P. Luttikhuizen. Themes in Biblical Narrative 1. Leiden: Brill, 1998.

Benjamins, H. S. "Noah, the Ark, and the Flood in Early Christian Theology: The Ship of the Church in the Making." Pages 134-49 in *Interpretations of the Flood*. Edited by Florentino García Martínez and Gerard P. Luttikhuizen. Themes in Biblical Narrative 1. Leiden: Brill, 1998.

Bernard Beer, *Das Buch der Jubiläen und sein Verhältnis zu den Midrashim*. Leipzig: Wolfgang Gerhard, 1856.

Bernstein, Moshe J. "4Q252: From Re-written Bible to Biblical Commentary." *Journal of Jewish Studies* 45 (1994): 1-27.

———. "4Q252 i 2 לא ידור רוחי באדם לעולם: Biblical Text or Biblical Interpretation? (1) *Revue de Qumran* 16 (1994): 421-27.

———. "Contours of Genesis Interpretation at Qumran: Contents, Context, and Nomenclature." Pages 57-85 in *Studies in Ancient Midrash*. Edited by James L. Kugel. Cambridge, Mass.: Harvard University Press, 2001.

———. "From the Watchers to the Flood: Story and Exegesis in the Early Columns of the *Genesis Apocryphon*." Pages 39-63 in *Reworking the Bible: Apocryphal and Related Texts at Qumran. Proceedings of a Joint Symposium by the Orion Center for the Study of the Dead Sea Scrolls and Associated Literature and the Hebrew University Institute for Advanced Studies Research Group on Qumran, 15-17 January 2002*. Edited by Esther G. Chazon, Devorah Dimant, and Ruth A. Clements. Studies on the Texts of the Desert of Judah 58. Leiden: Brill, 2005.

---. "Noah and the Flood at Qumran." Pages 199–231 in *The Provo International Conference on the Dead Sea Scrolls: New Texts, Reformulated Issues, and Technological Innovations.* Edited by Donald W. Parry and Eugene C. Ulrich. Studies on the Texts of the Desert of Judah 30. Leiden: Brill, 1999.

---. "Pentateuchal Interpretation at Qumran." Pages 128–59 in vol. 1 of *The Dead Sea Scrolls after Fifty Years.* Edited by Peter W. Flint and James C. VanderKam. Leiden: Brill, 1998.

---. " קשט in the Genesis Apocryphon and the Remainder of the Qumran Corpus." Paper presented at the annual meeting of the Society of Biblical Literature. Atlanta, Georgia, November 24, 2003.

---. "Rearrangement, Anticipation and Harmonization as Exegetical Features in the Genesis Apocryphon." *Dead Sea Discoveries* 3 (1996): 37–57.

Bhayro, Siam. "Noah's Library: Sources for *1 Enoch* 6–11." *Journal for the Study of the Pseudepigrapha* 15 (2006): 163–77.

Boccaccini, Gabriele. *Beyond the Essene Hypothesis: The Parting of the Ways between Qumran and Enochic Judaism.* Grand Rapids: Eerdmans, 1998.

---. "The Covenantal Theology of the Apocalyptic Book of Daniel." Pages 39–44 in *Enoch and Qumran Origins: New Light on a Forgotten Connection.* Edited by Gabriele Boccaccini. Grand Rapids: Eerdmans, 2005.

---. "From a Movement of Dissent to a Distinct Form of Judaism." Paper presented to the Fourth Enoch Seminar. Camaldoli, Italy, July 8–12, 2007.

---. *Middle Judaism: Jewish Thought, 300 B.C.E. to 200 C.E.* Minneapolis: Fortress, 1991.

Boersma, Hans. *Violence, Hospitality and the Cross: Reappropriating the Atonement Tradition.* Grand Rapids: Baker Academic, 2004.

Bosshard-Nepustil, Erich. *Vor uns die Sintflut: Studien zu Text, Kontexten und Rezeption der Fluterzählung Genesis 6–9.* Beiträge zur Wissenschaft vom Alten (und Neuen) Testament 165. Stuttgart: Kohlhammer, 2005.

Bowker, John. *The Targums and Rabbinic Literature: An Introduction to Jewish Interpretations of Scripture.* Cambridge: Cambridge University Press, 1969.

Brooke, George J. "4Q252 as Early Jewish Commentary." *Revue de Qumran* 17 (1996): 385–401.

---. "4Q500 1 and the Use of Scripture in the Parable of the Vineyard." *Dead Sea Discoveries* 2 (1995): 268–94.

---. "4QTestament of Levi[d](?) and the Messianic Servant High Priest." Pages 83–100 in *From Jesus to John: Essays on Jesus and New Testament Christology in Honour of Marinus de Jonge.* Edited by Martinus C. de Boer. Journal for the Study of the New Testament: Supplement Series 84. Sheffield: Sheffield Academic Press, 1993.

---. "Between Authority and Canon: The Significance of Reworking the Bible for Understanding the Canonical Process." Pages 85–104 in *Reworking the Bible: Apocryphal and Related Texts at Qumran. Proceedings of a Joint Symposium by the Orion Center for the Study of the Dead Sea Scroll and Associated*

Literature and the Hebrew University Institute for Advanced Studies Research Group on Qumran, 15-17 January 2002. Edited by Esther G. Chazon, Devorah Dimant, and Ruth A. Clements. Studies on the Texts of the Desert of Judah 58. Leiden: Brill, 2005.

———. "Biblical Interpretation in the Wisdom Texts from Qumran." Pages 201-20 in *The Wisdom Texts from Qumran and the Development of Sapiential Thought*. Leuven: Peeters, 2001.

———. "'The Canon within the Canon at Qumran and in the New Testament." Pages 242-66 in *The Scrolls and the Scriptures: Qumran Fifty Years After*. Edited by Stanley E. Porter and Craig A. Evans. Journal for the Study of the Pseudepigrapha: Supplement Series 26. Sheffield: Sheffield Academic Press, 1997.

———. "The Deuteronomic Character of 4Q252." Pages 121-35 in *Pursuing the Text: Studies in Honor of Ben Zion Wacholder on the Occasion of his Seventieth Birthday*. Edited by John C. Reeves and John Kampen. Journal for the Study of the Old Testament: Supplement Series 184. Sheffield: Sheffield Academic Press, 1994.

———. "Exegetical Strategies in Jubilees 1-2: New Light from 4QJubilees[a]." Pages 39-57 in *Studies in the Book of Jubilees*. Edited by Matthias Albani, Jörg Frey, and Armin Lang. Texte und Studien zum antiken Judentum 65. Tübingen: Mohr Siebeck, 1997.

———. "Ezekiel in Some Qumran and New Testament Texts." Pages 317-37 in vol. 1 of *The Madrid Qumran Congress: Proceedings of the International Congress on the Dead Sea Scrolls, Madrid, 18-21 March 1991*. Edited by Julio Trebolle Barrera and Luis Vegas Montaner. Studies on the Texts of the Desert of Judah 12. Leiden: Brill, 1992.

———. "From 'Assembly of Supreme Holiness for Aaron' to 'Sanctuary of Adam': The Laicization of Temple Ideology in the Qumran Scrolls and Its Wider Implications." *Journal for Semitics* 8 (1996): 119-45.

———. "Levi and the Levites." Pages 115-39 in *The Dead Sea Scrolls and the New Testament*. Minneapolis: Fortress, 2005.

———. "Miqdash Adam, Eden and the Qumran Community." Pages 285-301 in *Gemeinde ohne Tempel*. Edited by Beate Ego, Armin Lange, and Peter Pilhofer. Tübingen: Mohr Siebeck, 1999.

———. "Psalms 105 and 106 at Qumran." *Revue de Qumran* 14 (1990): 267-92.

———. "Reading the Plain Meaning of Scripture in the Dead Sea Scrolls." Pages 67-90 in *Jewish Ways of Reading the Bible*. Edited by George J. Brooke. Oxford Oxford University Press, 2000.

———. "Some Remarks on 4Q252 and the Text of Genesis." *Textus* 19 (1998): 1-25.

———. "Thematic Commentaries on Prophetic Scriptures." Pages 134-57 in *Biblical Interpretation at Qumran*. Edited by Matthias Henze. Grand Rapids: Eerdmans, 2005.

Broshi, Magen. *The Damascus Document Reconsidered.* Jerusalem: Israel Exploration Society, 1992.

Brown, William P. "Atonement in Scripture." *Interpretation* 52 (1988): 5–69.

Brownlee, W. H. *The Dead Sea Manual of Discipline.* Bulletin of the American Schools for Oriental Research: Supplement Series 10–12. New Haven: American Schools of Oriental Research, 1951.

Brueggemann, Walter. *The Land.* Philadelphia: Fortress, 1977.

Burns, Joshua Ezra. "Practical Wisdom in 4Q Instruction." *Dead Sea Discoveries* 11 (2004): 12–42.

Carmignac, Jean. "Les citations de l'Anciènt Testament, et specialment des Poèmes du Serviteur, dans les *Hymnes* de Qumran. *Revue de Qumran* 2 (1959/60): 357–94.

Chabot, I. B. *Scriptores Syri 36: Chronicon ad annum Christi 1234 Pertinens.* Corpus scriptorum christianorum orientalium 81. Leuven: Peeters, 1953.

Chamberlain, John V. "Toward a Qumran Soteriology." *Novum Testamentum* 3 (1959): 305–13.

Charlesworth, James H. "The Portrayal of the Righteous as an Angel." Pages 135–47 in *Ideal Figures in Ancient Judaism: Profiles and Paradigms.* Edited by George W. E. Nickelsburg and John J. Collins. Chico, Calif.: Scholars Press, 1980.

Chazon, Esther G. "The Creation and Fall of Adam in the Dead Sea Scrolls." Pages 13–24 in *The Book of Genesis in Jewish and Oriental Interpretation: A Collection of Essays.* Edited by Judith Frishman and Lucas Van Rompay. Traditio exegetica Graeca 5. Leuven: Peeters, 1997.

———. "*Dibre Hammerot*: Prayer for the Sixth Day (4Q504 1–2 v-vi)." Pages 23–27 in *Prayer from Alexander to Constantine: A Critical Anthology.* Edited by Mark Kiley. London: Routledge, 1997.

———. "Prayers from Qumran and Their Historical Implications." *Dead Sea Discoveries* 1 (1994): 265–84.

Chazon, Esther G., and Moshe J. Bernstein. "An Introduction to Prayer at Qumran." Pages 9–13 in *Prayer from Alexander to Constantine: A Critical Anthology.* Edited by Mark Kiley. London: Routledge, 1997.

Collins, John J. *The Apocalyptic Imagination: An Introduction to the Jewish Matrix of Christianity.* 2nd ed. Grand Rapids: Eerdmans, 1998.

———. *Apocalypticism in the Dead Sea Scrolls.* London/New York: Routledge, 1997.

———. "Asking for the Meaning of a Fragmentary Qumran Text: The Referential Background of 4QAaron A." Pages 579–90 in *Texts and Contexts: Biblical Texts in Their Textual and Situational Contexts.* Edited by Tord Fornberg and David Hellholm. Oslo: Scandinavian University Press, 1995.

———. "Before the Fall: The Earliest Interpretation of Adam and Eve." Pages 293–308 in *The Idea of Biblical Interpretation: Essays in Honor of James L. Kugel.* Edited by Hindy Najman and Judith H. Newman. Supplements to the Journal for the Study of Judaism 83. Leiden: Brill, 2004.

———. "In the Likeness of the Holy Ones: The Creation of Humankind in a

Wisdom Text from Qumran." Pages 609-18 in *The Provo International Conference on the Dead Sea Scrolls: Technological Innovations, New Texts, and Reformulated Issues*. Edited by Donald W. Parry and Eugene C. Ulrich. Studies on the Texts of the Desert of Judah 30. Leiden: Brill, 1999.

———. "The Place of Apocalypticism in the Religion of Ancient Israel." Pages 539-58 in *Ancient Israelite Religion: Essays in Honor of Frank Moore Cross*. Edited by Patrick D. Miller, Jr., Paul D. Hanson, and S. Dean McBride. Philadelphia: Fortress, 1987.

———. *The Sceptre and the Star: the Messiahs of the Dead Sea Scrolls and Other Ancient Literature*. Anchor Bible Reference Library 10. New York: Doubleday, 1995.

———. "Theology and Identity in the Early Enoch Literature." *Henoch* 24 (2002): 57-62.

Cook, Edward C. *Solving the Mysteries of the Dead Sea Scrolls*. Grand Rapids: Zondervan, 1994.

———. "A Thanksgiving for God's Help (4Q434 II-III)." Pages 14-17 in *Prayer from Alexander to Constantine: A Critical Anthology*. Edited by Mark Kiley. London: Routledge, 1997.

Crawford, Sidnie White. *Rewriting Scriptures in Second Temple Times*. Grand Rapids: Eerdmans, forthcoming.

Daley, Stephanie. *Myths from Mesopotamia: Creation, the Flood, Gilgamesh and Others*. Oxford/New York: Oxford University Press, 1989.

Davenport, Gene L. *The Eschatology of the Book of Jubilees*. Studia Post Biblica 20. Leiden: Brill, 1971.

Davidson, Maxwell. *Angels at Qumran: A Comparative Study of I Enoch 1-36, 72-108 and Sectarian Writings from Qumran*. Journal for the Study of the Pseudepigrapha: Supplement Series 11. Sheffield: Sheffield Academic Press, 1992.

Davies, Philip R. "Calendrical Change and Qumran Origins: An Assessment of VanderKam's Theory." *Catholic Biblical Quarterly* 45 (1983): 80-89.

———. *The Damascus Covenant: an Interpretation of the "Damascus Document*. Journal for the Study of the Old Testament: Supplement Series 25. Sheffield: University of Sheffield, 1983.

———. "The 'Damascus' Sect and Judaism." Pages 70-84 in *Pursuing the Text: Studies in Honor of Ben Zion Wacholder on the Occasion of his Seventieth Birthday*. Edited by John C. Reeves and John Kampen. Journal for the Study of the Old Testament: Supplement Series 184. Sheffield: Sheffield Academic Press, 1994.

———. "The Judaism(s) of the Damascus Document." Pages 27-43 in *The Damascus Document: A Centennial of Discovery. Proceedings of the Third International Symposium of the Orion Center for the Study of the Dead Sea Scrolls and Associated Literature, 4-8 February 1998*. Edited by Joseph M. Baumgarten, Esther G. Chazon, and Avital Pinnick. Studies on the Texts of the Desert of Judah 34. Leiden: Brill, 2000.

———. "Sons of Cain." Pages 35–56 in *A Word in Season: Essays in Honour of William McKane*. Edited by James D. Martin and Philip R. Davies. Journal for the Study of the Old Testament: Supplement Series 42. Sheffield: JSOT Press, 1986.

———. "The Torah at Qumran." Pages 23–44 in vol. 2 of *Judaism in Late Antiquity. Part 5, The Judaism of Qumran: A Systematic Reading of the Dead Sea Scrolls*. Edited by Alan J. Avery-Peck, Jacob Neusner, and Bruce D. Chilton. Leiden: Brill, 2001.

Davies, Philip R., George J. Brooke, and Phillip R. Callaway. *The Complete World of the Dead Sea Scrolls*. London: Thames & Hudson, 2002.

Davies, William D. *The Gospel and the Land*. Berkeley: University of California Press, 1974.

Davila, James R. "4QMess ar (4Q534) and Merkavah Mysticism." Pages 367–81 in *Qumran Studies Presented to Eugene Ulrich on His Sixtieth Birthday*. Special Issue. *Dead Sea Discoveries* 5 (1998).

———. "The Flood Hero as King and Priest." *Journal of Near Eastern Studies* 54 (1995): 199–214.

———. *Liturgical Works*. Eerdmans Commentaries on the Dead Sea Scrolls. Grand Rapids: Eerdmans, 2000.

Dimant, Devorah. "1 Enoch 6–11: A Fragment of a Parabiblical Work." *Journal of Jewish Studies* 8 (2002): 223–37.

———. "1 Enoch 6–11: A Methodological Perspective." Pages 323–39 in *SBL Seminar Papers 1978*. Society of Biblical Literature Seminar Papers 13. Atlanta: Scholars Press, 1978.

———. "Apocrypha and Pseudepigrapha At Qumran." *Dead Sea Discoveries* 1 (1994): 151–59.

———. "The Biography of Enoch and the Books of Enoch." *Vetus Testamentum* 33 (1983): 14–29.

———. "'The Fallen Angels' in the Dead Sea Scrolls and in the Apocryphal and Pseudepigraphic Books Related to Them." English summary of Ph.D. dissertation. Hebrew University, 1974.

———. "Noah in Early Jewish Literature." Pages 123–50 in *Biblical Figures Outside the Bible*. Edited by Michael E. Stone and Theodore A. Bergren. Harrisburg, Pa.: Trinity Press International, 1998.

———. "The 'Pesher on the Periods'(4Q180) and 4Q181." *Israel Oriental Studies* 9 (1979): 77–102.

———. "Qumran Sectarian Literature." Pages 483–550 in *Jewish Writings of the Second Temple Period: Apocrypha, Pseudepigrapha, Qumran Sectarian Writings, Philo*. Edited by Michael Stone. Compendia rerum iudaicarum ad Novum Testamentum 2. Philadelphia: Fortress, 1984.

———. "Two 'Scientific' Fictions: The So-Called *Book of Noah* and the Alleged Quotation of *Jubilees* in CD 16:3–4." Pages 230–49 in *Studies in the Hebrew Bible, Qumran and the Septuagint Presented to Eugene Ulrich*. Edited by Peter

W. Flint, Emanuel Tov, and James C. VanderKam. Supplements to Vetus Testatmentum 101. Leiden/Boston: Brill, 2006.

Dohmen, C. "Zur Gründung der Gemeinde von Qumran (1QS VIII–IX)." *Revue de Qumran* 11 (1982): 81–96.

Drawnel, Henryk. *An Aramaic Wisdom Text from Qumran: A New Interpretation of the Levi Document.* Supplements to the Journal for the Study of Judaism 86. Leiden: Brill, 2004.

Eisenman, Robert H., and Michael O. Wise. *The Dead Sea Scrolls Uncovered.* Shaftesbury: Element, 1992.

Elgvin, Torleif. "Admonition Texts from Qumran Cave 4." Pages 179–96 in *Methods of Investigation of the Dead Sea Scrolls and the Khirbet Qumran Site: Present Realities and Future Prospects*. Edited by Michael O. Wise, Norman Golb, John J. Collins, and Dennis G. Pardee. New York: New York Academy of Sciences, 1994.

———. "The Genesis Section of 4Q422 (4QParaGenExod)." *Dead Sea Discoveries* 1 (1994): 180–96.

———. "Priestly Sages? The Milieus of Origin of 4QMysteries and 4QInstruction." Pages 67–87 in *Sapiential Perspectives: Wisdom Literature in Light of the Dead Sea Scrolls: Proceedings of the Sixth International Symposium of the Orion Center for the Study of the Dead Sea Scrolls and Associated Literature, 20–22 May 2001*. Edited by John J. Collins, Gregory E. Sterling, and Ruth A. Clements. Studies on the Texts of the Desert of Judah 51. Leiden/Boston: Brill, 2004.

———. "The Reconstruction of Sapiential Work A." *Revue de Qumran* 16 (1995): 559–80.

———. "Renewed Earth and Renewed People: 4Q475." Pages 577–91 in *The Provo International Conference on the Dead Sea Scrolls: Technological Innovations, New Texts, and Reformulated Issues*. Edited by Donald W. Parry and Eugene C. Ulrich. Studies on the Texts of the Desert of Judah 30. Leiden: Brill, 1999.

———. "Wisdom and Apocalypticism in the Early Second Century." Pages 226–47 in *The Dead Sea Scrolls Fifty Years after Their Discovery: Proceedings of the Jerusalem Congress, July 20–25, 1997*. Edited by Lawrence Schiffman, Emanuel Tov, and James C. VanderKam. Jerusalem: Israel Exploration Society/Shrine of the Book, Israel Museum, 2000.

———. "Wisdom, Revelation, and Eschatology in an Early Essene Writing." Pages 440–63 in *SBL Seminar Papers 1995*. Edited by E. H. Lovering. Society of Biblical Literature Seminar Papers 34. Atlanta: Scholars Press, 1995.

———. "Wisdom With and Without Apocalyptic." Pages 15–38 in *Sapiential, Liturgical and Poetical Texts from Qumran: Proceedings of the Third Meeting of the International Organization for Qumran Studies Oslo 1998*. Edited by Daniel K. Falk, Florentino García Martínez, and Eileen M. Schuller. Studies on the Texts of the desert of Judah 35. Leiden: Brill, 2000.

Ellis, E. Earle. "The Old Testament Canon in the Early Church." Pages 653–89 in *Mikra: Text, Translation, Reading and Interpretation of the Hebrew Bible in Ancient Judaism and Early Christianity*. Edited by Martin J. Mulder. Assen/Maastricht: Van Gorcum, 1988.

Endres, John C. *Biblical Interpretation in the Book of Jubilees*. Catholic Biblical Quarterly Monograph Series 18. Washington, D.C.: Catholic Biblical Association of America, 1989.

———. "Prayer of Noah: Jubilees 10:3–6." Pages 53–58 in *Prayer from Alexander to Constantine: A Critical Anthology*. Edited by Mark Kiley. London: Routledge, 1997.

———. "Prayers in Jubilees." Pages 31–47 in *Heavenly Tablets: Interpretation, Identity and Tradition in Ancient Judaism*. Edited by Lynn LiDonnici and Andrea Lieber. Journal for the Study of Judaism: Supplement Series 119. Leiden: Brill, 2007.

Eshel, Esther. "4Q414 Fragment 2: Purification of a Corpse-Contaminated Person." Pages 3–10 in *Legal Texts and Legal Issues: Proceedings of the Second Meeting of the International Organization for Qumran Studies, Cambridge 1995. Published in Honour of Joseph M. Baumgarten*. Edited by Moshe J. Bernstein, Florentino García Martínez, and John Kampen. Studies on the Texts of the Desert of Judah 23. Leiden: Brill, 1997.

———. "Hermeneutical Approaches to Genesis in the Dead Sea Scrolls." Pages 1–12 in *The Book of Genesis in Jewish and Oriental Christian Interpretation: A Collection of Essays.*. Edited by Judith Frishman and Lucas Van Rompay. Traditio exegetica Graeca 5. Leuven: Peeters, 1997.

———. "The Identification of the 'Speaker' of the Self-Glorification Hymn." Pages 619–35 in *The Provo International Conference on the Dead Sea Scrolls: Technological Innovations, New Texts, and Reformulated Issues*. Edited by Donald W. Parry and Eugene C. Ulrich. Studies on the Texts of the Desert of Judah 30. Brill: Leiden, 1999.

———. "The *Imago Mundi* of the *Genesis Apocryphon*." Pages 111–31 in *Heavenly Tablets: Interpretation, Identity and Tradition in Ancient Judaism*. Edited by Lynn LiDonnici and Andrea Lieber. Journal for the Study of Judaism: Supplement Series 119. Leiden: Brill, 2007.

Eshel, Esther, and Hanan Eshel. "New Fragments from Qumran: 4QGen^f, 4QIsa^b, 4Q226, 8QGen, and XQ papEnoch." *Dead Sea Discoveries* 12 (2005): 134–57.

Eshel, Hanan. "Three New Fragments from Cave 11." *Tarbiz* 68 (1999): 273–78.

Evans, Craig A. "Covenant in the Qumran Literature." Pages 55–80 in *The Concept of the Covenant in the Second Temple Period*. Edited by Stanley E. Porter and Jacqueline C. R. de Roo. Supplements to the Journal for the Study of Judaism 71. Leiden: Brill, 2003.

———. "'The Two Sons of Oil': Early Evidence of Messianic Interpretation of Zechariah 4:14 in 4Q254 4 2." Pages 566–75 in *The Provo International*

Conference on the Dead Sea Scrolls: Technological Innovations, New Texts, and Reformulated Issues. Edited by Donald W. Parry and Eugene C. Ulrich. Studies on the Texts of the Desert of Judah 30. Leiden: Brill, 1999.

Falk, Daniel. *Daily, Sabbath, and Festival Prayers in the Dead Sea Scrolls*. Studies on the Texts of the Desert of Judah 27. Leiden: Brill, 1998.

———. "God's Covenant with Noah: Analysis of a Scene in the Genesis Apocryphon." Paper presented at the annual meeting of the West Coast Qumran Study Group. Mayne Island, B.C., October 23, 2004.

———. "In the Door of the Ark: Noah's Prayer and Sacrifice in Genesis Apocryphon." Paper presented at the Society of Biblical Literature Pacific Northwest regional meeting. Eugene, Oregon, May 3–5, 2002.

———. *The Parabiblical Texts: Strategies for Extending the Scriptures among the Dead Sea Scrolls*. Companion to the Qumran Scrolls 8. Library of Second Temple Studies 63. New York: T&T Clark, 2007.

———. "Reconstructions in *Genesis Apocryphon*." Paper presented at the annual meeting of the West Coast Qumran Study Group. Eugene, Oregon, October 23, 2003.

Feldman, Ariel. "*Mikra* and *Haggada* in the Flood Story According to 4Q370." Paper presented to the Graduate Enoch Seminar. Ann Arbor, Michigan, May 2–4, 2006.

———. "The Story of the Flood in 4Q422." In *Proceedings of the Symposium 'The Dynamics of Exegesis and Language at Qumran' held on May 14–16, 2007 at Göttingen*. Edited by Devorah Dimant and Reinhard Kratz. Forthcoming.

Feldman, Louis. "Hellenization in Josephus' *Antiquities*: The Portrait of Abraham." Pages 133-153 in *Josephus, Judaism, and Christianity*. Edited by Louis H. Feldman and Gohei Hata. Leiden: Brill, 1987.

Finkelstein, Louis. "The Book of Jubilees and the Rabbinic Halakah." *Harvard Theological Review* 16 (1923): 39-61.

Fitzmyer Joseph A. "The Aramaic 'Elect of God' Text from Qumran Cave 4." Pages 127–60 in *Essays on the Semitic Background of the New Testament*. Edited by Joseph A. Fitzmyer, S.J. Missoula, Mont.: Scholars Press, 1974. Repr. from *Catholic Biblical Quarterly* 27 (1965): 348–72.

———. "The Aramaic Levi Document." Pages 453–64 in *The Provo International Conference on the Dead Sea Scrolls: Technological Innovations, New Texts, and Reformulated Issues*. Edited by Donald W. Parry and Eugene C. Ulrich. Studies on the Texts of the Desert of Judah 30. Leiden: Brill, 1999.

———. *The Genesis Apocryphon of Qumran Cave I: A Commentary*. 2nd ed. Biblica et Orientalia 34. Rome: Pontifical Biblical Institute, 1971. 3rd ed., 2004.

Fletcher-Louis, Crispin H. T. *All the Glory of Adam*. Leiden: Brill, 2002.

Flint, Peter W. "The Greek Fragments of Enoch from Qumran Cave 7." Pages 224–33 in *Enoch and Qumran Origins: New Light on a Forgotten Connection*. Edited by Gabriele Boccaccini. Grand Rapids: Eerdmans, 2005.

Fraade, Steven D. *Enosh and His Generation: Pre-Israelite Hero and History in*

Postbiblical Interpretation. Society of Biblical Literature Monograph Series 30. Chico, Calif.: Scholars Press, 1984.

Frankel, Z. "Das Buch der Jubiläen." Pages 311–16 and 380–400 in *Monatsschrift fuer Geschichte und Wissenschaft des Judentums*. Breslau, 1856.

Frey, Jörg. "Different Patterns of Dualistic Thought in the Qumran Library: Reflections on Their Background and History." Pages 275–335 in *Legal Texts and Legal Issues: Proceedings of the Second Meeting of the International Organization for Qumran Studies, Cambridge 1995. Published in Honour of Joseph M. Baumgarten*. Edited by Moshe J. Bernstein, Florentino García Martínez, and John Kampen. Studies on the Texts of the Desert of Judah 23. Leiden: Brill, 1997.

———. "Flesh and Spirit in the Palestinian Jewish Sapiential Tradition and in the Qumran Texts: An Inquiry into the Background of Pauline Usage." Pages 367–404 in *The Wisdom Texts from Qumran and the Development of Sapiential Thought*. Edited by Charlotte Hempel, Armin Lange, and Hermann Lichtenberger. Bibliotheca Ephemeridum Theologicarum Lovaniensium 159. Leuven: Peeters, 2002.

Freyne, Sean. "The Geography of Restoration: Galilee–Jerusalem Relations in Early Jewish and Christian Experience." Pages 405–33 in *Restoration: Old Testament, Jewish, and Christian Perspectives*. Edited by James M. Scott. Supplements to the Journal for the Study of Judaism 72. Leiden: Brill, 2001.

Fröhlich, Ida. "'Narrative Exegesis' in the Dead Sea Scrolls." Pages 81–99 in *Biblical Perspectives: Early Use and Interpretation of the Bible in Light of the Dead Sea Scrolls. Proceedings of the First International Symposium of the Orion Center for the Study of the Dead Sea Scrolls and Associated Literature, 12–14 May 1996*. Edited by Michael E. Stone and Esther G. Chazon. Studies on the Texts of the Desert of Judah 28. Leiden: Brill, 1998.

———. "The Symbolical Language of the Animal Apocalypse of Enoch (*1 Enoch 85–90*)." *Revue de Qumran* 14 (1989): 629–36.

———. "Themes, Structure and Genre of Pesher Genesis: A Response to George J. Brooke." *Jewish Quarterly Review* 85 (1994): 81–90.

Gane, Roy E. "Moral Evils in Leviticus 16:16, 21 and Cultic Characterization of YHWH." Paper presented at the annual meeting of the Society of Biblical Literature. Denver, Colorado, November 2001.

García Martínez, Florentino. "4QMess ar and the Book of Noah." Pages 1–44 in *Qumran and Apocalyptic: Studies on the Aramaic Texts from Qumran*. Edited by R. Aguirre and Florentino García Martínez. Studies on the Texts of the Desert of Judah 9. Leiden: Brill, 1992.

———. "Interpretations of the Flood in the Dead Sea Scrolls." Pages 86–108 in *Interpretations of the Flood*. Edited by Florentino García Martínez and Gerard P. Luttikhuizen. Themes in Biblical Narrative 1. Leiden: Brill, 1998.

———. "Man and Woman: Halakah Based upon Eden in the Dead Sea Scrolls."

Pages 95–115 in *Paradise Interpreted: Representations of Biblical Paradise in Judaism and Christianity.* Edited by Gerard P. Luttikhuizen. Leiden: Brill, 1999.

García Martínez, Florentino, and Julio Trebolle Barrera. *The People of the Dead Sea Scrolls: Their Writings, Beliefs and Practices.* Translated by W. G. E. Watson. Leiden: Brill, 1995.

García Martínez, Florentino, and Eibert J. C. Tigchelaar. "1 Enoch and the Aramaic Fragments from Qumran." *Revue de Qumran* 14 (1989): 131–46.

Garnet, Paul. *Salvation and Atonement in the Qumran Scrolls.* Tübingen: J. C. B. Mohr, 1977.

Gebhardt, Oscar. "Die 70 Hirten des buches Henoch und ihre Deutungen mit besonderer Rücksicht auf die Barkochba-Hypothese." *Archiv für wissenschaftliche Erforschung des Alten Testaments* 2.2 (1872): 163–246.

Gilders, William K. "Where Did Noah Place the Blood? A Textual Note on *Jubilees* 7:4." *Journal of Biblical Literature* 124 (2005): 745–49.

Ginzberg, Louis. *The Legends of the Jews.* Translated by Henrietta Szold. Philadelphia: Jewish Publication Society, 1937–66.

Goff, Mathew J. "The Mystery of Creation in 4QInstruction." *Dead Sea Discoveries* 10 (2003): 163–86.

———. "Reading Wisdom at Qumran: 4QInstruction and the Hodayot." *Dead Sea Discoveries* 11 (2004): 264–88.

———. *The Worldly and Heavenly Wisdom of 4QInstruction.* Studies on the Texts of the Desert of Judah 50. Leiden/Boston: Brill, 2003.

Goldin, Judah. *Studies in Midrash and Related Literature.* Edited by Barry L. Eichler and Jeffrey H. Tigay. Philadelphia: Jewish Publication Society, 1988.

Greenfield, Jonas C., and Elisha Qimron. "The Genesis Apocryphon Col. XII." *Abr-Nahrain Supplement* 3 (1992): 70–77.

Grossman, Maxine. "Priesthood as Authority: Interpretive Competition in First-Century Judaism and Christianity." Pages 117–31 in *The Dead Sea Scrolls as Background to Postbiblical Judaism and Early Christianity: Papers from an International Conference at St. Andrews in 2001.* Edited by James R. Davila. Studies on the Texts of the Desert of Judah 46. Leiden: Brill, 2003.

———. *Reading for History in the Damascus Document: A Methodological Study.* Studies on the Texts of the Desert of Judah 45. Leiden: Brill, 2002.

Gruenwald, Ithamar. "Midrash and the 'Midrashic Condition': Preliminary Considerations." Pages 6–22 in *The Midrashic Imagination: Jewish Exegesis, Thought, and History.* Edited by Michael Fishbane. Albany: State University of New York Press, 1993.

Gunkel, Hermann. *The Legends of Genesis: The Biblical Saga of History.* Translated by W. H. Carruth. New York: Schocken Books, 1964. Translation of *Die Sagen der Genesis* (1901).

Gunn, David M. "Deutero-Isaiah and the Flood." *Journal of Biblical Literature* 94 (1975): 493–508.

Habel, Norman C. *The Land Is Mine: Six Biblical Land Ideologies*. Overtures to Biblical Theology. Minneapolis: Fortress, 1995.

Halivni, David Weiss. "From Midrash to Mishnah: Theological Repercussions and Further Clarifications of 'Chate'u Yisrael.'" Pages 23–44 in *The Midrashic Imagination: Jewish Exegesis, Thought, and History*. Edited by Michael Fishbane. Albany: State University of New York Press, 1993.

Halpern-Amaru, Betsy. *Rewriting the Bible: Land and Covenant in Postbiblical Jewish Literature*. Valley Forge, Pa.: Trinity Press International, 1994.

Hannah, Darrell D. "The Book of Noah, the Dead of Herod the Great, and the Date of the Parables of Enoch." Pages 469–77 in *Enoch and the Messiah Son of Man: Revisiting the Book of the Parables*. Edited by Gabriele Boccaccini. Grand Rapids: Eerdmans, 2007.

Harland, P. J. *The Value of Human Life: A Study of the Story of the Flood (Genesis 6–9)*. Supplements to Vetus Testamentum 64. Leiden: Brill, 1996.

Harrington, Daniel J. "Sirach Research since 1965: Progress and Questions." Pages 164–76 in *Pursuing the Text: Studies in Honor of Ben Zion Wacholder on the Occasion of His Seventieth Birthday*. Edited by John C. Reeves and John Kampen. Journal for the Study of the Old Testament: Supplement Series 184. Sheffield: Sheffield Academic Press, 1994.

———. "Two Early Jewish Approaches to Wisdom: Sirach and Qumran Sapiential Work A." Pages 123–32 in *SBL Seminar Papers 1996*. Society of Biblical Literature Seminar Papers 35. Atlanta: Scholars Press, 1996.

Hartman, Lars. "Comfort of the Scriptures: An Early Jewish Interpretation of Noah's Salvation, 1 En. 10:16–11:2." *Svensk Exegetisk Årsbok* 41–42 (1976–77): 87–96.

Heinrich, Ewald. *Abhandlung über des Äthiopischen Buches Henókh: Entstehung Sinn und Zusammensetzung*. Göttingen: Dieterichschen Buchhandlung, 1854.

Hendel, Ronald S. "4Q252 and the Flood Chronology of Genesis 7–8: A Text-Critical Solution." *Dead Sea Discoveries* 2 (1995): 72–79.

———. "The Nephilim Were on the Earth: Genesis 6:1–4 and Its Ancient Near Eastern Context." Pages 11–34 in *The Fall of the Angels*. Edited by Christoph Auffarth and Loren T. Stuckenbruck. Themes in Biblical Narrative 6. Leiden: Brill, 2004.

Himmelfarb, Martha. "The Book of the Watchers and the Priests of Jerusalem." *Henoch* 24 (2002): 131–35.

Horst, Pieter W. van der. "Antediluvian Knowledge: Graeco-Roman and Jewish Speculations about Wisdom from before the Flood." Pages 139–58 in *Japheth in the Tents of Shem: Studies on Jewish Hellenism in Antiquity*. Contributions to Biblical Exegesis and Theology 32. Leuven: Peeters, 2002.

Huggins, Ronald V. "A Canonical 'Book of Periods' at Qumran?" *Revue de Qumran* 15 (1991–92): 421–36.

———. "Noah and the Giants: A Response to John C. Reeves." *Journal of Biblical Literature* 114 (1995): 103–10.

Hughes, Maldwyn. *The Ethics of Jewish Apocryphal Literature*. London: Robert Culley, 1910.
Jackson, David R. *Enochic Judaism: Three Defining Paradigm Exemplars*. London: T&T Clark International, 2004.
Jacobs, Irving. *The Midrashic Process: Tradition and Interpretation in Rabbinic Judaism*. Cambridge: Cambridge University Press, 1995.
Jassen, Alex P. "Sapiential Revelation in Apocalyptic Literature Preserved at Qumran." Pages 260-78 in *Mediating the Divine: Prophecy and Revelation in the Dead Sea Scrolls and Second Temple Judaism*. Studies on the Texts of the Desert of Judah 68. Leiden: Brill, 2007.
Jastram, Nathan. "Hierarchy at Qumran." Pages 349-76 in *Legal Texts and Legal Issues: Proceedings of the Second Meeting of the International Organization for Qumran Studies, Cambridge 1995. Published in Honour of Joseph M. Baumgarten*. Edited by Moshe J. Bernstein, Florentino García Martínez and John Kampen. Studies on the Texts of the Desert of Judah 23. Leiden: Brill, 1997.
Jellinek, Adolph. *Über das Buch der Jubiläen and das Noah-Buch*. Leipzig, 1855.
Jonge, Marinus de. "Levi in Aramaic Levi and in the Testament of Levi." Pages 71-89 in *Pseudepigraphic Perspectives: The Apocrypha and Pseudepigrapha in Light of the Dead Sea Scrolls. Proceedings of the International Symposium of the Orion Center for the Study of the Dead Sea Scrolls and Associated Literature, 12-14 January 1997.* Edited by Esther G. Chazon and Michael E. Stone. Studies on the Texts of the Desert of Judah 31. Leiden: Brill, 1999.

―――――. "The Testaments of the Twelve Patriarchs and Related Qumran Fragments." Pages 63-77 in *For a Later Generation: The Transformation of Tradition in Israel, Early Judaism, and Early Christianity*. Edited by Randal A. Argall, Beverly A. Bow, and Rodney A. Werline. Harrisburg, Pa.: Trinity Press International, 2000.
Joosten, Jan. *People and Land in the Holiness Code: An Exegetical Study of the Ideational Framework of the Law in Leviticus 17-26*. Supplements to Vetus Testamentum 67. Leiden: Brill, 1996.
Kaminski, Carol. *From Noah to Israel: Realization of the Primaeval Blessing after the Flood*. London: T&T Clark International, 2004.
Kampen, John. "Knowledge, Truth, and 'Wisdom' in the Cave 1 Texts?" Paper presented to the VIth Congress of the International Organization of Qumran Studies. Ljubljana, Slovenia, July 16, 2007.
Kasher, Rimon. "The Interpretation of Scripture in Rabbinic Literature." Pages 547-94 in *Mikra: Text, Translation, Reading and Interpretation of the Hebrew Bible in Ancient Judaism and Early Christianity*. Edited by Martin J. Mulder. Assen/Maastricht: Van Gorcum, 1988.
Kister. Menahem. "5Q13 and the 'Avodah: A Historical Survey and Its Significance." *Dead Sea Discoveries* 8 (2001): 136-48.
―――――. "Some Aspects of Qumranic Halakhah." Pages 576-86 in vol. 2 of *The Madrid Qumran Congress: Proceedings of the International Congress on the*

Dead Sea Scrolls, Madrid 81–21 March 1991. Edited by Julio Trebolle Barrera and Luis Vegas Montaner. Studies on the Texts of the Desert of Judah 12. Leiden: Brill, 1992.

———. "Wisdom Literature and Its Relation to Other Genres." Pages 13–47 in *Sapiential Perspectives: Wisdom Literature in Light of the Dead Sea Scrolls. Proceedings of the Sixth International Symposium of the Orion Center for the Study of the Dead Sea Scrolls and Associated Literature, 20–22 May 2001.* Edited by John J. Collins, Gregory E. Sterling, and Ruth A. Clements. Studies on the Texts of the Desert of Judah 51. Leiden/Boston: Brill, 2004.

Klawans, Jonathan. *Impurity and Sin in Ancient Judaism.* Oxford: Oxford University Press, 2000.

Klijn, A. F. J. "From Creation to Noah in the Second Dream-Vision of the Ethiopic Enoch." Pages 147–60 in *Miscellanea Neotestamentica.* Edited by T. Baarda. Leiden: Brill, 1978.

Knibb, Michael A. "The Book of Enoch in the Light of Qumran Wisdom Literature." Pages 193–210 in *Wisdom and Apocalypticism in the Dead Sea Scrolls and in the Biblical Tradition.* Edited by Florentino García Martínez. Bibliotheca Ephemeridum theologicarum Lovaniensium 168. Leuven: Leuven University Press, 2003.

———. "Jubilees and the Origins of the Qumran Community." Inaugural address delivered at King's College, London, January 17, 1989.

———. "The Structure and Composition of the Parables of Enoch." Pages 48–64 in *Enoch and the Messiah Son of Man: Revisiting the Book of Parables.* Edited by Gabriele Boccaccini. Grand Rapids: Eerdmans, 2007.

Knohl, Israel. *The Messiah before Jesus.* Translated by David Maisel. Berkeley: University of California Press, 2000.

Koltun-Fromm, Naomi. "Aphrahat and the Rabbis on Noah's Righteousness in Light of the Jewish-Christian Polemic." Pages 56–71 in *The Book of Genesis in Jewish and Oriental Christian Interpretation: A Collection of Essays.* Edited by Judith Frishman and Lucas Van Rompay. Traditio exegetica Graeca 5. Leuven: Peeters, 1997.

Krasovec, Joze. "Sources of Confession on Sin in 1QS 1:24–26 and CD 20:28–30." Pages 306–21 in *The Dead Sea Scrolls Fifty Years after Their Discovery: Proceedings of the Jerusalem Congress, July 20–25, 1997.* Edited by Lawrence H. Schiffman, Emanuel Tov, and James C. VanderKam. Jerusalem: Israel Exploration Society, 2000.

Kudan, David B. "Sabbath Worship in the Parables of Enoch (1 Enoch 37–71)." Paper presented to the Graduate Enoch Seminar. Ann Arbor, Michigan, May 2–4, 2006.

Kugel, James. "How Old Is the *Aramaic Levi Document?" Dead Sea Discoveries* 14 (2007): 291–312.

———. "Levi's Elevation to the Priesthood in Second Temple Writings." *Harvard Theological Review* 86 (1993): 1–64.

———. "Two Introductions to Midrash." Pages 77–103 in *Midrash and Litera-*

ture. Edited by Geoffrey H. Hartman and Sanford Budick. New Haven and London: Yale University Press, 1986.

Kugel, James L., and Rowan A. Greer. *Early Biblical Interpretation*. Philadelphia: Westminster, 1986.

Kugler, Robert A. *From Patriarch to Priest: The Levi-Priestly Tradition from Aramaic Levi to Testament of Levi*. Society of Biblical Literature Early Judaism and Its Literature 9. Atlanta: Scholars Press, 1996.

———. "A Note on 1QS 9:14: The Sons of Righteousness or the Sons of Zadok?" *Dead Sea Discoveries* 3 (1996): 315-20.

———. "The Priesthood at Qumran: The Evidence of References to Levi and the Levites." Pages 465-79 in *The Provo International Conference on the Dead Sea Scrolls: Technological Innovations, New Texts, and Reformulated Issues*. Edited by Donald W. Parry and Eugene C. Ulrich. Studies on the Texts of the Desert of Judah 30. Leiden: Brill, 1999.

———. "Some Further Evidence for the Samaritan Provenance of *Aramaic Levi* (1QTestLevi; 4QTest Levi) (1)." *Revue de Qumran* 17 (1996): 351-58.

———. *The Testaments of the Twelve Patriarchs*. Guides to Apocrypha and Pseudepigrapha. Sheffield: Sheffield Academic Press, 2001.

Kvanvig, Helge. "Enochic Judaism—A Judaism with the *Torah* and the Temple?" Paper presented to the Fourth Enoch Seminar. Camaldoli, Italy, July 8-12, 2007.

———. "The Watchers Story, Genesis, and *Atra-hasis*, a Triangular Reading." *Henoch* 24 (2002): 17-21.

Lambert, David. "Last Testaments in the Book of Jubilees." *Dead Sea Discoveries* 11 (2004): 82-107.

Lange, Armin. "Wisdom and Predestination in the Dead Sea Scrolls." *Dead Sea Discoveries* 2 (1995): 340-52.

Lee, Thomas R. *Studies in the Form of Sirach 44-50*. Society of Biblical Literature Dissertation Series 75. Atlanta: Scholars Press, 1986.

Leszynsky, Rudolf. *Die Sadduzäer*. Berlin: Mayer & Mueller, 1912.

Levenson, Jon D. *The Hebrew Bible, The Old Testament, and Historical Criticism*. Louisville: Westminster John Knox, 1993.

Lewis, Jack P. *A Study of the Interpretation of Noah and the Flood in Jewish and Christian Literature*. Leiden: Brill, 1968.

Licht, J. מגילת הסרכים (*The Rule of the Community*). Jerusalem: Bialik Institute, 1965.

Lim, Timothy H. "The Chronology of the Flood Story in a Qumran Text (4Q252)." *Journal of Jewish Studies* 43 (1992): 288-98.

Loader, William. *Enoch, Levi, and Jubilees on Sexuality: Attitudes Towards Sexuality in the Early Enoch Literature, the Aramaic Levi Document, and the Book of Jubilees*. Grand Rapids: Eerdmans, 2007.

Longenecker, Bruce W. "Lukan Aversion to Humps and Hollows: The Case of Acts 11:27-12:25." *New Testament Studies* 50 (2004): 185-204.

Ludlow, Jared. "Progression to the Angelic Realm in Second Temple Literature."

Paper presented at the annual meeting of the Society of Biblical Literature. Denver, Colorado, November 19, 2001.

MacCormac, Earl R. *Metaphor and Myth in Science and Religion*. Durham, N.C.: Duke University Press, 1976.

Machiela, Daniel A. "Divinely Revealed History and Geography in the Genesis Apocryphon Columns 13–17." Paper presented at the annual meeting of Society of Biblical Literature. Philadelphia, November 22, 2005.

———. "Geography as an Evaluative Tool in the Genesis Apocryphon." Forthcoming in *Dead Sea Discoveries*.

Magness, Jodi. *The Archaeology of Qumran and the Dead Sea Scrolls*. Studies in the Dead Sea Scrolls and Related Literature. Grand Rapids: Eerdmans, 2002.

Martin, M. Francoise. "Le Livre des Jubilés." *Revue biblique* 8 (1911): 321–44, 502–33.

Metso, Sarianna. "In Search of the *Sitz Im Leben* of the *Community Rule*." Pages 306–15 in *The Provo International Conference on the Dead Sea Scrolls: Technological Innovations, New Texts, and Reformulated Issues*. Edited by Donald W. Parry and Eugene C. Ulrich. Studies on the Texts of the Desert of Judah 30. Brill: Leiden, 1999.

———. "The Primary Results of the Reconstruction of 4QS^e." *Journal of Jewish Studies* 44 (1993): 303–8.

———. *The Textual Development of the Qumran Community Rule*. Studies on the Texts of the Desert of Judah 21. Brill: Leiden, 1997.

———. "The Textual Traditions of the Qumran Community Rule." Pages 132–47 in *Legal Texts and Legal Issues: Proceedings of the Second Meeting of the International Organization for Qumran Studies, Cambridge 1995. Published in Honour of Joseph M. Baumgarten*. Edited by Moshe J. Bernstein, Florentino García Martínez, and John Kampen. Studies on the Texts of the Desert of Judah 23. Leiden: Brill, 1997.

Milik, Jozef T. "Milkî-ṣedeq et Milkî-rešaʿ." *Journal of Jewish Studies* 23 (1972): 95–144.

———. *Ten Years of Discovery in the Wilderness of Judaea*. Translated by J. Strugnell. Studies in Biblical Theology 26. London: SCM, 1959.

Molenberg, Corrie. "A Study of the Roles of Shemihaza and Asael in 1 Enoch 6–11." *Journal of Jewish Studies* 35 (1984): 136–46.

Morgenstern, Matthew. "Language and Literature in the Second Temple Period." *Journal of Jewish Studies* 48 (1997): 130–45.

———. "A New Clue to the Original Length of the Genesis Apocryphon." *Journal of Jewish Studies* 47 (1996): 345–47.

Morgenstern, Matthew, Elisha Qimron, and Daniel Sivan. "The Hitherto Unpublished Columns of the Genesis Apocryphon." *Abr-Nahrain* 33 (1995): 30–54.

Murphy-O'Connor, Jerome. "The Essenes and Their History." *Revue biblique* 81 (1974): 221–22.

———. "La genèse littéraire de la Règle de la Communauté." *Revue biblique* 76 (1969): 528–49.

———. "The Judaean Desert." Pages 119–56 in *Early Judaism and Its Modern Interpreters*. Edited by Robert A. Kraft and George W. E. Nickelsburg. Atlanta: Scholars Press, 1986.

Neusner, Jacob. *The Idea of Purity in Ancient Judaism*. Studies in Judaism in Ancient Antiquity 1. Leiden: Brill, 1973.

———. *Invitation to Midrash: The Workings of Rabbinic Bible Interpretation*. San Francisco: Harper & Row, 1989.

Newsom, Carol A. "4Q370: An Admonition Based on the Flood." *Revue de Qumran* 13 (1988): 23–43.

———. "'Sectually Explicit' Literature from Qumran." Pages 167–87 in *Hebrew Bible and Its Interpreters*. Winona Lake, Ind.: Eisenbrauns, 1990.

Nickelsburg, George W. E. *Ancient Judaism and Christian Origins: Diversity, Continuity and Transformation*. Minneapolis: Fortress, 2003.

———. "Apocalyptic and Myth in 1 Enoch 6–11." *Journal of Biblical Literature* 96 (1977): 383–405.

———. "The Books of Enoch at Qumran: What We Know and What We Need to Think About." Pages 99–113 in *Antikes Judentum and Frühes Christentum: Festschrift für Hartmut Stegemann zum 65 Geburtstag*. Edited by Bernd Kollmann, Wolfgang Reinbold, und Annette Steudel. Berlin: W. de Gruyter, 1999.

———. "Enoch, Levi, and Peter: Recipients of Revelation in Upper Galilee." Pages 427–57 in vol. 2 of *George W. E. Nickelsburg in Perspective: An Ongoing Dialogue of Learning*. Edited by Jacob Neusner and Alan J. Avery-Peck. Leiden: Brill, 2003.

———. *Faith and Piety in Early Judaism: Texts and Documents*. Philadelphia: Fortress, 1983.

———. *Jewish Literature between the Bible and the Mishnah*. Philadelphia: Fortress, 1987.

———. "The Nature and Function of Revelation of 1 Enoch, Jubilees, and Some Qumranic Documents." Pages 91–119 in *Pseudepigraphic Perspectives: The Apocrypha and Pseudepigrapha in Light of the Dead Sea Scrolls. Proceedings of the International Symposium of the Orion Center for the Study of the Dead Sea Scrolls and Associated Literature, 12–14 January 1997*. Edited by Esther G. Chazon and Michael E. Stone. Studies on the Texts of the Desert of Judah 31. Leiden: Brill, 1999.

———. "Patriarchs Who Worry about Their Wives: A Haggadic Tendency in the Genesis Apocryphon." Pages 137–58 in vol. 1 of *Biblical Perspectives: Early Use and Interpretation of the Bible in Light of the Dead Sea Scrolls. Proceedings of the First International Symposium of the Orion Center for the Study of the Dead Sea Scrolls and Associated Literature, 12–14 May 1996*. Edited by Michael E. Stone and Esther G. Chazon. Studies on the Texts of the Desert of Judah 28. Leiden: Brill, 1998.

———. "The Qumranic Transformation of a Cosmological and Eschatological Tradition (1QH 4:29–40)." Pages 649–59 in vol. 2 of *The Madrid Qumran Congress: Proceedings of the International Congress on the Dead Sea Scrolls, Madrid, 18–21 March 1991*. Edited by Julio Trebolle Barrera and Luis Vegas Montaner. Studies on the Texts of the Desert of Judah 12. Leiden: Brill, 1992.

———. "Reflection on Ideology and Date of the Apocalypse of Weeks." Pages 200-203 in *Enoch and Qumran Origins: New Light on a Forgotten Connection*. Edited by Gabriele Boccaccini. Grand Rapids: Eerdmans, 2005.

———. "Response: Context, Text, and Social Setting of the Apocalypse." Pages 237–39 in *Enoch and Qumran Origins: New Light on a Forgotten Connection*. Edited by Gabriele Boccaccini. Grand Rapids: Eerdmans, 2005.

———. "Revealed Wisdom as a Criterion for Inclusion and Exclusion: From Jewish Sectarianism to Early Christianity." Page 73–91 in *"To See Ourselves As Others See Us": Christians, Jews, 'Others' in Late Antiquity*. Edited by Jacob Neusner and Ernest S. Frerichs. Chico, Calif.: Scholars Press, 1985.

———. "Scripture in *1 Enoch* and *1 Enoch* as Scripture." Pages 333–54 in *Texts and Contexts: Biblical Texts in Their Textual and Situational Contexts*. Edited by Tord Fornberg and David Hellholm. Oslo: Scandinavian University Press, 1995.

Nitzan, Bilhah. "The Concept of the Covenant in Qumran Literature." Pages 85–104 in *Historical Perspectives from the Hasmoneans to Bar Kokhba in Light of the Dead Sea Scrolls*. Edited by David Goodblatt, Avital Pinnick, and Daniel R. Schwartz. Studies in the Texts of the Desert of Judah 37. Leiden: Brill, 2001.

———. "Repentance in the Dead Sea Scrolls." Pages 145–70 in vol. 2 of *The Dead Sea Scrolls after 50 Years*. Edited by Peter W. Flint and James C. Vanderkam. Brill: Leiden, 1999.

Oegema, Gerbern S. "Tradition-Historical Studies on 4Q252." Pages 155–74 in *Qumran-Messianism: Studies on the Messianic Expectations in the Dead Sea Scrolls*. Edited by James H. Charlesworth, Hermann Lichtenberger, and Gerbern S. Oegema. Tübingen: Mohr Siebeck, 1998.

Orlov, Andrei A. "The Heir of Righteousness and the King of Righteousness: The Priestly Noachic Polemics in 2 Enoch and the Epistle to the Hebrews." *Journal of Theological Studies* 58 (2007): 45–65.

———. "'Noah's Younger Brother': The Anti-Noachic Polemics in *2 Enoch*." *Henoch* 22 (2000): 207–21.

Peters, Dorothy M. "'Atoning for the Land' in the Dead Sea Scrolls: The Day of Atonement Revisited." In *Studies in Biblical Law*. Edited by George J. Brooke. Journal of Semitic Studies: Supplement Series 25. Oxford: Oxford University Press, 2008. Forthcoming.

———. "Noah the 'Righteous' in the *Genesis Apocryphon*: Enoch's Noah Rebiblicized?" Paper presented at the annual meeting of the Society of Biblical Literature, Philadelphia, Pennsylvania, November 2005.

———. "Noah Traditions in *Jubilees*: Evidence for the Struggle between Enochic and Mosaic Authority." *Henoch* 2008/2. Forthcoming.

———. "The Recombination and Evolution of Noah Traditions as Found in the *Genesis Apocryphon* and *Jubilees*: The DNA of Fraternal Twins." Paper presented to the VIth Congress of the International Organization of Qumran Studies. Ljubljana, Slovenia, July 16, 2007.

———. "The Tension between Enoch and Noah in the Aramaic Enoch Texts at Qumran." *Henoch* 29 (2007): 11–29.

Poirier, John C. "4Q464: Not Eschatological." *Revue de Qumran* 20 (2002): 583–87.

Puech, É. "Sept fragments de la lettre d'Hénoch (1Hén 100, 103 et 105) dans la grotte 7 de Qumrân." *Revue de Qumran* 18/70 (1997): 313–23.

———. "Une Apocalypse Messianique (4Q521)." *Revue de Qumran* 15 (1992): 475–519.

Qimron, Elisha. *The Hebrew of the Dead Sea Scrolls*. Harvard Semitic Studies 29. Atlanta: Scholars Press, 1986.

———. "Toward a New Edition of 1QGenesis Apocryphon." Pages 106–9 in *The Provo International Conference on the Dead Sea Scrolls: Technological Innovations, New Texts, and Reformulated Issues*. Edited by Donald W. Parry and Eugene C. Ulrich. Studies on the Texts of the Desert of Judah 30. Leiden: Brill, 1999.

Rast, Walter E. *Tradition History and the Old Testament*. Philadelphia: Fortress, 1972.

Reed, Annette Yoshiko. "Angels, Demons, and the Dangerous Ones in between: Reflections on Enochic and Mosaic Traditions in *Jubilees*." Paper presented to the Fourth Enoch Seminar. Camaldoli, Italy, July 8–12, 2007.

———. *Fallen Angels and the History of Judaism and Christianity: The Reception of Enochic Literature*. Cambridge: Cambridge University Press, 2005.

Reeves, John C. "Utnapishtim in the Book of Giants?" *Journal of Biblical Literature* 112 (1993): 110–15.

———. "What Does Noah Offer in 1QapGen X, 15?" *Revue de Qumran* 12 (1986): 415–19.

Rendtorff, Rolf. "Noah, Abraham, and Moses: God's Covenant Partners." Pages 127–36 in *In Search of True Wisdom*. Edited by Edward Ball. Sheffield: Sheffield Academic Press, 1999.

Ringgren, Helmer. *The Faith of Qumran: Theology of the Dead Sea Scrolls*. Expanded Edition. New York: Crossroad, 1995.

Roberts, J. J. M. "Wicked and Holy (4Q180–181)." Pages 204–13 in *Damascus Document, War Scroll and Related Documents*. Vol. 2 of *The Dead Sea Scrolls Hebrew, Aramaic, and Greek Texts with English Translations*. Edited by James H. Charlesworth. Princeton Theological Seminary Dead Sea Scrolls Project. Tübingen: Mohr Siebeck, 1995.

Rogerson, J. W. *Myth in Old Testament Interpretation*. Berlin: de Gruyter, 1974.

Rothstein, David. "Joseph as Pedagogue: Biblical Precedents for the Depiction of

Joseph in *Aramaic Levi* (4Q213)." *Journal for the Study of the Pseudepigrapha* 14 (2005): 223–29.

Rudolph, David J. "Festivals in Genesis 1:14." *Tyndale Bulletin* 54 (2003): 23–40.

Ruiten, Jacques T. A. G. M. van. "The Covenant of Noah in *Jubilees* 6.1–38." Pages 167–90 in *The Concept of the Covenant in the Second Temple Period*. Edited by Stanley E. Porter and Jacqueline C. R. de Roo. Supplement to the Journal for the Study of Judaism 71. Leiden: Brill, 2003.

———. "Eden and the Temple: The Rewriting of Genesis 2:4–3:24 in the Book of Jubilees." Pages 63–94 in *Paradise Interpreted: Representations of Biblical Paradise in Judaism and Christianity*. Edited by Gerard P. Luttikhuizen. Leiden: Brill, 1999.

———. "The Interpretation of Genesis 6:1–12 in Jubilees 5:1–19." Pages 59–75 in *Studies in the Book of Jubilees*. Edited by Matthias Albani, Jörg Frey, and Armin Lang. Texte und Studien zum Antiken Judentum 65. Tübingen: Mohr Siebeck, 1997.

———. *Primaeval History Interpreted: The Rewriting of Genesis 1–11 in the Book of Jubilees*. Supplements to the Journal for the Study of Judaism 66. Leiden: Brill, 2000.

Safrai, S., and M. Stern, eds. *The Jewish People in the First Century*. 2 vols. Assen: Van Gorcum, 1974–76.

Sanders, E. P. *Judaism: Practice & Belief 63 BCE–66 CE*. London: SCM, 1992.

Saukkonen, Juhana. "From the Flood to the Messiah: Is 4Q252 a History Book?" Paper presented at the annual meeting of the Society of Biblical Literature, San Antonio, Texas, November 21, 2004.

Schiffman, Lawrence H. "The Case of the Day of Atonement Ritual." Pages 181–88 in *Biblical Perspectives: Early Use and Interpretation of the Bible in Light of the Dead Sea Scrolls. Proceedings of the First International Symposium of the Orion Center for the Study of the Dead Sea Scrolls and Associated Literature, 12–14 May 1996*. Edited by Michael E. Stone and Esther G. Chazon. Studies on the Texts of the Desert of Judah 28. Leiden: Brill, 1998.

———. "The Concept of Covenant in the Qumran Scrolls and Rabbinic Literature." Pages 259–89 in *The Idea of Biblical Interpretation: Essays in Honor of James L. Kugel*. Edited by Hindy Najman and Judith H. Newman. Supplements to the Journal for the Study of Judaism 83. Leiden: Brill, 2004.

———. *The Halakhah at Qumran*. Studies in Judaism in Late Antiquity 16. Leiden: Brill, 1975.

———. "Modification of Biblical Law and the Temple Scroll." Paper presented at the annual meeting of the Society of Biblical Literature. Toronto, Ontario, November 24, 2002.

———. *Reclaiming the Dead Sea Scrolls*. Philadelphia: Jewish Publication Society, 1994.

Schniedewind, William M. *How the Bible Became a Book: The Textualization of Ancient Israel*. Cambridge: Cambridge University Press, 2004.

Schüller, Eileen. "Prayer, Hymnic, and Liturgical Texts." Pages 153-71 in *The Community of the Renewed Covenant: The Notre Dame Symposium on the Dead Sea Scrolls*. Edited by Eugene Ulrich and James C. VanderKam. Notre Dame: University of Notre Dame Press, 1994.

Schürer, Emil. *A History of the Jewish People in the Time of Jesus Christ*. 3 vols. Edinburgh: Clark, 1886.

Schwartz, Martin. "Qumran, Turfan, Arabic Magic, and Noah's Name." Pages 231-38 in *Charmes Et Sortligès*. Edited by R. Gyselen. Res Orientales 14. Bures-sur-Yvette: Groupe pour l'Étude de la Civlisation du Moyen-Orient, 2002.

Scott, James M. *On Earth as in Heaven: The Restoration of Sacred Time and Sacred Space in the Book of Jubilees*. Supplements to the Journal for the Study of Judaism 91. Leiden: Brill, 2005.

———. "Exile and the Self-Understanding of Diaspora Jews in the Greco-Roman Period." Pages 171-218 in *Exile: Old Testament, Jewish, and Christian Conceptions*. Edited by James M. Scott. Supplements to the Journal for the Study of Judaism 56. Leiden: Brill, 1997.

———. "Geographic Aspects of Noachic Materials in the Scrolls at Qumran." Pages 368-81 in *The Scrolls and the Scriptures; Qumran Fifty Years after*. Edited by Stanley E. Porter and Craig A. Evans. Sheffield: Sheffield Academic Press, 1997.

———. "Jubilees 8-9." Pages 23-43 in *Geography in Early Judaism and Christianity: The Book of Jubilees*. Cambridge: Cambridge University Press, 2002.

Segal, Michael. "The Origin of Evil in Jubilees: Eden, Watchers, and Mastema." Paper presented at the annual meeting of Society of Biblical Literature. Atlanta, Georgia, November 24, 2003.

Seifrid, Mark A. "Righteousness Language in the Hebrew Scriptures and Early Judaism." Pages 415-42 in *Justification and Variegated Nomism*. Vol. 1 of *The Complexities of Second Temple Judaism*. Edited by D. A. Carson, Peter T. O'Brien, and Mark A. Seifrid. Tübingen: Mohr Siebeck, 2001.

Singer, W. *Das Buch der Jubiläen oder die Leptogenesis*. Stuhlweissenberg, Hungary: Ed. Singer'sche Buchhandlung, 1898.

Skehan, Patrick W. "Jubilees and the Qumran Psalter." *Catholic Biblical Quarterly* 37 (1975): 343-47.

Stanley, Christopher D. "The Importance of 4QTanḥumim (4Q176)." *Revue de Qumran* 15 (1991-92): 569-82.

Starcky, Jean. "Le Maître de Justice et Jésus." *Le Monde de la Bible* 4 (1978): 53-57.

———. "Les Quatre Étapes du Messianisme." *Revue biblique* 70 (1963): 481-505.

Steiner, R.C. "The Heading of the Book of the Words of Noah on a Fragment of the Genesis Apocryphon: New Light on a 'Lost' Work." *Dead Sea Discoveries* 2 (1995): 66-71.

Steinmetz, Devora. "Vineyard, Farm, and Garden: The Drunkenness of Noah in the Context of Primeval History." *Journal of Biblical Literature* 113 (1994): 193–207.

Stern, David. "Midrash and the Language of Exegesis: A Study of Vayikra Rabbah, Chapter 1." Pages 105–24 in *Midrash and Literature*. Edited by Geoffrey H. Hartman and Sanford Budick. New Haven: Yale University Press, 1986.

———. "The Rabbinic Parable and the Narrative of Interpretation." Pages 78–95 in *the Midrashic Imagination: Jewish Exegesis, Thought, and History*. Edited by Michael Fishbane. Albany: State University of New York Press, 1993.

Stone, Michael E. "Aramaic Levi in Its Contexts." *Jewish Studies Quarterly* 9 (2002): 307–26.

———. "The Axis of History at Qumran." Pages 133–49 in *Pseudepigraphic Perspectives: The Apocrypha and Pseudepigrapha in Light of the Dead Sea Scrolls. Proceedings of the International Symposium of the Orion Center for the Study of the Dead Sea Scrolls and Associated Literature, 12–14 January 1997*. Edited by Esther G. Chazon and Michael E. Stone. Studies on the Texts of the Desert of Judah 31. Leiden: Brill, 1999.

———. "The Book(s) Attributed to Noah." *Dead Sea Discoveries* 13 (2006): 4–23.

———. "Ideal Figures and Social Context: Priest and Sage in the Early Second Temple Age." Pages 575–86 in *Ancient Israelite Religion: Essays in Honor of Frank Moore Cross*. Edited by Patrick D. Miller, Jr., Paul D. Hanson, and S. Dean McBride. Philadelphia: Fortress, 1987.

Stone, Michael E., and Theodore A. Bergren. *Biblical Figures Outside the Bible*. Harrisburg, Pa.: Trinity Press International, 1998.

Stone, Michael E., and Esther Eshel. "An Exposition on the Patriarchs (4Q464) and Two Other Documents (4Q464^a and 4Q464^b)." *Muséon* 105 (1992): 243–64.

Strugnell, John. "Moses-Pseudepigrapha at Qumran: 4Q375, 4Q376, and Similar Works." Pages 221–56 in *Archaeology and History in the Dead Sea Scrolls: The New York University Conference in Memory of Yigael Yadin*. Edited by Lawrence H. Schiffman. Journal for the Study of the Pseudepigrapha: Supplement Series 8. Sheffield: JSOT Press, 1990.

———. "Notes en marge du volume V des Discoveries in the Judaean desert of Jordan." *Revue de Qumran* 7 (1970): 163–276.

Stuckenbruck, Loren T. "The Origins of Evil in Jewish Apocalyptic Tradition: The Interpretation of Genesis 6:1–4 in the Second and Third Centuries B.C.E." Pages 87–118 in *The Fall of the Angels*. Edited by Christoph Auffarth and Loren T. Stuckenbruck. Leiden: Brill, 2004.

Sutcliffe, E. F. "The First Fifteen Members of the Qumran Community. A Note on 1QS 8:1 ff." *Journal of Semitic Studies* 4 (1959): 134–38.

Suter, David W. "Fallen Angel, Fallen Priest: The Problem of Family Purity in 1 Enoch 6–16." *Hebrew Union College Annual* 50 (1979): 115–35.

Suter, David W. "Revisiting 'Fallen Angel, Fallen Priest.'" *Henoch* 24 (2002): 137–42.

Swarup, Paul N. W. "An Eternal Planting, a House of Holiness: The Self-Understanding of the Dead Sea Scrolls Community." *Tyndale Bulletin* 54 (2003): 151–56.

Talmon, Shemaryahu. "The Community of the Renewed Covenant: Between Judaism and Christianity." Pages 3–24 in *The Community of the Renewed Covenant: The Notre Dame Symposium on the Dead Sea Scrolls*. Edited by Eugene Ulrich and James C. VanderKam. Notre Dame, Ind.: University of Notre Dame Press, 1994.

———. "Fragments of Hebrew Writings without Identifying Sigla of Provenance from the Literary Legacy of Yigael Yadin." *Dead Sea Discoveries* 5 (1998): 149–57.

Tigchelaar, Eibert J. C. "Eden and Paradise: the Garden Motif in Some Early Jewish Texts (1 Enoch and Other Texts Found at Qumran)." Pages 37–62 in *Paradise Interpreted: Representations of Biblical Paradise in Judaism and Christianity*. Edited by Gerard P. Luttikhuizen. Leiden: Brill, 1999.

———. "Evaluating the Discussions concerning the Original Order of Chapters 91–93 and Codicological Data Pertaining to 4Q212 and Chester Beatty XII Enoch." Pages 220–23 in *Enoch and Qumran Origins: New Light on a Forgotten Connection*. Edited by Gabriele Boccaccini. Grand Rapids: Eerdmans, 2005.

———. *To Increase Learning for the Understanding Ones: Reading and Reconstructing the Fragmentary Early Jewish Sapiential Text 4QInstruction*. Leiden: Brill, 2001.

Tiller, Patrick. "The 'Eternal Planting' in the Dead Sea Scrolls." *Dead Sea Discoveries* 4 (1997): 312–35.

Tisserant, E. "Fragments syriaques de Livre des Jubilés." *Revue biblique* 30 (1921): 55–86, 206–32.

Toews, Casey. "Moral Purification in 1QS." *Bulletin for Biblical Research* 13 (2003): 71–96.

Torrey, Charles C. "A Hebrew Fragment of Jubilees," *Journal of Biblical Literature* 71 (1952): 39–41.

Tov, Emanuel. "Biblical Texts as Reworked in Some Qumran Manuscripts with Special Attention to 4QRP and 4QParaGen-Exod." Pages 111–34 in *The Community of the Renewed Covenant: The Notre Dame Symposium on the Dead Sea Scrolls*. Edited by Eugene Ulrich and James VanderKam. Notre Dame, Ind.: University of Notre Dame Press, 1994.

Tsumura, David T. "Genesis and Ancient Near Eastern Stories of Creation and Flood: An Introduction." Pages 44–57 in *"I Studied Inscriptions from before the Flood": Ancient Near Eastern, Literary, and Linguistic Approaches to Genesis 1–11*. Edited by Richard S. Hess and David T. Tsumura. Sources for Biblical and Theological Study 4. Winona Lake, Ind.: Eisenbrauns, 1994.

Ulrich, Eugene. "The Bible in the Making: The Scriptures at Qumran." Pages 77–93 in *The Community of the Renewed Covenant: The Notre Dame Symposium on the Dead Sea Scrolls*. Edited by Eugene Ulrich and James C. VanderKam. Notre Dame, Ind.: University of Notre Dame Press, 1994.

———. "The Septuagint Manuscripts from Qumran: A Reappraisal of Their Value." Pages 49–80 in *Septuagint, Scrolls and Cognate Writings: Papers Presented to the International Symposium on the Septuagint and Its Relations to the Dead Sea Scrolls and Other Writings*. Edited by George J. Brooke and Barnabas Lindars. SBL Septuagint and Cognate Studies 33. Atlanta: Scholars Press, 1992.

VanderKam, James C. "The Angel Story in the Book of Jubilees." Pages 151–70 in *Pseudepigraphic Perspectives: The Apocrypha and Pseudepigrapha in Light of the Dead Sea Scrolls. Proceedings of the International Symposium of the Orion Center for the Study of the Dead Sea Scrolls and Associated Literature, 12–14 January 1997*. Edited by Esther G. Chazon and Michael E. Stone. Studies on the Texts of the Desert of Judah 31. Leiden: Brill, 1999.

———. "Biblical Interpretation in *1 Enoch* and *Jubilees*." Pages 96–125 in *The Pseudepigrapha and Early Biblical Interpretation*. Edited by James H. Charlesworth and Craig A. Evans. Journal for the Study of the Pseudepigrapha Supplement Series 14. Sheffield: Sheffield Academic Press, 1993.

———. "The Birth of Noah." Pages 213–31 in *Intertestamental Essays in Honour of Józef Tadeusz Milik*. Edited by Zdzislaw Jan Kapera. Kroków: Enigma Press, 1992.

———. *The Book of Jubilees*. Guides to Apocrypha and Pseudepigrapha. Sheffield: Sheffield Academic Press, 2001.

———. *Calendars in the Dead Sea Scrolls: Measuring Time*. London/New York: Routledge, 1998.

———. "Calendrical Texts and the Origins of the Dead Sea Scroll Community." Pages 371–88 in *Methods of Investigation of the Dead Sea Scrolls and the Khirbet Qumran Site: Present Realities and Future Prospects*. Edited by Michael O. Wise. New York: New York Academy of Sciences, 1994.

———. "Covenant and Biblical Intepretation in Jubilees 6." Pages 92–104 in *The Dead Sea Scrolls Fifty Years after Their Discovery: Proceedings of the Jerusalem Congress, July 20–25, 1997*. Edited by Lawrence H. Schiffman, Emanuel Tov, and James C. VanderKam. Jerusalem: Israel Exploration Society, 2000.

———. *The Dead Sea Scrolls Today*. Grand Rapids: Eerdmans, 1994.

———. *Enoch, A Man for All Generations*. Studies on Personalities of the Old Testament. Columbia: University of South Carolina Press, 1994.

———. *Enoch and the Growth of an Apocalyptic Tradition*. Catholic Biblical Quarterly Monograph Series 16. Washington, D.C.: Catholic Biblical Association of America, 1984.

———. *From Revelation to Canon: Studies in the Hebrew Bible and Second Temple Literature*. Leiden: Brill, 2000.

———. "The Granddaughters and Grandsons of Noah." *Revue de Qumran* 16 (1993-94): 457–61.

———. "The Interpretation of Genesis in *1 Enoch*." Pages 129–48 in *The Bible at Qumran: Text, Shape, and Interpretation*. Edited by Peter W. Flint. Grand Rapids: Eerdmans, 2001.

———. "Isaac's Blessing of Levi and His Descendants in *Jubilees* 31." Pages 497–519 in *The Provo International Conference on the Dead Sea Scrolls: Technological Innovations, New Texts, and Reformulated Issues*. Edited by Donald W. Parry and Eugene C. Ulrich. Studies on the Texts of the Desert of Judah 30. Leiden: Brill, 1999.

———. "Jubilees' Exegetical Creation of Levi the Priest." *Revue de Qumran* 17 (1996): 359–73.

———. "The Jubilees Fragments from Qumran Cave 4." Pages 635–48 in *The Madrid Qumran Congress: Proceedings of the International Congress on the Dead Sea Scrolls, Madrid, 18-21 March 1991*. Edited by Julio Trebolle Barrera and Luis Vegas Montaner. Studies on the Texts of the Desert of Judah 12. Leiden: Brill, 1992.

———. "The Origins and Purposes of the Book of Jubilees." Pages 3–24 in *Studies in the Book of Jubilees*. Edited by Matthias Albani, Jörg Frey, and Armin Lange. Texte und Studien zum antiken Judentum 65. Tübingen: Mohr Siebeck, 1997.

———. "The Righteousness of Noah." Pages 13–32 in *Ideal Figures in Ancient Judaism: Profiles and Paradigms*. Edited by John J. Collins and George W. E. Nickelsburg. SBL Septuagint and Cognate Studies 12. Chico, Calif.: Scholars Press, 1980.

———. "The Scriptural Setting of the Book of Jubilees," *Dead Sea Discoveries* 13 (2006): 61–72.

———. *Textual and Historical Studies in the Book of Jubilees*. Harvard Semitic Studies 14. Missoula, Mont.: Scholars Press, 1977.

VanderKam, James C. and J.T. Milik, "The First *Jubilees* Manuscript from Qumran Cave 4: A Preliminary Publication." *Journal of Biblical Literature* 110 (1991): 243–70.

Vasholz, Robert I. "An Additional Note on the 4Q Enoch fragments and 11QtgJob." *Maarav* 3.1 (1982): 115–18.

Vermes, Geza. "Bible and Midrash: Early Old Testament Exegesis." Pages 199–31 in vol. 1 of the *Cambridge History of the Bible*. Edited by P. R. Ackroyd and C. F. Evans. Cambridge: Cambridge University Press, 1970.

———. "La communauté de la Nouvelle Alliance d'après ses écrits récemment découverts." *Ephemerides theologicae louvanienses* 27 (1951): 70–80.

Wacholder, Ben Zion. *The Dawn of Qumran: The Sectarian Torah and the Teacher of Righteousness*. Cincinnati: Hebrew Union College Press, 1983.

———. "Ezekiel and Ezekielism As Progenitors of Essenianism." Pages 186–96 in *The Dead Sea Scrolls: Forty Years of Research*. Edited by Devorah Dimant and Uriel Rappaport. Studies on the Texts of the Desert of Judah 10. Leiden: Brill, 1992.

———. "Jubilees as Super Canon." Pages 195–211 in *Legal Texts and Legal Issues: Proceedings of the Second Meeting of the International Organization for Qumran Studies, Cambridge 1995. Published in Honour of Joseph M. Baumgarten*. Edited by Moshe J. Bernstein, Florentino García Martínez, and John Kampen. Studies on the Texts of the Desert of Judah 23. Leiden: Brill, 1997.

———. "The Preamble to the Damascus Document: A Composite Edition of 4Q266–4Q268." *Hebrew Union College Annual* 69 (1998): 31–47.

———. "The Relationship between 11QTorah (The Temple Scroll) and the Book of Jubilees: One Single or Two Independent Compositions?" Pages 205–16 in *SBL Seminar Papers 1985*. Society of Biblical Literature Seminar Papers 24. Atlanta: Scholars Press, 1985.

Weigold, Matthias. "The Deluge and the Flood of Emotions: The Use of Flood Imagery in 4 Maccabees in Its Ancient Jewish Context." Pages 197–210 in *The Book of the Maccabees: History, Theology, Ideology. Papers of the Second International Conference on the Deuterocanonical Books, Pápa, Hungary, 9–11 June, 2005*. Edited by G. G. Xeravits and J. Zsengellér. Journal for the Study of Judaism: Supplement Series 118. Leiden: Brill, 2007.

Weinfeld, Moshe. "Prayer and Liturgical Practice in the Qumran Sect." Pages 241–58 in *The Dead Sea Scrolls: Forty Years of Research*. Edited by Devorah Dimant and Uriel Rappaport. Studies on the Texts of the Desert of Judah 10. Leiden: Brill, 1992.

Weissenberg, Hanne von. "Covenant Motives in 4QMMT." Paper presented to the Graduate Enoch Seminar, Ann Arbor, Michigan, May 2–4, 2006.

Wenham, Gordon J. "The Coherence of the Flood Narrative." Pages 436–47 in *"I Studied Inscriptions from before the Flood": Ancient Near Eastern, Literary, and Linguistic Approaches to Genesis 1–11*. Edited by Richard S. Hess and David Toshio Tsumura. Sources for Biblical and Theological Study 4. Winona Lake, Ind.: Eisenbrauns, 1994.

Werman, Cana. "Qumran and the Book of Noah." Pages 171–81 in *Pseudepigraphic Perspectives: The Apocrypha and Pseudepigrapha in Light of the Dead Sea Scrolls. Proceedings of the International Symposium of the Orion Center for the Study of the Dead Sea Scrolls and Associated Literature, 12–14 January 1997*. Edited by Esther G. Chazon and Michael E. Stone. Studies on the Texts of the Desert of Judah 31. Leiden: Brill, 1999.

Wernberg-Møller, Preben. *The Manual of Discipline*. Studies on the Texts of the Desert of Judah 1. Edited by J. Van Der Ploeg OP. Leiden: E.J. Brill, 1957.

Wernberg-Møller, Preben. "צדק, צדיק and צדוק in the Zadokite Fragments (CDC), the Manual of Discipline (DSD) and the Habakkuk-Commentary (DSH)." *Vetus Testamentum* 3 (1953): 310–15.

Wolde, Ellen van. "A Text-Semantic Study of the Hebrew Bible, Illustrated with Noah and Job." *Journal of Biblical Literature* 113 (1994): 19–35.

Woude, A. S. van der. "Fragmente des Buches Jubiläen aus Qumran Höhle XI (11QJub)." In *Tradition und Glaube: Das frühe Christentum in seiner Umwelt. Festgabe für Karl Georg Kuhn*. Edited by G. Jeremias, H. W. Kuhn, and H. Stegemann. Göttingen: Vandenhoek & Ruprecht, 1972.

Wright, Benjamin G., III. "'Fear the Lord and Honor the Priest': Ben Sira as Defender of the Jerusalem Priesthood." Pages 189–222 in *The Book of Ben Sira in Modern Research: Proceedings of the First International Ben Sira Conference, 28–31 July 1996*. Edited by Pancratius C. Beentjes. Berlin/New York: de Gruyter, 1997.

———. "Putting the Puzzle Together: Some Suggestions Concerning the Social Location of the Wisdom of Ben Sira." Pages 133–49 in *SBL 1996 Seminar Papers*. Society of Biblical Literature Seminar Papers 35. Atlanta: Scholars Press, 1996.

Yinger, Kent L. *Paul, Judaism, and Judgment According to Deeds*. Society for New Testament Studies Monograph 105. Cambridge: Cambridge University Press, 1999.

Zeitlin, Solomon. "The Book of Jubilees: Its Character and Significance." *Jewish Quarterly Review* 30 (1939): 1-31.

Biblical and Apocryphal Books

Genesis		5:1–32	17
1	143	5:1–6:8	17, 19
1–4	15	5:2	19
1–5	145	5:4	79
1:4	61	5:5	76, 79
1:6	161	5:6–18	76
1:7	161	5:6–27	76
1:11	131	5:9	15
1:14	143, 161	5:19	79
1:14–18	34	5:21–24	30
1:15, 17	143	5:21–27	17
1:18	161	5:21–28	5
1:21	21	5:22	59
1:24–25	21	5:24	41, 176
1:26–27	20	5:28–29	76
1:28	5, 16, 21	5:28–32	17
1:29	22	5:29	19, 23, 27, 37,
2–3	21		43, 108, 134
2:7	20	5:32	5, 76
2:9	147	6	65, 66
2:17	147	6:1–2	17
3	66	6:1–4	17, 19, 27, 35,
3–4	140		48, 78
3:2–6	140	6:1–5, 11	77
3:5	147	6:1–12	36
3:6	19	6:1–13	78
3:17	21, 108	6:2	16, 19, 108
3:22	147	6:3	17, 19
4:8	76	6:4	16, 17, 20, 133
4:10–11	36	6:5	17, 27, 71, 137, 140,
4:11	21, 108		146, 152, 156, 160
4:17–24	76	6:5, 11	116
4:25	76	6:5–7	20
5	48	6:5–8	17
5–10	17, 22, 28	6:5–11	41
5:1	19	6:6	36
5:1–10:32	19	6:6–7	17, 19
5:1–20	17	6:7	19, 20, 79

Genesis (continued)		7:23a	20, 24
6:8	17, 20, 79, 80	7:23b	20
6:8–9	153	7:24	20, 27, 133
6:9	5, 19, 27, 43, 79, 111, 112, 160	7:23	18, 27, 104
		7:24	18
6:9–7:12	18	7:24–8:1	13
6:9–7:24	18, 19	8:1	18, 21, 25, 28
6:9–13	18	8:1–2	133
6:9–9:29	18	8:1–14	18, 21
6:7b–8a	5	8:1–9:29	18, 21
6:9	27, 59	8:2	131
6:11–13	27	8:2–5	18, 26
6:12	108	8:4	19
6:13	24, 28, 36, 64, 77, 89, 108	8:6–14	18
		8:9	19
6:13–21	15, 37	8:12–17	28
6:14–16	28	8:15–19	18
6:14–7:5	18, 27	8:15–9:17	18, 21
6:17	108	8:17	108
6:19	108	8:18–19	27
6:18	81, 113	8:18–20	81
6:20	16, 21	8:20	27, 80, 83
6:22	20	8:20–21	15, 18
7:1	27, 111	8:21	16, 19, 21, 23, 27, 28, 77, 108, 135, 137, 146
7:4	21		
7:4–8:14	27	8:21–9:7	81
7:5	36	8:22	19, 27, 135, 143, 164
7:6–12	18	9:1	5, 16, 19, 22, 27, 36
7:11	26, 131	9:1–3	16
7:13–14	18	9:1–17	18
7:13–18	18	9:2	21
7:14	21	9:3	22
7:15	108	9:4–7	28, 36
7:15–16	18, 108	9:5–6	36
7:16	19	9:6	19
7:16 (LXX), 130		9:7	22
7:17–18	18	9:8	83
7:18	20, 133	9:8–17	28, 81, 135
7:18–20	27	9:9	81, 113
7:19	20, 133	9:10	21
7:19–20	143	9:11	24, 108, 113, 143
7:19–22	18	9:12	113, 141
7:19–24	18	9:13–14	81, 113
7:20	20, 133	9:15	24, 108, 113
7:21	20, 108	9:16	108, 113
7:22	20	9:17	108, 113
7:23	70, 133	9:18–28	18

9:18–29	22	23:10–22	75
9:20	85	24	75
9:21	5	24:8	85
9:21–27	86	24:1–8	83, 90
9:25	27	30:21	112
9:25–27	27, 186	32:11	23
9:28–29	86	32:25–29	59
10	22, 27		
10:1–32	18, 27, 86	**Leviticus**	
10:1	19	6:18	112
10:20	16	6:22	112
10:25	86	7:34	112
10:32	22	10:10	161
11	81	10:15	112
11:7	131	11:47	161
11:10–26	86	16	13
12:1–3	92	16:1–34	82
13	15	16:11	80, 83
15	81	16:15–16	82, 83
15:13	131	18:27–28	25
15:14	71?	20:22	25
17–50	15	20:25	161
18:16–33	23	24:8	154
22	15	24:9	112
22:12	132	26	24
24	59	26:22–26	24
27	15	26:31	23
34	15, 59	26:40	137
35	15		
36	15	**Numbers**	
37	15	18:8,11,19	112
39	15	35:33–34	25, 82
41:39	187	25:6–13	59
45	15	25:13	154
47	15		
48	15	**Deuteronomy**	
49	15	1:39	147
50:26	15	8:7–20	146
		8:19	146
Exodus		11:29	87
1–9	15	26:3–10	139
10:15	140	26:5	187
13:10	161	27:12–14	87
14:4	141	27:13–14	168
14:21	131	27:14–15	87
15:5, 8	26	27:14–26	165
19	75	27:15–26	139

Deuteronomy (continued)
29:10–20	162, 171
29:11–21	162
29:21	162
29:22	162
32:43	36
33:8–11	59

Joshua
24:2	131

Psalms
1	5
14	65, 99
14:1	99
14:2	99
14:5	99
18:12	140
18:16[15]	26
29:10	26
42:7	26
48:13	162
48:14	162
65:6–9 [6–8]	26
69:2[1]	26
76:17	26
77:16	26
78:4	162
78:6	162
78:50	142
89:4	104, 105
93:3	26
102:18	162
102:19	162
103:12–14	137
106:6	137
106:23	104, 105
106:38	25

Job
22:15–20	26

2 Samuel
7:10–11	37
22:12	140

1 Kings
3:9	147

1 Chronicles
1:4	22

2 Chronicles
29:16	160

Daniel
9	61
9:4–5	137
9:26	26

Malachi
2:4–5	154
2:4–7	54, 59
2:4–8	59
2:6	57, 59, 112
2:10	179
3:3–4	160
3:16	67
3:16–18	66, 67, 159, 165
3:18	66, 137, 138

Ezekiel
	22
7:2, 3, 6	24
7:23	24
13	22
14:12	82
14:13–23	23
14:14	27
14:22–23	23
18:9	112
21:4–5	108
22:26	161
25:13	24
26:19	26
29: 8	24
31:15	26
32:7	143
36:16–18	143
36:19–33	143
36:33	147
36:35	147
36:24–36	113
42:20	161
44:15	160
48:11	154, 172

BIBLICAL AND APOCRYPHAL BOOKS

Ezra		54:7–10	25
9	25	54:10	25
		54:10a	134
Nehemiah		60:21	68
9:33	137	61:3	68
13:23–31	25	65:9	134
		66:16	108
Jeremiah			
3:1	25	**Amos**	
3:2	25	7:4	26
3:9	25		
23:3	70	**Joel**	
25:31	108	4:15–16	146
33:17	161		
45:5	108	**Jonah**	
46:8	143	2:5	26
47:1–2	143		
51:58	66	**Habbakuk**	
51:62	24	3:10	26
Isaiah		**Micah**	
5:7	68	4:7	70
24:1	26		
24:4–5	26	**Zechariah**	
24:5–7	25	4:14	159, 161
24:5–18	146	13:2	160
24:18	26		
29:6	146	**Nahum**	
29:20–21	26	1:8	26
30:26	34		
36:10	131	**Zephaniah**	
36:11	131	1:3	24
40:1–5	134	3:5	111
41:4	162	3:9	131
42:1	104, 105		
43:20	104, 105	**Tobit**	
44:27	26	4:12	87
45:4	104, 105, 134	6:6–7	87
46:3	70		
50:2	26	**Sirach**	
51:10	26	1	68
52:1–3	135	6:14–15	69
54	22, 134, 175	6:20–31	69
54:1–10	133	16:7	71
54:4–10a	134, 135	16:18	153
54:8	147	16:18–19	26
54:9	27, 135, 143, 147	24	68

Sirach (*continued*)

33:7–13	71
34:5	71
35:13–14	77
36:4–9	77
39:27–44:17	69
43:6	71
44:1–50:21	68
44:16	71, 80
44:17	69
44:17–18	69
45:6–7	154
45:15	154
45:24	57
48:8	70
49:16	68, 69
51:13–20, 30b	69

Baruch

3:9–4:4	68

2 Maccabees

8:3–4	36

4 Ezra

14:50	61

Luke

17:26–27	4

Hebrews

11:7	4

Romans

5:12–18	140

1 Peter

3:18–19	4
3:19–20	4

2 Peter

2:5	4

Dead Sea Scrolls and Related Texts

CD (*Cairo Damascus Document*)
I, 4	70, 104, 154
I, 10–18	100
I, 11–12	170
I, 12–13	162
II, 2–III, 12	152
II, 6–7	70
II, 12–13	153
II, 14–III	152
II, 16	152
III, 1–2	138
III, 2–4	154
III, 10–13	169
III, 21–IV, 2	160
III, 21–IV, 4	154, 172
XII, 11	138, 154
XV, 12–XVI, 2	84
XIX, 35	157
XX	160
XX, 13–14	170
XX, 20–21	136
XX, 28–29	137

1QH^a (1QHodayot^a)
	57
VII, 19	57
IX, 5	143
IX, 7	143
IX, 8	143
IX, 9	143
IX, 12	143
IX, 13	143
IX, 15–16	143
IX, 19	143
IX, 23	104
XI, 22	109
XI, 23	133
XII, 5–27	100
XII, 28	104

XIV, 14–18	109
XV, 15	136
XV, 30	104
XVI, 10–11	87, 109
XIX, 27	57
XXIV, 27	104
XXVI, 15	104

1QpHab (1QPesher to Habakkuk)
II, 6–8	162
VII, 4–5	104
VII, 8–10	159
X, 9–12	100
X, 9–13	105
X 13	104

1QIsaiah^a   25

1QM (1QWar Scroll)
XIV, 5	70

1QS (1QRule of the Community)
I–II	83, 93, 114 171
I, 10	161
I, 16	156
I, 18– II, 19	87
I, 18–19	168, 171
I, 20	168
I, 21–24	168
I, 22–24	171
I, 24–25	137
II, 1–4	168
II, 4	57
II, 4–5	165
II, 4–9	168
II, 4–10	165
II, 4–18	153
II, 10	168

1QS (continued)	
II, 11–16	161
II, 12	169
II, 16	171
II, 16 – III,	185
II, 18	168
II, 19	167, 168, 169
II, 25	157
II, 25–IIII, 6	169
III, 4	167
III, 5	167
III, 6	167
III, 15	155
IV, 14	70
IV, 22	109
V, 8–10	84
V, 13	70
VII 8, 1–10a	179, 180
VIII	83
VIII, 5	109
VIII, 6–7	43
VIII, 6, 10	83
IX, 3–5	179
IX, 4	83
IX, 4–5	160
X, 1–2	140
XI, 7–8	157
XI, 15	103
XI, 16	105
XI, 17–19	104

1QSa (1QRule of the Congregation)	
I, 1–3	179
I, 10–11	147
III	83

1QSb (1QRule of Benedictions)	
III, 22–23	142, 147

1Q14 (1QPesher to Micah)	
17–19 3–5	162

1Q17–18 (1QJubilees[a–b])	72

1Q18 (1QJubilees[b])	
1–2, 3–4	73, 77

1Q19 (1QBook of Noah)	
1 2	107
1 2–4	132
3	102
3 1–5	131
13–14	109
13–14 1–3	132
13–14 3	133
15 2	104, 105, 106, 131, 13

1Q19bis (1QBook of Noah)	
2 1	107
2 1–5	132
2 5	133

1Q20 (Genesis Apocryphon)	57, 87, 112, 114, 159, 184
0–1	120
0, 5	109, 111
0, 5–8	107
0 10–11	107
0, 12	107, 119
0, 13	107
0, 15	107, 119
0, 1 –I, 29	107
I, 1	119
I, 13	107
I, 25	107, 108
II	102, 103, 105
II–V	89, 108
II, 1 – V, 25	119
II, 1–7	108
II, 4	133
II, 5	109
II, 7	109
II, 8–10	117
II, 9–16	109
II, 10	109
II, 15	133
II, 18	109
II, 20	109
II, 1–V, 27	108
III, 13	109
V, 2–22	116
V, 2	111
V, 3–4	133

DEAD SEA SCROLLS AND RELATED TEXTS

V, 2–4	117, 120	XIII, 8 – XVII, 19	114
V, 3–10	109	XIII, 8–17	120
V, 8	109	XIII, 16	107, 120
V, 9	109	XIV, 9	120
V, 16	103	XIV, 9–14	109, 111
V, 18	109	XIV, 11–14	57, 120
V, 22	109	XIV, 12	120
V, 29–XII, 17	110	XIV, 13	115
V, 29	57, 103, 105, 110, 123, 173	XV, 20	105
VI	111, 116	XV, 20–23	115
VI–VII	110, 111	XV, 23	111
VI, 1	41, 109, 111	XVI–XVII	119
VI, 1–2	80, 115	XVI, 1– XVII, 19	115, 120
VI, 1–6	110	XVII, 19	120
VI, 2	103, 106	XIX, 7	120
VI, 2–3	57, 112	XIX, 8	120
VI, 4	57, 103, 106, 112, 120	XIX, 12–15	120
VI, 6	120	XIX, 14	120
VI, 8	57, 111, 112, 120	XIX, 14–15	120
VI, 11	109, 112	XIX, 15–17	120
VI, 11–12	106, 104	XIX, 24–26	116
VI, 16	112, 173	XIX, 25	103, 105, 120, 123
VI, 19	112	XX, 8–31	119, 121
VI, 19–23	111	XX, 14	107, 120
VI, 23	115	XX, 19	108
VIII–IX	112	XX, 21–22	88
IX, 3	114	XX, 31–33	119, 121
X, 10–12	107	XXI, 8–14	120
X, 12–14	112	XXI, 15–19	120, 121
X, 13–17	57, 120, 160	XXI 21–22	120
XI	116	XXI, 23 – XXII, 11	119, 121
XI, 1	141	XXII, 31	108, 120
XI, 3	105	XXII, 34	120
XI, 11–12	113, 120		
XI, 11–13	1	**1Q21 (1QTestament of Levi)**	53
XI, 11–14	97		
XI, 13–14	57, 100, 113, 116, 137, 180	**1Q34(bis) (1QFestival Prayers)**	
		3 I, 4–5	135, 136
XI, 14	111	3 II, 5–6	139
XI, 15–19	114		
XI, 16	57	**2Q18 (2QBen Sira)**	69
XII, 1	113		
XII, 7–17	114	**2Q19–20 (2QJubilees**[a-b]**)**	72
XII, 8–9	120		
XII,9	113	**2Q26 (2QBook of Giants)**	33
XII, 13–17	57		
XII, 16–17	120	**3Q5 (3QJubilees)**	72

4Q156 (4QTargum of Leviticus)	23	4Q181 (4QAges of Creation B)	157
		1 1–2	157
4Q157 (4QTargum of Job)	23	1 2	108, 133, 157
		1 3–4	157
4Q169 (4QNahum Pesher)		1 1–6	157
3–4 II, 8	100		
		4Q201–202 (4QEnoch^a–b)	187
4Q171 (4QPsalms Pesher^a)			
1–2 I, 17–28	100	4Q201 (4QEnoch^a)	33
3–10 IV, 14	105	1 II, 1	38
		1 II, 13	38
4Q174		1 IV, 5	104
1–3 II, 2	104	1 IV, 7–8	36
		1 V, 3–4	35, 50, 109
4Q176 (4QTanhumim)	25, 134,	1 VI, 17	114
	135, 143, 147		
1–2 I, 1–4	134	4Q202 (4QEnoch^b)	33
8–10 13–15	134	1 II	133
8–11	134, 135	1 II, 20 – 1 III, 6	133
8–11	3, 135	1 III, 5	104
8–11 9–10	135	1 III, 12	114
8–11 11–15	160	1 IV, 6, 10	114
8–11 12	134		
		4Q203, (4QEnoch Giants^a)	33, 44
4Q176a (4QJubilees?)	72, 184	8 4	105
		8, 12	114
4Q177 (4QCatena A)			
9 8	162	4Q204, (4QEnoch^c)	33, 39, 44, 87
		1 V, 4	37
4Q196–200 (4QTobit^a–e)	87	1 VI, 11b–12	108
		1 VI, 17	114
4Q180–181(4QAges of Creation A–B)		1 VI, 19	105
	154, 156, 169, 172, 184	4 10	40
		5 I–II	44
4Q180 (4QAges of Creation A)	156	5 II, 16–30	44
1–2	155	5 II, 17–19	38
1 1–2	156	5 II, 20	109, 114
1 1–5	155	5 II, 21–23	43
1 3–4	156	5 II, 23–24	41
1 4	155	5 II, 26	104
1 7–10	156	5 II, 28	52, 99
2	156		
2–4 I	155	4Q206 (4QEnoch^e)	33
2–4 II, 1–10	156	1 XXVI, 21–XXVII, 10	113
5–6 5	156	4 I, 13–14	40, 50
6–9	155	4 II, 4–5	40, 50

4Q209 (4QAstronomical Enoch[b])	33	VII, 17	73
		XIV, 10	115
4Q212 (4QEnoch[g])	29, 33, 40		
	42, 87, 187	4Q218 (4QJubilees[c])	
1 II, 13–17	41	1, 1–4	73
1 II, 18–21	41		
1 II, 19–20	58	4Q219 (4QJubilees[d])	
1 II, 22–23	103, 104	II, 17–37	85
1 III, 23–25	51	II, 28–29	73
1 III, 24	57	II, 30	87, 109
1 III, 24–25	40, 51, 100	II, 31	73
1 IV	100	II, 33	104
1 IV, 12–13	103	II, 35	73
1 IV, 12–14	41, 57		
1 IV, 14	41	4Q221 (4QJubilees[f])	
1 IV, 15–17	42	1 5–7	73
1 IV, 19	42	1 5 5	73
1 IV, 23	42	7 10	73
4 V, 24–25	41		
		4Q223–224 (4QpapJubilees[h])	
4Q213 (4QAramaic Levi[a])	53	2 II, 5–8	77
4Q213 1 I, 9–21	103	2 I, 49–50	73
4Q213 1 I, 13	57		
4Q213 1 II, 8–12	103	4Q225–227 (4Qpseudo-Jubilees[a–c?])	73
4Q213 4 5–6	57		
		4Q242 (4Q Prayer of Nabonidus)	187
4Q213a (4QAramaic Levi[b])	53		
4Q213a 1 14	103	4Q243–245 (4QPseudo-Daniel[a–c])	99,
4Q213a 1 14	57		187
4Q213a 1 17	57, 114		
4Q213a 1 17–18	114	4Q243–244 (4QPseudo-Daniel[a–b])	141
4Q213a 2 6–7	57		
		4Q243 (4QPseudo-Daniel[a])	
4Q213b (4QAramaic Levi[c])	53	9 I	99
		28 1	99
4Q214 (4QAramaic Levi[d])	53		
		4Q244 (4QPseudo-Daniel[b])	
4Q214a (4QAramaic Levi[e])	53	8 2–3	99
4Q214b (4QAramaic Levi[f])	53	4Q245 (4QPseudo-Daniel[c])	
		1 I, 4–5	99
4Q216 (4QJubilees[a])	73		
V, 12–14	143	4Q249[g] (4Qpap cryptA Serekh ha-Edah[g])	
VII	73	1–2 3	179
VII, 6–7	73		
VII, 10–11	73	4Q252–254a (4QCommentary on	
VII, 12–13	73	Genesis A–D)	22, 67, 87,
VII, 13	73	143, 151, 158, 165, 184	

4Q252 (4QCommentary on Genesis A)
                                9, 158, 159, 161,
                                162, 163, 164, 165, 184
I   167
I, 3–II, 4   164
I, 1   163
II, 4–5   162
II, 6–7   165
V, 2   161, 165

4Q253 (4QCommenary on Genesis B)
                                           159, 160, 161
1   159
1 4   164
1 I, 4   158
2   159
2 1–5   160
3   159, 160

4Q253a (4QCommentary on Malachi)
                                           159, 160, 161
1   159
1 I   159
1 I, 1–5   159
1 I, 4–5   136
1 II   159
1 II, 1–4   160

4Q254 (4QCommenary on Genesis C)
                                                159, 161
1 3–4   165
2   161
3   161
4   161
4 2   161
5–6   161
7   161
8 7   161, 165

4Q254a (4QCommenary on Genesis C)
                                                162, 165
1–2 1   162
1–2 2–4   162
3 1–2   162
3 4–5   162

4Q265 (4QMiscellaneous Rules)
3 1–3   179

7, 7–14   179
7 9–10   83

4Q266 (4Q Damascus Document^a)
2 1, 3–6   153
2 1, 15–16   162
2 II, 5–7   153
2 II, 11–12   153
11 16–17   84, 93, 153
11 17   165

4Q269 (4Q Damascus Document^d)
16 14   84

4Q270 (4Q Damascus Document^e)
1 I, 1   152
1a II, 1   160
2 II, 13   104
7 II, 10   84
7 II, 11–12   93, 153

4Q275 (4QCommunal Ceremony)
1 1–3   103

4Q280 (4QCurses)
2 5   70

4Q370 (4QExhortation Based on the Flood)   113, 144, 145
1 I, 1–2   146
1 I, 1–9   146
1 I, 3a   146
1 I, 3b–4   146
1 I, 7–9   146
1 II, 1–4   147
1 II, 1–9   145
1 II, 6   147

4Q400 (4Q Songs of the Sabbath Sacrifice^a)
2 2   133

4Q416 (4QInstruction^b)   64, 65, 111
1 10–16   66, 99
1 11–12   66
1 14–16   66

1 15	66
1 15–16	67
1 16	146
2 III, 18	104

4Q417 (4QInstruction^c)

1 I	155
1 I, 14	155
1 I, 14–17	160
1 I, 14–18	67
1 I, 16–18	66, 67
1 I, 17	146
1 I, 18–19	104
1 II, 8	135

4Q418 (4QInstruction^d)

2 7	66
69 II, 2–13	133
73, 201	64
81+81a	68
201 1	65
201 1–2	65

4Q422 (4QParaphrase of Genesis and Exodus) 9, 113, 139, 140, 143, 144

I, 6–12	140
I 6	143
I, 9	140
I, 13	143
II, 2–7	141, 142
II, 3–7	142
II, 5	142
II, 6	142
II, 7	143
II, 8–11	141
II, 9–11	143
II, 11	143
II, 12	143
III	141
III, 7	141
III, 9	142
III, 10	143
7	140
8	140, 143
9	143
frg. M	143
frg. Q	143

4Q427 (4Q Hodayot^a)

7 II, 18	133

4Q464 (4QExposition on the Patriarchs) 130

1 1–2	131
3 I, 5–9	131
3 II, 3–4	131
5 II, 1–5	130
6 3	132
7 2	132
10 1–2	132

4Q500 (4QBenediction)

1, 2–6	87

4Q503 (4QDaily Prayers^a)

24–25 4	142

4Q507–509 (4QFestival Prayers^{a–c}) 136

4Q508 (4QFestival Prayers^b) 67, 83, 114, 136, 137, 138, 139, 165

1 1	136, 138, 158, 184
1 1–2	135
1 2–6	129
2–3	135
2 1–3 2	4
2 2–5	137
2 2–6	135, 147
2 5	137
3 1	137, 138
3 2	138, 142, 158
3 1–2	129, 147
3 1–3	135
4 2	135, 142, 147
30 1–2	83

4Q509 (4QFestival Prayers^b) 136

13–14	133
16 4	133
17 2–3	147

4Q512 (4QRitual of Purification B)

29–32 10	160

4Q525 (4QBeatitudes) 68

4Q521 (4QMessianic Apocalypse)
14 2	136

4Q529 (4QWords of Michael)
1 1	105

4Q530 (4Q Book of Giants^b)
1 I, 3–5	36
2 II+6–12(?), 7–8	39

4Q531 (4Q Book of Giants^c)
22 1	39
22 12	9

4Q532 (4Q Book of Giants^d)
2 9	43

4Q533 (4QGiants or Pseudo-Enoch)
4, 1–3	41

4Q534 (4QNoah) — 103, 134, 159, 184
1 I, 1–3	103
1 I, 3	103
1 I, 5	103, 105
1 I, 6	103, 106
1 I, 7–8	103, 104, 106
1 I, 9	105, 106
1 I, 10	106, 134,138
1 II + 2 1–5	103
1 II + 2 13–14	106
1 II + 2 15–17	106
7 0–1	56
7 2	114
7, 3–4	123

4Q535 (4QAramaic N)
3 3	103

4Q536 (4QAramaic C)
2 I +3 8–9	104, 106
2 II +3 9–13	106
2 II + 3 11–13	106
2 II + 3 12	105, 106
2 II + 3 13	104
2 II, 12	56
2 II, 12–13	123
2 II, 3 9	104

4Q537 (4Q Testament of Jacob?) — 87, 100, 187
1+2+3 1	104
1+2+3 3	99, 100, 123

4Q538 (4Q Testament of Judah) — 187
9 8	105

4Q539 (4Q Apocryphon of Joseph B)
	187

4Q540 (4Q Apocryphon of Levi^a)
1 1	100

4Q541 (4Q Apocryphon of Levi^b?) — 100, 101, 106
1 3	105
2 I, 3	100
2 I, 6	103
2 II, 6	103
2 II, 3	100
2 II, 8; 3 1	100
6 1, 3	100
7, 2	123
7 4–6	103
9 I, 1–7	100
9 I, 2	100

4Q542 (4Q Testament of Qahat) — 53, 98
1 I, 3–4	99
1 I, 5–9	98
1 I, 8–9	108
1 II, 9–14	103
1 II, 9–13	103, 123
1 II, 12	99, 105, 123

4Q543 (4Q Visions of Amram^a) — 58, 99, 100, 187
1 I, 7	102
1a–c 1	105, 120
2 a–b 2–4	103, 105

4Q544 (4Q Visions of Amram^b) — 58
2, 16 – 3, 1	114
3 1	114

4Q545 (4Q Visions of Amram^c)
1a I, 1	99, 103, 123

DEAD SEA SCROLLS AND RELATED TEXTS 241

4Q547 (4Q Visions of Amram^e)	58, 83, 99	**7Q4 (7QEnoch)**	32
1–2 III,7–8	98	**7Q8–13 (7QEnoch)**	32
5 1–4	98		
6 1–4	98	**11QT (11QTemple)**	
8 1–3	98	XIV	113
9 1–6	98	XXVI, 5–7	137
9 8	123		
		11Q5 (11QPsalms^a)	69
4Q548 (4Q Visions of Amram^f?)			
1 II–2 12	103	**11Q10 (11QTargum of Job)**	23
4Q550 (4Q Proto- Esther^a)	187	**11Q12 (11QJubilees)**	73, 78
		4 1–3	103, 123
4Q558 (4QVision^d)	105		
		11Q13 (11QMelchizedek)	67
4Q577 (4QText Mentioning the Flood)		II, 10	167
	67, 184	II,11–13	167
1 3	67		
2 1	67	**XQ**	
3 3	105	8 3	36
5Q13 (5QRule)	4, 7, 166, 184	*Aramaic Levi Document (ALD)*	
1	164	2:1	57
1 1–13	168	2:5–3:4–5	56
1 6	167	3:4	57
		3:6	57
1 6–7	151	3:9	57
1 6–13	166	3:15	57
1 7	167	3:21–24	71
1 7, 11	159	5:1–9:18	57
1 12–13	167	6:4	57, 58
1 13	168	10	53
2 4–9	166	10:10	53, 123
2 4–11	168	11:5–6	53
3 2	168	12:3	53
4 1–4	167	12:6–7	55
4 2–3	169	13:7	57
4 4	168, 169	13:7–15	99
6 2	168	10:10	57
		11:1	57
6Q1 (6QGenesis)	16	12:6	57
6Q8 (6QGiants)		*1 Enoch*	
2 1–3	39	1–5	61, 90
		1–36	49, 90
7Q1 (7QSeptuagint Exodus)	32	1;1	102

1 Enoch (continued)		
1:2	37, 49	
2:1	38	
5:4	38	
6–11	33, 35, 48, 49, 60, 90	
6–16	38, 105	
6–19	105	
7:1	36	
7:1–8:3	92	
7:2–8:4	133	
7:5–6	36	
8:1–2	36	
8:3	104	
8:4	36	
9:1	36	
9:3	114	
10:1–3	35, 90, 109	
10:3	37, 59, 64, 116	
10:4	41	
10:9, 12	114	
10:16	30, 37, 87, 109	
10:20	4	
12:6	114	
12–16	90	
14:3	108	
14:6	114	
17–36	105	
18:15	38	
32:3		
32:3–6	113	
34:1–8	71	
40:5	102	
45:3	102	
53:6	102	
54:7–55:2	44	
60	44	
65:1–69:1	44	
65:11–12	45	
66:1–2	45	
67:1–3	45	
67:4–7	45	
68:1	45, 102	
72–82	105	
72:1	34	
81:6	123	
82:1	102, 123	
83–90:40	105	
84:1	90	
84:1–6	51	
86:1–3	38	
89:1	40, 50	
89:9	40, 50	
89:36	40	
90:34	42	
91:1–10	40	
91:11	41, 57, 100	
91:12–13	41	
91:14	42	
91:18–19	41	
91:19	58	
92:1	104	
93:3–4	29, 40	
93:3–5A	51	
93:4	51, 57, 59, 61, 90, 100	
93:6	61	
93:9–10	41, 57	
93:10	40, 102	
94:1	41	
98:11	36	
99:2	42	
103:3–8	32	
104:11–13	123	
106	36, 89, 104	
106–7	44, 46	
106–8	102	
106:5	108	
106:13	38	
106:13–107	44	
106:15	114	
106:16–18	41, 43, 90	
106:18	41, 43, 51	
106:19	104	
107:1	52	
107:2	109	

Jubilees	6
1:1	84
1:1–5	75
1:5	123
1:16	86
2:2–3	113
2:3	143

2:17	73	6:2	24
2:20–22	73	6:4	81
2:21–22	73	6:4–16	90
2:23	73	6:10–11	63
2:25	73	6:10–12	84
3:17–20	78	6:11	
4:3	76	6:11–14	81
4:4	74	6:11–38	90
4:7	76	6:13–17	84
4:7–33	74	6:14	85
4:9	76, 77	6:17	162
4:11–27	76	6:17–18	75, 91
4:15	76	6:17–20	81
4:15–28	78, 89	6:23–32	162
4:16–19	76	6:26	92
4:16–24	105	6:28–29	84
4:17	61, 187	7:1–2	85
4;17–19	89	7:1–6	82
4:17–22	102	7:3	80
4:21	78	7:3–4	113
4:21–24	91	7:3–6	85
4:22	82	7:4	82
4:28–29	76, 81, 89	7:7–13	85, 86
4:31	76	7:10–13	86
4:33	87	7:13–19	86
4–10	102	7:20	77, 86
5:1–2	76, 78, 89	7:20–21	86
5:1–32	74	7:20–33	87
5:2	78, 82	7:27–34	36
5:4	79, 89	7:30–33	86
5:5	79	7:34	109
5:5–19	138	7:34–39	86, 87
5:5–8	79	7:37	87
5:6–16	80	7:38	102
5:6–19	4, 79	8:1–4	88
5:7	77	8:1–9	87
5:7–9	78	8:8–9:13	86
5:12–19	79	8:10–9:15	87
5:13–18	80	9:14–15	86
5:14	67	10–11	74
5:17–18	82, 137, 147	10:1	91
5:19	79	10:1–3	80
5:21–32	164	10:1–4	88
5:23	130	10:1–9	86
6:1–3	80, 90, 160	10:6	80
6:1–4	81	10:12	92
6:1–11:6	74	10:13	123

1 Enoch (continued)

10:13–14	86	22:11–31	92
10:15–17	85, 86	22:13–14	80
10:18–26	88	23:19	77
10:18–11:6	88	23:23	77
10:26	132	25:1–27:11	77
10:27–34	88	27:1	95
11:1	88	27:21	95
11:2	88	30:18	55
11:3–6	88	31	82
11:4–5	91	31:3	92
12:16–26	92	32:1	92
12:20	88	32:21	95
12:25–27	132	35:9	77
14:1–4	92	37:13	73
15:1–16	92	38:–42–42:57	77
15:1–14	85	40:5	187
15:25–34	92	44:5–6	92
16:13–19	92	46:1	77
17:1–14	92		
17:11	95	**SirA**	
19:28	88	6r:25	71
20:1–21	77	6v:11	70, 153
20–26	92	6v:23–25	26
21:2	104		
21:10b	85	**SirB**	
21:18–22:1	85	14r:1–3	70
21:24	87, 109	17:11	70
22:1	73, 92	19r:6	69
22:1–5	85	**SirE**	
22:11–23	92	1r:15–23	67, 71

Other Ancient Literature

Old Testament Pseudepigrapha
2 Enoch	49
3 Enoch	61

Sibylline Oracles 5
i. 147-98	5
3.818-28	5

Testament of Joseph
3:9	73

Testament of Levi
2:2-3	55
5:2-3	55
12:5-7	55
17:11-18:4	100
18:3-4	100

Testament of Moses
9:7	36

Targums
Tg. Ps.-Jon.
Mal 2:6	111

Tg. Jon.
Mal 2:6a	100

Other Rabbinic Writings
'Abot R. Nat.
2	6

Genesis Rabbah 5
28.8	5
26.1	5
30.6	5
30:9	5
36.4	5
31:7	24

Deuteronomy Rabbah
11.3	5

Numbers Rabbah
4:8	5
14.12	5

Midrash Tanhuma
Zeph 3:9	130

Mishnah, Talmud
b. Git. 45a	162
b. Sanh. 70a	5
Yoma 3:8	137
Sotah 7:2	139

Greek and Latin Writings
Josephus, 3, 4, 7
Ant.
1.74	4
1.93-94	4
13.171-73	7
18.11-22	7

J.W.
2.119-66	7

Philo, 3, 7
Det.
170	4

Hypoth.
11.1-11	7

Praem.
23	4

Prob.
75-91	7

QG
1.96	4

Pliny the Elder		Justin	
Nat.		*Dial.*	
5.15.73	7	92.2	4
		19.4	6
Early Christian Writings		46	6
Cyril of Jerusalem		Origen	
Catech.		*Cels.*	
17.10	4	4.21	4
Ephraem Syrus		Pseudo-Clement	
Hymns on the Nativity		*Rec.*	
1	4	1.29	4
		4.12	4
Eusebius of Caesarea		*Hom.*	
Praeparatio Evangelica		8.17	4
9.17.1-9	46		
9.18.2	46	Tatian	
		Pros Hellenas	
Gregory of Nazianzus	4	39.2	4
Or. Bas.			
28.18	4	Tertullian	
43.70	4	*Mon.*	
		5.5	4
Jerome			
Jov.			
1.17	4		

MODERN AUTHORS

Abegg, Jr., Martin G., 1, 69, 70, 132, 139, 158, 159
Akhmim, George Syncellus, 31
Alexander, Philip S., 37, 43, 48, 59, 61, 118
Alter, Robert, 14, 18–19, 20
Avigad, N., 107
Argall, Randal A., 72

Baillet, M., 136
Barker, Margaret, 36
Barrera, J. Trebolle, 7
Baumgarten, Joseph, 56, 152
Beckwith, Roger T., 9
Bedenbender, Andreas, 61
Beentjes, Pancratius C., 69
Beer, G., 31
Bekkum, Wout J. van, 3
Benjamins, H.S, 3
Bergren, T. A., 47
Bernstein, Moshe J., 11, 36, 78, 81, 107, 113, 163, 164
Bhayro, Siam, 35
Black, Matthew, 31, 32, 38, 40, 43, 50, 122

Boccaccini, Gabriele, 7, 32, 40, 42, 61, 69, 71, 91, 101
Bosshard-Nepustil, Erich, 13
Bowley, James E., 1
Brooke, George J., 7, 52, 67, 101, 130, 158, 162, 163, 165, 166, 171

Callaway, Phillip R., 7
Carmignac, Jean, 105
Cassuto, Umberto, 14
Charles, R. H., 9, 31
Charlesworth, James H., 136
Chazon, Esther, 144

Collins, John J., 33, 38, 48, 61, 67, 99, 101
Cook, Edward M., 1, 101, 106, 132

Davies, Philip R., 7, 9, 19, 21, 84, 108, 169, 170
Davila, J. R., 102, 136
Dimant, Devorah, 10, 32, 35, 36, 38, 39, 47, 82, 110, 122, 155, 156
Drawnel, Henryk, 54,

Eisenman, Robert H., 163
Elgvin, Torleif, 9, 64, 65, 68, 140, 142
Endres, John C., 72, 88
Eshel, Esther, 15, 36, 53, 56, 118, 119, 130, 163
Eshel, Hanan, 15, 36

Falk, Daniel K., 9, 16, 17, 22, 112, 113, 114, 136, 164
Feldman, Ariel, 8, 140, 144, 146
Fitzmyer, J. A., 102
Fletcher-Louis, Cripsbin H. T. 10
Flint, Peter W., 32, 38, 99
Fleming, Johannes, 31
Fraade, Steven D., 10
Fretheim, Terence E., 19
Frey, Jörg, 66
Fröhlich, Ida, 92, 117, 118, 152, 163

García Martínez, Florentino, 7, 10, 11, 34, 102, 110, 122
Gilders, William K., 82
Gordon, N., 132
Greenfield, Jonas C., 53, 54, 56, 107
Grossman, Maxine, 66, 153, 154
Gunkel, Hermann, 13, 14
Gunn, David M, 26

Hamilton, Victor P., 13
Harland, P. J., 21
Harrington, Daniel J., 69, 71, 72
Hendel, Ronald, 9, 14
Hiebert, Robert J. V., 16
Himmelfarb, Martha, 38

Jassen, Alex P., 42, 123
Jonge, Marinus de, 55, 56,

Kaminski, Carol, 22
Kampen, John, 56
Kister, Menahem, 72, 166
Knibb, Michael A., 31, 32, 43, 44, 45, 68, 74, 123
Koltun-Fromm, Naomi, 3, 5, 6
Kugel, James L., 3, 54, 55, 59
Kugler, Robert A., 10, 55, 59
Kvanvig, Helge S., 14, 48, 90

Lambert, David, 86
Lange, Armin, 154, 155
Lee, Thomas R., 68
Lewis, Jack P., 3, 4, 8, 16, 26, 122
Lim, Timothy, 9, 163, 164, 165
Loader, William, 43

Machiela, Daniel A., 114, 115, 119
Martin, Françoise, 31
Milik, Jozef T., 31, 34, 39, 45, 54, 105, 154, 155, 156, 158, 159
Molenberg, Corrie, 32, 35
Morgenstern, Matthew, 107, 126, 130
Murphy-O'Connor, Jerome, 9

Nelson, Milward Douglas, 69
Newsom, Carol A., 144, 145, 147
Nickelsburg, George W. E., 7, 31, 32, 33, 35, 36, 37, 38, 40, 42, 43, 45, 61, 89, 94

Olson, D. T., 136
Orlov, Andrei, 4, 49

Parker, Benjamin H., 69
Peters, Dorothy M., 17, 24, 31, 159
Poirier, John C., 131
Puech, Émile, 32, 98, 100, 104, 105, 106

Qimron, Elisha, 107, 126

Rad, Gerhard von, 13
Radermacher, Ludwig, 31
Reed, Annette Yoshiko, 36, 37, 91
Reeves, John C., 46, 112, 113
Ruiten, Jacques T. A. G. M. van, 85, 118

Sarna, Nahum M., 13, 18, 20, 25
Saukkonen, Juhana, 163
Schiffman, Lawrence H., 137
Schüller, Eileen, 136
Schürer, Emil, 31
Scott, James M., 37, 78, 89, 94, 118, 122
Sivan, Daniel, 107, 126
Speiser, E.A., 13
Stanley, Christopher D., 134
Steinmetz, Devora, 22
Stone, Michael, E., 53, 55, 56, 122, 123, 130, 144
Strugnell, J., 134, 154, 155
Stuckenbruck, Loren, 33, 34, 39, 41, 46, 47, 68, 111
Suter, David W., 38

Tigchelaar, Eibert J. C., 9, 34, 42, 65
Tiller, Patrick A., 31, 32, 37
Toews, Casey, 1, 70
Tsumura, David T., 14

Van Bekkum, Woute J., 3
Van der Horst, Pieter W., 47
VanderKam, James C., 7, 9, 10, 32, 34, 35, 36, 37, 38, 40, 41, 48, 63, 72, 73, 79, 82, 83, 84, 87, 90, 102, 112, 118, 122
Vermes, Geza, 10
Vosté, J.M., 131

Wacholder, Ben Zion, 24, 152, 158, 159
Weigold, Matthias, 3, 8
Weinfeld, Moshe, 135
Wenham, Gordon J., 14, 21
Werman, Cana, 118, 119
Westermann, Claus, 13
Williams, Ronald J., 179
Wise, Michael O., 132, 163
Wright, Benjamin G., III, 69, 71, 72

Yadin, Y., 107

www.ingramcontent.com/pod-product-compliance
Lightning Source LLC
Chambersburg PA
CBHW021805220426
43662CB00006B/190